A SEMANTIC AND STRUCTURAL ANALYSIS OF HEBREWS

SIL International

SEMANTIC AND STRUCTURAL ANALYSIS SERIES

JOHN C. TUGGY, GENERAL EDITOR

A SEMANTIC AND STRUCTURAL ANALYSIS OF HEBREWS

Ellis W. Deibler, Jr.

SIL International®
Dallas, Texas

© 2017 by SIL International®

Library of Congress Control Number: 2017937857
ISBN: 978-1-55671-411-5

Printed in the United States of America

The Greek text used in this SSA is from the fourth revised edition
of the United Bible Societies' *Greek New Testament*.

All Rights Reserved
No part of this publication may be reproduced, stored in a retrieval system,
or transmitted in any form or by any means without the express permission
of SIL International. However, brief excerpts, generally understood to be
within the limits of fair use, may be quoted without written permission.

Copies of this and other publications of SIL International®
may be obtained through distributors such as Amazon,
Barnes & Noble, other worldwide distributors and, for
select volumes, www.sil.org/resources/publications:

SIL International Publications
7500 West Camp Wisdom Road
Dallas, TX 75236-5629, USA

General inquiry: publications_intl@sil.org
Pending order inquiry: sales_intl@sil.org
www.sil.org/resources/publications

CONTENTS

Acknowledgements 7

Abbreviations 8

GENERAL INTRODUCTION 9
Theoretical Basis 9
Communication Relations and Paragraph Patterns 10
Structural Forms of Paragraph Pattern in Various Discourse Types 11
Chart of Communication Relations 12
The Format of an SSA 13
The Display of the Unit 13
Example of the Display 14
Statement of the author's Intent 16
The Exegetical Notes 16
The Evidence for the Analysis of the Unit 16

INTRODUCTION TO THE ANALYSIS OF THE EPISTLE TO THE HEBREWS 17
Overview 17
Comment on the Epistle's Content 17
The Identification of the Recipients and Their Location 18
Place and Date of Writing 18
The Author of the Epistle to the Hebrews 18
Thematic outline of the epistle to the Hebrews 20
The Constituent Organization of Hebrews 26

THE SEMANTIC UNITS OF HEBREWS 27
HEBREWS 1:1—13:25 (Epistle) 27
    Epistle Constituent 1:1–4 (Paragraph: Opening of the Epistle) 28
    Epistle Constituent 1:4—12:29 (Part: BODY of the Epistle) 31
        Part Constituent 1:4—2:18 (Sub-Part: Mitigated Appeal$_1$ of 1:4—12:29) 32
        Part Constituent 3:1—4:16 (Section: Appeal$_2$ of 1:4—12:29) 52
        Part Constituent 5:1—9:28 (Section: Appeal$_3$ of 1:4—12:29) 78
        Part Constituent 10:1–39 (Section: Appeal$_4$ of 1:4—12:29 150
        Part Constituent 11:1—12:6 (Hortatory Sub-Part: Appeal$_5$ of 1:4—12:29) 172
        Part Constituent 12:7–11 (Paragraph: Appeal$_6$ of 1:4—12:29) 212
        Part Constituent 12:12–29 (Paragraph: Summary Appeals of 1:4—12:29) 216
    Epistle Constituent 13:1–19 (Part: Final Appeals of 1:1—13:25) 228
        Part Constituent 13:1–14 (Hortatory Paragraph: Appeal$_1$ of 13:1–19) 229
        Part Constituent 13:15 (Hortatory Paragraph: Appeal$_2$ of 13:1–19) 236
        Part Constituent 13:16 (Hortatory Paragraph: Appeal$_3$ of 13:1–19) 237
        Part Constituent 13:17–19 (Hortatory Paragraph: Appeal$_4$ of 13:1–19) 238
    Epistle Constituent 13:20–25 (Paragraph: Conclusion of the Epistle) 240

Appendix 245

Bibliography 255

Commentaries, Lexicons, and Other General References 255

Greek Texts and Translations 256

ACKNOWLEDGEMENTS

The author benefitted from a semantic and structural analysis of Hebrews done under the author's supervision by James L. Courter in 1985 for a thesis to fulfill requirements for his M.A. degree at the University of Texas at Arlington.

John Banker, the general editor of the SSA series, contributed very heavily to this work until his death in 2012, giving his expert insights into the theme statements, the semantic relationships, the text of the displays, and other material, for each paragraph. His place was taken by John Tuggy, and he and I have worked on this SSA both at his place of residence and at a distance. Copy editor Betty Eastman edited the manuscript at an early stage and gave significant advice on formatting. In more recent years, Linda Boehm has done a tremendous amount of work on the relational structure of the displays, as well as general editing and proofreading.

Most of all, I thank the Lord for the wisdom and strength he has given me for this project day by day, and for the spiritual blessings I have received in doing it. I trust that many others will benefit from using this SSA, both personally and as they translate this difficult book into other languages.

Ellis W. Deibler Jr.
April 2016

ABBREVIATIONS IN THE DISPLAYS

[CHI]	chiasmus		[LIT]	litotes
[DOU]	doublet		[MET]	metaphor
[EUP]	euphemism		[MTY]	metonymy
[HEN]	hendiadys		[PRS]	personification
[HYP]	hyperbole		[RHQ]	rhetorical question
[IDI]	idiom		[SYN]	synecdoche

ABBREVIATIONS IN THE TEXT

BAGD	Bauer, Arndt, Gingrich, Danker
CEV	Contemporary English Version
GNT	Greek New Testament
JB	Jerusalem Bible
JBP	J.B. Phillips
KJV	King James Version
LB	Living Bible
LXX	The Septuagint
NCV	New Century Version
NEB	New English Bible
NIV	New International Version
NLT	New Living Translation
REB	Revised English Bible
RSV	Revised Standard Version
SSA	Semantic and Structural Analysis
TCNT	Twentieth Century New Testament
TEV	Today's English Version (Good News Bible)
TFT	Translation for Translators
TNIV	Today's New International Version
TNT	Translator's New Testament
UBS	United Bible Societies

GENERAL INTRODUCTION TO SEMANTIC AND STRUCTURAL ANALYSES

The Semantic and Structural Analysis (SSA) commentaries are designed to assist Bible translators and Bible translation consultants. Due to the careful attention to meaning at all levels of the discourse, they should also be useful for Bible scholars, teachers, preachers, and anyone interested in a thorough understanding of the biblical text. The analysis is firmly based on discourse linguistics and assumes that each New Testament book is an integrated whole. The analytical process involves detailed study of the grammar, lexicon and discourse structure of the Greek, with the aim of clearly presenting the meaning of the text and the linguistic evidence on which the meaning is established.

THEORETICAL BASIS

The theoretical basis of these studies is Beekman, Callow and Kopesec's theory of discourse analysis, presented in *The Semantic Structure of Written Communication* (1981) and further developed by Kathleen Callow in *Man and Message* (1998). However, other theoretical approaches have not been ignored. A large body of biblical scholarship has been considered, and some of the weaknesses in their works have been supplemented.

This commentary is called *A Semantic and Structural Analysis* because its primary interest is the organized meaning of the text. The aim is to present, as far as possible, the organization and meaning that the biblical author intended his audience to understand. The text is approached with several underlying assumptions about language as a communicative medium:

1. The writer used written language signals in his attempt to communicate meaning, emotion, and social relations to his readers.
2. The writer assumed a vast body of shared information with his audience, such as language, culture, world-view, social relations, socio-political circumstance, specific circumstances, and time of the writing. Beekman, Callow and Kopesec call this the "communication situation."
3. The writer's own intended purpose and communication meaning were prior to and have priority over the written surface forms, but today our main access to the biblical writer's purpose and meaning is through the written text.
4. Communicated meaning consists of units of meaning logically related to other units of meaning.
5. Some meaning units are nuclear, or central, while others are satellitic or supportive to these nuclear units. These bundles of meaning are also bundled together with other, larger, units of meaning. In other words, meaning units are organized hierarchically in a discourse, giving rise to the "natural prominence" of the units (so Beekman, Callow and Kopesec).
6. The ways in which units are related to each other, that is, their "communication relations," are relatively few. These relationships are basic to human intelligence and makeup and are used in all languages whether or not there is a corresponding surface form expressing them. Moreover, even in the same language a specific relation is not always expressed by the same surface form, and conversely one surface form may be used to express *more* than one semantic relation.
7. When two meaning units are related to each other, each unit in this relationship carries out a "communication role."
8. Every language has certain grammatical and lexical devices which may be used by an author to mark specific meaning units as prominent. This is called "marked prominence."
9. There are limited ways in which communication relations can be arranged so that a whole arrangement is a purposive and complete unit. Such an arrangement forms a communication paragraph, or "paragraph pattern."
10. Each unit has a "theme," that is, a central topic and an argument about that topic, understandable from the prominence structure of the unit. (This is not to be confused with *motif*, which is a prosodic and coherence feature that runs through units of various sizes.)

In order to present the meaning and structure of any written communication, the editors of the SSA series have developed their own metalanguage and diagramming devices, which are explained in what follows.

COMMUNICATION RELATIONS AND PARAGRAPH PATTERNS

Semantic relationships between propositions, "communication relations," are the basic joining elements at all levels of a discourse. "Paragraph patterns" are made up of these relations with the additional elements of purposiveness and completeness. (An explanation of the total array of semantic relations between propositions is available in Beekman, Callow and Kopesec.)

Of the two charts that follow, the first shows the paragraph patterns used in this analysis, and the second shows the communication relations and unit roles. Most of the terms in the charts are self-explanatory, but for further explanations see Tuggy (1992) and Beekman, Callow and Kopesec (1981).

In the chart of communication roles, the relations are given in the usual order in which they are found in the Greek of the New Testament, e.g., reason–RESULT. Where there is no natural prominence on one part (i.e. where there is only *contextual* prominence), both relations are shown in lowercase letters, e.g. generic-specific.

		SOLUTIONALITY	CAUSALITY	VOLITIONALITY
I D E A S	EXPOSITORY −sequence	+problem(expo) +SOLUTION ±evidence^n ±(complication +SOLUTION)	+cause^n +EFFECT or +major +minor +INFERENCE or +evidence^n +INFERENCE^n or +application^n +PRINCIPLE	+justification^n +CLAIM
	NARRATIVE +sequence	+problem +RESOLUTION ±resolving incident^n ±(complication +RESOLUTION)	+occasion +OUTCOME	+step^n +GOAL
E M O T I O N S	EXPRESSIVE −sequence	+problem(emot) +SOLUTION ±seeking ±(complication +SOLUTION)	+situation^n +REACTION ±belief	+belief^n +CONTROL
	DESCRIPTIVE +sequence	+problem(desc) +SOLUTION ±experience^n ±(complication +SOLUTION)	+situation^n +REACTION	+description^n +DECLARATION
B E H A V I O U R	HORTATORY −sequence	+problem(hort) +APPEAL ±evidence^n ±(complication +SOLUTION)	+basis^n +APPEAL or +APPEAL +application^n	+motivation +ENABLEMENT^n or +motivation^n +ENABLEMENT
	PROCEDURAL +sequence	+problem(proc) +SOLUTION ±step^n ±(complication +SOLUTION)	+APPEAL +outcome^n	+STEP^n +accomplishment

STRUCTURAL FORMS OF PARAGRAPH PATTERN IN VARIOUS DISCOURSE TYPES

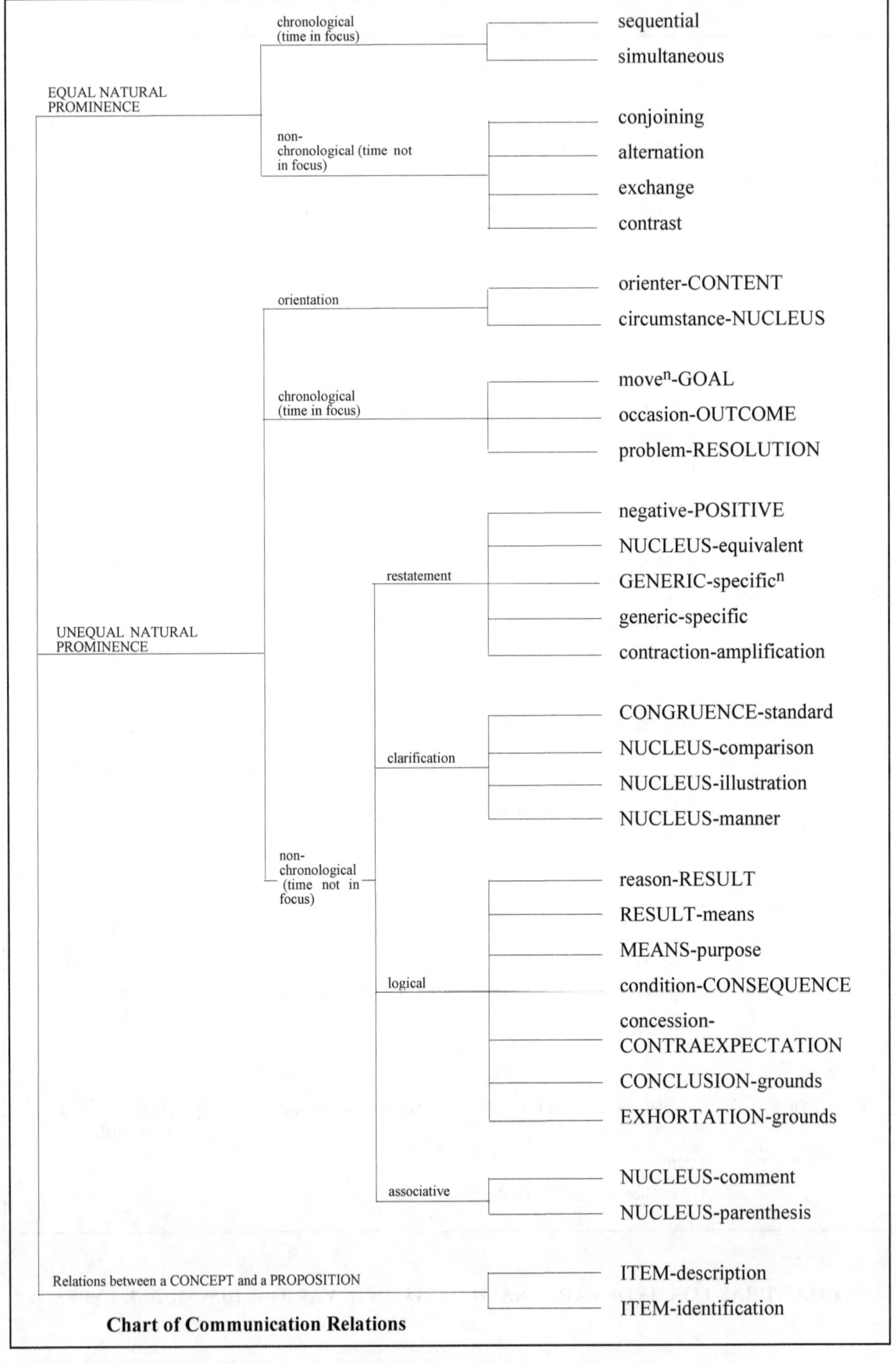

Chart of Communication Relations

THE FORMAT OF AN SSA

Following the General Introduction and a specific introduction to the book being studied, the main part of each Semantic and Structural Analysis (SSA) consists of displays and discussions of the semantic units which comprise the book. All units are considered, from the macrostructure or overall structure of the book, through the intermediate level structures such as parts and sections, down to the semantic paragraphs. Within each semantic paragraph smaller units are discussed, such as concepts, which relate to each other to form propositions (the basic unit of meaning) and the relationship of the propositions to one another.

Each semantic unit, whether semantic paragraph or something larger, is presented in the following order: (1) a display of the unit, (2) an explanation of the structure of the unit and a statement of how the original author intended to affect his audience by it, (3) exegetical notes about specific words and phrases as presented in the Display, and (4) arguments supporting the analysis of the unit under discussion as a whole.

THE DISPLAY OF THE UNIT

The Display is a schematic representation of the structure of the meaning of the unit. It contains a number of elements, as detailed in the following example (from the SSA of the Gospel of John):

14 A SEMANTIC AND STRUCTURAL ANALYSIS OF HEBREWS

PART CONSTITUENT 1:1-5 (Descriptive Paragraph: Generic Declaration of 1:1-5)

THEME: Jesus Christ expresses to us God's character being himself eternally God. He expresses by creating everything, giving humans life and knowledge, and by evil humans not overcoming him.

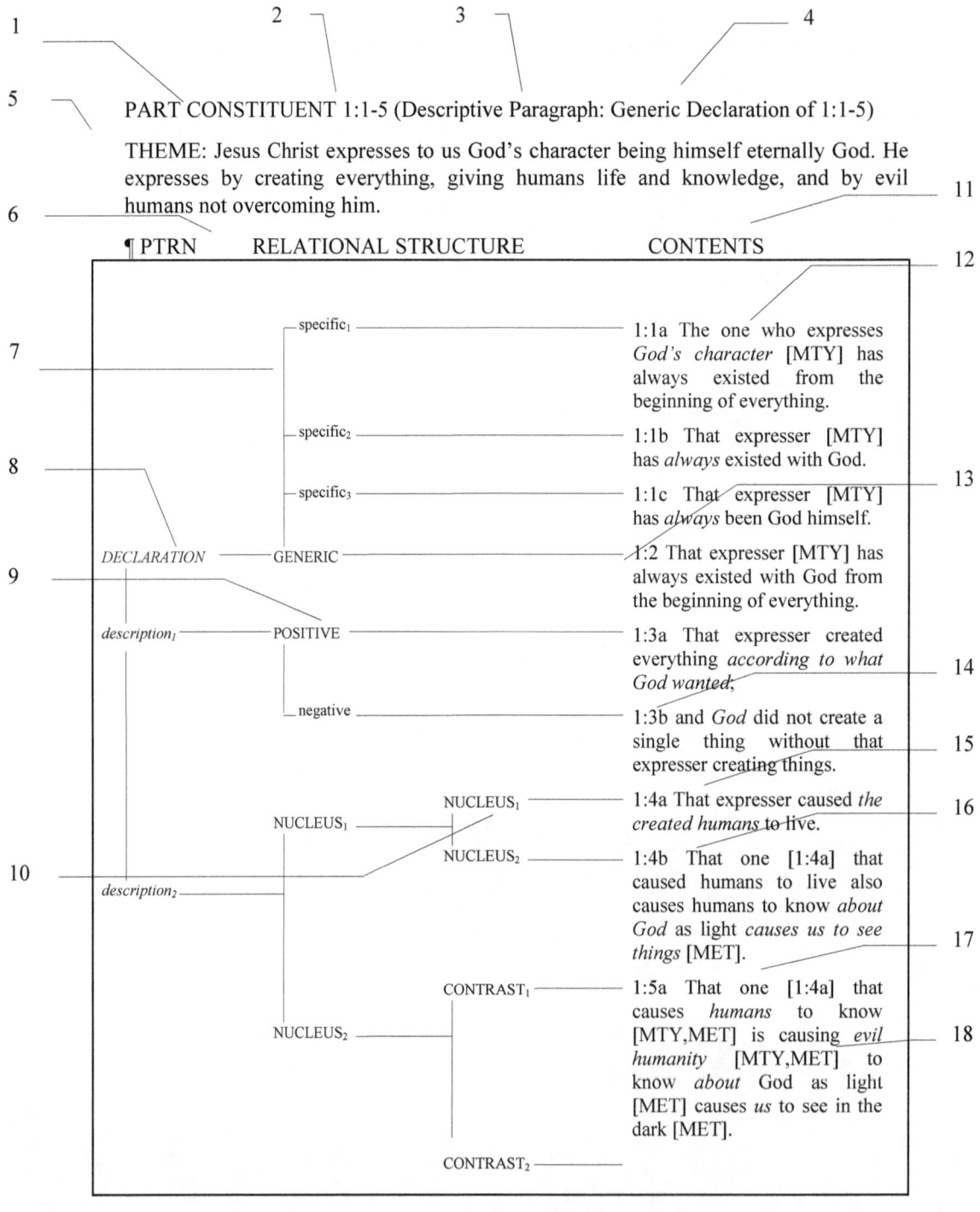

Key:

1. 'Part Constituent' shows that the unit goes together with some other similar unit(s) to form a 'Part', i.e., it gives the broader context of the unit.

2. '1:1–5' defines the specific text span of the unit.

3. 'Descriptive Paragraph' shows that the author was describing something with the intent of effecting the emotions of his audience (see the chart of Structural Forms of Paragraph Pattern, above) within the specific semantic level of this unit, which here is a semantic paragraph.

4. 'Generic Declaration of 1:1–5' states that the unit functions as a generic declaration within the larger context of the text span identified.

5. The second line is a statement of what the unit is all about. The Theme Statement presents the most prominent or nuclear parts of the unit, stating the topic and what is said about that topic.

6. The middle box contains column headers showing the type of information found below in the body of the Display.

The main body of the Display is in two main columns: on the left are the internal relations and structure of the unit, and on the right is the message content.

7. The text is assumed to be structured hierarchically and is therefore displayed with a form of tree diagram showing levels of dependency and branching.

8. The labels farthest to the left show the interdependent highest level units.

9. The next level from the left shows the units that support the highest level units.

10. Each succeeding column shows a lower supportive level and branching of units.

Units with labels in upper-case letters (capitals) are prominent or nuclear. In this particular example, the highest level of interdependent units are a declaration (prominent) with two descriptions supporting the declaration. The declaration is made up of four units, a generic statement with its specifics, as shown by the second level from the left.

It should also be noted that although the vertical lines indicate direct interdependency between units, a dotted vertical line is used to signify a proposition's relationship to those that follow as a group. (This is used mainly for the orienter–content relationship.)

11. The right-hand column of the display, under the title 'CONTENTS', has its own characteristics.

12. This column shows the results of a careful study of the grammatical structure of the Greek text and its semantic significance. The meaning is stated here in propositions with verbs in the active voice (as far as possible) and all participants explicit. The Greek text from which these propositions are derived may be a clause, a phrase, a verb, an abstract noun, or some other grammatical unit.

13. In the example the declaration unit is made up of four propositional statements. Each propositional statement is numbered as a part of a verse (1:1a, 1:1b, 1:1c, and 1:2). However, propositions are not numbered separately unless they require separate treatment. Here 1:3a is made up of two separate propositions in one propositional statement.

14. At the beginning of most propositional statements, a conjunction is used to signify its relationship to some other proposition. In 1:3b the negation is a restatement of the previous positive statement, and is therefore given the conjunction 'and'. In 1:5b the contrastive statement is introduced by 'but'.

15. The meaning is expressed unambiguously 'we are united to God'. In 1:4b the Greek term 'the life,' is expressed as 'the one that caused humans to live'.

16. The referents of pronouns and demonstratives are made explicit. In 1:4b the Greek has 'he' referring back in the text to 1:4a. This is signalled unambiguously in square brackets: 'that one [1:4a]'.

17. Italic words represent implicit information which is judged to have been part of the original message communicated by the writer. The exegetical notes give justifications for the inclusion of this information in the meaning of the message.

18. Abbreviations in square brackets indicate where a figure of speech (e.g., metonymy, metaphor) was used in the Greek.

In addition, words in bold face indicate focal words or phrases in the Greek that cannot be appropriately reflected in the grammar of written English.

THE STATEMENT OF THE AUTHOR'S INTENT

Following the Display is a section entitled 'Intent and Macrostructure' or 'Intent and paragraph pattern'. It deals with discourse type: how the biblical author intended the unit to affect his audience (in terms of the chart of Structural Forms of Paragraph Pattern, above). Where there are alternative ways of interpreting the author's intent, the reasons for the preferred analysis are given. Also, the unit's structure is discussed in terms of the author's strategy for accomplishing the intended effect on the audience.

THE EXEGETICAL NOTES

The section entitled 'Notes' contains comments on words and phrases from the Display. Most of the notes consider the Greek text and its meaning, stating different opinions found in the commentaries and reasons for choices made in the analysis. In particular, discussion is focused on relationship with other units, prominence, purpose, meaning, plus historical and cultural matters required for understanding the text, and translational problems.

THE EVIDENCE FOR THE ANALYSIS OF THE UNIT

The Notes are followed by two sections that present the textual and semantic evidence for the analysis of the unit.

In the section entitled 'Boundaries and Coherence' argumentation is given for the analysis of the beginning and ending points of the unit. In view of the wide variation in ways that commentaries and translations divide the material of biblical books into smaller units (sections, paragraphs etc.) it is important to consider the linguistic evidence provided by discourse study of the Greek text. For each unit there need to be not only convincing indicators of its boundaries but also elements within it showing its coherence.

Under 'Prominence and Theme' the textual and semantic prominence features within the unit are set out. These include both the features of natural prominence, as in the relationships between propositions and sub-units, and the grammatical and lexical devices indicators of marked prominence, such as forefronting and emphatic words. In this section there is also an explanation of how these prominence features determine the unit's Theme Statement (as given in the Display).

INTRODUCTION TO THE ANALYSIS OF THE EPISTLE TO THE HEBREWS

OVERVIEW

Most, if not all, of the contemporary commentaries on the "Epistle to the Hebrews" offer thorough discussions of possible identification and location of the recipients, author, and date and place of writing. Internal evidence points to Hebrew Christians as the recipients. Suggestions on where they lived range from Rome to Jerusalem. The place of writing is unknown. Estimates of the date of writing range from 48 A.D. to 96 A.D.

Most of the introductory discussion in the commentaries is given to identifying the author. Sources for this information include Origen and the early Eastern and Western Churches. Calvin and Luther did not think Paul was the author, thus differing from Origen and the other early church fathers. Many current commentators agree that Paul did not write Hebrews. Textual analysis and form criticism point away from Paul. But if Paul did not write it, who did? We do not know. Therefore, the lack of any definite information about the author, date of writing, the recipients, and place of its writing, suggests that this introduction should be shorter than the commentaries' analyses. A review of their circumstantial evidence and speculation in support of the suggested author does not require a level of thoroughness herein, for to do so would leave the reader wondering.

COMMENT ON THE EPISTLE'S CONTENT

Hebrews' commentaries all give an overview of the content. All say that the epistle compares and contrasts Christ with things Jewish. The epistle gives warnings and encouragements. Warnings address loss of faith, failing to meet together, to pray, to work, to endure, and to listen to God. Other warnings stress neglecting the message of salvation and rejecting the gospel. The encouragement is to endure persecution and to keep trusting in Christ. The tendency to go back to Judaism is strongly presented in Hebrews: the recipients need to remain having a close relationship with Christ and to adhere to the new agreement. The content of the epistle to the Hebrews can be said to expound the words of the risen Christ to the two disciples on the road to Emmaus:

TFTLuke 24:25-27: He said to them, "You two foolish men! You are so slow to believe all that the prophets have written about the Messiah! You should certainly have known that it was necessary that the Messiah should suffer all those things and die, and then enter his glorious home in heaven!" Then he explained to them all the things that the prophets had written about him in the Scriptures. He started with what Moses wrote and what all the other prophets wrote.

THE IDENTIFICATION OF THE RECIPIENTS AND THEIR LOCATION

Shortly after Pentecost, the scattered Christian Jews settled in Judea, Samaria, Phoenicia, Cyprus, Antioch and Cyrene (Acts 8:1; 11:19ff).

Those scattered Christian Jews knew Jesus' prophecies that the temple would be utterly demolished and that Rome would surround and besiege Jerusalem. The Jews who were still in Jerusalem knew that they would have to flee, and they did so. These Jews learned of the soon and awful fulfillment of those prophecies. They could not return, for nothing would remain of their city and sacrifices. The writer of Hebrews probably realized that this disaster would make the Levitical sacrifices obsolete. He felt the anxiety, terror and confusion that filled their daily lives—threatening the salvation initiated by Christ. He explains the relation between the old and new agreements—the two great epochs of God dealing directly with his human creation. Jeremiah foretold this new agreement. Now, the new agreement superseded the old, leaving the Jews of that day no access to God via the old system. The author explains this singular access to God for everyone through Jesus the Messiah—the new and living way. To explain this new agreement, the author leads the recipients through the Torah, into Kings and Chronicles, into the Psalms, and introduces several prophets—all of the foregoing pointing to Jesus fulfilling every Hebrew Messianic prophecy and the new agreement to the fullest extent by what he did.

Hebrews does not offer again in detail the gospel to the diaspora. Instead it refers to the old and new agreements fifteen times. Only Paul (3 times) and Luke-Acts (3 times) mention "agreement." The Diaspora Jews related best to words like "agreement" and "unshakable kingdom." Those Jews already knew the gospel.

In sum, the recipients of this epistle are Jewish Christians identified as the diaspora. Their spiritual situation as Jews would change from instability to impossibility with the destruction of Jerusalem. It did not matter where they lived, because their culture never depended on location, but on their religion. Bruce (p. 18) comments on the mass of unverifiable opinion regarding the location of the recipients with: "Where did they live? We do not know" (p.10).

PLACE AND DATE OF WRITING

Internal evidence regarding the place of writing is confined to the words "they of Italy" (13:24). But is that Rome? Lenski (p.15) thinks so. Does this mean "they of Italy who are here with me" or "they who are with me here in Italy?" Perhaps it refers to Italians who are elsewhere. Does it refer to Priscilla and Aquila, Italians who were with the author and who send their greetings? The reference to Timothy (13:23) suggests his release from imprisonment in Rome, but not as Rome being the place of writing. Rather than listing places of writing and scenarios supporting each, I will shorten this section to leave this question unanswered—to avoid a guessing game. The least important information and most unlikely to advance our knowledge of The Letter to the Hebrews is its place of writing.

The writing of Hebrews must be within the first century (Bruce, et al.), since Clement of Rome quoted it in A.D. 96. Kistemaker (pp. 14–16) puts the date range at A.D. 80-85. Attridge chooses anywhere between A.D. 60 to 100. This is the final possible time of writing. The author states that Timothy is still alive. The recipients of the letter endured a persecution (10:32–36). Three Roman persecutions occurred in the first century: under Claudius (A.D. 49-54), under Nero (A.D. 58-64), and under Domitian (A.D. 81-96). Most commentators look to the reign of Claudius for the earliest date of writing. The persecutions of Nero and Domitian were murderous but probably future. The persecutions under Claudius were probably recent. The persecution by the Sanhedrin in A.D. 33 began the diaspora. The Jewish Christians are told to "Remember those earlier days..." (10:32). But that referred to a distant past persecution—removed from the date of the writing of Hebrews. That persecution cannot date the composition. It serves to remind the recipients of something past. The text in Hebrews 10:32–34 uses athlēsis - contest, struggle or fight, denoting resistance, not bloodshed:

The TFT for Hebrews 10:32–34 has "Recall the former times when you first understood the message about Christ. You endured a hard struggle and continued to trust him when you suffered for your faith in Christ. At times people publicly insulted you and persecuted you. At other times you showed great concern for those who were treated like that. 34 You not only were kind to those who were in prison for their faith in Christ, but you also accepted it joyfully when unbelievers took away your possessions... because you knew very well that you have eternal possessions in heaven that are much better than those they took from you."

Hughes (1977) lists eighteen Hebrews' passages that pertain to the "still operative" Levitical priesthood services, such as: "...what is obsolete and aging will soon disappear."(8:13); "...the high priest enters the Most Holy Place every year with blood..." (8:25) and "...every priest stands and performs his religious duties..." (10:11). The verbs in these passages are all present tense, not past tense. Therefore the destruction of Jerusalem could not have occurred yet. The destruction of Jerusalem and the temple in A.D. 70 mitigates against all later dates for the writing of this epistle.

To sum up: To date the Hebrews writing beyond A.D. 70 would have been inconceivable to any first century Jewish Christian of the diaspora. They knew Jesus' prophecy concerning Jerusalem, and they felt sure that now it was imminent. This puts Hebrews within the apostles' lifetimes. The Roman siege of Jerusalem sets the date of Hebrews well after the persecution mentioned in Acts and within sight of the destruction of Jerusalem.

THE AUTHOR OF THE EPISTLE TO THE HEBREWS

Most current scholars remove Paul as a possibility of being the writer of the epistle. But other nominations abound. However, nearly every candidate nominated as author lacks convincing evidence to be "elected." Early church leaders suggested Paul, Apollos and Barnabas. Origen named Luke and Clement of Rome as possible writers. The Eastern Church stuck with Paul; the Western Church accepted Paul as the writer three centuries later. Luther picked Apollos; so did Lo Bue, and Montefiore—and with impressive, but inconclusive documentation. Spicq gave ten reasons for Barnabas being the author. Guthrie (p. 21) agreed, and lists Apollos, Priscilla, Philip, Peter, Silvanus, Ariston and Jude as modern guesses. Bruce quotes Manson: "...attempts to discover the writer's identity have no greater interest than a parlour-game." (Epistle to the Hebrews, p. 171f.)

Paul is disqualified in the minds of most scholars because 1) of a missing Pauline salutation; 2) Hebrews 2:3 makes the author a "second-generation" Christian; 3) textual criticism points elsewhere. Origen said, ". . . who wrote the epistle, in truth, God knows." But he also said, "... the style and composition belonged to one who called to mind the apostle's teachings...."

Defenders of non-Pauline authorship suggest that identifying Paul as the author would offend the Jews who knew him as "the apostle to the Gentiles." They also note Paul's ubiquitous form of greeting at the end of every epistle and found (in a truncated form) in Hebrews: "The grace of our Lord Jesus Christ be with you."

Origen is lightly regarded today as the author. But he identified three factors to be considered later in this introduction: 1) the author (known by the apostle's thoughts), 2) the writer of Hebrews. His truncated quote often found is "...who wrote the epistle, in truth, God knows..." and 3) the style and diction of the Greek text of the Epistle to the Hebrews.

One by one each nominee drops out as the evidence or argument fails to be to convincing. A question germane to identifying the author or writer is, "What prior writing do we have of this person?" Two men who were not apostles, Mark and Luke, wrote treatises that became part of the canon and are considered to be inspired by God. An argument that an excellent speaker (Apollos) could have written Hebrews begs the question of whether excellent speaking and writing are identical twin gifts; but the proposal of Apollos as being the author is at least as good as any other suggestion.

For further discussion of the author of the epistle, giving an alternate suggestion, see the Appendix.

Thematic outline of the epistle to the Hebrews

HEBREWS 1:1—13:25 (Epistle)
THEME: God has communicated to us through what his Son taught and did. His Son possesses everything that belongs to God, he created the universe, he manifests God's glory and exact nature, he sustains everything, he cancels our guilt, and is now with God in heaven. Since Jesus is superior to all aspects of the Jewish sacrificial system, and since there are many people who kept trusting God under that system, and since the purpose of our sufferings is to discipline us, renew yourselves spiritually and go forward in your Christian life.
I appeal to you that you love and help one another, respect your marriages, and be content. Imitate your former leaders and obey well their teachings about Christ. Also I want you to praise God, and do good to others. I want you to share with others. Submit to your spiritual leaders, and pray for me.
Greet the believers; those from Italy send their greetings. May God act graciously to you all.

   EPISTLE CONSTITUENT 1:1–4 (Paragraph: Opening of the Epistle)
   THEME: God has communicated to us through what his Son taught. His Son possesses everything that belongs to God, he created the universe, he manifests God's glory and exact nature, he sustains everything, cancels our guilt, and is now with God in heaven.

   EPISTLE CONSTITUENT 1:4—12:29 (Part: BODY of the Epistle)
   THEME: Since Jesus is superior to all aspects of the Jewish sacrificial system, and since there are many people who kept trusting God under that system, and since the purpose of our sufferings is to discipline us, renew yourselves spiritually and go forward in your Christian life.

      PART CONSTITUENT 1:4—2:18 (Sub-Part: Mitigated Appeal$_1$ of 1:4—12:29)
      THEME: We must pay careful attention to what we have heard about God's Son, since we will not escape God's punishment if we ignore it.

         SECTION CONSTITUENT 1:4–14 (Expository Paragraph: Basis$_1$ of 1:4—12:29)
         THEME: We know Christ is greater than the angels, since the Scriptures state that angels are transient and must worship him. What the Scriptures say that God said about his Son, he never said to any angel; God called Christ his Son who would rule righteously forever, being the creator of the universe and ruler over all his enemies.

         SECTION CONSTITUENT 2:1–4 (Paragraph: Mitigated Appeal of 1:4—12:29)
         THEME: We must pay careful attention to what we have heard about God's Son, since we will not escape God's punishment if we ignore it.

         SECTION CONSTITUENT 2:5–13 (Paragraph: Basis$_2$ of 1:4—12:29)
         THEME: It is not angels, but Jesus who has been appointed ruler over everything in God's new world, since now Jesus, who has been crowned as king, has authority over everything.

         SECTION CONSTITUENT 2:14–18 (Paragraph: Basis$_3$ of 1:4—12:29)
         THEME: Since it is not angels but we believers who are Abraham's spiritual descendants that Jesus helps, he became human just like us in order that by his death he might make powerless the devil, who has the power to cause people to be separated from God. Jesus became human so that he also might be a merciful and faithful Supreme Priest.

      PART CONSTITUENT 3:1—4:16 (Section: Appeal$_2$ of 1:4—12:29)
      THEME: Jesus deserves that we honor him much more than we honor Moses.

         SECTION CONSTITUENT 3:1–6 (Hortatory Paragraph: Mitigated Appeal$_1$ of 3:1—4:16)
         THEME: Jesus deserves that we honor him much more than we honor Moses, since Jesus is God/Divine and since he is faithful as he cares for all of us who are God's people.

         SECTION CONSTITUENT 3:7–19 (Hortatory Paragraph: Basis of 3:1—4:16)
         THEME: God is warning you, saying, "Your ancestors repeatedly disobeyed me as if they were irritating me to know whether I would be patient with them." Therefore, each one of you

must exhort each other every day, since you benefit in all that Christ has done, only if you keep firmly trusting in him.

SECTION CONSTITUENT 4:1–16 (Sub-Section: Mitigated Appeal$_2$ of 3:1—4:16)
THEME: We must strive to enter that place of eternal rest and firmly continue to hold as true what we believe about our powerful Supreme Priest.

SUB-SECTION CONSTITUENT 4:1–5 (Paragraph: Appeal$_1$ of 4:1–16)
THEME: Some of you should be afraid that God might consider that you will have not qualified to enter the place of resting with God. We/you have heard the good news about Christ, but it won't benefit you if you don't continue to believe it. Certainly we who have believed in Christ are able to experience/enter the place of resting with God.

SUB-SECTION CONSTITUENT 4:6–10 (Paragraph: Basis$_2$ of 4:1–16)
THEME: We conclude that God has appointed a time when his people can enter their eternal rest, since he would not have spoken about it if Joshua had led the Israelites to a place of rest.

SUB-SECTION CONSTITUENT 4:11–13 (Paragraph: Mitigated Appeal$_1$ of 4:1–16)
THEME: We must strive to enter that place of eternal rest and be sincere in doing so, since God's message can powerfully penetrate our thoughts.

SUB-SECTION CONSTITUENT 4:14–16 (Paragraph: Mitigated Appeal$_2$ of 4:1–16)
THEME: We should firmly continue to hold as true what we believe about our powerful Supreme Priest. We should pray boldly to him in order that we might experience his acting mercifully toward us and in order that we might experience his graciously helping us.

PART CONSTITUENT 5:1—9:28 (Section: Appeal$_3$ of 1:4—12:29)
THEME: You should request that we(exc.) teach you how to become spiritually mature, because it is not possible that anyone can persuade to repent again those who have renounced the message about Christ. Part of that message is that we needed to be consecrated by a better sacrifice, one made by Christ.

SECTION CONSTITUENT 5:1—6:20 (Sub-Section: Appeal of 5:1—9:28)
THEME: You should request that we(exc.) teach you how to become spiritually mature, but it may not be possible that anyone can persuade to repent again those who have renounced the message that they believed about Christ.

SUB-SECTION CONSTITUENT 5:1–14 (Paragraph Cluster: Basis$_1$ of 5:1—6:20)
THEME: The Israelites had Supreme Priests, but now God has installed Christ as our Supreme Priest who resembled Melchizedek in many ways, but it is hard for me to explain that to you.

PARAGRAPH CLUSTER CONSTITUENT 5:1–10 (Paragraph: Claim of 5:1–14)
THEME: Every Israelite Supreme Priest was chosen from among humans. Each of them dealt gently with those who ignorantly sinned. Similarly, God installed Christ as our Supreme Priest. Since he resembled Melchizedek in many ways, he is fully qualified to be Supreme Priest; thus we can certainly know that he is able to eternally forgive us who obey him.

PARAGRAPH CLUSTER CONSTITUENT 5:11–14 (Paragraph: Complication of 5:1–14)
THEME: Although there is much that I might teach you about how Christ resembles Melchizedek, such teaching is hard for me to explain to you, since you continue to need that someone teach you again the basic truths about Christ. You are not yet able to learn any more profound teaching.

SUB-SECTION CONSTITUENT 6:1–12 (Paragraph Cluster: Appeal of 5:1—6:20)
THEME: You should request that we(exc.) teach you how to become spiritually mature, but it may not be possible that anyone can persuade to repent again those who have renounced the message that they believed about Christ.

PARAGRAPH CLUSTER CONSTITUENT 6:1–8 (Paragraph: Appeal of 6:1–12)
THEME: You should request that we teach you how to become spiritually mature. But it may be impossible for some of you to become spiritually mature because those who

have experienced the blessings of a relationship with Christ and who have said that they no longer believe the message about Christ cannot be persuaded by anyone to repent again.

PARAGRAPH CLUSTER CONSTITUENT 6:9–12 (Paragraph: Basis of 6:1–12)
THEME: I am certain concerning you that most of you are doing better than those who have rejected God's message. Therefore, I strongly desire that each one of you continue to expect with certainty that you will receive what God has promised you until you finally receive it all.

SUB-SECTION CONSTITUENT 6:13–20 (Paragraph: Basis$_2$ of 5:1—6:20)
THEME: God promised that he would bless Abraham. God also guaranteed his promise to us by saying that he would punish himself if he did not fulfill his promise.

SECTION CONSTITUENT 7:1—9:22 (Sub-Section: Basis of 5:1—9:28)
THEME: Just as Melchizedek was greater than the priests descended from Aaron, and the new agreement is better than the old one, we needed to be consecrated by better sacrifices.

SUB-SECTION CONSTITUENT 7:1–19 (Paragraph Cluster: Claim$_1$ of 5:1—9:28)
THEME: We may deduce that Melchizedek was greater than Abraham and the priests descended from Aaron, and now we have God's Son who is a perpetual Supreme Priest who was like Melchizedek.

PARAGRAPH CLUSTER CONSTITUENT 7:1–3 (Paragraph: Basis$_1$ of 7:1—9:22)
THEME: For several reasons, we may properly consider that God's Son is like Melchizedek, and that it is as though he continues to serve as a priest perpetually.

PARAGRAPH CLUSTER CONSTITUENT 7:4–10 (Paragraph: Basis$_2$ of 7:1—9:22)
THEME: We may deduce that Melchizedek was greater than Abraham. It is as if God wanted us to understand that Melchizedek is still living. Also it was as though Levi himself, and all the Supreme Priests who descended from him, gave gifts to Melchizedek.

PARAGRAPH CLUSTER CONSTITUENT 7:11–19 (Paragraph: Conclusion of 7:1—9:22)
THEME: Some people might suppose that those Supreme Priests who were descendants of Levi's descendant Aaron had completely helped the people. However, those Supreme Priests were not adequate to help us. Instead, God has appointed a new type of Supreme Priest, like Melchizedek. Thus we know that the regulations concerning how God appoints priests also have changed.

SUB-SECTION CONSTITUENT 7:20—9:22 (Paragraph Cluster: Claim$_2$ of 5:1—9:28)
THEME: Since Jesus guarantees us a better agreement than the old one, and since the rituals set up by Moses did not allow ordinary people to enter God's presence, Jesus went into that holy place only once to put into effect the new agreement to allow us to have those benefits.

PARAGRAPH CLUSTER CONSTITUENT 7:20—8:13 (Sub-Paragraph Cluster: Basis$_1$ of 7:20—9:22)
THEME: Since Jesus guarantees us a better agreement than the old one and will be a Supreme Priest forever, he can completely and eternally save those who come to God because of what Christ has done.

SUB-PARAGRAPH CLUSTER CONSTITUENT 7:20–25 (Paragraph: Claim$_1$ of 7:20—8:13)
THEME: Since Jesus guarantees us a better agreement than the old one and will be a Supreme Priest forever, he can completely and eternally save those who come to God because of what Christ has done.

SUB-PARAGRAPH CLUSTER CONSTITUENT 7:26—8:6 (Paragraph: Claim$_2$ of 7:20—8:13)

THEME: Jesus is the Supreme Priest, since God solemnly declared that Jesus is the one whom he has appointed as the eternal Supreme Priest. Jesus is the kind of Supreme Priest that we need and he ministers in the true place of worship in heaven. If he were now living on the earth, he would not be a Supreme Priest. But where he is now, Christ ministers in a more excellent way than the Jewish priests do, and the agreement he has validated is better than the former agreement.

SUB-PARAGRAPH CLUSTER CONSTITUENT 8:7–13 (Paragraph: Claim$_3$ of 7:20—8:13)
THEME: A new agreement was needed, as is supported by what the Scriptures say about God making a new agreement.

PARAGRAPH CLUSTER CONSTITUENT 9:1–10 (Sub-Paragraph Cluster: Basis$_1$ of 7:20—9:22)
THEME: God told Moses what rituals were to be performed and about the Sacred Tent for those rituals, but those rituals indicated that the way for ordinary people to enter God's presence was not yet revealed.

SUB-PARAGRAPH CLUSTER CONSTITUENT 9:1–5 (Descriptive Paragraph: Concession of 9:1–10)
THEME: When God gave Moses the first agreement, he told Moses exactly how the priests should do the rituals and exactly how to build the tent for those rituals. The tent had two rooms—the outer room, which they called the Holy Place, with its furniture, and the inner room, which they called the Very Holy Place, with its furniture.

SUB-PARAGRAPH CLUSTER CONSTITUENT 9:6–10 (Paragraph: Contraexpectation of 9:1–10)
THEME: These rituals indicated that the way for ordinary people to enter God's presence was not yet revealed; people who brought the sacrifices still sensed that they were guilty for their sins. The Holy Spirit has shown that the ordinary people could not enter the presence of God as long as the Jewish system of offering sacrifices was in effect.

PARAGRAPH CLUSTER CONSTITUENT 9:11–22 (Sub-Paragraph Cluster: Inference of 7:20—9:22)
THEME: It was as though Christ went into that very holy place only once, taking his own blood with him, thus putting into effect a new agreement.

SUB-PARAGRAPH CLUSTER CONSTITUENT 9:11–14 (Expository Paragraph: Grounds of 9:11–22)
THEME: Christ being our Supreme Priest enabled us to have many good benefits. It was as though he went into that very holy place only once, taking his own blood with him.

SUB-PARAGRAPH CLUSTER CONSTITUENT 9:15–22 (Expository Paragraph: Conclusion of 9:11–22)
THEME: Forgiveness for sins has, ever since the time of Moses, always required the shedding of blood. Therefore, since Christ by his death redeemed those who did not obey the first agreement, he puts into effect a new agreement by shedding his own blood.

SECTION CONSTITUENT 9:23–28 (Expository Paragraph: Basis$_2$ of 5:1—9:28)
THEME: Since those who would enter heaven had to be consecrated by better sacrifices than those of the old agreement, Christ has appeared once to cause people to be no longer guilty for sin.

PART CONSTITUENT 10:1–39 (Section: Appeal$_4$ of 1:4—12:29)
THEME: Since Christ offered one sacrifice which is eternally adequate, and since there is no other sacrifice to appease God but only judgment facing us, let us not become discouraged when we

are persecuted. Let us come to God sincerely, keep firmly professing the truth, incite one another to love and good deeds, and encourage each other.

SECTION CONSTITUENT 10:1–25 (Sub-Section: Appeal₁ of 10:1–39)
THEME: Since Christ offered one sacrifice which is eternally adequate, and since Christ is our great Supreme Priest, let us come to God sincerely, keep firmly professing the truth, incite one another to love and good deeds, and encourage each other.

> SUB-SECTION CONSTITUENT 10:1–18 (Paragraph Cluster: basis of 10:1–25)
> THEME: In fulfillment of the Scripture, God abolished the first way of atonement to establish the second way, that of Christ offering his body as a sacrifice.
>
>> PARAGRAPH CLUSTER CONSTITUENT 10:1–4 (Expository Paragraph: Grounds of 10:1–18)
>> THEME: These yearly sacrifices can never make those who offer them perfect, otherwise they would have ceased. Instead they remind people that their guilt remains.
>
>> PARAGRAPH CLUSTER CONSTITUENT 10:5–10 (Expository Paragraph: Conclusion₁ of 10:1–18)
>> THEME: In fulfillment of the Scriptures which state that Christ indicated these sacrifices were inadequate and that he had come to do what was truly needed, God abolished the first way of atonement to establish the second way, that of Christ offering his body as a sacrifice.
>
>> PARAGRAPH CLUSTER CONSTITUENT 10:11–18 (Expository Paragraph: Conclusion₂ of 10:1–18)
>> THEME: Christ offered one sacrifice, and now is ruling with God until all his enemies are completely subdued. We know his sacrifice is eternally adequate since we, by trusting in that sacrifice, are eternally made perfect, and since the Scriptures support this claim.
>
> SUB-SECTION CONSTITUENT 10:19–25 (Paragraph: Mitigated Appeal of 10:1–25)
> THEME: Since we can confidently enter God's presence and since Christ is our great Supreme Priest, let us come to God sincerely, keep firmly professing the truth, incite one another to love and good deeds, and encourage each other.

SECTION CONSTITUENT 10:26–39 (Sub-Section: Appeal₂ of 10:1–39)
THEME: Since there is no sacrifice to appease God if we keep sinning, but only judgment facing us, let us not become discouraged when we are persecuted.

> SUB-SECTION CONSTITUENT 10:26–31 (Paragraph: Warning basis of 10:26–39)
> THEME: If we deliberately keep sinning, no other sacrifice is available that can appease God for our sinning; instead we will face God's judgment, since anyone who thus despises Christ and his shed blood deserves to be greatly punished by God.
>
> SUB-SECTION CONSTITUENT 10:32–39 (Paragraph: Appeal of 10:26–39)
> THEME: You recall how previously you continued to believe when you suffered for your faith. So do not become discouraged now when you are persecuted, since God will greatly reward you if you keep believing, and since we are ones who will be saved because of our faith.

PART CONSTITUENT 11:1—12:6 (Hortatory Sub-Part: Appeal₅ of 1:4—12:29)
THEME: Since we know about many people who trusted in God during difficult circumstances, we must be like them—we must put aside the things that hinder us spiritually, and try to achieve God's will, imitating Jesus.

> SUB-PART CONSTITUENT 11:1–40 (Section: Basis of 11:1—12:6)
> THEME: We can confidently expect to receive the good things that God has promised, when we trust him. Whenever we read in the Scriptures about some of our ancestors, we can know that God esteemed their faith. But God did not give them the most important benefit, since he planned that they receive that benefit only as they join together with us who trust God now.
>
> SECTION CONSTITUENT 11:1 (Claim₁ of 11:1–40)

INTRODUCTION TO THE ANALYSIS OF HEBREWS 25

THEME: We can confidently expect to receive the good things that God has promised, because we trust him. We can confidently expect to finally see them.

SECTION CONSTITUENT 11:3 (Claim$_2$ of 11:1–40)
THEME: It is because we trust God that we know that when he created the world, he did not create it from things that can be seen.

SECTION CONSTITUENT 11:2, 4–38 (Expository Sub-Section: Claims$_3$ of 11:1–40)
THEME: It was because our ancestors trusted God that he commended them. Those included Abel, Enoch, Noah, Abraham, Isaac, Jacob, Moses, Rahab, Gideon, Barak, Samson, Jephthah, David, Samuel, and others who suffered torture and death, who, because they trusted in God, each did things that pleased God.

SECTION CONSTITUENT 11:39–40 (SUMMARY of 11:1–40)
THEME: God did not give these people all that he promised them, because he foresaw that what he would later give them and us together would be better.

SUB-PART CONSTITUENT 12:1–6 (Paragraph: Appeal of 11:1—12:6)
THEME: Since we know so many people with faith like that, let us put aside anything, especially sin, which hinders us, and let us strive to achieve God's will and concentrate on Jesus.

PART CONSTITUENT 12:7–11 (Paragraph: Appeal$_6$ of 1:4—12:29)
THEME: Endure what you suffer, because our sufferings are to discipline us, and if we haven't experienced God's discipline we are not his true children. We should accept God's discipline since it is always to help us.

PART CONSTITUENT 12:12–29 (Paragraph: Summary Appeals of 1:4—12:29)
THEME: Renew yourselves spiritually; go forward in your Christian life; endeavor to live peacefully with everyone; seek to be holy; guard against bitterness; do not be immoral; and do not refuse to listen to God.

EPISTLE CONSTITUENT 13:1–19 (Part: Final Appeals of 1:1—13:25)
THEME: I appeal to you that you love and help one another, respect your marriages, and be content. Imitate your former leaders and obey well their teachings about Christ. Also I want you to praise God. I want you to do good to others, and share with others. Submit to your spiritual leaders, and pray for me.

PART CONSTITUENT 13:1–14 (Hortatory Paragraph: Appeal$_1$ of 13:1–19)
THEME: I appeal to you to love one another, be hospitable, help imprisoned and other mistreated believers, respect the marriage relationship; avoid covetousness; remember the manner of life of your former spiritual leaders and imitate their faith. Since Christ never changes, don't be diverted to believe strange teachings.

PART CONSTITUENT 13:15 (Hortatory Paragraph: Appeal$_2$ of 13:1–19)
THEME: We should continually praise God. Specifically, we should say openly that we belong to Jesus.

PART CONSTITUENT 13:16 (Hortatory Paragraph: Appeal$_3$ of 13:1–19)
THEME: Be continually doing good for others and be continually sharing your things with people who lack.

PART CONSTITUENT 13:17–19 (Hortatory Paragraph: Appeal$_4$ of 13:1–19)
THEME: Submit to your spiritual leaders, and pray for me.

EPISTLE CONSTITUENT 13:20–25 (Paragraph: Conclusion of the Epistle)
THEME: May God equip you with everything good you need. Timothy will be able to come with me to see you. Greet the believers; those from Italy send their greetings. May God act graciously to you all.

The Constituent Organization of Hebrews

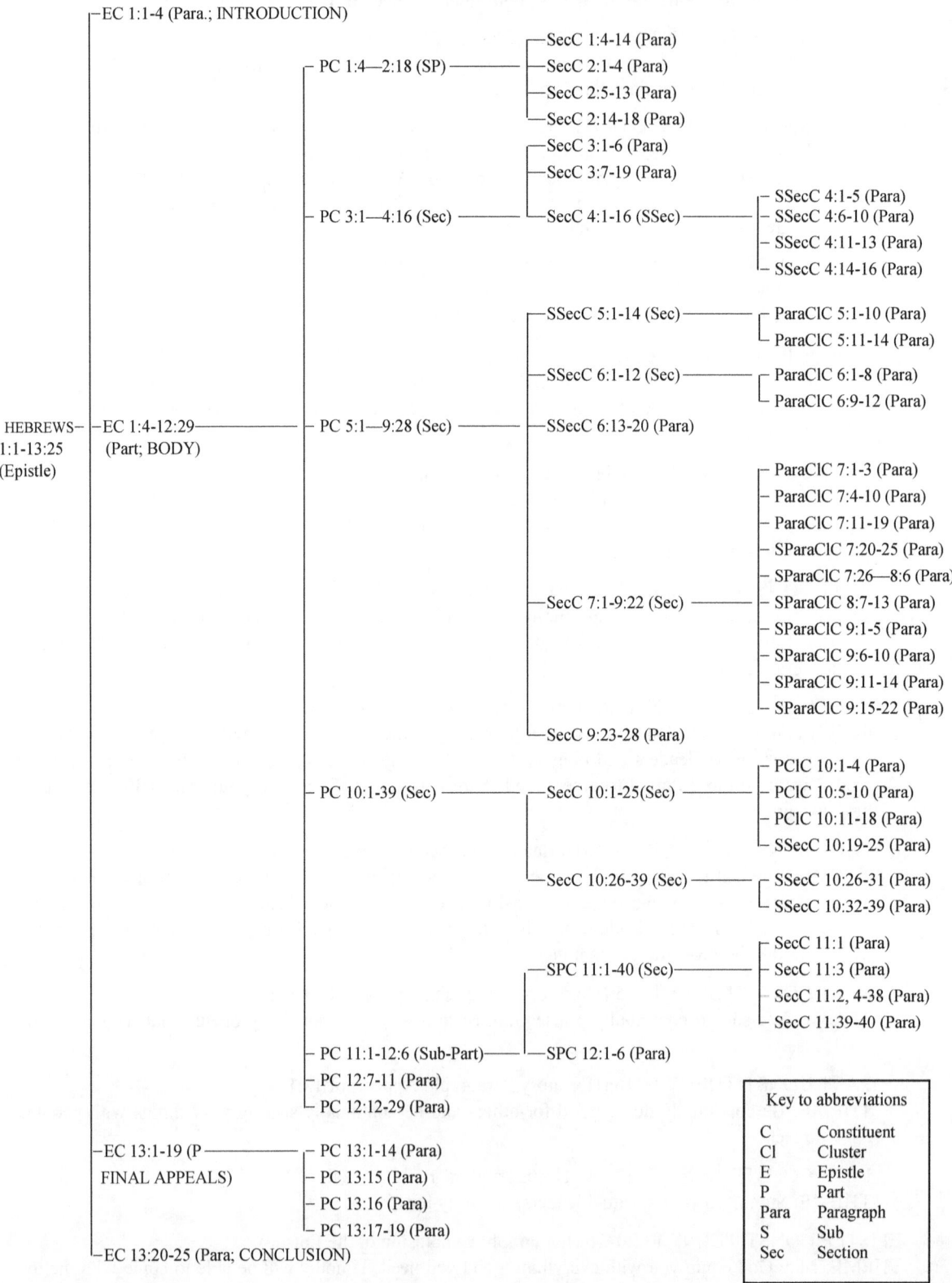

THE SEMANTIC UNITS OF HEBREWS

HEBREWS 1:1—13:25 (EPISTLE)

THEME: God has communicated to us through what his Son taught and did. His Son possesses everything that belongs to God, he created the universe, he manifests God's glory and exact nature, he sustains everything, he cancels our guilt, and is now with God in heaven. Since Jesus is superior to all aspects of the Jewish sacrificial system, and since there are many people who kept trusting God under that system, and since the purpose of our sufferings is to discipline us, renew yourselves spiritually and go forward in your Christian life.

I appeal to you that you love and help one another, respect your marriages, and be content. Imitate your former leaders and obey well their teachings about Christ. Also I want you to praise God, and do good to others. I want you to share with others. Submit to your spiritual leaders, and pray for me.

Greet the believers; those from Italy send their greetings. May God act graciously to you all.

MACROSTRUCTURE	CONTENTS
OPENING	1:1–4 God has communicated to us through what his Son taught. His Son possesses everything that belongs to God, he created the universe, he manifests God's glory and exact nature, he sustains everything, cancels our guilt, and is now with God in heaven.
BODY	1:4—12:29 Since Jesus is superior to all aspects of the Jewish sacrificial system, and since there are many people who kept trusting God under that system, and since the purpose of our sufferings is to discipline us, renew yourselves spiritually and go forward in your Christian life.
FINAL APPEALS	13:1–19 I appeal to you that you love and help one another, respect your marriages, and be content. Imitate your former leaders and obey well their teachings about Christ. Also I want you to praise God. I want you to do good to others, and share with others. Submit to your spiritual leaders, and pray for me.
CONCLUSION	13:20–25 May God equip you with everything good you need. Timothy will be able to come with me to see you. Greet the believers; those from Italy send their greetings. May God act graciously to you all.

COMMENTS ON OVERALL STRUCTURE

The structural coherence of the epistle consists of a number of features standard for epistles: an OPENING comparing what Christ has revealed to us with what the prophets revealed, a BODY, a set of FINAL APPEALS and a CONCLUSION containing a benediction, a brief message about Timothy, and a conveying of greetings.

EPISTLE CONSTITUENT 1:1–4 (Paragraph: Opening of the Epistle)

THEME: God has communicated to us through what his Son taught. His Son possesses everything that belongs to God, he created the universe, he manifests God's glory and exact nature, he sustains everything, cancels our guilt, and is now with God in heaven.

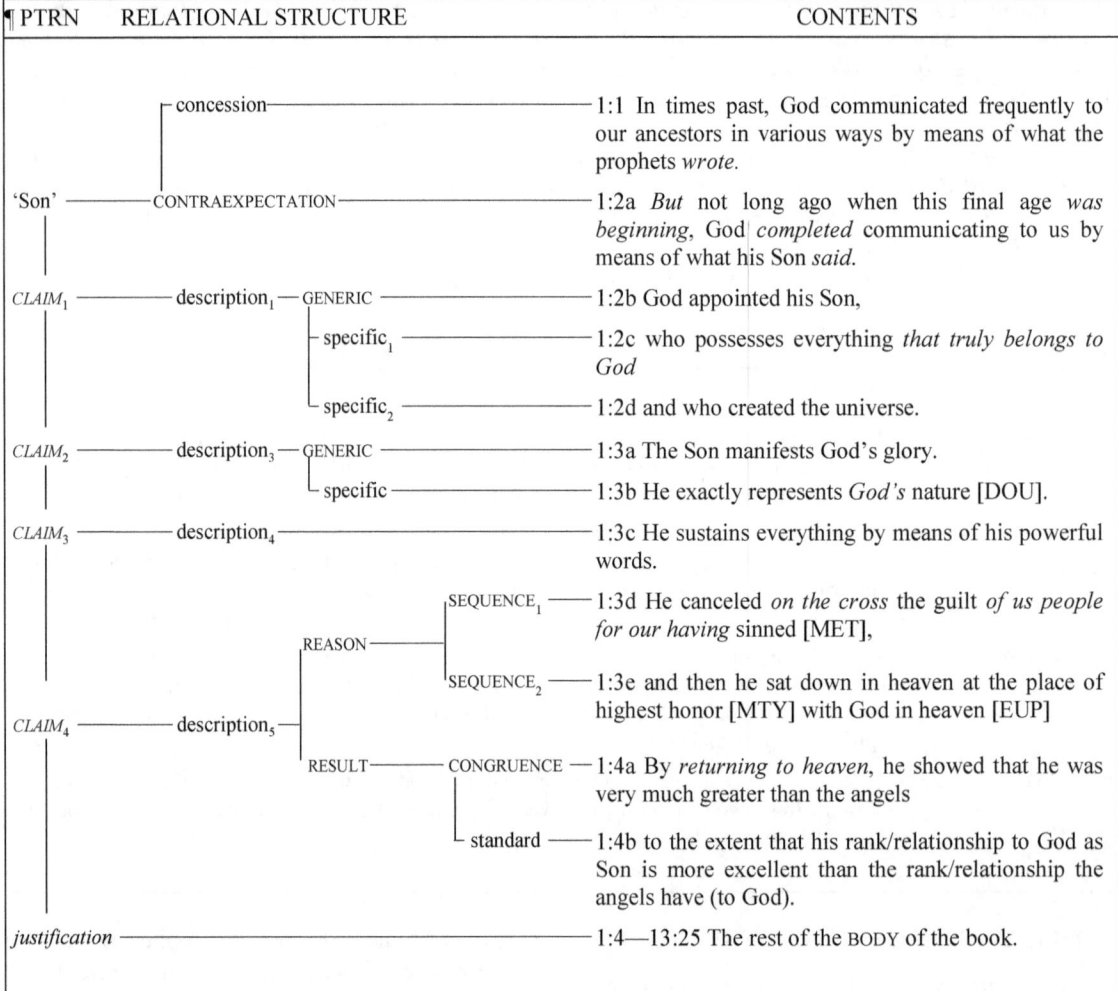

INTENT AND PARAGRAPH PATTERN

Hebrews is one of only two epistles in the New Testament which does not have the usual introductory paragraph containing the name of the author, the name of the intended recipients, and a blessing. But the 1:1–3 paragraph is still introductory, as is evident by the fact that it is difficult to classify as to paragraph pattern. It is clearly not hortatory. It is expressive or expository, but its constituents do not fit any of the patterns of those types of discourse. It consists of a set of four descriptions about the 'son', which are four CLAIMS with one *justification*.

Verse 4 provides a tail-head construction tying this OPENING closely to the following BODY of the epistle. This v. 4 is grammatically joined to the preceding but is the nucleus to the rest of chapter 1.

NOTES

1:1 In times past The Greek adverb πάλαι means 'long ago, formerly, in the past'. It is placed at the beginning of the clause in the display text because both this Greek word and the contrasting Greek phrase which begins v. 2 are forefronted to highlight the contrast between the two time periods.

communicated The verb λαλέω means 'to speak' but in the light of the word πολυτρόπως 'in many ways', the display uses a more generic word.

ancestors The plural of the word πατήρ 'father' is used in an extended sense to refer to the ancestors of the Jews.

by means of what the prophets *wrote* The phrase ἐν τοῖς προφήταις 'in the prophets' is a shortened form of a means proposition, requiring some verb to fill out the case frame. Thus 'wrote' is supplied; cf. CEV "God's prophets spoke."

1:2a *But* There is no conjunction in the Greek (the verb in v. 1 being only a participle). However, there is clearly a contrastive relation between the two verses, since the agent, time, and recipient in v. 1 contrast with those of v. 2.

Most modern English translations supply 'but' here (e.g., NIV, CEV, RSV, JB, NEB, TEV, NLT).

not long ago when this final *age was beginning* The phrase ἐπ' ἐσχάτου τῶν ἡμερῶν τούτων 'in these last days' seems to be a reflection of an Old Testament expression (Num. 24:14, Deut. 4:30), referring to the future Messianic period. The word 'days' is used in an extended sense, referring to an age or period of time. Several New Testament writers (Jude, Peter, and the author of Hebrews) use the expression to indicate that the whole Messianic age which Christ inaugurated has already begun. The inauguration might have been at the birth of Christ or at his death. The concept 'last' might refer to the close of the preceding age which was completed with the death of Christ, or it might refer to the present age as being the "final age" (NEB) before Christ's return. Since the whole focus in Hebrews is on what Christ accomplished for us by his death, and since the book has no references to his birth or his teaching ministry, it seems best to follow the great majority of commentators and assume the phrase refers to this period which was initiated with the death of Christ. The display is in agreement with this interpretation. One could translate the phrase as 'recently at the time that began with the death of Christ' to convey the idea more specifically.

***completed* communicating** The word 'completed' is included to convey the implied contrast with the πολυμερῶς 'many times' in v. 1; it is an implicature of the argument.

what his Son *said* See the discussion of 'prophets *said*' in v. 1.

1:2b God The agent of the verb is repeated from v. 1.

1:2c possesses everything *that truly belongs to God* The word κληρονόμος 'heir' is considered a dead metaphor, and is rendered as 'possess' (cf. TEV); the word 'inherit' is avoided because in English that word connotes the death of the original owner. The word πάντα 'all things' is rendered as 'everything that belongs to God' because it might be assumed that since Christ created everything (2e) he already possessed it; but Satan has temporarily gained control of much of God's creation.

1:2d–e God appointed his Son, who created the universe The additional clause is needed to unravel the Greek phrase δι᾽ οὗ 'through whom'. The word αἰῶνα usually means 'ages', but here most commentators support the sense of 'the universe' given by BAGD (p. 28.3).

1:3a manifests God's glory The Greek noun ἀπαύγασμα is given the sense of 'radiance' by BAGD (p. 82), which is followed by most commentators, though a few take the passive sense 'reflection'. Either way it is figurative; thus the display renders it 'manifests'. An alternative for 'glory' would be 'greatness.'.

1:3b exactly represents *God's* nature The Greek word χαρακτήρ originally meant representation (i.e., an image of some ruler stamped on coins) but in a figurative sense referring to God the whole phrase means "exact representation of his (= God's) nature." (BAGD, p. 876.1b).

Propositions 3a and 3b are listed as a doublet. Ellingworth says (p. 99), "In the present verse, χαρακτὴρ τῆς ὑποστάσεως αὐτοῦ (representation of his reality) reinforces ἀπαύγασμα τῆς δόξης (radiance of glory) in describing the essential unity and exact resemblance between God and his Son."

1:3c sustains Suggestions for the meaning of the verb φέρω are "holds together" (CEV), "bear up" (BAGD), "to govern" (Dods, Wilson).

his powerful words The Greek genitive construction τῷ ῥήματι τῆσ δυνάμεως αὐτοῦ 'by the word of the power of him' is simply a way of saying 'by his powerful words/commands' or 'by his words which act powerfully' (cf. NIV, TEV, NJB, and NCV).

1:3d He canceled *on the cross* the guilt *of us people for our having* sinned The word 'cleanse' in the participial phrase καθαρισμὸν τῶν ἁμαρτιῶν ποιησάμενος 'having made cleansing of sins' is taken as a dead metaphor. The display refers specifically to the act that cancelled the guilt. The word 'sins' here means specifically guilt for sins.

There is a slight textual problem here. The Textus Receptus follows manuscripts which add the words δι' ἑαυτοῦ (OR variants of that) 'by himself'. The words are omitted in the GNT Fourth Revised Edition with a B "almost certain" rating. It is more likely that some scribe added the words to reinforce the participle 'having made' than that some other scribe omitted them and then the omission was replicated in both Alexandrian and Western manuscripts.

1:3e sat down in heaven at the place of highest honor The words ἐν δεξιᾷ 'on the right (hand)' is a figure of metonymy, the place standing for the high honor that is associated with it (cf. LB "in highest honor"). Westcott (p. 15) suggests that the verb "expresses the solemn taking of the seat of authority, and not merely the act of sitting" and many commentators agree, and some translators may want to state or imply "to rule."

with God As BAGD points out (p. 497), the word μεγαλωσύνη 'greatness' is "a periphrasis for God Himself," being used by the writer somewhat euphemistically to avoid the name of God, likely for the sake of the Jews in his anticipated audience. It seems to be used to reinforce the majesty and greatness of God. Both TEV and LB/NLT use 'God'.

in heaven The phrase ἐν ὑψηλοῖς means literally 'in highest (places)'. This seems to be a shortened form of 'in the highest heavens,' a Jewish idiom meaning 'heaven,' and it is so rendered in TEV, NIV, NJB, CEV, and NCV.

1:4a By *returning to heaven,* he showed The participle γενόμενος 'having become' signifies an event that is related to his 'sitting down' (3f). As Bruce says (p. 18), "His exaltation to the right hand of God in itself marks Him out as being superior to the angels" (see also Miller, p. 14). These comments by Bruce and Miller support '*by returning to heaven*'.

much greater In languages where the word 'greater' must be more specific, it may be best to translate something like 'worthy of much more honor'.

1:4b to the extent that The Greek word τοσούτῳ means 'by so much as'.

his rank/relationship to God as Son is more excellent This represents the clause διαφορώτερον παρ' αὐτοὺς κεκληρονόμηκεν ὄνομα 'he has inherited a more excellent name than they (the angels)'. The word 'inherited' is a dead metaphor, indicating something a person receives. TEV has "that God gave him," but the perfect tense indicates a present possession and the display uses the present tense also. The word 'name' is a metonymy standing for Christ's "rank, dignity, authority, position" as God's son (Miller, p.14); see also Moffatt, Davies, Westcott; NJB and NEB have "title."

BOUNDARIES AND COHESION

It is possible to posit the paragraph boundary here at the end of v.3 or starting with v. 5. TEV and LB/NLT seem to be the only versions which make the break after v. 3, but six of twelve commentaries consulted that give paragraph divisions make the break before v. 5. This writer was persuaded by the semantic evidence instead of the grammatical evidence. Observe that there is a claim in v. 4 that is justified in the rest of the chapter. Thus, it is likely that v. 4 begins a new paragraph. Moreover, v. 4 introduces the subject of Christ's superiority over the angels, a theme continued through 2:18. Furthermore, v. 5 begins with γάρ 'for', an indication that what follows supports the statement made in v. 4. The main feature of cohesion in the first three verses is the pronominal references and the euphemistic references to both the Father and the Son.

The start of a new paragraph at v.4 is indicated by a switch from a brief discussion of the superiority of Christ's communicating to us, to a lengthy discussion of his superiority over angels: there is a tail-head structure, angels being mentioned briefly in v.4 but discussed at length through the rest of chapter 1 and all of chapter 2. Cohesion in the 1:1–4 paragraph is seen in the contrast between παλαι 'in the past' in v.1 and επ᾿ εξαστον των ψνερων 'in the last days' in v.2.

PROMINENCE AND THEME

The theme statement is drawn from the several *CLAIMS* in vv. 1 and 3.

EPISTLE CONSTITUENT 1:4—12:29 (Part: BODY of the Epistle)

THEME: Since Jesus is superior to all aspects of the Jewish sacrificial system, and since there are many people who kept trusting God under that system, and since the purpose of our sufferings is to discipline us, renew yourselves spiritually and go forward in your Christian life.

MACROSTRUCTURE	CONTENTS
APPEAL₁	1:4—2:18 We must pay careful attention to what we have heard about God's Son, since we will not escape God's punishment if we ignore it.
APPEAL₂	3:1—4:16 Jesus deserves that we honor him much more than we honor Moses.
APPEAL₃	5:1—9:28 You should request that we(exc.) teach you how to become spiritually mature, because it is not possible that anyone can persuade to repent again those who have renounced the message about Christ. Part of that message is that we needed to be consecrated by a better sacrifice, one made by Christ.
APPEAL₄	10:1–39 Since Christ offered one sacrifice which is eternally adequate, and since there is no other sacrifice to appease God but only judgment facing us, let us not become discouraged when we are persecuted. Let us come to God sincerely, keep firmly professing the truth, incite one another to love and good deeds, and encourage each other
APPEAL₅	11:1—12:6 Since we know about many people who trusted in God during difficult circumstances, we must be like them—we must put aside the things that hinder us spiritually, and try to achieve God's will, imitating Jesus.
APPEAL₆	12:7–11 Endure what you suffer, because our sufferings are to discipline us, and if we haven't experienced God's discipline we are not his true children. We should accept God's discipline since it is always to help us.
SUMMARY APPEALS	12:12–29 Renew yourselves spiritually; go forward in your Christian life; endeavor to live peacefully with everyone; seek to be holy; guard against bitterness; do not be immoral; and do not refuse to listen to God.

INTENT AND PARAGRAPH PATTERN

Each of these part constituents is hortatory, containing a lot of expository material but ending with an appeal. The writer's intention is to remind his readers of all the ways that Christ is superior to everything that the Jews had known and cherished, and that therefore they needed to keep trusting in what he did for them, otherwise they would face eternal punishment.

BOUNDARIES AND COHERENCE

A new unit at 13:1 is indicated by a change from the topic of worship to individual exhortations concerning various aspects of Christian behavior. This *body* of the epistle is a sandwich structure with 'worship' at 1:6 and at 12:28.

PROMINENCE AND THEME

The theme for the BODY of the epistle is drawn from summaries of the *APPEALS*.

PART CONSTITUENT 1:4—2:18 (Sub-Part: Mitigated Appeal₁ of 1:4—12:29)

THEME: We must pay careful attention to what we have heard about God's Son, since we will not escape God's punishment if we ignore it.

MACROSTRUCTURE	CONTENTS
basis₁	1:4–14 We know Christ is greater than the angels, since the Scriptures state that angels are transient and must worship him. What the Scriptures say that God said about his Son, he never said to any angel; God called Christ his Son who would rule righteously forever, being the creator of the universe and ruler over all his enemies.
MITIGATED APPEAL	2:1–4 We must pay careful attention to what we have heard about God's Son, since we will not escape God's punishment if we ignore it.
basis₂	2:5–13 It is not angels, but Jesus who has been appointed ruler over everything in God's new world, since now Jesus, who has been crowned as king, has authority over everything.
basis₃	2:14–18 Since it is not angels but we believers who are Abraham's spiritual descendants that Jesus helps, he became human just like us in order that by his death he might make powerless the devil, who has the power to cause people to be separated from God. Jesus became human so that he also might be a merciful and faithful Supreme Priest.

INTENT AND MICROSTRUCTURE PATTERN

This unit consists of a MITIGATED APPEAL and three *bases* supporting that APPEAL. The author here is presenting one of his strong warnings to his Jewish readers of the severe consequences if they reject the message about God's Son.

BOUNDARIES AND COHERENCE

A new unit at 3:1 is signaled by the conjunction οὖν 'therefore' and a vocative phrase ἀδελφοὶ ἅγιοι 'holy brothers'.

PROMINENCE AND THEME

The theme for this unit is drawn from condensations of the most naturally prominent propositions in several of the *bases* and in the MITIGATED APPEAL.

SECTION CONSTITUENT 1:4–14 (Expository Paragraph: Basis₁ of 1:4—12:29)

THEME: We know Christ is greater than the angels, since the Scriptures state that angels are transient and must worship him. What the Scriptures say that God said about his Son, he never said to any angel; God called Christ his Son who would rule righteously forever, being the creator of the universe and ruler over all his enemies.

¶ PTRN	RELATIONAL STRUCTURE	CONTENTS

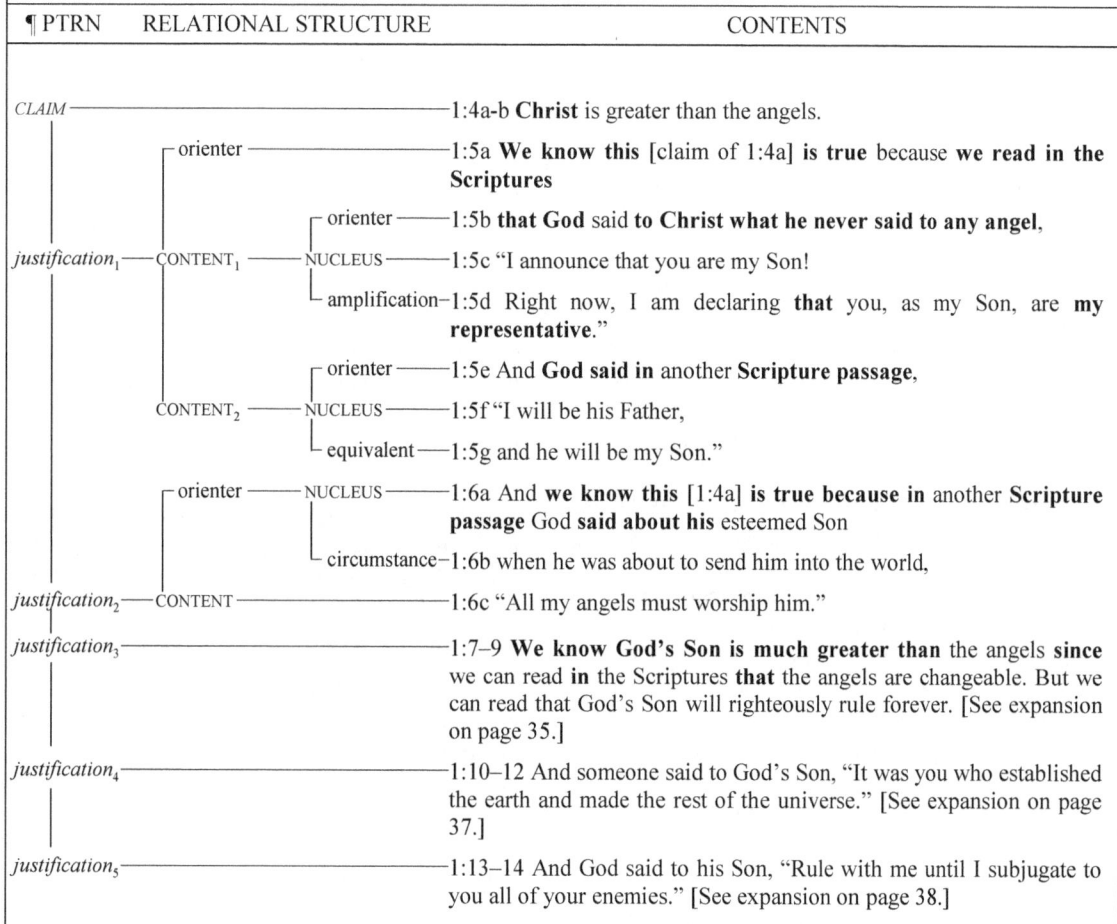

INTENT AND PARAGRAPH PATTERN

The 1:4–14 paragraph is clearly expository, having no emotive elements or hortatory elements directed to his addressees. It consists of an initial CLAIM about Christ's superiority to angels, followed by five *justifications*, each of which cites an Old Testament passage to support the claim. 1:4 is a tail-head construction which serves as a turning point between the introduction and the BODY of the epistle. This verse is grammatically joined to the preceding but is the nucleus to the rest of chapters 1 and 2.

NOTES

1:4a-b This verse is treated here and in the introduction because it functions in both places.

1:5a *We know this* [claim of 1:4a] *is true because* The words in italics are part of the implicature of the argument: v. 5 is not the reason the Son is superior to the angels, but the grounds by which we know the statement in v. 4 is true.

in the Scriptures These words supply what the writer assumed his audience would know; namely, that the passages he is citing are from the Scriptures.

1:5b *that God said to Christ* These words are both part of the implicature of the argument and a specification of the pronominal referent of 'you' in the quote. Alternatively 'to Jesus' could be used. NLT puts it quite clearly: "But God said it about Jesus," although it is true that both

'Jesus' and 'Christ' would be somewhat anachronistic.

It is recognized that the word 'son' when referring to Jesus is metaphorical, and probably a live metaphor. In some languages it may be necessary to adjust the translation accordingly. The author meant "I declare you to be my fully accredited Representative, as a son represents his father in accomplishing the father's plans."

what he never said to any angel The display makes clear the real force of the rhetorical question. The same is done in TEV, NLT, NEB, NJB. The words in italics are a contextual implicature: God said this to his Son, not to any angel.

1:5d Right now We must not suppose that the original sentence in Psalm 2:7 or its citation here referred to a specific day in the life of the speaker. God meant "on this occasion." This writer agrees with Morris who says, "We should not concern ourselves overmuch with trying to identify the day meant in 'today.' " Trying to specify what day does too much violence to the doublet, which is basically saying the same thing in both lines.

I am declaring that you, as my Son The display tries to take a middle road with 'declared to all.' The Greek ἐγὼ σήμερον γεγέννηκά σε 'today I have begotten thee' could be considered a doublet with the line preceding it; it is from Psalm 2:7 and is typical Hebrew parallelism. As Barnes notes, the word begotten must "be understood figuratively; and must mean, substantially, 'I have constituted, or appointed thee.' "

1:5e And *God said in* **another** *Scripture passage* The parts in italics are simply repeated from 5a. In some languages it may be necessary to state it in a fuller form, such as 'and we know this because God never said to any angel what he said in another Scripture passage.' TEV has "Nor did God say to any angel ..."

1:5f-g In some languages, the parallel statements of the Hebrew poetry is not natural. In such cases, the translation might render these two sentences as a doublet.

1:6a See the notes on 5a and 5d. The word 'God' is supplied as the agent of 'said' to fit the context.

esteemed As most commentators note, the word πρωτότοκος does not mean firstborn in the temporal sense, but 'preeminent in every respect.' It could be considered a metonymy, in which the temporal word stands for "the superior dignity and honor due to a firstborn in any household" (Miller, p. 18). A literal translation is likely to imply God had many other sons; and indeed, any adjective used here could imply there were other sons to whom that adjective did not apply.

1:6b when he was about to send him into the world The author implied that God spoke a ritual sentence in order to show the importance of his Representative. Some commentators suggest that this sentence will be spoken in the future when Jesus returns to earth to rule. It is not likely that the author would have supposed that this sentence would have supported his argument here by referring to an event that had not yet happened by the time of his writing this message.

1:6c "All my angels must worship him." This was the ritual sentence with which God authenticated his Son as his Representative.

BOUNDARIES AND COHESION

The boundary at 2:1 is clearly marked by the conjunction Διὰ τοῦτο 'therefore'. followed by the verb δεῖ 'it is necessary' which is conveying an appeal. Cohesion is seen in several occurrences of ἄγγελος 'angel' in the paragraph (vv. 5, 6, 7 (2X), 13) contrasting with its absence in the following paragraph.

PROMINENCE AND THEME

The theme consists first of all of the naturally prominent congruence proposition of the CLAIM followed by 'the Scriptures state' to summarize that what follows are five OT passages providing *justifications* for the CLAIM. The rest of the theme reverses the order of the most thematic propositions of each of the justifications for brevity and simplicity, giving first what was said in the Scriptures about the angels and then what was said to or about God's Son but what was not said to or about any angels.

EXPANSION OF *JUSTIFICATION*₃ IN THE 1:4–14 DISPLAY

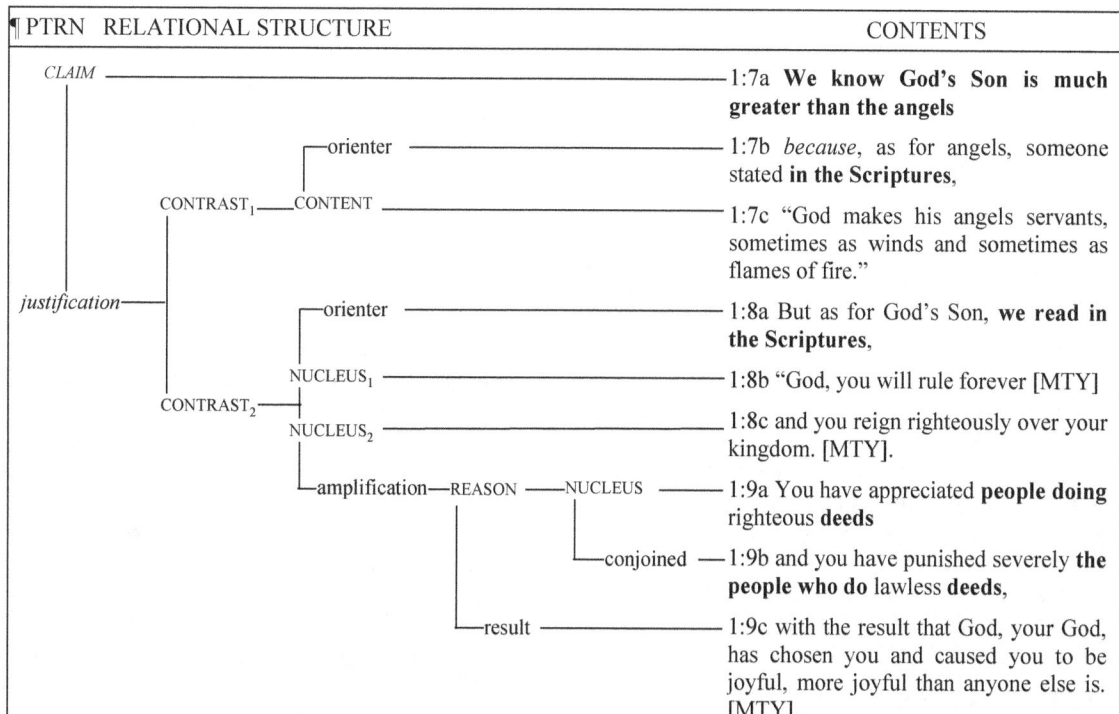

NOTES

1:7a We know God's Son is much greater than the angels

This is simply repeated from 4a. Such a repetition might be necessary in some languages to make sure the theme clearly is maintained.

1:7b *as for angels* The author used the Greek construction μὲν...δέ 'in regard to ... in regard to'. He wrote here the words πρὸς μὲν τοὺς ἀγγέλους 'in regard to the angels' in v. 7, then he introduced v. 8 with πρὸς δὲ τὸν υἱόν 'in regard to the Son'. He was indicating that he was contrasting the unimportance of angels (the first clause) with the much greater worthiness of Jesus (the second clause). The author used this idiom also in 3:5–6, 7:8, 7:20, 7:23, 9:6–7, 9:23, 10:11, 10:33, 11:15, probably in 12:9, certainly in 12:10 and in 12:11.

someone stated The Greek simply has λέγει 'he/it says'. which does not indicate the agent. But since the quote itself (7c) has 'his angels' the agent of 'says' cannot be God. An alternative to that given in the display would be 'someone wrote'.

in the Scriptures These words make clear that this is an Old Testament quotation. (It is from Ps. 104:4.)

1:7c makes his angels servants, sometimes as winds and sometimes as flames of fire Various commentators suggest subservient, changeable, or swift as the point of comparison, but some of those qualities do not fit well with the author's intention to show that they are not worthy of worship. The display does not supply the point of comparison, but if a translator needs to supply one, the majority of commentators suggest 'changeable'. One factor that supports "changeable" as the point of comparison between the image of the metaphor and the angels' character is the fact that in v. 8 they are contrasted with the Son whose throne is forever unchangeable.

1:8a But as for God's Son The author completed his contrast between angels and Jesus.

See notes on 7b. Since the quotation here (from Ps. 45:6–7) addresses Christ directly (taking the words ὁ θεός 'God' in 8b as a vocative, as do all the versions examined and most commentators), the πρός has to be expressed as 'as for' and not 'concerning' as in 7b.

1:8b rule forever The word θρόνος 'throne' is here as elsewhere in the NT (e.g., Luke 1:52,

22:30, Heb. 4:16, 8:1, Rev. 3:21) a metonymy, here standing for the event of ruling associated with it.

1:8c you reign righteously The Greek, ἡ ῥάβδος τῆς εὐθύτητος ῥάβδος τῆς βασιλείας σου 'the scepter of righteousness (is) the scepter of thy kingdom' has a couple of problems. First, scepter is again a metonymy standing for the event of ruling; cf. TEV's "you rule over." Second, there is a textual problem as to whether the final pronoun of the phrase is 'thy' or 'his'. The display follows the GNT which is now given a B "almost certain" rating. The OT passage uses 'thy'. Although four of the best early manuscripts have 'his'. the range of manuscripts supporting 'thy' is far greater and wider. Metzger suggests that it seems likely that it was changed by some scribe who thought ὁ θεός 'God' was a predicate nominative instead of a vocative, which is regarded as very improbable. Having a 3rd person pronoun here would also severely conflict with the five 2nd person singular pronouns in v. 9, which is part of the same quotation.

1:9a You have appreciated The Greek word ἠγάπησας literally refers to 'loving' people. However, it seems that the Psalmist is referring to the king esteeming the actions of righteous people.

people doing righteous deeds
The Greek word is δικαιοσύνη 'righteousness' which, being an abstract noun, has been made a gerundive clause.

1:9b you have punished severely The primary sense of the Greek word ἐμίσησας is 'hating'. Here, the Psalmist is using a figure of metonymy with the cause 'hating' standing for the effect of punishing, focusing on the result of the king's actions towards evil-doers. The word 'severely' seems to be implied by the word 'hating'.

the people who do lawless deeds This expresses the abstract noun ἀνομία 'lawlessness'.

1:9c chosen you The expression ἔχρισέν σε...ἔλαιον 'anointed thee (with) oil' is a metonymy in which the cause (the event of anointing with oil) stands for the effect (choosing) associated with it. Some commentators say with the word 'oil' there is also a metaphor involved, referring to the joyful time when a king was anointed at his coronation, or else to the custom of anointing guests at a feast to honor them. But to spell out the image of such a metaphor would probably detract from the main point more than it would add. TEV's with "gave you the joy," also omits the figure of anointing. Kistemaker (p. 44) states it well: "The application of justice fills him with joy and happiness, and constitutes his anointing."

and caused you to be joyful This spells out the genitive abstract noun ἀγαλλιάσεως 'of gladness'.

anyone else Commentators are greatly divided as to whom τοὺς μετόχους σου 'thy partners/companions' refers. Opinions range from men, to kings, to angels, to an indefinite 'anyone else'. There seems no good way to decide; therefore the 'indefinite' interpretation is chosen here.

EXPANSION OF *JUSTIFICATION*₄ IN THE 1:4–14 DISPLAY

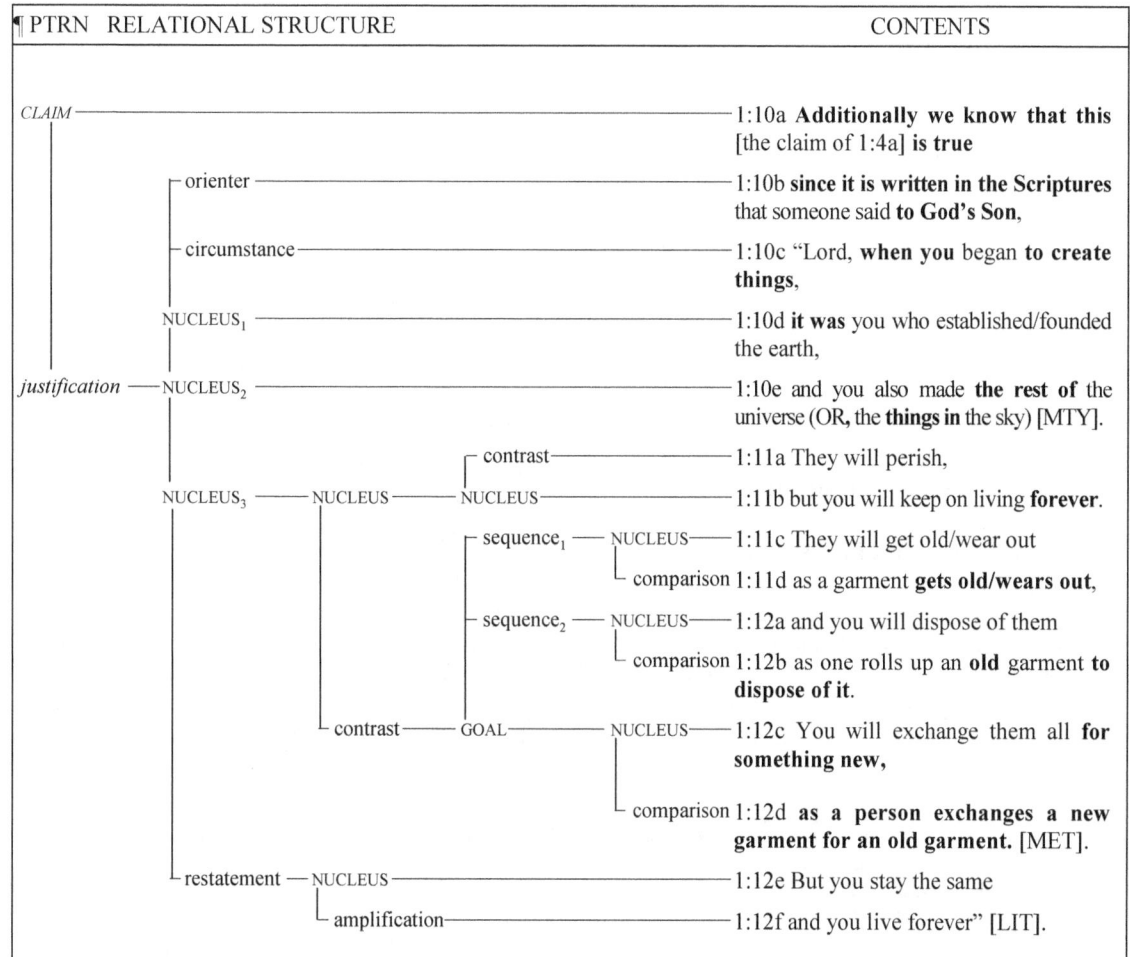

NOTES

1:10a–b ***we know*** See the notes on 7a–b. The Greek simply has καί 'and'. but it introduces an additional Scriptural (Ps. 102:25–27) justification for the CLAIM made in 4a, and again the quote itself records what someone else (the Psalmist) was saying directly to God. F. F. Bruce says (p. 23) "That our author understood this quotation from Ps. 102 as an utterance of God seems plain from the way in which it is linked by the simple conjunction 'and' to the preceding quotation from Ps. 45. Both quotations fall under the same rubric: 'But to the Son [God says].' If in the preceding quotation the Son is addressed by God as 'God,' in this one he is addressed by God as 'Lord.' ".

1:10c ***began to create things*** The phrase κατὰ ἀρχάς 'in the beginning' is a metonymy standing for a specific beginning; the beginning of the universe.

1:10d ***it was*** **you** The prominence given the second person singular pronoun σύ by its being clause-initial is conveyed by the cleft construction in English.

established/founded The Greek verb θεμελιόω means literally 'lay the foundation of' but is used in a figurative sense here; cf. TEV's "created," LB/NLT's "made."

1:10e ***you also made*** The words ἔργα τῶν χειρῶν σού 'the works of thy hands' are a metonymy and also an anthropomorphism, and therefore are rendered non-figuratively in the display.

the rest of **the universe (OR,** ***the things in*** **the sky)** As Miller notes (p. 24), the word οὐρανοί 'heavens' reflects a Jewish understanding of the universe and "would include all else besides the earth."

1:11b keep on living *forever* As Lenski (p. 59) says, the present tense of the verb διαμένεις 'you remain' is just a way of stating the Son will live forever; LB/NLT has "remain forever."

1:11c get old/wear out The two alternatives here are simply to call attention to the fact that a literal translation of παλαιωθήσονται 'become old' may result in a collocational clash in some languages.

1:12b an *old* **garment** *to dispose of it* As Barnes notes, this is figurative language "borrowed from folding up and laying aside garments that are no longer fit for use." The implied function of the action is stated.

1:12c You will exchange them all It seems best in a sentence of adoration to translate the passive as an active clause. Most English translations use the word 'change', but to change clothes in English means 'to put on clean clothes'. Here 'exchange' avoids this wrong meaning.

all *for something new* These words are simply a summary of what was stated in 10d–e, to identify the pronoun αὐτούς 'them'.

1:12d *as a person exchanges a new garment for an old garment.* The word ἀλλαγήσονται means 'will be changed' (BAGD, p. 39.1); but as Miller notes (p. 27) "in the context of changing clothes, it means to exchange them for others, not alter them so that they can be worn longer." The display agrees with Miller, and spells out all the parts of the live metaphor. LB captures the sense quite well with "and replace them."

The words ὡς ἱμάτιον 'as a garment' are included in the GNT with a C "difficulty in deciding" rating but omitted in the TR. Their inclusion has strong manuscript support. Since these words are not found in the LXX text of Ps. 102:26, it seems quite certain that they were omitted by some scribe who wanted to make the two texts conform to each other.

1:12e In some languages, the words *you are not like what you have created* may need to be supplied simply to make clearer the contrast being made between the creation and the Creator.

1:12f you live forever The expression τὰ ἔτη σου οὐκ ἐκλείψουσιν 'thy years will not end' is very poetic: it is both a metonymy, years standing for the event of living, and a litotes, stating the denial of the negative to emphasize the positive.

EXPANSION *JUSTIFICATION*₅ IN THE 1:4–14 DISPLAY

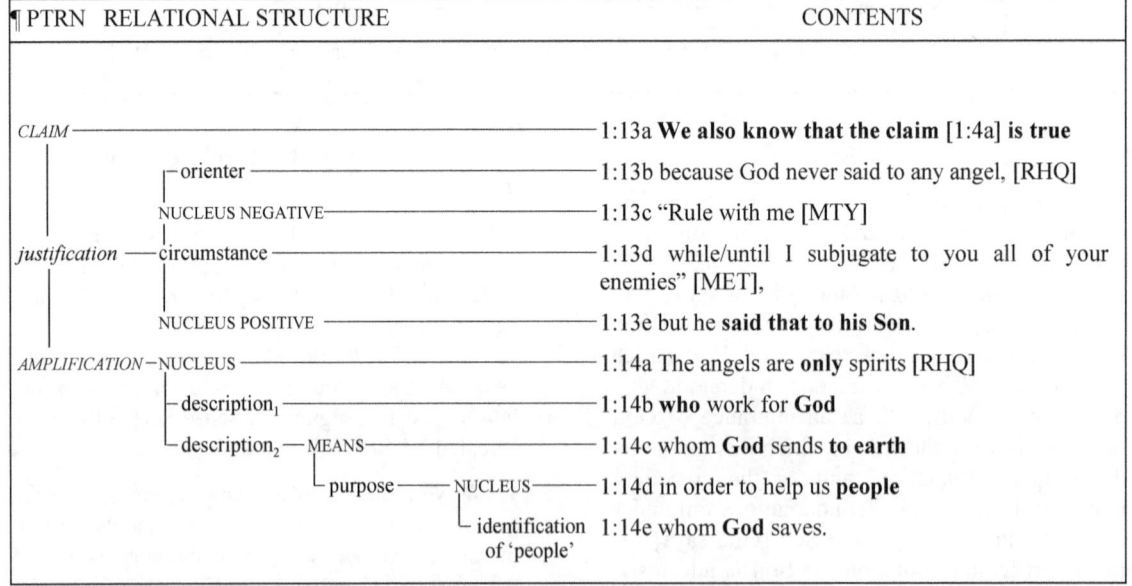

NOTES

1:13a See notes on 1:7a.

1:13b See notes on 4a.

because God never said to any angel, The author uses a rhetorical question that implies that God authenticated only his Son, not any angel.

1:13c The citation here is from Ps. 110:1. Here the words 'sit down' were included, because sitting down after finishing work is probably universally appropriate. LB departs partially from a literal rendering here with "Sit here beside me in honor." But in this context the whole clause κάθου ἐκ δεξιῶν μου 'sit at my right' is probably best taken as a metonymy for 'rule with me'. Miller says (p. 28) the clause refers to Christ's being "associated with the Father in His royal dignity."

1:13d I subjugate to you all of your enemies The clause θῶ τοὺς ἐχθρούς σου ὑποπόδιον τῶν ποδῶν σου 'I put thy enemies a footstool of thy feet' is very figurative. Kistemaker (p. 49) says it refers to a practice of kings in those times: "A victorious king or general would place his feet on the neck of a defeated king (Josh. 10:24; Isa. 51:23) to demonstrate his triumph over his enemy." Miller (p. 29) adds that "to perpetuate the memorial and effect of the victory, a conqueror would have a footstool made for his feet to rest upon as he sat upon his throne, depicting the fallen enemy on it." Regardless of whether the latter is true or not, since the figure is mentioned twice in the Old Testament, it is thus considered dead, and made non-metaphorical here. Miller (p. 29) says the meaning is simply "until I completely conquer all your enemies." TFT has "put all of your enemies completely under your control."

1:13e but he *said that to his Son* Changing the rhetorical question to a statement fits well.

1:14a are *only* spirits The negative word οὐχί introducing the rhetorical question indicates a positive answer is called for; the component of emphasis conveyed by the question is maintained by the word 'only'.

1:14b work for *God* The adjective λειτουργικός means 'engaged in holy service' (BAGD, p. 471); the words 'to God' complete the case frame. "Serve God" (TEV) is a good alternative.

1:14c *God* sends *to earth* The italicized words simply complete the case frame.

1:14d us The Greek has 'those who,' but the display renders this in the first person plural (inclusive) because it refers to the writer and his anticipated readers.

1:14e whom *God* saves In the Greek phrase τοὺς μέλλοντας κληρονομεῖν σωτηρίαν 'those about to inherit salvation', 'inherit' is considered a dead metaphor (cf. 1:2e) and rendered non-metaphorically but expressing the concept by the verb 'receive'. Rendering the abstract noun 'salvation' by a full clause entails completing the case frame. The writer is referring to eschatological aspects of our salvation, but it should not be taken to mean salvation is completely future.

SECTION CONSTITUENT 2:1–4 (Paragraph: Mitigated Appeal of 1:4—12:29)

THEME: We must pay careful attention to what we have heard about God's Son, since we will not escape God's punishment if we ignore it.

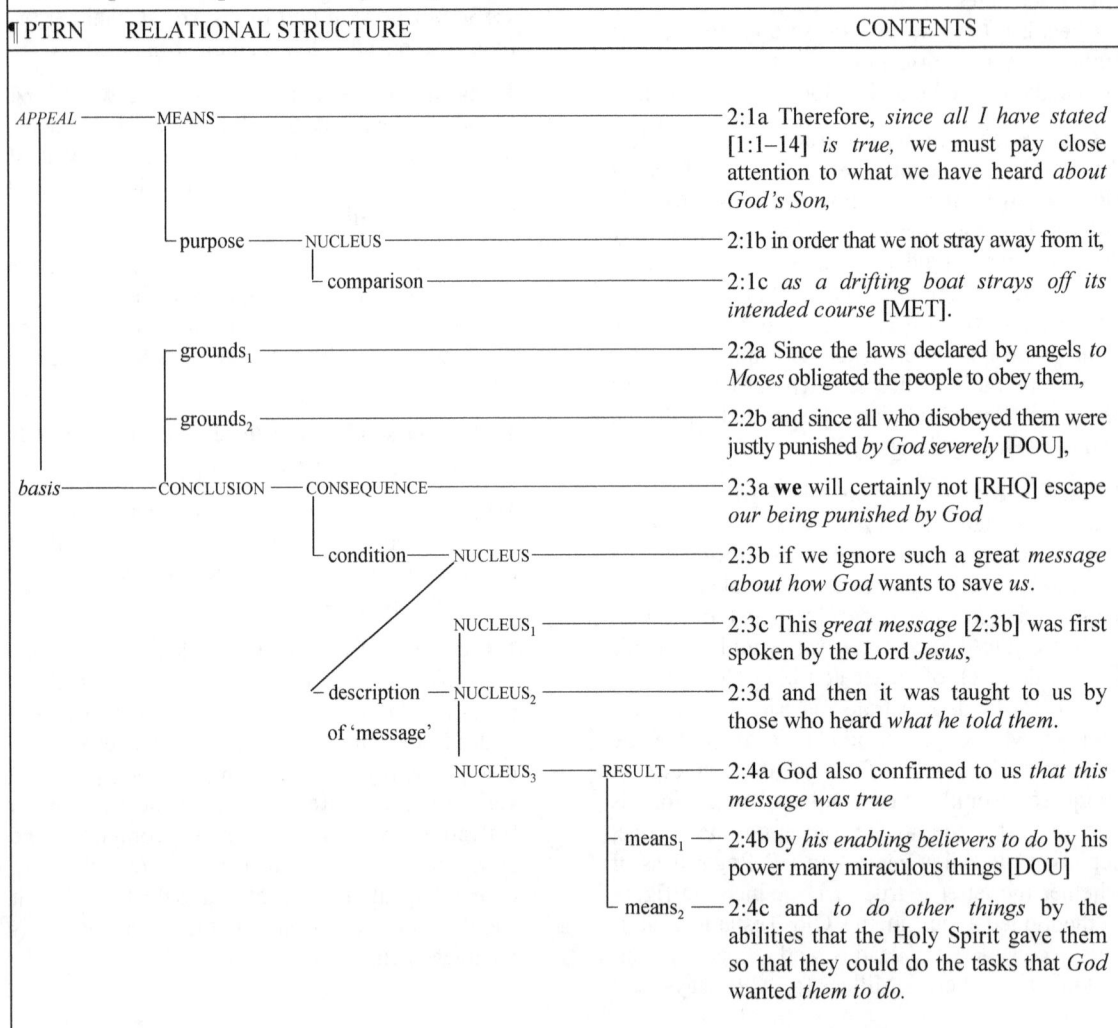

INTENT AND PARAGRAPH PATTERN

The 2:1–4 paragraph is considered to be hortatory, with a somewhat MITIGATED APPEAL 'we must pay close attention' in v. 1 followed by its *basis* in vv. 2–4.

NOTES

2:1a *since all I have stated* [1:1–14] *is true* The author connected the following to his affirmation of the greatness of Jesus.

we The author used the Greek first person plural pronoun 'ἡμᾶς' 'we', inferring that he was urging something that both he and his audience needed to do. He himself was already obeying the truths that he had heard. Thus, in some languages it may be necessary to change the pronouns in this paragraph to an imperative 'you(pl)', though in many languages the first person plural inclusive will be best.

what we have heard *about God's Son* The words in italics are a contextual implicature. Lane (p. 37) suggests the referent is "the words spoken to the Son, in the Son, and about the Son," but 'about' captures these more than any other preposition. Several versions include the words 'the truths' but the rendering in the display specifies what truths are meant.

we must pay close attention The Greek δεῖ περισσοτέρως προσέχειν 'must more abundantly heed' has the meaning 'we certainly should pay great attention to'. The word 'heed' implies listening to and obeying a message.

2:1b–c stray away from it, *as a drifting boat strays off its intended course* The verb παραρρέω is given meanings of "flow by, slip away, be washed away, drift away" in BAGD (p. 622), but listed as 'drift away' for this reference (its only occurrence in the NT). Louw and Nida (31.69) also assign it this meaning. Commentators are divided as to whether it is a nautical metaphor, but the majority believe it is, and therefore it is considered a live metaphor and the image is specified. In cultures where little is known about boats, it may be necessary to say 'as a drifting boat goes wherever the wind takes it' instead of 'veers off course'.

2:2a Since The εἰ followed by the indicative expresses "a true-to-fact condition rather than a future contingent condition, and as such it presents the grounds for the conclusion drawn in verse 3." (Miller, p. 32–33). Lane agrees; cf. also LB/NLT, CEV, and NCV.

the laws Commentators agree that the word λόγος here means "the law that God gave to the Israelites from Mount Sinai" (Kistemaker (p. 57). But 'law' means all the Mosaic laws, not just one law.

declared by angels *to Moses* The actual account of the giving of the law on Mt. Horeb does not mention angels, but they are clearly alluded to in Deut. 33:2 and mentioned by Stephen in Acts 7:38, 53 and by Paul in Gal. 3:19.

obligated the people to obey them The Greek ἐγένετο βέβαιος 'was confirmed' refers to the obligation on the people to obey, since it is amplified by the next clause πᾶσα παράβασις καὶ παρακοὴ ἔλαβεν ἔνδικον μισθαποδοσίαν 'every transgression and disobedience received its punishment'. Several commentators (Alford, Hagner, Dods, Lünemann) note that the phrase signifies that the laws could not be violated without punishment; it is, in effect, a metonymy, the cause standing for the effect.

2:2b all who disobeyed them The phrase πᾶσα παράβασις 'every transgression' is a personification which is expressed in a non-figurative way in the display text. TEV, LB, NCV, and CEV have translated it similarly.

by God severely This indicates the agent of the punishment.

2:3a we will certainly not The force of the rhetorical question beginning with πῶς 'how?' is that of an emphatic negative statement. It is rendered similarly by NJB, NCV. The pronoun ἡμεῖς 'we' is emphatic, and is so indicated by bold type. It "reinforces comparison with the people of the Old Covenant" (Miller, p. 34).

our being punished by God These words complete the case frame and are implied by the context. NCV has "surely we also will be punished."

2:3b *message about how God* wants to save *us* The italicized words can be looked at as spelling out the case frames for the abstract noun σωτηρία 'salvation', which can also be considered as a metonymy, the act standing for the message proclaiming it.

2:3c This *great message* Miller (p. 34) states that the relative pronominal adjective ἥτις 'which' "will introduce two amplifications to emphasize the greatness of the salvation," but they are more accurately labeled descriptions.

the Lord *Jesus* Commentaries agree the reference is to Jesus; LB/NLT makes it specific.

2:3d heard *what he told them* The Greek has only τῶν ἀκουσάντων 'the ones having heard'; the display fills out the case frame. JBP has "the men who had heard him speak;" cf. LB/NLT also.

2:4a confirmed to us *that this message was true* The wording here spells out the case frames of συνεπιμαρτυρέω 'witness with'; cf. NLT's "verified the message," CEV's "showed that his message was true."

2:4b *enabling believers to do* by his power The record seems to indicate that it was the apostles themselves who were the immediate instruments of the miracles, as in Acts 5:12 (RSV): "many signs and wonders were done ... by the hands of the apostles." See also Acts 14:3.

many miraculous things The expression σημεῖα καὶ τέρατα 'signs and wonders', says Lane (p. 40), "is to be taken as a fixed expression, in which the original distinction between the terms has not been maintained." It is thus considered a doublet used to emphasize the various kinds of miracles.

2:4c to do other things The word μερισμοῖς 'by distributions' is an abbreviated way of saying 'gifts which were distributed'; but in the context, the confirmation of the message would have to be not so much by the gifts themselves but by the things they did as they exercised those gifts.

so that they could do the tasks that *God* wanted *them to do*. The Greek κατὰ τὴν αὐτοῦ θέλησιν 'according to his will' refers to God helping them to do the tasks that he wanted someone to do. Alternatively, the phrase might be translated 'as God apportioned to them', as referring to God deciding which abilities he would give to them.

BOUNDARIES AND COHESION

The boundary of a new paragraph at 2:5 introduced by γάρ 'for' is marked by another negative reference to angels (5a) and a return to expository discourse. The author was continuing his focus on Jesus, however. Cohesion within the 2:1–4 paragraph is provided by several expressed and implied references to the message of salvation: τοῖς ἀκουσθεῖσιν 'to the things heard' (1a), σωτηρία 'salvation' (3b), ἥτις λαλεῖσθαι 'which was spoken' (3c), ἐβεβαιώθη 'confirmed' (3d), συνεπιμαρτυροῦντος 'confirmed at the same time' (4a).

THEME AND PROMINENCE

The theme for the 2:1–4 paragraph is drawn from the most prominent propositions of the *APPEAL* in v. 1a and the *basis* in v. 3a-b. The latter includes both the condition (3b) and consequence (3a) propositions, since both are considered equally thematic and one is incomplete without the other.

SECTION CONSTITUENT 2:5–13 (Paragraph: Basis₂ of 1:4—12:29)

THEME: It is not angels, but Jesus who has been appointed ruler over everything in God's new world, since now Jesus, who has been crowned as king, has authority over everything.

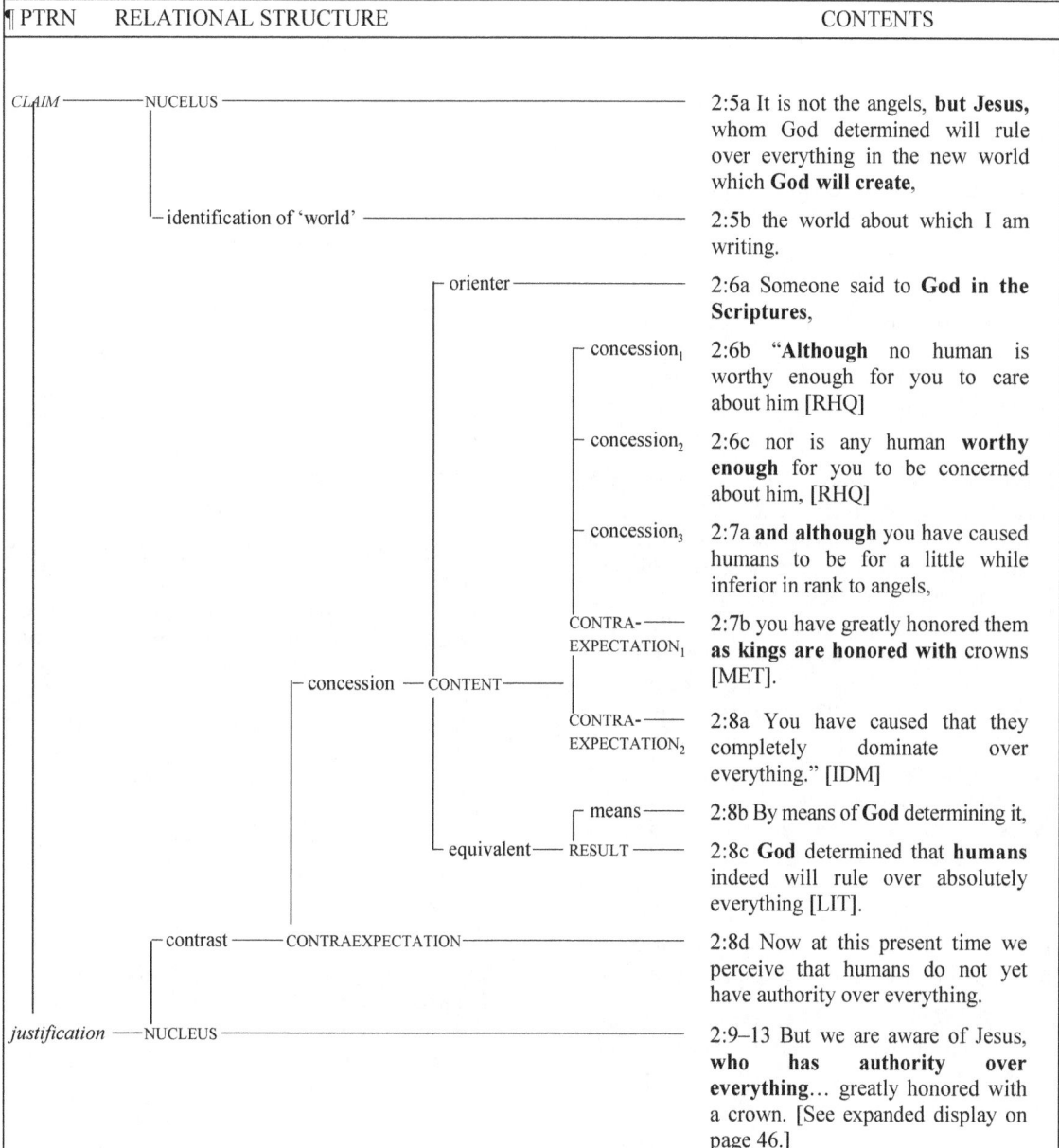

INTENT AND PARAGRAPH PATTERN

The 2:5–13 paragraph continues the author's affirmation of the importance of Jesus, in an expository mode. It consists of one CLAIM and its *justification*.

NOTES

2:5a This paragraph is a return to the presentation of the superiority of God's Son over the angels. Thus the γάρ is resumptive, rather than introducing a reason or grounds of what precedes.

but Jesus This is a clear contextual implicature and it is implied by the forefronting of οὐ ἀγγέλοις 'not to angels'.

God determined will rule The text has ὑπέταξεν 'he subjected', but since the subjection is still future, the past event is considered to be God's determining that it will happen.

everything in the new world which God will create The Greek phrase τὴν οἰκουμένην means 'the place for humans to live'. We are not to suppose that the author was referring to an already existing place, such as "the inhabited earth, the world," (BAGD p. 561.1a). It refers to a place that will be created in the future. Most commentators suggest this phrase refers to something which has begun but which is not yet completed. But the phrase τὴν μέλλουσαν 'the coming one' cannot refer to something already in existence; it must refer to something that will exist in the future. The word 'coming' does not refer to physical movement but to something God will create. This is made clear in the display by the adjective 'new' and the verb 'create.'

2:5b I am writing The Greek has λαλοῦμεν 'we are speaking', but the author was writing sentences here. He was not speaking. He referred to himself in the plural in the modest way that teachers of that time often did (as at 5:11, 6:9).

2:6a said to God The author used διεμαρτύρατο 'testified'. This idiom commonly referred to someone speaking to a king. The author is implying that the speaker was talking to God; the words 'to God' thus make clear the identification of the addressee in the following quote. This is made specific in LB and CEV.

in the Scriptures The Greek πού 'somewhere' is an indefinite expression used as a Jewish idiom for referring to the Scriptures. It does not necessarily imply that the author was uncertain as to the location of the text. The words 'in the Scriptures' are thus implied and made explicit in TEV, CEV, and NCV. The passage in 6b–8a is cited from Ps. 8:4–6. LB makes it much more specific with "in the book of Psalms David says," but such a notation is more suitable in a footnote than in the text.

2:6b, 7a Although The concessional force of these propositions is carried by the semantics, not by any grammatical signal; it is expressed also in LB, NCV, CEV.

2:6b no human is worthy The τί ἐστιν ἄνθρωπος 'what is man?' express a rhetorical question whose semantic function is a belittlement. This is conveyed by a negative statement in the display text. The word 'man' is used in a generic sense; CEV has "us humans," TNIV has "mere mortals."

care about The verb μιμνῄσκομαι has the sense "remember, think of, care for, be concerned about" (BAGD p. 522.1c).

2:6c any human The GNT has υἱὸς ἀνθρώπου 'son of man'. Of all the sources examined, only Bruce among the commentators and LB among the versions takes this as referring to Christ. As Lane notes (p. 47), with only one exception (John 5:27), "In the Gospels...the title by which Jesus designated himself is uniformly the articular expression ὁ υἱὸς τοῦ ἀνθρώπου 'the Son of Man'... The fact that υἱὸς ἀνθρώπου is anarthrous in Ps. 8 supports the presumption that the writer to the Hebrews did not find a christological title in the designation. He cites Ps. 8:5 because he wishes to emphasize that Jesus in a representative sense fulfilled the vocation intended for humankind." The Psalmist was writing poetically; Moore (p. 57) classifies 2:6b–c as a near-synonymous rhetorical parallelism.

to be concerned about The verb ἐπισκέπτομαι means literally 'to visit', but in this passage it has the sense "be concerned about." The word is used in the Septuagint to refer to visits for a good purpose. This is a figurative doublet with the previous statement.

2:7a a little while The word βραχύς 'short, little' can refer to a short distance, a short time, or a small amount. BAGD (p. 147.2) says the meaning here is "for a short time." Louw and Nida (78.43) say, "In Heb. 2.7...the expression βραχύ τι as a lexical unit refers to rank. However, Heb. 2.8–9 suggests that the writer of Hebrews probably interpreted βραχύ as meaning a small quantity...and as referring to time in the sense of a 'little (while)'. "

caused...inferior in rank to The verb ἐλαττόω means 'make lower, inferior' (BAGD p. 248.1); the sense is lower in rank or status, not in elevation.

2:7b greatly honored them *as kings are honored with* **crowns** The Greek words δόξῃ καὶ τιμῇ ἐστεφάνωσας αὐτόν 'with glory and with honor you have crowned him' are very figurative. The words 'glory and honor' are considered a doublet, the function being to intensify the one concept, not to express two different ones. They are classified as a near-synonymous doublet (Moore p. 57).

The KJV follows manuscripts which add a clause here, καὶ κατέστησας αὐτὸν ἐπὶ τὰ ἔργα τῶν χειρῶν σου 'and hast set him over the works of thy hands'. The added part is omitted in the GNT and given a C "difficulty in deciding" rating. Following the principle that the shorter reading is more likely to be original, and the likelihood that some scribe added the extra words to include Psalm 8:6a, the display text follows the GNT.

2:8a completely dominate over everything See the notes on 1:13d. 'Put under one's feet' is considered a dead metaphor; cf. TEV's "made him rulers over all things," JB's "put him in command of everything."

2:8b–c *God...humans* The Greek pronouns are disambiguated in the display text. The agent of both ὑποτάξαι 'to subject' and ἀφῆκεν 'he allowed to remain' is God; the referent of αὐτῷ is ἄνθρωπος 'human' in 2:6b, which refers to mankind, not to an individual man.

2:8c rule over absolutely everything The Greek has a double negative, οὐδὲν ἀφῆκεν ἀνυπότακτον 'he left nothing unsubjected (to him)'. This is a litotes, a way of emphasizing the positive by denying the negative. TEV treats b-c as a doublet and seems to omit this clause.

2:8d, 9a we perceive...we are aware of The Greek uses two verbs, ὁρῶμεν and βλέπομεν, both of which mean 'we see'. It is true that ὁράω is used to express various kinds of sense perception and βλέπω is normally used to express physical sight; but βλέπω is also used to express various kinds of mental functions (see BAGD p. 143.3–7). When the writer says in 9a 'we see Jesus', he did not intend that we understand this literally. Davidson says the word in 9a "embraces the knowing and apprehension of things beyond the region of actual eyesight." The display has tried to recognize the extended sense of both verbs and yet capture a difference in sense that the author seems to intend.

humans The 3rd person singular pronoun here again refers to 'humans' in 6b; it is rendered as "man" in TEV, REB; CEV handles it as "our power."

EXPANSION OF THE *JUSTIFICATION* IN THE 2:5–13 DISPLAY

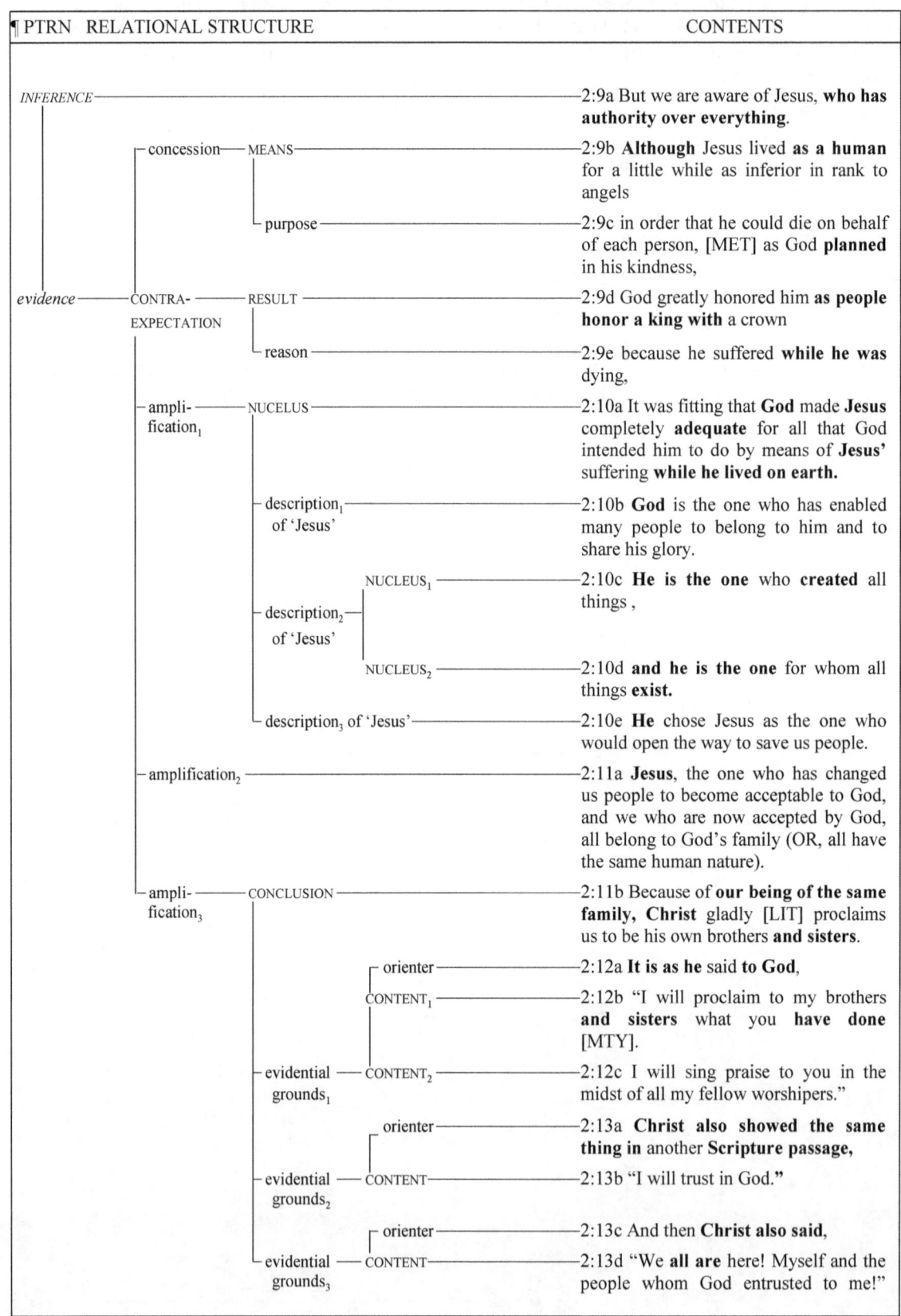

NOTES

2:9a ***who has authority over everything*** The words in italics are included to maintain coherence with what is stated in 8a. This is an important implicature of the argument. The writer has said in v. 8 that we have not experienced everything under our control, and here he affirms that, in contrast, we should be aware of who Jesus is and his present exalted position, following his having been temporarily in a position inferior to angels.

2:9b–e There are great differences between versions and commentators on the relationships within this verse. Some have tried to make the διά 'because' (9e) express purpose, but, with the accusative (as here), διά always expresses reason. The main difficulty is that it is impossible to follow the Greek order and the normal meanings of the conjunctions and still maintain English order unambiguously (NIV and REB try to do so, but unsuccessfully). The only set of relationships which coheres relationally is to make the ὅπως 'so that' purpose clause (9c) relate to the concession clause (9b). As Hughes notes (p. 90), 9b–e is a chiasm. This forces 9c in English to immediately follow 9b. This is exactly what TEV has done, as do CEV and NCV, but these versions fail to make all the relationships clear.

2:9b ***Although*** The concession relationship here conveys the writer's train of thought. An argument against Jesus' superiority to angels cannot be based on his having lived for a certain amount of time with a status that was lower than angels, because that inferior position was only temporary. The author reinforces his argument by putting βραχύ τι 'a little (while)' in an emphatic position. It is the same expression that he used in 7a.

Jesus lived *as a human*...as inferior in rank The Greek ἠλαττωμένον 'was made lower' usually refers to someone demoting another person. However, the author seems to imply that he was merely referring to the result of Jesus becoming a human. For 'inferior in rank' see note on 7a.

2:9c on behalf of each person The Greek clause ὑπὲρ παντὸς γεύσηται θανάτου 'taste death on behalf of every (man)' is a figurative way of saying 'experience death'; but there does not seem to be a way of avoiding the abstract noun 'death' without simply using the verb 'die'.

as God *planned* in his kindness The phrase χάριτι θεοῦ 'by the grace of God' would normally express means, but since 'grace' is semantically an attribute modifying an implied event, and since a means proposition would require a clause such as 'by doing what God graciously planned', the display shortens this a bit.

2:9e he suffered *while he was* dying The noun phrase τὸ πάθημα τοῦ θανάτου 'the suffering of death' is expressing two events, but the genitive 'of death' puts more focus on Jesus' dying, since the author repeats the word θανάτου 'death' of 9c. CEV and NCV say "suffered and died" but the Greek implies more than just two successive actions.

2:10a The γάρ here is taken as introducing an amplification, not a reason or grounds for 2:9. In v. 10 the author discusses further Jesus' death, which was mentioned in 9e, but this verse does not state the reason for his death. At least seven modern English versions have no conjunction here.

God ... Jesus The display follows TEV, LB/NLT, and CEV in making the pronominal referents specific.

It was fitting that *God* made *Jesus* completely *adequate* for all that God intended him to do The rendering here follows the meaning suggested for this reference by BAGD (p. 809.2a): "bring to its goal or to its accomplishment." Miller says (p. 52), "In the N.T. a person is τέλειος when he fully carries out the purpose for which God designed him and sent him into the world. So the verb will mean basically to make fully adequate for, able for the task for which the person is purposed and designed."

by means of *Jesus'* suffering *while he lived on earth* The preposition in the phrase διὰ παθημάτων 'by sufferings' expresses means (BAGD, p. 180.AIII1). But since the agent of a means proposition must be the same as the agent of the result proposition to which it relates, and the agent of the result proposition (10a) is 'God', God is kept as the agent of 10a. Miller notes (p. 52), "The plural 'sufferings' indicates...the many experiences He went through from birth to Calvary."

2:10b–d It may be necessary in some languages to translate these as independent clauses preceding 10a (as is done by CEV, NCV).

2:10b *God* is the one who has enabled many people to belong to him and to share his glory All commentaries consulted say that the agent of the expression πολλοὺς υἱοὺς εἰς δόξαν ἀγαγόντα 'leading many sons to glory' is God. The word 'sons' is a dead metaphor standing for all those who belong to God; and 'bring to glory' is considered a way of stating purpose 'so that they might share his glory'. TEV has "bring ... to share his glory." NCV has "wanted to have ... share his glory," CEV has "led ... to share in his glory."

2:10c–d *who created* **all things ... for whom all things** *exist* The Greek expression διʼ ὃν τὰ πάντα καὶ διʼ οὗ τὰ πάντα 'because of whom all things and through whom all things' lacks verbs, and the display supplies alternatives; NCV's "for his glory" is a good alternative for the second clause. In some languages it may be necessary to use an active form for 10c; e.g., "who creates... all things" (TEV).

2:10e *He* **chose Jesus as the one who would open the way to save us people** The GNT has τὸν ἀρχηγὸν τῆς σωτηρίας αὐτῶν 'the leader/beginner of their salvation'. As Miller says (p. 51), ἀρχηγός "is a challenging term to find adequate translation for." The word means 'originator, founder' (BAGD p. 112.3). The problem is somewhat compounded by the fact that σωτηρία 'salvation' is an abstract noun. Of the versions, NEB handles that the best by rendering this as "the leader who delivers them." Ellingworth suggests (p. 161) that this "is a hellenistic metaphor of a pioneer opening a path on which others can follow." The display follows this interpretation, and unskews the two abstract nouns to make them into full clauses by rendering the concept of "opening a path" as 'made a way'.

2:11a *Jesus,* **the one who has changed us people to become acceptable to God** The γάρ introduces the amplification for all of v. 10 and most specifically for 10b. The display makes specific the agent and patient of ὁ ἁγιάζων 'the (one) sanctifying'. The word ἁγιάζω can mean 'consecrate, set apart for God' or 'purify'. The rendering here tries to capture some of both meanings. In some places 'make holy' would have wrong connotations.

we who are now accepted by God The previous clause focused on the one who produced the change. This clause focuses on the objects of the change.

all belong to God's family The Greek for 'belong to God's family' is ἐξ ἑνός 'from one'. Although several alternative suggestions have been made, nearly all commentators agree that the 'one' referred to is God. The context supports this. Miller states (p. 54), "Jesus is related to 'brothers' because He and His brothers have the same Father." It is true, of course, that Jesus is related to the Father in a different way than believers are, but spiritually he and we have the same origin, making us to spiritually belong to one family.

2:11b gladly The words οὐκ ἐπαισχύνεται 'is not ashamed' is a litotes, a denial of the negative concept to emphasize the positive one.

his own brothers *and sisters* The feminine is included (as in CEV, NLT, and NCV) to avoid the notion that only males were meant.

2:12a *It is as* This implied information might have to be spelled out in some languages by saying something like: *There is evidence in the Scriptures that Christ considers us to be his siblings from what ....* This makes clear what the author wanted to communicate in vv. 12–13 by citing Old Testament Scriptures (v. 12 being from Psalm 22:22) as evidence for his statement in 11b. LB has "in the book of Psalms."

2:12b proclaim to my brothers *and sisters* **what you** *have done* The word 'name' in the clause ἀπαγγελῶ τὸ ὄνομά σου 'I will proclaim thy name' is a metonymy. Morris says (p. 28), "In antiquity 'name' generally ... stood for the whole character, the whole person." But in the context in Psalm 22 David was praising God for what he had done, more than for God's character. Probably both are involved; both could be included in a translation.

The words 'and sisters' are again included (as in TNIV, NLT) to avoid the implication that only males were meant.

2:12c in the midst of all my fellow worshipers The Greek ἐν μέσῳ ἐκκλησίας 'in the middle of the group' refers to a group of people whom the speaker considered his fellow-worshipers. For the Psalmist it meant the people of Israel assembled for religious purposes (the quotation is from Psalm 22:22).

2:13a-b See notes on 12a. The word πάλιν 'again' means 'in another Scripture passage'; BAGD (606.3) says the word is used "very often in a series of quotations from scripture."

2:13a *Christ also showed the same thing in another Scripture passage* The author implied a meaning that Isaiah did not mean, that the singer was identifying himself with his siblings. Isaiah was affirming that he and his biological descendants were committed to worshipping Yahweh. Thus some of the author's implication must be built into the orienter. See note in NIV Study Bible.

2:13b I will trust in God Here the quotation is from Is. 8:17; the words 'in God' clarify the referent of 'him' in the quote.

2:13c The author cited the next sentence in Isaiah's prophecy (Isa. 8:18). Thus, this is a continuation of the quote from Isaiah.

2:13d We *all are* here! Myself and the people whom God entrusted to me! Isaiah referred to his own biological children. The author implied that the speaker was referring to other people in a family, particularly siblings, as the reference in v. 12b. See notes on 12a. The words 'people whom God entrusted to me' explain the metaphorical use of 'children' in 13d. No modern version supplies a lexical equivalent for the attention-eliciting word ἰδού and it is not discussed in commentaries, but the statement 'We *are* all here!" in the display shows its function with an exclamation mark.

BOUNDARIES AND COHESION

The main lexical cohesion in the 2:5–13 paragraph is seen in three occurrences of the verb ὑποτάσσω 'subject' (v. 5 and twice in v. 8) and two occurrences (vv. 7, 9) of a word in the same semantic domain, ἐλαττόω 'be made inferior'. A new paragraph at v. 14 (marked by οὖν 'therefore') carries a new CLAIM and its *justification*. There is a tail-head linkage between the two paragraphs exhibited by the word παιδία 'children' in 13d and 14a.

THEME AND PROMINENCE

The theme of 2:5–13 has drawn from the nuclei of the CLAIM and *justification* clusters. For the sake of abbreviation the final relative clause of the first nucleus and the initial orienter 'we are aware of' of the second nucleus are omitted.

SECTION CONSTITUENT 2:14–18 (Paragraph: Basis₃ of 1:4—12:29)

THEME: Since it is not angels but we believers who are Abraham's spiritual descendants that Jesus helps, he became human just like us in order that by his death he might make powerless the devil, who has the power to cause people to be separated from God. Jesus became human so that he also might be a merciful and faithful Supreme Priest.

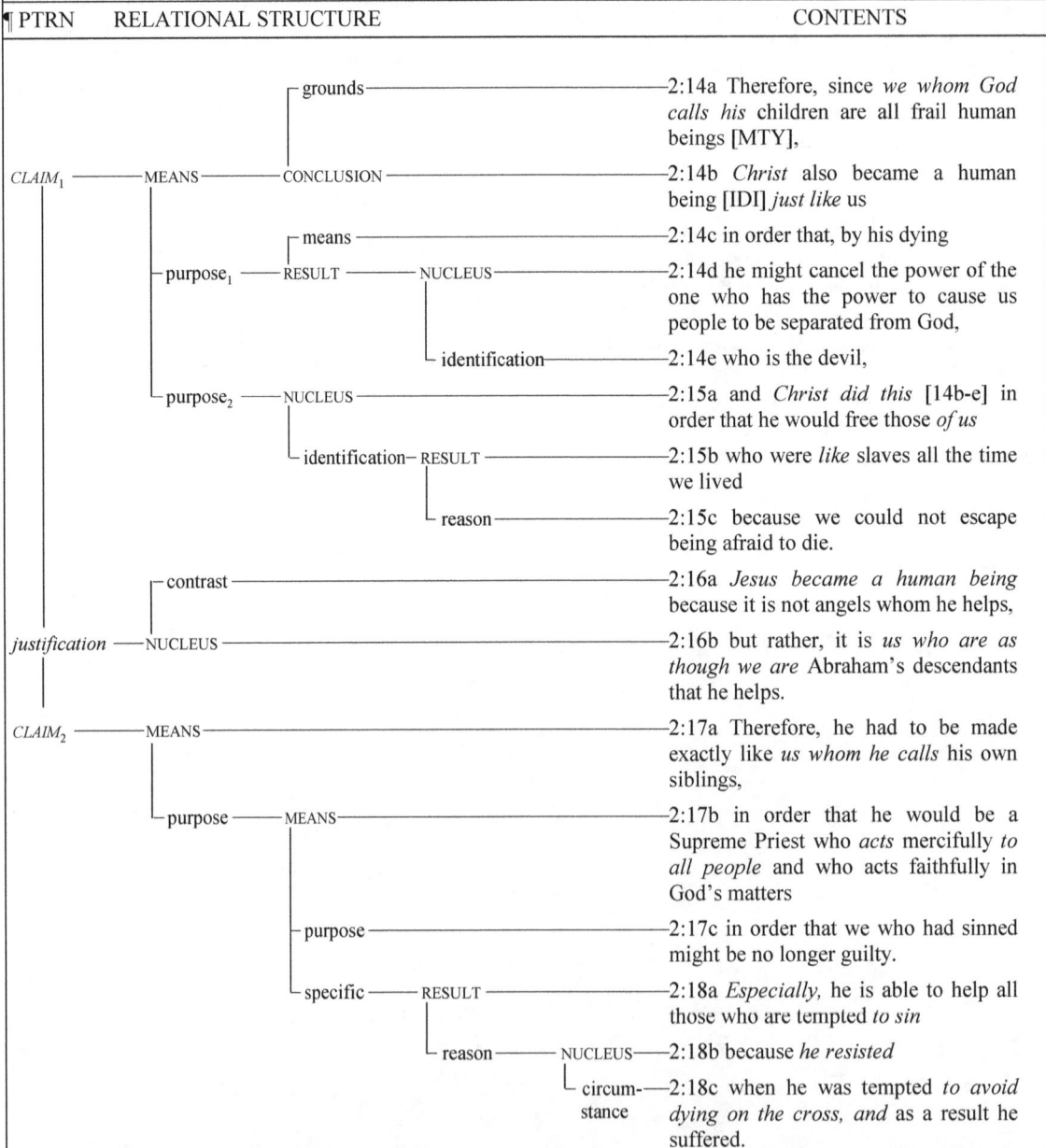

INTENT AND PARAGRAPH PATTERN

The writer continues to expound the greatness of Christ as our Supreme Priest with another expository paragraph. It consists of an initial claim in vv. 14–15 introduced by οὖν 'therefore', a justification in v. 16 introduced by γάρ 'since', and a second claim in vv. 17–18 introduced by ὅθεν 'wherefore'.

NOTES

2:14a *we whom God calls* The author used the third person plural to refer to the people whom Christ saved. However, he was referring to all Christians and thus including himself. Thus the subject of the clause is 'we'.

***his* children** In the display it is clear that τὰ παιδία 'the children' is not to be taken in its literal sense. TEV renders it "the children, as he calls them."

all frail human beings The words κεκοινώνηκεν αἵματος καὶ σαρκός 'have shared in blood and flesh' are, first of all, a designation of becoming human, but the usual order of the nouns is reversed. Commentators are divided as to whether there is any significance in this reversal, which also occurs in Eph. 6:12. Kistemaker (p.75) argues that "the prominence of the word *blood* indicates that the ties that bind us are blood ties;" but since the expression is an idiom either way, the decision is irrelevant. As Attridge says (p. 92), "Both terms in any case suggest the weakness and frailty of humankind." See also Montefiore, Ellingworth and Nida, Lane.

2:14d cancel the power The Greek verb phrase καταργήσῃ τὸν 'destroy the one' is referring to God destroying Satan's power.

the one who has the power to cause us people to be separated from God In the phrase τὸν τὸ κράτος ἔχοντα τοῦ θανάτου 'the one having the power of death' it is difficult to determine just what the genitive phrase means. Some (e.g., Miller, Kistemaker (p. 75–76) suggest we are set free from the fear of death, which is true, but this is not what v. 14 says. It seems best to say that the writer refers to the fall of mankind in Gen. 3, at which time Satan gained the power to cause Adam and his descendants to die—which here refers to eternal death (= separation from God), so Kistemaker, p. 75.

2:15b who were *like* slaves all the time we lived This unskews the phrase ὅσοι διὰ παντὸς ζῆν ἔνοχοι ἦσαν δουλείας 'as many as through all their (time) to live were subject to slavery' and makes clear that 'slavery' is conveying a metaphor.

2:15c because we could not escape being afraid to die The phrase φόβῳ θανάτου 'by fear of death' is a personification since death is the agent that holds people in slavery. The personification is eliminated in the display by transforming it into a reason clause (as in TEV, NCV). The words 'could not escape' express the point of comparison in the slavery metaphor. (If the whole metaphor were made complete, one would add 'as slaves cannot escape from doing what their masters tell them.')

2:16a *Jesus became a human being* The γάρ here indicates that this entire paragraph is the basis for the preceding paragraph. The main proposition of 14b is repeated for the γάρ 'because' clause to relate to.

whom he helps BAGD (p. 295.2c) says the meaning of ἐπιλαμβάνομαι here is 'be concerned with, take an interest in; help'. Louw and Nida (30:42 and 35.1) say both those meanings are possible here, adding in a footnote, "It is difficult to know whether ἐπιλαμβάνομαι in a context such as Heb. 2:16 refers principally or even in a significant measure to the intellectual concern rather than the more practical implication of giving help." But since the primary meaning of the verb is 'take hold of', it is rendered "he takes to himself" by NEB (but "helps" in REB), and "he took to himself" by JB. Nearly all the modern commentators reject that sense and suggest the meaning includes both taking hold of and helping; e.g., "he takes hold to help" (Lane, p. 63). But since the 'takes hold of' is then only figurative, it is omitted in the display.

2:16b *us who are as though we are* Abraham's descendants The first person plural pronoun is included to make clear that the writer and his audience are included. Commentators are about evenly divided as to whether σπέρματος ἀβραάμ 'seed of Abraham' is to be read as meaning literal descendants of Abraham (i.e., the Jews) or to all believers as being his spiritual descendants. The telling point in favor of the interpretation chosen for the display is that the other interpretation would lead to the conclusion that Christ did not come to help non-Jews.

2:17a *us whom he calls* his own siblings Again the display makes clear that the writer and his audience are included. For 'siblings' see note on 11b. In some languages it might be necessary to include *since he came to help us humans* to show the connection with v. 16.

2:17b acts mercifully *to all people* Grammatically the adjective ἐλεήμων modifies the noun 'Supreme Priest' but semantically it qualifies the implied verb 'act'.

2:17c in order that we who had sinned might be no longer guilty The verb in the phrase ἱλάσκεσθαι τὰς ἁμαρτίας τοῦ λαοῦ 'to make propitiation for the sins of the people' means 'to expiate' (BAGD p. 375.2). Since that is not a common word in English, the display spells out the meaning following Webster (p. 437:2a): "to extinguish the guilt incurred by."

2:18a *Especially* Although Miller suggests the γάρ here introduces a grounds for v. 17, its contents does not fit as such. The display here agrees with Lenski (p. 97) who says it "does not introduce a proof; it only adds an elucidation;" it states a specific way Christ acts mercifully towards us.

2:18b because Nearly all versions and commentators take the words ἐν ᾧ to mean 'because', which coheres well semantically, but a few commentators take a literal meaning 'wherein' which does not seem to make much sense (for the causal sense of ἐν ᾧ see Rom. 8:3).

he resisted The Greek word πέπονθεν 'he has suffered' does not focus on the pain, but rather on his enduring the temptation or resisting when it would have been easy to give in to the temptation.

2:18c when The aorist participle πειρασθείς 'having been tempted' following the main verb could express means, but it is more natural to take it as expressing attendant circumstance. Quite a few versions simply join the actions by 'and' (e.g., TEV, LB/NLT, RSV, NCV, CEV) but the two different verb forms suggest the one action was closely associated with the other. Scholars disagree on what the Greek verb πειρασθείς 'he has suffered' refer to. The author does not focus on the pain, but rather on Christ enduring the temptation or resisting when it would have been easy to do otherwise. What temptations of Jesus are being referred to? Some say that in connection with suffering, the temptation was to avoid death on a cross (cf. Moffatt, Lenski (p. 97); also Ellingworth) and this is the interpretation chosen here.

BOUNDARIES AND COHERENCE

A new paragraph unit at 3:1 is signaled by a vocative, a prominence orienter 'consider Jesus', and a new CLAIM and its *justifications* on a new topic, namely the superiority of Jesus over Moses. Coherence in the 2:14–18 paragraph is seen in the fact that the one being described, Jesus, is not referred to by name but is referred to at both the beginning and end (14b and 18a) by the pronoun αὐτός 'he'.

PROMINENCE AND THEME

The theme for the 2:14–18 paragraph is taken from the most naturally prominent propositions of the *justification* and the two CLAIMS. The two contrastive propositions of the *justification* are both considered prominent, and these are given first in the theme to maintain the flow of the sentence better. The theme includes both MEANS and PURPOSE propositions from both CLAIMS because a means proposition by itself would be incomplete. According to SSA theory, a means proposition is considered more important than its related purpose proposition, but in many actual situations they are of equal prominence.

PART CONSTITUENT 3:1—4:16 (Section: Appeal₂ of 1:4—12:29)

THEME: Jesus deserves that we honor him much more than we honor Moses.	
MACROSTRUCTURE	CONTENTS
MITIGATED APPEAL₁	3:1–6 Jesus deserves that we honor him much more than we honor Moses, since Jesus is God/Divine and since he is faithful as he cares for all of us who are God's people.
basis	3:7–19 God is warning you, saying, "Your ancestors repeatedly disobeyed me as if they were irritating me to know whether I would be patient with them." Therefore, each one of you must exhort each other every day, since you benefit in all that Christ has done, only if you keep firmly trusting in him.
MITIGATED APPEAL₂	4:1–16 We must strive to enter that place of eternal rest and firmly continue to hold as true what we believe about our powerful Supreme Priest.

INTENT AND MICROSTRUCTURE PATTERN

This unit consists of two MITIGATED APPEALS, and one *basis*. It is thus considered to be hortatory. The author's purpose here is to strongly urge his readers to continue to hold fast their faith in Jesus.

BOUNDARIES AND COHERENCE

A new unit at 5:1 is marked by a switch from an APPEAL in which Jesus is referred to as our Supreme Priest to an extensive discussion about the Jewish Supreme Priests. Coherence is provided by ten occurrences of κατάπαυσις 'rest' and three occurrences of σκληρύνω 'harden'.

PROMINENCE AND THEME

The theme for this unit is drawn from condensations of the most naturally prominent propositions in the *basis* and in the two *MITIGATED APPEALS*.

SECTION CONSTITUENT 3:1–6 (Hortatory Paragraph: Mitigated Appeal₁ of 3:1—4:16)

THEME: Jesus deserves that we honor him much more than we honor Moses, since Jesus is God/Divine and since he is faithful as he cares for all of us who are God's people.

¶ PTRN	RELATIONAL STRUCTURE	CONTENTS
APPEAL — orienter		3:1a Therefore, my fellow believers, who are dedicated to **God** and who have also/like me been invited by God,
CONTENT		3:1b consider Jesus' **qualities** carefully.
NUCLEUS₁		3:1c **He is God's** very special messenger to us
NUCLEUS₂		3:1d and he is the Supreme Priest whom we affirm that we believe in,
NUCLEUS₃ — NUCLEUS		3:2a and he faithfully **served God** who appointed him,
comparison		3:2b just as Moses faithfully **served** God's people [MTY].
basis₁ — NUCLEUS₄		3:3a Jesus deserves that we honor him much more than we honor Moses
comparison — RESULT		3:3b just as the one who makes a house deserves to be honored more than the house **does,**
reason — contrast		3:4a since every house is made by someone,
nucleus		3:4b but Jesus, who made everything, is God/Divine.
contrast — NUCLEUS — CONGRUENCE		3:5a As for Moses, **he** very faithfully **served God as he cared for** his people
standard		3:5b just as a servant **faithfully serves his master**
basis₂ — simultaneous		3:5c as he told **the people** what **Jesus** would say later.
NUCLEUS — NUCLEUS		3:6a But as for Christ, he **faithfully serves God as he cares for us** his people [MTY],
comparison		3:6b just as a son **cares for his younger siblings.**
MITIGATED APPEAL — CONSEQUENCE		3:6c And we continue to be God's people [MTY]
condition₁		3:6d only if we are continuing to confidently **believe in Christ**
condition₂		3:6e and **if** we continue to proudly wait for **what God will do for us**.

INTENT AND PARAGRAPH PATTERN

The writer here continues in the expository mode, continuing his exposition (v. 1 ὅθεν 'because of' introduces a new appeal which is the outcome of the previous context) of the ways Christ is greater than every being, as well as the whole institution of the Jewish religion. In this paragraph he states why Christ is greater than Moses. After an opening set of descriptive statements about Jesus (vv. 1–2) the paragraph consists of an APPEAL to consider Jesus as compared to Moses (v. 3), two *justifications*, and a MITIGATED APPEAL (vv. 4–6).

In this analysis Hebrews 3:1–6 is considered a chiasmus. But it would not seem wise to try to unite the separated pairs.[1]

NOTES

3:1a who are dedicated to *God* The word in italics completes the case frame; in languages with no passives it may be necessary to say 'whom God dedicated/set apart for himself', or possibly even 'who are God's people'. Montefiore says the term ἅγιοι "refers to those who are chosen to be set aside for divine use."

have also/like me been invited by God In the phrase κλήσεως ἐπουρανίου μέτοχοι 'sharers of a heavenly calling' the abstract noun 'calling' is represented by the verb 'invite'. In some languages it may be necessary to add something like 'to follow him'.

The verb 'share' implies an action common to various participants. It could mean they share it among themselves or share it along with the writer. The word 'heavenly' is taken as a euphemism referring to God. Louw and Nida say (12:17), "Though it is possible to interpret Heb. 3.1 as a 'calling which comes from heaven', it seems more appropriate in terms of the frequent references to 'calling' to recognize that the use of ἐπουράνιος in this context is simply a substitute for a direct reference to God. Accordingly, the passage may be effectively rendered as 'those who have been called by God'…" For the same reason this writer rejects the suggestions by some commentators that the meaning is 'a call to come to heaven'.

3:1b consider Jesus' *qualities* carefully The author wanted the readers and listeners to think carefully about how great Jesus was.

3:1c God's very special messenger Although the word ἀπόστολος means 'apostle', that gloss is avoided here because it is nowhere else applied to Christ, but instead reserved for that special group appointed by Christ. The display follows LB. An alternative used by TEV and NCV is "God sent." Miller (p. 65) notes the word means "one sent forth with a commission."

3:1d whom we affirm that we believe in The noun ὁμολογία can here be understood to mean 'that which is professed' or 'the act of professing'. Though several versions translate it as 'of the faith we profess' or something similar, unraveling the genitive leads to the meaning given in the display.

3:2b Moses faithfully *served* God's people The Greek here is πιστὸν…ἐν [ὅλῳ] τῷ οἴκῳ αὐτοῦ 'faithful…in [all] his house' Since the word 'faithful' here is semantically qualifying some event (cf. Barnes, "He performed with fidelity all the offices entrusted to him"), the word 'served' is supplied. The word 'house' is a dead figure of metonymy standing for the people in the house. Bruce says (p. 56–57), "The 'house' of Num. 12:7 in which Moses served so faithfully is not the tent of meeting but the people of Israel, the family of God."

There is a very difficult textual problem here. The word 'all' is included in the GNT with a D rating indicating the Committee had great difficulty in arriving at a decision. As Metzger notes (p. 594), "Both external evidence and transcriptional probabilities are singularly difficult to evaluate." On the side of its inclusion, it is found in the vast majority of manuscripts of various text types. Favoring its exclusion is the fact that the word is omitted in a number of very excellent and early manuscripts and translations. More telling is the fact that it also occurs when the phrase is repeated in v. 5, (and this verse alludes to it). Metzger suggests (p. 594) that it could have been deliberately omitted "in order to render the Old Testament quotation more appropriate to the argument (in v. 2 'whole' disturbs the parallelism between Moses and Jesus.)" However, such a possibility seems very far-fetched and unlikely, and the likelihood of its being deliberately added to correspond with v. 5

---

[1] The chiasm goes like this:
- **A** Christ deserves more honor than Moses (1-3)
    - **B** Moses faithfully served God as he cared for his people (4-5)
    - **B'** Christ faithfully served God as he cares for all of his family (6a-b)
- **A'** We continue to be God's family if we keep waiting for what he will do for us (6d-e)

and Num. 12:7 is far greater. Therefore the display assumes the word was not in the original. Versions are about equally divided as to its inclusion or omission.

3:3a Jesus deserves that we honor him much more than we honor Moses The γάρ here introduces a new aspect of the topic of Moses. It seems clearer to recast the Greek passive ἠξίωται 'has been found worthy' as an active statement, since the author was urging the people to recognize the greatness of Jesus. The display translated this verb as 'deserves to be', similar to the renderings in JB, CEV, and NLT. The author used the Greek evaluative phrase καθ' ὅσον πλείονα τιμήν 'by very much more honor' to refer to the believers' obligation to honor Jesus.

3:4a–b The RSV has translated the Greek text literally "(For every house is built by someone, but the builder of all things is God.)" However, it is rather difficult to see how such a translation fits into the argument. Some commentators (e.g., Morris, Attridge, Hughes, Kistemaker (p. 86)) consider the verse parenthetical. But the whole epistle shows too much of a tight logical argument to accept this viewpoint. Others (Miller, Hewitt) consider it clarificational: the 'house' was declared to be God's in v. 2 but Jesus was declared the builder in v. 3. But the word 'house' in v. 2 is figurative and its use in vv. 3–4 is literal. Lane is much nearer the mark when he recognizes the chiastic structure in the two verses. However, his rendering of the chiasmus fails to cohere as a logical argument, because Jesus is the topic of the first element in the chiasm and God is the topic in the fourth element in his translation. The solution is to take the chiasm and supplement it with the insights of Peake, Barnes, and Hughes (and mentioned as a possibility by several other commentators). As Hughes says (p. 134), "the implication is that 'he who' in the preceding verse was designated the builder of the house is indeed God." In support of this interpretation is the fact that the word 'God' occurs in the predicate position and has no article, allowing it to have the sense, "Almost as a substitute for the adj. divine" (BAGD p. 457.3fδ). The final clause in v. 4 does not say 'God is the builder of all things' but "he, who is the builder of all things, (is) God." The argument then is quite clear. When we eliminate the center parts of the chiasm, we have the statement that Jesus is more worthy of honor than Moses because he, who made everything, is God. (Implicit in the argument is that if Jesus made everything, he made Moses too.) The chiasm in a somewhat shortened form is thus as follows:

> A Jesus is more worthy of honor than Moses
>   B just as a builder is worthy of more honor than his house,
>   B' since just as every house is made by someone,
> A' Jesus, who made everything, is God.

3:5a As for Moses The author again used the Greek construction μὲν...δέ 'in regard to...in regard to', indicating that Moses and Christ were equally faithful to God.

very faithfully *served God...cared for* his people See comments on 2a–b. Since 'faithful' again modifies some event, one which fits the context is supplied. The phrasing could be shortened to say 'faithfully cared for'.

3:5b *faithfully serves his master* These words fill in the ellipsis and complete the comparison.

3:5c what *Jesus* would say later The Greek has only εἰς μαρτύριον τῶν λαληθησομένων 'unto a testimony of the to-be-spoken (things)'. The majority of commentators take the agent of 'spoken' to be God, assuming a 'divine' passive here (e.g., Hughes, p. 135). Some take the agent as Christ. Miller notes (p. 72) that if Moses' witness "would serve to point to future revelation, to things that would later be spoken when Christ came, then the future in the participle is accounted for." Kistemaker agrees, saying what Moses testified to was "specifically the gospel that Jesus proclaimed as the fullness of God's revelation (p. 87)." If one chooses to interpret that God is the agent, an alternative choice to that taken in the display would be to say 'what God would later say about Jesus', but making God the agent of the passive does fit well with the author's argument.

3:6a But as for Christ, he *faithfully* The author completed his comparison between Moses and Christ.

serves God as he cares for us **his people** These words are all elliptical, simply repeated from 5a.

3:6a-b-c *us* his people...*his younger siblings*... God's people Here the figurative meaning of οἶκος 'house' is 'family' or 'siblings', a metonymy (the place standing for the people who live there) following the motif that the author affirmed in 2:9–13.

3:6b son *cares for his younger siblings* The Greek has only ὡς υἱός 'as a son'. The display simply fills out the ellipsis, and completes the comparison. Barnes says "he was like a son over the affairs of a family."

3:6c–e This propositional cluster is introduced by the relative clause οὗ οἶκός ἐσμεν ἡμεῖς 'whose house we are', Grammatically it seems to present only a comment prompted by the word 'house,' it does not seem to relate to the theme of the superiority of Christ over Moses. However, it is very thematic for the whole book: the main theme of the book is a warning against turning away from the truths of the gospel and the salvation offered by Christ.

3:6c we continue to be God's people The author continues his theme, that Jesus is our elder brother in God's family.

3:6d only if we are continuing to confidently believe in Christ This represents the Greek ἐὰν τὴν παρρησίαν κατάσχωμεν 'if we hold fast the confidence'. But 'confidence' is semantically an attribute modifying 'hold fast,' and 'hold fast' is idiomatic. What the writer is stating is the necessity for holding fast to their faith in Christ, in contrast to returning to the Jewish rituals. The display makes this clear with the word 'only' cf. REB, TNT; also NCV's "if we hold on to our faith". As Bruce points out, the conditional clauses in this epistle (here, and in v. 14 and 10:26) are crucial; the conjunction ἐάν 'if' could be rendered as 'assuming that' or as JB has it, "as long as." Kistemaker (p. 87) agrees: "They were exhorted to hold on to their faith in Christ." Since παρρησία means "courage, confidence, boldness, fearlessness" (BAGD p. 630.3), the word 'boldly' could be considered as an alternative to 'confidently', in which case the words καύχημα 'boasting' and παρρησία 'confidence' could be taken as a hendiadys, but it is not so indicated in the display.

3:6e *if* we continue to proudly wait for *what God will do for us* In translating the phrase τὸ καύχημα τῆσ ἐλπίδος 'the boast of hope', the second object of the verb 'hold fast', the display unskews the abstract nouns. The word ἐλπίς 'hope' as always in the New Testament refers to a confident expectation of God doing something for us.

The Textus Receptus and Byzantine text follow a number of manuscripts which insert the words μέχρι τέλους βεβαίαν 'firm until the end' before the verb. But following the rule that the shorter is more likely the original, and because of the fact that the same words are found in v. 14 and no doubt repeated from there, they are omitted here. The GNT omits them with a B "almost certain" rating. Metzger further notes that if the alternate reading were genuine, it should have read βέβαιον (neuter) to agree with its most likely antecedent.

BOUNDARIES AND COHERENCE

The boundary at 3:7 is marked by the conjunction διό 'wherefore' and a change from an expository to a hortatory paragraph. The main lexical items providing cohesion to the 3:1–6 paragraph are the words οἶκος 'house' which occurs in verses 2, 3, 4, 5, and twice in v. 6, and πιστός 'faithful' in vv. 2 and 5 (and implied from ellipsis in v. 6).

PROMINENCE AND THEME

The theme of 3:1–6 is drawn from the most naturally prominent propositions of the CLAIM and its two *bases*. It also includes a condensation of the MITIGATED APPEAL in 6c-e, because that is such an integral part of the main message of the whole book: that we remain God's children only as long as we keep trusting in the sacrifice made for us by Christ.

SECTION CONSTITUENT 3:7–19 (Hortatory Paragraph: Basis of 3:1—4:16)

THEME: God is warning you, saying, "Your ancestors repeatedly disobeyed me as if they were irritating me to know whether I would be patient with them." Therefore, each one of you must exhort each other every day, since you benefit in all that Christ has done, only if you keep firmly trusting in him.

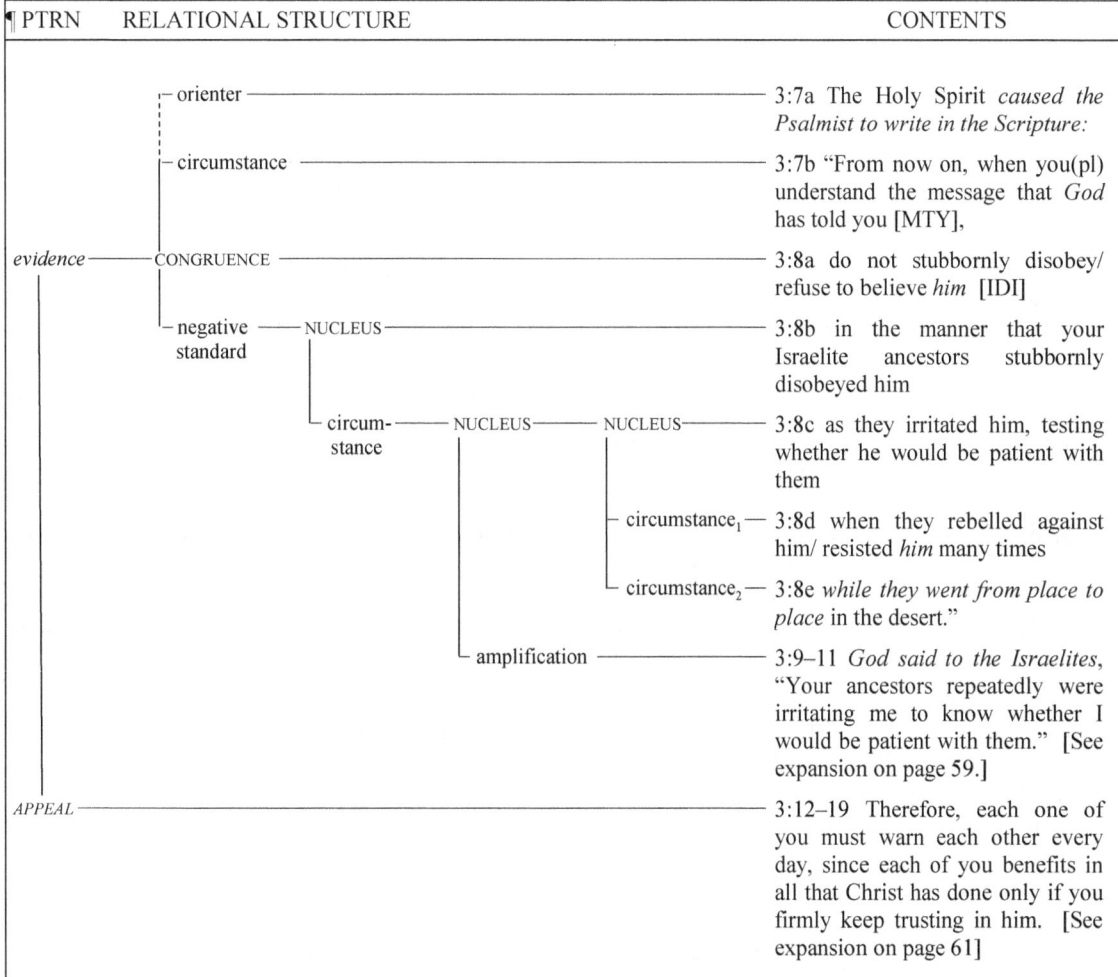

INTENT AND PARAGRAPH PATTERN

The 3:7–19 paragraph is considered to be hortatory because of the imperatives βλέπετε 'beware' in v. 12 and παρακαλεῖτε 'exhort' in v. 13. It consists of an implied *warning* in vv. 7–11 and the *APPEAL* in vv. 12–19. In this paragraph the writer warns his readers, by citing a warning given by the Psalmist, about not sinning and about not continuing to trust in God.

NOTES

3:7 The Greek διό 'therefore' indicates that the content of vv. 7–19 is another *APPEAL* following the *APPEAL* in vv. 1–6.

The majority of commentators point out that the διό 'therefore' relates to the imperative 'see' in v. 12. In other words, the one sentence continues from the beginning of v. 7 through v. 14 or 15: 'Therefore, as was written in the Scriptures... beware that no one ...' The wording in the display renders vv. 7–11 by three sentences, and the καθώς 'as' which introduces v. 7 is expressed by the words 'In accordance with that' in v. 12 to start another new sentence. JB similarly starts v. 7 with "The Holy Spirit says." But all versions examined start v. 12 with a new sentence; in other words, none of them makes the connection between vv. 7–11 and v. 12ff. clear. The alternative is to supply a dummy imperative clause here as a main verb for vv. 7–8, such as 'Keep in mind what', JBP starts v. 7 with "We ought to take note of." The problem with such a solution is it would suggest that the vv. 7–11 unit is hortatory, but that would be inappropriate considering the fact that vv. 7–11 constitutes the *evidential grounds* for the APPEAL in v. 12.

The Holy **Spirit caused *the Psalmist to write in the Scripture*** The Psalmist was warning his fellow-Israelites that they should not behave like their ancestors. The author affirmed that the Holy Spirit had inspired the Psalmist to do that. The writer counted on his Jewish audience to know that the passage is cited from Psa. 95:7–11.

It is very difficult to determine the relationship between the Holy Spirit, the Psalmist, the pronoun 'his' in v. 7 and the pronoun 'me' in v. 9. There seem to be three alternative ways of understanding and handling it:

1. The Holy Spirit can be considered as the speaker for the whole citation. God can be the referent of 'his voice'. Then the third person would be the pronoun all the way to the end of verse 11, instead of switching to first person in v. 9. But this does violence to all the first person singular pronouns in vv. 8–11.
2. One may consider only "Today if you hear his voice, do not harden your hearts" as inspired by the Holy Spirit. The remainder of the citation could be quoted as direct citation from God or as a description of the event. The CEV makes the pronouns referring to God in vv. 7–9 third person singular, and returns to first person singular in v. 10.
3. One may quote the passage as a selection from a Psalm that was inspired by the Holy Spirit. Then one could make all the pronouns referring to God as first person.

This third choice is the solution chosen for the display; the words "*God said to King David*" are included at v. 9a as being implied.

3:7b understand the message that *God* has told you This conveys the sense of τῆς φωνῆς αὐτοῦ 'the voice of him'. The Psalmist was not expecting the people to literally hear God's voice; he was instead expecting them to respond to what God has proclaimed to them through the prophets.

3:8a do not stubbornly disobey/ refuse to believe *him* This rendering conveys in a straightforward way the idiom μὴ σκληρύνητε τὰς καρδίας ὑμῶν 'do not harden your hearts'. NCV has "Do not be stubborn." Several other versions are similar.

3:8b in the manner that your Israelite ancestors stubbornly disobeyed him The display text fills in the ellipsis and specifies the pronominal referent. The Holy Spirit accused the Jewish ancestors of rebelling against God. It is not likely that those people were actually hostile to God, but rather their repetitions of disobedience were as painful to God as if they had been bullying him.

3:8c testing whether he would be patient with them This rendering has tried to give some of the meaning in 'testing' in this context. If necessary one could make it more specific: to determine how many things that displeased God they could do without God punishing them.

3:8d many times The Psalmist was referring to many events of disobedience, not just a single rebellion.

3:8e *while they went from place to place* in the desert The Psalmist and the author referred to the situations in which those people disobeyed God. The word ἔρημος is sometimes rendered 'wilderness' but 'wilderness' sometimes denotes a heavily forested area. The word 'desert' is more appropriate, and is so rendered in TEV, CEV, NEB, NIV, and LB.

EXPANSION OF THE AMPLIFICATION IN THE 3:7–19 DISPLAY

RELATIONAL STRUCTURE	CONTENTS
reason — CONTENT — orienter	3:9a **That is: God said to the Israelites,**
reason — CONTENT — CONTRAEXPECTATION	3:9b "Your ancestors repeatedly tested whether **I would be patient with them in spite of their disobeying me**
concession	3:9c even though they saw all the ways I helped them (OR, ways I punished them) for forty years.
RESULT₁	3:10a As a result **of their disobedience,** I became disgusted with those people who saw those things,
orienter	3:10b and I said **about them,**
reason₁	3:10c 'They are constantly disloyal to me
reason₂	3:10d and they did not want to learn how I **desired them** to live',
orienter — RESULT	3:11a **with the result that** I solemnly declared
reason	3:11b because I was angry **with them,**
RESULT₂ — CONTENT — RESULT — CONTENT	3:11c '**I certainly** will not allow them to enter **the land** which I **provided for them to** rest' [MTY].

NOTES

3:9a *That is: God said to the Israelites* There is a shift from the Psalmist warning his fellows in v. 7, to God speaking directly to the Israelites here. This is quite common in other Psalms and other Old Testament writings. See the alternative options listed in the notes on v. 3:7b.

3:9b Your ancestors repeatedly tested whether *I would be patient with them* The phrase οὗ ἐπείρασαν... ἐν δοκιμασίᾳ 'in (the circumstance of) being tempted in testing' can be considered a doublet to emphasize the repetitive nature of the testing. But to give some lexical representation to the noun, the phrase 'whether *I would be patient*' is included; cf. NCV's "tested me and my patience." The word 'testing' means it resulted in seeing "how long His patience would hold out in face of their stubbornness of heart" (Bruce, p. 64) or "seeing how far one can go and get away with it" (Miller, p. 79); (i.e., seeing how much sin one can commit without being punished for it.)

3:9c even though The καί here is "emphasizing a fact as surprising or unexpected or noteworthy: 'and yet, and in spite of that, nevertheless'" (BAGD p. 392.2g); cf. also Miller, TEV, LB, JB.

ways I helped them (OR, ways I punished them) The Greek has the generic τὰ ἔργα μου 'my works', which is ambiguous, as noted by Louw and Nida. It could mean, as Lenski (p. 114) says, that it "refers to all the miracles which God did for them," cf. LB's "his mighty miracles." But some commentators say it refers to the ways God punished them. Both alternatives are given in the display.

3:10a people who saw those things The phrase τῇ γενεᾷ ταύτῃ 'this generation' refers to the people just mentioned in v. 9. It could thus be rendered as in TEV, "those people." Technically the word γενεά refers to "the sum total of all those born at the same time, expanded to include all those living at a given time" (BAGD p. 154:2); but since it refers only to those at a given place, and in the NT almost always refers to people who have observed miraculous events, it is rendered here as 'people who saw those things'.

3:10c disloyal to me The phrase πλανῶνται τῇ καρδίᾳ 'go astray in the heart' is a dead figure; the sense of being "disposed to wander from God" (Barnes) is shown non-figuratively (cf. TEV's "disloyal," NCV's "are not loyal").

3:10d did not want to learn how I *desired them* to live' The words οὐκ ἔγνωσαν τὰς ὁδούς μου 'did not know my ways' means that those Israelites refused Moses' instructions repeatedly. The idiom 'did not know' is a Hebrew understatement that emphasizes the disobedient attitude of the people. The word ὁδός 'path' means "way of life, way of acting, conduct" (BAGD p. 554:2b) and is rendered non-metaphorically in the display by 'how I *desired them* to live.'

3:11a *with the result* This sense for ὡς is supported by BAGD (p. 898.IV2) and Louw and Nida, as well as the great majority of commentators.

solemnly declared The verb ὀμνύω, 'swear, take an oath' (BAGD p. 566) is somewhat figurative here; with God as the agent it means "a strong affirmation" (Lenski, p. 115–116).

3:11c *the land* which I *provided for them to rest* The phrase τὴν κατάπαυσίν μου 'my rest' involves an abstract noun representing an event; it is a metonymy using the event for the place where it would occur. The sense is fully stated by Davies as "the land destined by God where they would come to rest from their desert wanderings." The writer develops the theme of 'God's rest' much further in chapter 4, but without the component 'in the land of Canaan' which is implied here.

EXPANSION OF THE *APPEAL* IN THE 3:7–19 DISPLAY

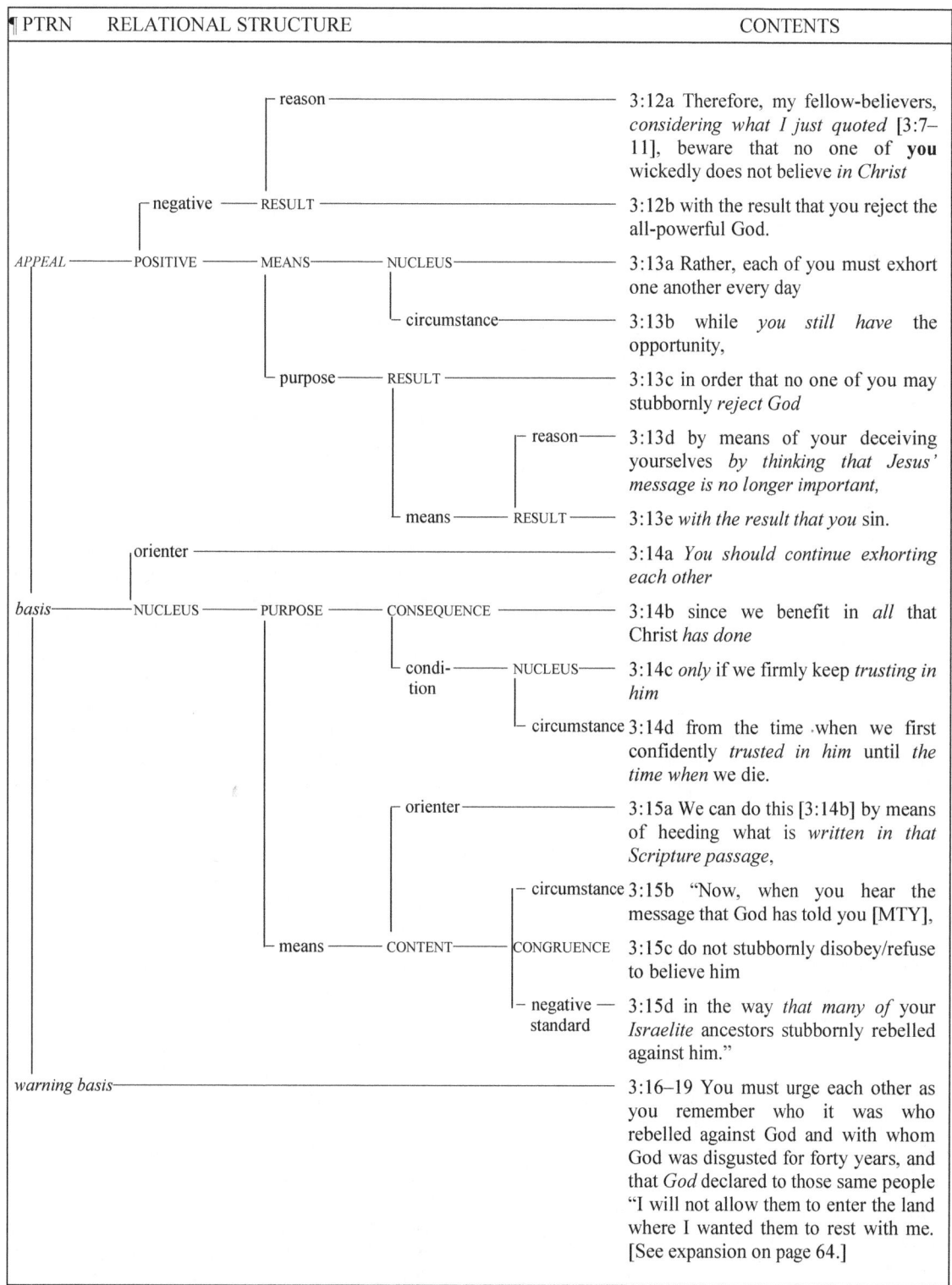

NOTES

3:12a Therefore The Greek dio 'therefore' actually occurs in v. 7a introducing one long sentence with no main verb until this point. So, the display presents it here.

considering what I just quoted [3:7–11] This simply represents the καθώς at the beginning of v. 7. See note on v. 3:7a. Grammatically the sentence that began with καθώς in v. 7 is completed in v. 12.

no one of you wickedly does not believe *in Christ* This simply unskews the very figurative ἔσται ἔν τινι ὑμῶν καρδία πονηρὰ ἀπιστίας 'will be in any of you an evil heart of unbelief', and fills out the case frames. 'Heart' here stands for "the moral life" (BAGD p. 404.1bδ). There is a difficulty concerning the force of the genitive, whether it refers to evil actions which lead to unbelief or result from the unbelief. Some commentators recommend 'leads to unbelief'. Some suggest 'result from unbelief'. Some say it doesn't matter. Since the whole thrust of the epistle is on unbelief, the display assumes the chronological sequence is unbelief—first evil attitudes, then discontinuing to obey God. Semantically the verb phrase 'not believe' requires some content of what is not believed. Therefore, 'in Christ' is supplied as the goal of the verb 'believe'.

3:12b with the result that Most versions and commentators take the ἐν in the RSV sense of "leading you to." Miller says (p. 86) "a means-result relationship is inherent" in the preposition here.

reject This follows Louw and Nida (34.26). BAGD (p. 126.2) suggests "desert." Morris (p. 36) suggests an even stronger sense, "rebel against."

all-powerful God In several contexts where the phrase θεὸς ζῶν 'living God' occurs in the NT, the connotation is much more than "not subject to death" (BAGD, p. 336.1aε). The connotation is always one who, because he is alive and not just an idol or imaginary, is omnipotent. That connotation is very much in focus here.

3:13a every day The GNT has καθ᾽ ἑκάστην ἡμέραν 'according to each day', which is, of course, somewhat idiomatic; the sense is 'day by day, continually'.

3:13b while *you still have* the opportunity The text is ἄχρις οὗ τὸ Σήμερον καλεῖται 'while it is being called the today'. The 'today' refers back to its occurrence in v. 7, but the expression is very idiomatic here. Moffatt (p.47) is representative of a number of commentators in saying it refers to a period "during which God's call and opportunity still hold out;" LB has "while there is still time."

3:13c stubbornly *reject* God The verb σκληρύνω is rendered here very similarly to how it was in 3:8; see note on 3:8a.

reject The Greek σκληρυνθῇ 'hardened' is a figurative way to refer to stubbornness, and the display supplies in what way they were stubborn.

3:13d–e by means of your deceiving yourselves *by thinking that Jesus' message is no longer important with the result that you* sin. The phrase ἀπάτῃ τῆς ἁμαρτίας 'by deceit of sin' contains two abstract nouns which are rendered by verbs in the display. Several commentators note that sin is personified here. In removing the personification, the question arises as to what relationship is signaled by the genitive construction connecting the two nouns. Montefiore and Hughes suggest that there is a reference to Satan's deception of Eve in the Garden of Eden. If so, the deception preceded and led to the sin; therefore the sinning is given a result relation to the deception in the display. Some commentators assume sin in general is being referred to, and many think it is some particular sin, but they are divided as to what sin is meant. Most (e.g., Miller, Attridge, Davidson, Hughes) state it is apostasy, which is probably correct in the immediate context as well as the context of the whole epistle.

3:14a *You should continue exhorting each other* The display supplied this from v. 13a in order to show that this is the *basis* of that *APPEAL*.

3:14b we The Greek text refers to the first person plural in the verbs of the *basis*. It is true that he was actually warning only a few among those who might read the document, but he used the first person plural to indicate that his statement applied to all believers, including himself.

benefit in *all* that Christ *has done* Regarding the clause μέτοχοι τοῦ Χριστοῦ γεγόναμεν 'we have become sharers of Christ', commentators are divided as to whether the sense is 'participators in Christ' or 'participators with Christ'. The former interpretation is followed by RSV, LB, NIV, JBP, NCV, the latter by REB, TEV, NJB. Morris's argument (p. 36–37) in favor of the former seems good: "it is the privilege we have in being Christians that is stressed, not the kind of work Christians do alongside Christ... it is important that the believer hold firmly to what God has given him." The display follows this interpretation, taking 'Christ' as a metonymy, the name of the person standing for what the person has done.

3:14c *only* if The display follows JB in giving this sense to ἐάνπερ. Miller (p. 90) gives the meaning as "only if indeed." Louw and Nida (89.68) say the word is "an emphatic marker of condition." The word 'only' is a crucial implicature of the argument of the whole book; (cf. JB, NEB.)

3:14c–d we firmly keep *trusting in him* from the time when we first confidently *trusted in him* until...we die The GNT has τὴν ἀρχὴν τῆς ὑποστάσεως μέχρι τέλους βεβαίαν κατάσχωμεν 'we keep the beginning of the situation firm until the end'. Most versions translate ὑπόστασις as 'confidence', but BAGD is most emphatic that such a sense "must be eliminated, since examples of it cannot be found" (p. 847.2). But the noun 'confidence' is semantically not a thing but an attribute, which must modify some implicit event; and in the context 'trusting in Christ' is implied, and is also the event referred to by the words ὦἠν ἀρχήν 'the beginning'. 'The beginning' is a metonymy, a generic word standing for some specific beginning. NLT puts it most clearly: "trusting God just as firmly as when we first believed." CEV represents the metonymy by "when we first became his people." No versions examined specified what end was being referred to, and very few commentators mention it either. Morris (p. 37) suggests it could be "the end of the age or the end of the believer's life," but since the former is hardly possible, the display follows Barnes who says it means "the end of life."

3:15a We can do this [3:14b] by means of heeding It is difficult to determine how the words ἐν τῷ λέγεσθαι 'in the to-be-said' function. It is true that they introduce the following quote, which is a repeat of the first part of Psa. 95:7–8 already quoted in vv. 7–8. Some suggest v. 15 connects more directly with what follows instead of with v. 14. But the fact that v. 16 begins with γάρ 'for' is strongly against this view. Some suggest it simply recapitulates v. 13, making v. 14 a parenthesis (so Montefiore). But v. 14, as the clear *basis* for the APPEAL in v. 13, is too central to the argument to be demoted to a parenthesis. Barnes is representative of perhaps the majority in saying the verse "connects easily and aptly with 'we hold'." Miller (p. 91) calls it a "specific to the grounds of the exhortation given in verses 13 and 14." But since the quote itself in v. 15b-d is an exhortation, and the grounds in vv. 14–15 (here called the basis) is a condition-consequence couplet, the quote cannot be a specific. The display does follow Montefiore in saying it expresses a means proposition; but to do so, one has to supply the 'by means of heeding' as an orienter to the quote.

what is *written* The 'to-be-said' is referring to Scripture and therefore 'written' is more straightforward. Several versions have 'the Scripture says' which is a personification.

3:15b the message that God has told you See notes on 3:7–8.

3:15d in the way This translates the Greek ὡς 'as' to indicate the example of undesirable attitudes.

many of your Israelite ancestors This clarifies the Greek ἐν τῷ παραπικρασμῷ 'during the rebellion'. The Psalmist referred to most of the Israelite ancestors while singing to his fellow Israelites. It might be possible to use first person plural 'our', but it seems that the Psalmist was warning his audience. Thus, the second person plural seems more fitting in English.

EXPANSION OF THE *WARNING BASIS* IN THE 3:12–19 DISPLAY

RELATIONAL STRUCTURE	CONTENTS
NUCLEUS₁ — NUCLEUS — CONTRAEXPECTATION	3:16a *You must urge each other* [3:13a–c] *as you* remember [RHQ] who it was who rebelled against *God*
└ concession	3:16b although they heard *God speaking to them*.
└ identification of 'who'	3:16c They were all those *who saw God do many miracles as Moses led them from Egypt* [RHQ], *with the result that no one would have expected those people to rebel!*
NUCLEUS₂ — NUCLEUS	3:17a And *you must remember* [RHQ] who it was that God was disgusted with for forty years.
└ identification of 'who' — REASON	3:17b It was those *same* people who had sinned *by rebelling like that*
└ result	3:17c *and whose bodies, as a result,* lay where they died in the desert [RHQ].
NUCLEUS₃ — NUCLEUS	3:18a And *you must remember* [RHQ] about whom *God* solemnly declared *"I certainly* will not allow them to enter *the land* which I *provided for them to* rest."
└ identification of 'whom'	3:18b It was those *same people*, who disobeyed God.
┌ orienter	3:19a Therefore, we know *from their example* [3:16a–18b]
summary — RESULT	3:19b that they could not enter *the land where they would rest,*
└ reason	3:19c because they did not believe *God*.

NOTES

3:16a *You must urge each other* The GNT begins with γάρ 'for'. The display starts a new sentence with words that indicate how this subparagraph relates to what precedes it.

as you **remember** These words convey the function of the rhetorical question that begins with τίνες 'who?'. By its nature the question calls upon the readers to think carefully about what follows.

3:16b although they heard The participle ἀκούσαντες 'having heard' has a concessive force as in REB and RSV.

God speaking to them These words simply complete the case frame in an appropriate way; (cf. REB's "God's voice.")

3:16c They were all those *who saw God do many miracles* **as Moses led them from Egypt** The writer's answer to his own rhetorical question is another rhetorical question. The answer gives an implied contrast of contraexpectation which is made specific. The emphasis implied by the use of the rhetorical question is conveyed in the display by a cleft construction, 'they were all those who…'

with the result that no one would have expected those people to rebel As Hughes notes (p. 153), "The point is that this generation, which had firsthand experience of the goodness of God in bringing them from slavery to freedom, comprised the very last group of persons one would have expected to rebel against their Savior God."

as Moses led them The GNT has οἱ ἐξελθόντες… διὰ Μωϋσέως 'those coming out through Moses'. Several versions are similar to NIV which renders as "those Moses led out," but the focus in the argument here is on God, who is not mentioned, probably for euphemistic reasons. The prepositional phrase is thus rendered by 'as Moses led them'. The word 'miraculously' is implicit Old Testament knowledge which is essential to the argument.

3:17a, 18a *you must remember* See the note on 16a.

3:17b sinned *by rebelling like that* The rendering here indicates that the sin meant is the one just referred to in 16a.

3:17c whose *bodies, as a result,* **lay where they died** Barnes says of the Greek ἔπεσεν 'fell down'. "That is, they all died and were left on the sands of the desert." The word κῶλα means literally 'limbs of a body' but Ellingworth says (p. 293) the sense here is "dead bodies, carcasses, unburied but not necessarily dismembered."

as a result The GNT has no conjunction here, but as several commentators (e.g., Hughes, Miller) point out, there is an implied reason-result relationship here; (cf. also LB.)

3:18a *I certainly* will not allow them The verb 'vowed' indicates not just a prediction of what would happen, but that God was not going to permit it to happen.

***I certainly* will not allow them to enter *the land* which I *provided for them to* rest** See note on v. 11c. The display changes the form from an indirect to a direct quote.

3:18b It was those *same people,* who disobeyed God This completes the rhetorical question's function. This might be translated by an emphatic device in the main statement, one that focuses on the people.

3:19a Therefore, we know *from their example* As Miller notes (p. 97), "The καί 'and so' is here used to introduce a summary which gathers together the preceding grounds [and its conclusion]." (cf. NIV, TFT,) NET Bible says: "Here καί has been translated as 'So' to indicate a summary or conclusion to the argument of the preceding paragraph."

BOUNDARIES AND COHERENCE

A new paragraph at 4:1 is indicated by a new appeal 'let us fear' followed by an extensive exposition of 'entering his rest'. Lexical Cohesion within the 3:7–19 paragraph is provided by the noun παραπικρασμός 'rebellion' in vv. 8, 15 and a cognate verb in v. 16; a repetition of Psalm 95:7–8 in vv. 7–8, 15 and the noun ἔρημω 'desert' in vv. 8, 17.

PROMINENCE AND THEME

The theme of the 3:7–19 paragraph is drawn from the *evidencial* Scripture quotation and the prominent propositions of the APPEAL. The implicit portion of the orienter in v. 7 is not included, but the vv. 7b–8c are considered thematic. The nuclear proposition of the positive constituent of the main APPEAL is, of course, thematic, and the consequence and condition propositions of 14b-c that support the *basis* in 3:14a are also prominent enough as the main point of the *basis* to be included in the theme.

SECTION CONSTITUENT 4:1–16 (Sub-Section: Mitigated Appeal₂ of 3:1—4:16)

THEME: We must strive to enter that place of eternal rest and firmly continue to hold as true what we believe about our powerful Supreme Priest.

MACROSTRUCTURE	CONTENTS
APPEAL₁	4:1–5 Some of you should be afraid that God might consider that you will have not qualified to enter the place of resting with God. We/you have heard the good news about Christ, but it won't benefit you if you don't continue to believe it. Certainly we who have believed in Christ are able to experience/enter the place of resting with God.
basis	4:6–10 We conclude that God has appointed a time when his people can enter their eternal rest, since he would not have spoken about it if Joshua had led the Israelites to a place of rest.
MITIGATED APPEAL₂	4:11–13 We must strive to enter that place of eternal rest and be sincere in doing so, since God's message can powerfully penetrate our thoughts.
MITIGATED APPEAL₃	4:14–16 We should firmly continue to hold as true what we believe about our powerful Supreme Priest. We should pray boldly to him in order that we might experience his acting mercifully toward us and in order that we might experience his graciously helping us.

INTENT AND PARAGRAPH PATTERN

This paragraph consists of an APPEAL, one *basis*, and two MITIGATED APPEALS. The appeals are considered mitigated because they are in the form of 1st person plural subjunctives, not imperatives. In the light of his exposition of Christ's superiority to angels and to Moses, and his promising us an eternal rest, he makes his first appeal to his readers to make sure they do what is necessary to enter that heavenly rest.

BOUNDARIES AND COHERENCE

The boundary at 5:1 has already been discussed. Coherence is provided by three occurrences of καταπαύω 'rest'.

PROMINENCE AND THEME

The APPEALS are more thematic than the *basis*; the theme is therefore drawn from the three APPEALS. The first part of the first APPEAL is considered more thematic than the last part containing the *basis* for the APPEAL, and the first part of the MITIGATED APPEAL₂, being more general, is considered more thematic than the MITIGATED APPEAL₃.

SUB-SECTION CONSTITUENT 4:1–5 (Paragraph: Appeal₁ of 4:1–16)

THEME: Some of you should be afraid that God might consider that you will have not qualified to enter the place of resting with God. We/you have heard the good news about Christ, but it won't benefit you if you don't continue to believe it. Certainly we who have believed in Christ are able to experience/enter the place of resting with God.

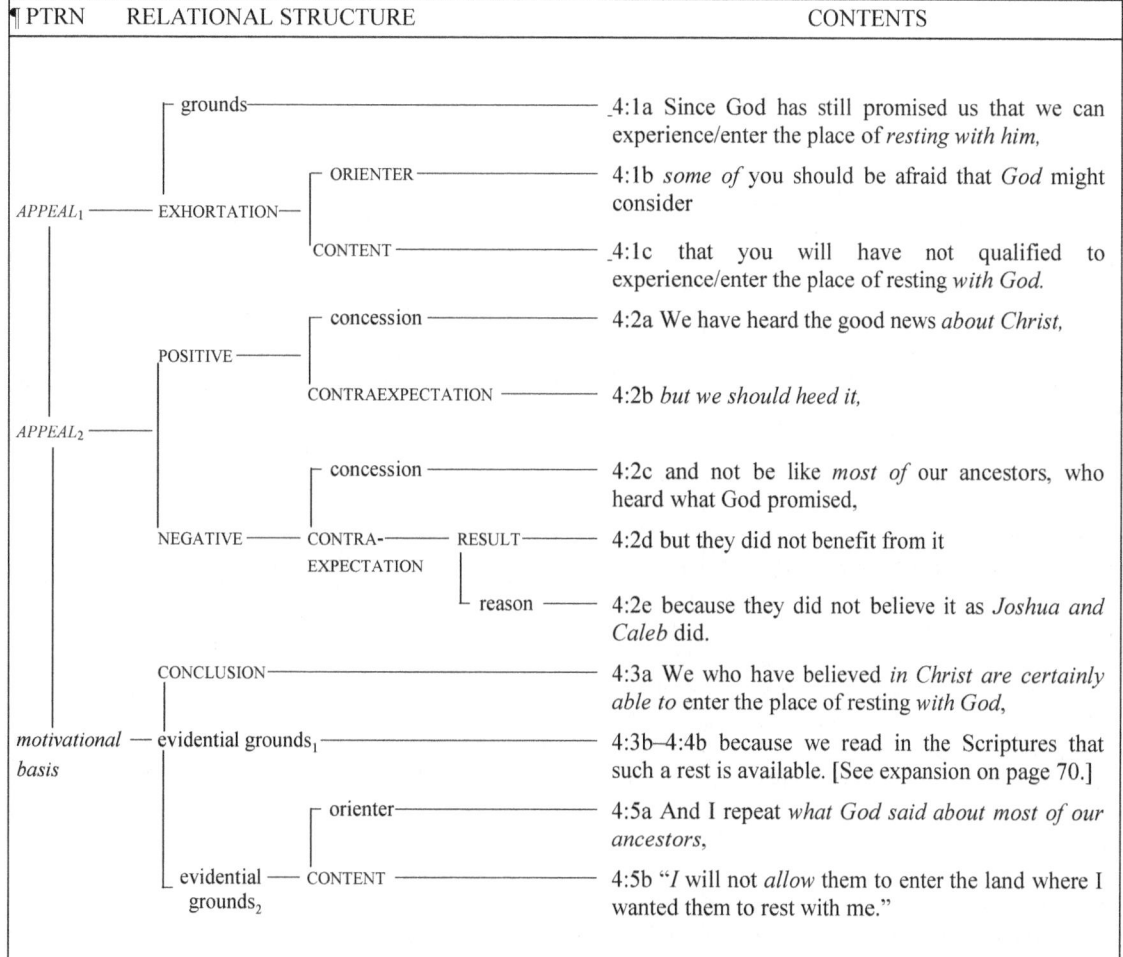

INTENT AND PARAGRAPH PATTERN

The first verb in the 4:1–5 paragraph, φοβηθῶμεν 'let us fear', being a first plural aorist subjunctive, points to this as being a hortatory paragraph. It consists of an APPEAL (v. 1) followed by a *warning basis* (v. 2) and a *motivational basis* (vv. 3–5).

NOTES

4:1a Since The verse begins with οὖν 'therefore' but it is considered "merely transitional" (Lenski, p. 125) and not represented in the display. NLT and CEV similarly do not represent it. The 'since' represents the function of the participle καταλειπομένης 'being left open'.

experience/enter the place of *resting with him* Here the writer of Hebrews is not talking about the Israelites entering the land of Canaan (as in 3:11) but about believers experiencing its ultimate counterpart. It is difficult to know whether the writer was referring to something believers experience now or experience in heaven. Barnes says, "There can be no doubt that Paul [sic] refers here to heaven." See also Lane.

4:1b *some of* you should be afraid that The verb is φοβηθῶμεν 'let us fear', which is a strong word, but the writer's concern is very strong. NCV's rendering, "Let us be very careful," is a good one. Since many of the writer's intended audience did not need this warning, the verb uses a first person plural subject, which probably is intended to soften the exhortation a bit, but the author's intent is clearly second person plural. The display tries to soften the exhortation somewhat by the words 'some of you'. Miller says (p. 99) the word 'anyone' "indicates that within the Christian community each one is now to take stock of himself and look for signs in his own life of any neglect, complaint, rebellion…"

God might consider There is a division among commentators as to whether the word δοκῇ should be interpreted to mean (1) be adjudged to, (2) seem to, or (3) think he has. Those who choose the *second* interpretation say the verb "is a way of softening the warning so that the writer refrains from saying that any of them actually missed or will miss the promise" (Morris, p. 39). But while the writer is not naming any names, his warnings throughout the book are very strong, and there does not seem to be any softening here or elsewhere. Those who choose the *third* interpretation assume the author is trying to encourage persecuted Christians who "were finding it hard to believe that rest was attainable in Christ" (Miller, p. 100). But the *first* interpretation fits the theme of the whole book much better: Hebrews is not an encouragement but a series of strong warnings. And as Miller notes, that interpretation fits the immediate context of the Israelites' experience in the desert: their continued rebellion angered God and "brought on an oath excluding them from the promised rest of God. They continued to exist until they died along the way, but… they were considered as having been already excluded."

4:1c that you will have not qualified to experience/enter The word ὑστερέω means "through one's fault to miss, fail to reach, be excluded" (BAGD, p. 849.1). Inasmuch as 'fail to enter' has geographical overtones and could easily be interpreted as 'failed to reach heaven', 'experience' is given as an alternative.

4:2a We have heard the good news *about Christ* This spells out in a straightforward way the periphrastic construction ἐσμεν εὐηγγελισμένοι 'we have been evangelized'; cf. TEV's "we have heard the Good News." The display does not represent the conjunction γάρ because it signals "a rather loose causal relationship" (Ellingworth and Nida, p. 73).

4:2b *but we should heed it* The statement in v. 1 that we should be afraid implies that we should do something about it. The above supplies that implicature.

4:2c and not be like *most of* our ancestors, who heard what God promised Parts of this proposition complete the comparison implied by the words καθάπερ κἀκεῖνοι 'just as they also' and the preceding context. The comparisons here and in 4:2d focus prominence on the warning.

There is a rather complex logical argument here:

The Israelites heard the good news
   They didn't act on it
      So they didn't enter God's rest
The readers have heard the good news:
   Some of them may not have acted on it
      So they will not enter God's rest

The final two steps in the argument, the necessary conclusion to be drawn from 2a, are not stated by the author. They can be combined to say 'All people who hear the good news but don't believe it will not benefit from it'.

4:2d but they did not benefit from it The Greek participle συγκεκερασμένους 'having been united' implies that there were some who did have faith. The words 'most of' are included to make clear that historically Caleb and Joshua were exceptions.

As many commentators note, there is an "analogy being drawn from the experience of the children of Israel in the wilderness generation" (Miller, p. 100)). This analogy is made specific in the display.

4:2e believe it as The accusative plural form of the participle in the expression συγκεκερασμένους τῇ πίστει 'having been united by faith' is the one that is now supported in the GNT with a B "almost certain" rating. As Metzger notes (p. 595), the preferred reading is supported by a much greater and wider selection of early manuscripts, and more importantly, some scribe would have been much more likely to alter it to the nominative singular form to agree with the nominative singular antecedent λόγος 'word', than the other way around. Then, as Hewitt notes, "the passage can mean only that the word which they heard did not benefit them because they were not united by faith with those who (truly) heard, i.e., with Moses, Joshua and Caleb, who not only heard but believed." The display makes explicit the participants involved. The phrase 'not mixed with faith with' is a figurative way of saying 'they did not believe as…', with the ones being compared with not stated. Thus the participle 'mixed with' is represented by the clause 'as Joshua and Caleb did'.

4:3a We who have believed *in Christ* There are a few manuscripts that support a conjunction οὖν 'therefore' here instead of γάρ, but support for οὖν is very weak. However, since "the first clause of verse 3 is not the cause for the last part of verse 2" (Louw and Nida), no conjunction is given in the display. The words 'in Christ' supply the content of the cognitive event 'believe'; as usual, an alternative would be 'trusted in what Christ has done for us'.

certainly The display attempts to show that the author was motivating the believers to continue to believe.

able to These words are supplied to indicate that 'entering' is a potential opportunity, not a given. Cf. NLT, "can enter."

Although the Greek verb is in the present tense, commentators are divided as to whether the sense is referring to a present experience of believers, or to an emphatic futuristic experience, primarily referring to something yet to be attained. The majority of commentators prefer the future sense. It seems likely that the writer was not specifically meaning one or the other, but both.

The GNT here begins with καθὼς εἴρηκεν 'as he has said' which introduces the Old Testament passage he has already cited twice. But the question is, how does the quotation support the author's affirmation that the believers are able to enjoy living with God? The verse starts with 'we enter that rest' and the quote says only 'they shall never enter my rest'. The answer is that a true heavenly rest must exist because David referred to it existing long after the Israelites entered Canaan. In the mind of the author, God's referring to such a place proves its existence. The author supports his affirmation in the context of v. 7.

To make this connection clear, in some languages it may be necessary to include the clause *We know there is a place where we will rest* **because....**

4:5a And I repeat *what God said about most of our ancestors* The GNT here has only καὶ ἐν τούτο πάλιν 'and in this again'. The display makes clear that the word 'this' refers to the passage previously cited; cf. NIV, "again in the passage above." As to the relationship of this verse to the context, Miller (p. 110) is no doubt correct in saying it is "an additional grounds for the conclusion drawn in verse 3." However, we must also consider why the author cited this sentence for the third time. Kistemaker's (p. 108) comments make good sense: "This recurring warning ought not to be taken lightly by the reader. And no one can ever say, 'It will never happen to me'. If the Israelites...had...obeyed the commands of God, they would have been the recipients of all the blessings God had promised." The display makes the author's purpose clear with the words "I want you to think again about what God said..."

I repeat These words convey the sense of πάλιν 'again'.

EXPANSION OF EVIDENTIAL GROUNDS₁ IN THE 4:1–5 DISPLAY

RELATIONAL STRUCTURE	CONTENTS
┌ orienter	4:3b because *we read in the Scriptures that* God said,
│ ┌ orienter — RESULT	4:3c "I solemnly declared
│ └ reason	4:3d because I was angry with them,
CONTENT — CONTENT	4:3e 'I will not *allow* them to enter the land where I wanted them to rest with me.' "
│ ┌ concession	4:3f Although *God had finished his work of* creating things after he created the world,
CONCLUSION — CONTRAEXPECTATION	4:3g *his promise of giving his people rest was not fulfilled when he finished creating the world.*
│ ┌ orienter	4:4a There is evidence for this from what *Moses wrote* in the Scriptures about the seventh day after God had worked six days creating the world,
└ grounds — CONTENT	4:4b "Then God rested on the seventh day, after he had finished creating everything."
	4:5 [See main chart 'SUB-SECTION CONSTITUENT 4:1–5 on page 67.

NOTES

4:3b because *we read in the Scriptures that* God said These words make clear again that what follows is again cited from the Old Testament.

4:3f work of creating things The display makes clear what work is being referred to, i.e., "his work of creation" (Kistemaker, p. 108). A translation should not convey the idea that God has done exactly nothing since creation.

4:3g *his promise of giving his people rest was not fulfilled when he finished creating the world* As Ellingworth and Nida note (p. 75), v. 4g "involves a number of complications, both linguistic and theological." The main problem is, how does the statement in v. 4f relate to the context? The answer is that v. 3g begins with the word καίτοι 'although' which indicates a concession-CONTRAEXPECTATION relationship. Other than Ellingworth and Nida, only Lane seems to have faced the problem squarely, and thus, following Lane, the display supplies the contraexpectation proposition which allows the passage to make sense.

4:4a There is evidence for this from what These words convey the sense of the γάρ 'for' here in introducing a supportive quotation, here probably taken from Gen. 2:2.

Moses wrote The verb again is ἔιρηκεν 'he said'; but since the following quote has God as the agent, the 'he' must refer to the writer of the OT passage, and to what he wrote, not what he said; cf. LB's "it is written." CEV avoids that problem with "the Scriptures say," but that rendering involves a personification.

seventh day after God had worked six days creating the world The GNT has only τῆς ἑβδόμῃ 'the seventh'. Clearly he means "the seventh day of creation" (LB), but it is very difficult to put that in a propositional form which eliminates the abstract noun and the genitive construction ('of creation').

4:4b after he had finished creating everything See the note on 3f: ἀπὸ πάντων τῶν ἔργων αὐτοῦ 'from all his works' again means his works of creation only. LB translates as "having finished all that he had planned to make."

BOUNDARIES AND COHERENCE

A new paragraph at v. 6 is marked by the conjunction οὖν 'therefore', a change from a hortatory to an expository unit, and a change in topic from the failure of the Israelites to enter God's rest to the logical necessity of there being a different rest still available to God's people. The vv. 6–10 unit cannot simply be "a conclusion for the grounds that is so carefully laid out in verses 3–5" (so Miller, p. 111) and thus be a part of the paragraph to which vv. 3–5 belong, because vv. 3–5 are part of a hortatory paragraph, not an expository paragraph.

PROMINENCE AND THEME

The theme is drawn from the most naturally prominent propositions of the APPEAL and the two supporting *bases*. The *warning basis* has as its most natural propositions two contrastive nuclei, but although the second of these (2e) is all implicit, it is the most crucial proposition of the syllogism, and therefore the most prominent.

SUB-SECTION CONSTITUENT 4:6–10 (Paragraph: Basis$_2$ of 4:1–16)

THEME: *We conclude that God has appointed a time when his people can enter their eternal rest, since he would not have spoken about it if Joshua had led the Israelites to a place of rest.*		
¶ PTRN RELATIONAL STRUCTURE		CONTENTS

INFERENCE$_1$ — CONCLUSION
- grounds$_1$ — 4:6a God continues *to invite us people* to enjoy *resting with him.*
- grounds$_2$ — RESULT — 4:6b And *our ancestors, those* who first heard the good news *about what God promised them,* did not enter *that place of resting,*
  - reason — 4:6c because they refused to believe *God.*
- RESULT — 4:7a Therefore, God has offered another opportunity *for us to begin resting with him, and he is offering it to us* now.
- means
  - orienter — 4:7b *The Israelites rebelled against God in the desert. Many years later,* God caused *King* David to write these words *that* I have already quoted:
  - CONTENT — 4:7c "From now on when you understand the message that God has told you, do not stubbornly disobey/refuse to believe him."

evidence — CONSEQUENCE
- condition — 4:8a If Joshua had led our ancestors to the true place of resting,
- 4:8b God would not have spoken later about another time *when we might rest.*

INFERENCE$_2$
- GENERIC
  - NUCLEUS — 4:9a Therefore, *I want you to know that* God continues to offer an opportunity for his people to rest with him [MET]
  - comparison — 4:9b *just like God* rested *on the seventh day.*
- specific
  - NUCLEUS — 4:10a Specifically, whoever enjoys resting with God has ceased doing things *to gain God's favor*
  - comparison — 4:10b just as God ceased doing his work *of creating everything.*

INTENT AND PARAGRAPH PATTERN

The 4:6–10 paragraph, with no imperatives, is in the expository mode, but here instead of the usual *CLAIMS* there are two *INFERENCES* and one bit of logical *evidence* from the OT to support the two *INFERENCES*.

The paragraph begins with οὖν 'therefore' which introduces the APPEAL which follows the information in the preceding unit 4:1–5.

NOTES

4:6a God continues *to invite us people* to enjoy resting with him As Miller notes (p. 112), the sense of ἀπολείπεται 'it remains' is "It is certain;" cf. NCV's "it is still true." Other good alternatives are LB's "the promise remains," or possibly "the opportunity is still available." Cf. Hewitt, "the promise of rest still remains open."

4:6b good news *about what God promised them* The participle εὐαγγελιθέντες 'having been evangelized' does not mean they had the gospel of salvation by Christ declared to them, but in the Old Testament context they heard the good news about God's promise (to give them the land of Canaan).

4:6c refused to believe God The word ἀπείθεια usually means 'disobey' but in this book the sense is probably closer to 'refused to believe'.

4:7a Therefore In the Greek, v. 6 begins with ἐπεί 'since', and v. 8 continues the same sentence. The display breaks it into two sentences and puts the relater word here.

Therefore, God has offered The verb ὁρίζει 'he appoints' uses the present tense. As Ellingworth and Nida note (p. 79), "this is evidently something which took place in the past but which is still relevant," so a perfect form of the verb is used in the display. An alternative explanation might be that he is referring not only to the historical act of appointing but to the present conclusion we can derive.

***he is offering it to us* now** The GNT has only the one word, Σήμερον, 'today'. Some versions supply a verb and/or quotation marks; e.g., "which is called 'Today' " (TEV). But since the word 'today' in these two chapters refers to 'the present time', here as elsewhere in the displays the word 'now' is used.

4:7b God caused *King* David to write The preposition in the phrase ἐν Δαυὶδ λέγων 'in David saying' is taken as introducing a means proposition; cf. TEV's "by means of David." Note that the means proposition is related to "God offered" in 7b and not to "we may conclude" in 7a. But since David's communication was by writing, the display has 'caused David to write.' The display also identifies David as a king; since the quote is from the Psalms; 'the Psalmist David' would also be appropriate.

***The Israelites rebelled against God in the desert.* Many years later** The display makes clear what time is being referred to by μετὰ τοσοῦτον χρόνον 'after so long a time'.

I have already quoted The subject of the verb προείρηται 'previously said' is technically third person singular; but the author is referring to his own quote, the display uses the first person singular; cf. CEV's "just as I have already said."

4:8a led our ancestors to the true place of resting According to BAGD (p. 416.1bβ) the verb καταπαύω 'bring to an end' here means "bring to a place of rest."

4:9a Therefore, *I want you to know* The conjunction ἄρα introduces an inference from what has preceded it. The part in italics strengthens the inferential function in English. The sense is captured well by NJB's "there must still be."

God continues to offer an opportunity for his people to rest with him The display makes clear that God is continuing to invite people to his place of rest. In some languages it may be necessary to translate as 'us people who belong to God' to indicate that the writer also belonged to God.

4:9b *just like God* rested *on the seventh* day We must understand what is meant by the word σαββατισμός. BAGD (p. 739) gives the meaning "Sabbath rest" which is followed in some versions. But that is a metaphor, and the italicized clause spells out the image of the metaphor. Moffatt says (p. 53) it "is the blissful existence of God's faithful in the next world."

4:10a Specifically Miller is incorrect in listing v. 10 as the grounds for v. 9, because it does not cohere as expressing a grounds proposition. Morris is much closer in saying (p. 43), "We now have a description of at least part of what the rest means." Bruce (p. 72) similarly says the verse "explains the description of the believers' coming rest."

ceased doing things *to gain God's favor* There is a question here regarding what is meant by κατέπαυσεν ἀπὸ τῶν ἔργων αὐτοῦ 'has rested from his works'. The meaning depends on whether 'rested' refers to what happens to believers at the time of conversion or at the time of death. Most commentators interpret that the author was thinking of a believer dying, perhaps pointing to Rev. 14:13 which speaks of those who 'die in the Lord' who "will rest from their labour" (NIV). Bruce says emphatically "it is evidently an experience which they do not enjoy in their present mortal life." On the other hand, Miller says (p. 118), "the author to Hebrews is not in chapter 4 promising his hearers rest after faithful service, but is *urging* them to complete their readiness to serve God effectively. He is trying also to head off possible defection from God altogether!.... What is at stake here is man's *redemption*, not a future reward for service." If that is the focus, then the author must be referring to the Sabbath that is "a full reliance upon God through the redemptive work of Christ...a perfect rest in a finished atonement" (Wiley), and the labors from which we cease would be those to gain our salvation. As was noted in 4:3a, it may well be that the author was not specifically focusing on one or the other. But if we interpret that the author was referring to our present life as believers, the translation needs to avoid implying that Christians cease all physical labor at the time of conversion. For that reason, the display supplies an implied purpose of 'works' 'to gain God's favor'. Even if one interprets it to refer to labors by believers up to the time of death, even if such labors "could involve specifically the persecution to which they, as Christians), have been subjected." (Attridge, p. 131), the words 'to gain God's favor' are not inappropriate.

4:10b work *of creating everything* See note on 4b.

BOUNDARIES AND COHERENCE

A start of a new paragraph at v. 11 is marked by a return to hortative genre and the connector οὖν, and a change from third person referents to first person plural ones. As in the previous paragraph, the 4:6–10 paragraph is bounded by occurrences of the verb 'enter'. Lexical cohesion is seen in verbal, nominal, or pronominal occurrences of 'rest' in vv. 6, 8, 9, and three times in v. 10 (one by ellipsis).

PROMINENCE AND THEME

The theme statement is drawn from the first INFERENCE in 7a (with the word 'know' changed to 'conclude' because of the grounds propositions that precede 7a) followed by the condition and consequence statements of the *evidence*. The second INFERENCE is not included in the theme because it is completely repetitious.

SUB-SECTION CONSTITUENT 4:11–13 (Paragraph: Mitigated Appeal₁ of 4:1–16)

THEME: *We must strive to enter that place of eternal rest and be sincere in doing so, since God's message can powerfully penetrate our thoughts.*

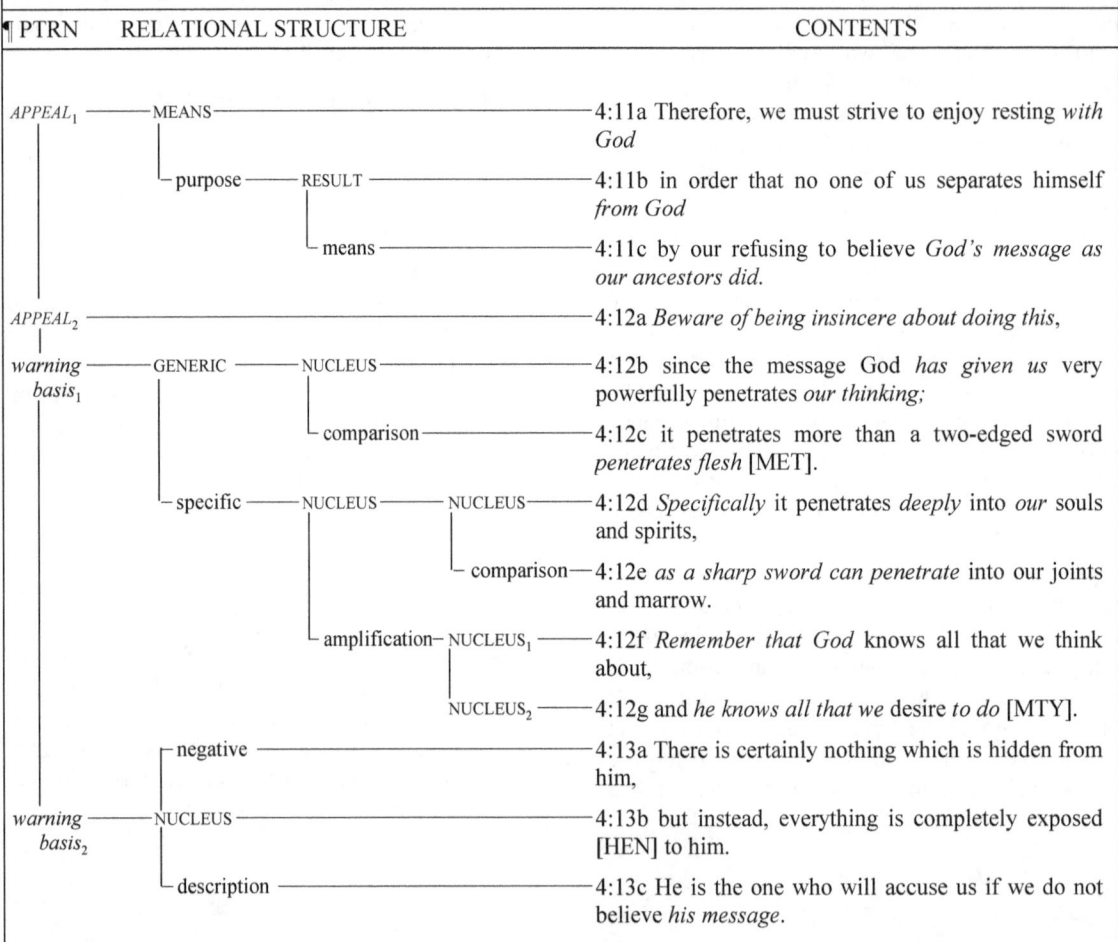

INTENT AND PARAGRAPH PATTERN

The 4:11–13 paragraph is hortatory because of its introductory first person plural subjunctive verb σπουδάσωμεν 'let us strive'. It consists of two APPEALS in vv. 11–12 and two *warning bases* in vv. 12–13.

The paragraph begins with οὖν 'therefore' which introduces the APPEAL which follows the information in the preceding unit.

NOTES

4:11a we must strive Here also the author uses first person plural pronouns to urge the people to continue believing. He is saying that the exhortation applies to himself as well as every other believer. But in some languages it may be necessary to use the second person plural to indicate the urgency of the appeal.

strive The verb σπουδάζω means 'be zealous or eager, make every effort' (BAGD, p. 763.2).

4:11b separates himself *from God* The verb here is πίπτω which can mean literally 'to fall', but here (as in Rom. 11:11, 1 Cor. 10:12) it has a figurative sense of "be completely ruined... = fall from a state of grace" (BAGD p. 660:2aβ). NJB has "be lost," which also carries a figurative sense but states the meaning well.

4:11c by our refusing to believe God's message See 4:6c for the meaning of this same word.

as our ancestors did This full proposition spells out the comparison expressed by ἐν τῷ αὐτῷ τις ὑποδείγματι 'by the same example'; cf. LB's "as the children of Israel did." In some languages it may be necessary to include *because they disobeyed/disbelieved God's message* to supply the reason.

4:12a *Beware of being insincere about doing this* There is a problem as to how vv. 12–13 relate to what precedes it. Some suggest this is from a poem that circulated in the early church; Attridge (p. 133) calls it "an elaborate bit of festive prose." But Kistemaker (p. 116) is much closer to the truth in saying, "The Bible demands a response, because God does not tolerate indifference and disobedience." Miller's comment (p. 123) is even more to the point: "Necessity for taking heed sincerely and immediately is found in the living power behind the promise." Lane (p. 102) is also good here: "Those who remain insensitive to the voice of God in Scripture may discover that God's word is also a lethal weapon." Since the exhortation is a positive one of urging that the addressees make every effort to enter God's eternal rest for us, and the grounds is a warning and so deals with the negative side of their ancestors' disobedience, a command to beware of being insincere is appropriate here. Thus 12a or its equivalent is a crucial implicature of the argument.

4:12b the message God *has given us* Some commentators think the phrase ὁ λόγος τοῦ θεοῦ 'the word of God' refers to the Scriptures, others think it refers to the Christian gospel, others that it means the spoken word of God. There is no good reason to confine it to any one of these. Kistemaker (p. 116) notes the phrase "occurs at least thirty-nine times in the New Testament and almost exclusively is the designation for the spoken or written Word of God." Miller (p. 123) states it means "God's declarations." Cf. CEV's "What God has said."

powerfully penetrates *our thinking* The phrase ζῶν...καὶ ἐνεργής 'living and active' is taken to be very nearly a doublet referring to being powerful. For 'living' see the note on 3:12b. Montefiore says the word means "it has within itself the dynamism and power associated with life." Kistemaker (p. 116) says the second adjective means "it is effective and powerful." Hughes says (p. 164) regarding both words together, "as God is the God who acts with power, his word cannot fail to be active and powerful." The phrase 'penetrates our thinking' spells out the point of comparison between God's message and a sword implied by the word τομώτερος 'sharper'.

4:12c *penetrates flesh* These words carry the rest of the image of the metaphor and fill out the case frame.

4:12d penetrates *deeply* into *our* souls and spirits The GNT says διϊκνούμενος ἄχρι μερισμοῦ ψυχῆς καὶ πνεύματος 'passing through unto a division of soul and spirit.' Miller states, (p. 125) "...the word is not dividing soul from spirit and joints from marrow. Rather, it is piercing through to lay open for examination what is deepest in man's nature." Cf. CEV's "His word can cut through our spirits and souls."

4:12e *as a sharp sword can penetrate* Here again the display separates the topic of the metaphor from the image. God's word penetrates "our innermost thoughts and desires" (NLT) as a sword can cut into our joints and bones.

4:12f *Remember that* The GNT here has καί 'and' but nearly all commentators agree that rather than presenting something new, 12f–g defines or enlarges on the preceding metaphor. Thus it is called an amplification here.

God knows God is made the agent here to remove the personification.

4:12f–g all that we think about...desire *to do* The display makes full clauses of the abstract nouns ενθυμήσεων καὶ ἐννοιῶν 'thoughts and intentions' and replaces the figurative word καρδίας 'heart' with the pronoun 'we'. Moore (p. 57) classifies 'thoughts and intentions' as a near-synonymous doublet and Attridge (p. 136) says they are "virtually synonymous," but most commentators seem to suggest there is a difference in the meanings. Thus the display follows Miller who says (p. 126) the sense is "The word tests what I am thinking about...and what I am deciding upon."

4:13a certainly This indicates that 4:13a-b amplifies and emphasizes the positive statements of 4:12f-g.

4:13c He is the one who will accuse us if we do not believe The words πρὸς ὃν ἡμῖν ὁ λόγος having the literal meaning 'before whom to us the word' are obviously an idiom, to which BAGD (p. 478.2e) give the sense as "with whom we have to do (i.e., to reckon)." Several versions use the expression 'give account', but this is still an idiom in English. NCV's translation, "explain the way we have lived," and LB's "explain all that we have done," are an attempt to explain the idiom. However, if we have persisted in disbelief, at the moment of reckoning, what we will be given is not an opportunity to defend our actions, but God's condemnation and judgment. The whole proposition is thus considered as somewhat of a euphemism.

BOUNDARIES AND COHERENCE

The beginning of a new section at 4:14 is marked by the conjunction οὖν 'therefore', the first of several occurrences of the term ἀρχιερεύς 'Supreme Priest' in the rest of chapter 4 and the early part of chapter 5, and no further discussion of God's rest.

PROMINENCE AND THEME

The occurrence of the metaphor of the sword gives marked prominence. The theme of the 4:11–13 paragraph is taken from the most naturally prominent propositions of the APPEAL in 11a, the IMPLIED APPEAL in 12a, and the two *warning bases* in 12–13.

SUB-SECTION CONSTITUENT 4:14–16 (Paragraph: Mitigated Appeal₂ of 4:1–16)

THEME: We should firmly continue to hold as true what we believe about our powerful Supreme Priest. We should pray boldly to him in order that we might experience his acting mercifully toward us and in order that we might experience his graciously helping us.

¶ PTRN	RELATIONAL STRUCTURE	CONTENTS
basis₁ — NUCLEUS		4:14a We have help *from such* a powerful Supreme Priest
— description of 'Supreme Priest'		4:14b who has ascended through the heaven/sky *into God's presence.*
— identification		4:14c That priest is Jesus, God's Son.
APPEAL₁		4:14d Therefore, we should firmly continue to hold as true *what we believe about him.*
basis₂ — RESULT — NUCLEUS		4:15a We certainly *can trust* a Supreme Priest [LIT] who can indeed compassionately help us
— description of 'us'		4:15b who are likely to sin,
— reason — CONCESSION		4:15c because he also was tempted *to sin* in every way that we are tempted to sin
— contraexpection		4:15d *and yet* he did not sin.
APPEAL₂ — MEANS — NUCLEUS		4:16a Therefore, we should pray boldly to *our Supreme Priest* [MTY],
— description of 'Supreme Priest'		4:16b who sits on the throne, to ask him to help us graciously [MTY]
— purpose — NUCLEUS — NUCLEUS₁		4:16c in order that we might experience *his acting mercifully toward us,*
— NUCLEUS₂		4:16d and *in order that* we might experience his graciously *helping us*
— circumstance		4:16e whenever we need *him.*

INTENT AND PARAGRAPH PATTERN

The 4:14–16 paragraph is again hortatory, having two verbs which are first person plural present subjunctives. In a sense one could say they are such forms which indicate slightly MITIGATED APPEALS. By saying 'let us hold fast' the author is including himself, whereas presumably he certainly does not need that exhortation. The paragraph consists of two APPEALS, each preceded by a basis.

The paragraph begins with οὖν 'therefore' which again introduces a MITIGATED APPEAL which follows the information in the preceding unit.

NOTES

4:14a We have help The Greek ἔχοντες 'having' merely refers to Jesus being in a close relationship to believers. The author wanted his people to understand that Jesus was beneficial to them because he was a priest before God.

from such These implied words help the readers to remember the claim the author made in 2:17–18 and 3:1.

a powerful Supreme Priest The author used the adjective μέγαν 'great' to describe Jesus. Other possible adjectives might be 'magnificent/wonderful/awesome/powerful' In English we are occustomed to the expression 'high priest' but since, in SSAs we try to avoid terms that are used in a non-primary sense, in this work the words 'Supreme Priest' are used.

4:14b has ascended through the heaven/sky *into* **God's** *presence* Nearly all the commentaries state something similar to Lenski, (p. 149), "through what we call the created heavens into the presence of God." The expression διεληλυθότα τοὺς οὐρανούς 'having gone through the heavens' "reflected the Jewish conception of several heavens..." (Miller, p. 130). Some versions focus on the destination rather than the area that is passed through. They give two possible alternatives, "to heaven itself" (LB) and "into the very presence of God" (TEV). They give one phrase or the other, not both.

4:14c See the note on 1:2c.

4:14d Therefore Miller notes (p. 129) "the οὖν 'therefore' summarizes the whole preceding section as grounds for the new exhortation."

firmly continue to hold as true *what we believe about him* The clause κρατῶμεν τῆς ὁμολογίας 'let us hold the confession' is somewhat figurative as well as having an abstract noun. These are unskewed in the display text. Since 'confession' is a communicative event, which implies some content of what is being communicated, 'what we believe about him' is supplied as suitable to the epistle; cf. CEV's "hold on to what we have said about him." Miller says (p. 130) the sense is "consent to something felt to be valid," which is very close to what is in the display.

4:15a We certainly *can trust* **a Supreme Priest** Verse 4:15 expresses the *basis* for the APPEAL in 4:16, and not the *basis* for the APPEAL in 4:14. Therefore, the γάρ which introduces verse 15 is represented by the communication relation, but not in the display. Cf. CEV, TEV, NLT.

The Greek text has the full verb of the participle that the author used in v. 14, ἔχομεν 'we have'. The words 'we have' do not imply possession, but 'the one who is acting on our behalf'.

who can indeed compassionately help us The GNT has a double negative here (i.e., a litotes) whose force is to emphasize the positive. The verb συμπαθῆσαι 'sympathize with' focuses on Jesus' compassion.

4:15b who are likely to sin The phrase ταῖς ἀσθενείαις ἡμῶν means 'our weaknesses', but what does the writer mean by 'weaknesses'? The context just does not support the notion that it refers to our "weaknesses, pressures, and trials" (Miller, p 131). BAGD (p. 115.2) suggests the meaning of this context is moral weakness. The immediately following context (15c–d) talks about temptation and sin. Attridge (p. 140) is right in saying the reference here is to "especially that weakness which results in sin."

4:15c in every way that we are tempted to sin This represents κατὰ πάντα καθ᾿ ὁμοιότητα 'according to all things according to (our) likeness' and follows TEV, NJB, CEV and NCV. It does not mean that he had exactly the same temptations as we have, but that "He has been tempted—in extent and range—in every way…just as intensely as we are" (Kistemaker, p. 125).

4:15d *and yet* **he did not sin** The display follows Miller, (p. 131), who says that the genitive expression χωρὶς ἁμαρτίας 'without sin' "plays a contra-expectation role."

4:16a The οὖν 'therefore' introduces the APPEAL, and is so represented in the communication relations.

pray boldly to *our Supreme Priest* The GNT has προσερχώμεθα μετὰ παρρησίας 'let us approach with confidence'. This is figurative, with the meaning that the author was urging the believers to be confident when they asked Jesus to help them.

A translator must often decide whether the person sitting on the throne is the Father or Christ. Most commentators suggest that the author implied the Father. However, it seems inconsistent to say 'since *Christ* is our Supreme Priest, let us approach *God*.' Furthermore, the paragraph is about the Supreme Priestly work of Christ, not about God; cf. Kistemaker, p. 126–127.

4:16b who sits on the throne, to ask him to help us graciously The GNT has τῷ θρόνῳ τῆς χάριτος 'the throne of grace'. The word 'throne' is a double metonymy, the place standing for the one associated with that place and for the event (ruling) that is associated with a throne. It is all very well to say with Dods that the throne of grace "is the source from which grace is dispensed," but this ignores the fact that grace is semantically not a thing but an attribute of some action; hence, 'to help us graciously'.

There is a question whether the one dispensing grace from the throne is God or Christ. Most commentators assume the former.

4:16c–d experience *his acting* mercifully *toward us*, ... *his graciously* helping *us* Again, the display recognizes that λάβωμεν ἔλεος καί χάριν εὕρωμενᾱεἰς... βοήθειαν 'we may receive mercy and we may find grace for help' are expressions using abstract nouns, which are transformed by making the first an adverb to modify the verb 'acting' and making the second modify the verb 'help'.

4:16e whenever we need *him* Bruce (p. 86–87) says that the words εἰς εὔκαιρον βοήθειαν 'for timely help' refer to "the constant availability of divine aid in all their need."

BOUNDARIES AND COHERENCE

The boundary at 5:1 is indicated by a return to expository discourse featuring a lengthy discussion of Christ as Supreme Priest, comparing him with the Jewish Supreme Priests. Coherence in the 4:14–16 paragraph is provided by two occurrences of ἀρχιερεύς 'Supreme Priest' (v. 14a; v. 15a, with reference to him all through those verses), plus the semantic oneness of the phrases 'able to sympathize with our weaknesses' (v. 15) and 'help us in our time of need' (v. 16).

PROMINENCE AND THEME

The theme of the paragraph 4:14–16 is taken from the naturally prominent propositions of each of the *APPEALS*. The second *APPEAL* has a *purpose* proposition which is considered equally prominent, and are therefore both included in the theme.

PART CONSTITUENT 5:1—9:28 (Section: Appeal₃ of 1:4—12:29)

THEME: You should request that we(exc.) teach you how to become spiritually mature, because it is not possible that anyone can persuade to repent again those who have renounced the message about Christ. Part of that message is that we needed to be consecrated by a better sacrifice, one made by Christ.

MACROSTRUCTURE	CONTENTS
APPEAL	5:1—6:20 You should request that we(exc.) teach you how to become spiritually mature, but it may not be possible that anyone can persuade to repent again those who have renounced the message that they believed about Christ.
basis₁	7:1—9:22 Just as Melchizedek was greater than the priests descended from Aaron, and the new agreement is better than the old one, we needed to be consecrated by better sacrifices.
basis₂	9:23–28 Since those who would enter heaven had to be consecrated by better sacrifices than those of the old agreement, Christ has appeared once to cause people to be no longer guilty for sin.

INTENT AND MACROSTRUCTURE PATTERN

This is a hortatory unit, one of the two most prominent in the epistle. This unit consists of an *APPEAL* and two *bases* for that *APPEAL*.

BOUNDARIES AND COHERENCE

A boundary at 10:1 is indicated by a switch from a discussion of the old sacrificial system to the sacrifice made by Christ. Cohesion within the 5:1—9:25 unit is provided by seven occurrences of Μελχισέδεκ 'Melchizedek' and nine occurrences of ἁμαρτία 'sin'.

PROMINENCE AND THEME

The theme for this unit is drawn from condensations of the most naturally prominent propositions in the two *bases* and in the *APPEAL*.

SECTION CONSTITUENT 5:1—6:20 (Sub-Section: Appeal of 5:1—9:28)

THEME: You should request that we(exc.) teach you how to become spiritually mature, but it may not be possible that anyone can persuade to repent again those who have renounced the message that they believed about Christ.

MACROSTRUCTURE	CONTENTS
basis₁	5:1–14 Although *there is much that I might teach you about how Christ resembles Melchizedek, such teaching is hard for me to* explain to you, since you continue to need that someone teach you again the basic truths about Christ. You are not yet able to learn any more profound teaching.
APPEAL	6:1–12 You should request that we(exc.) teach you how to become spiritually mature, but it may not be possible that anyone can persuade to repent again those who have renounced the message that they believed about Christ.
basis₂	6:13–20 God promised that he would bless Abraham. God also guaranteed his promise to us by saying that he would punish himself if he did not fulfill his promise.

INTENT AND MACROSTRUCTURE PATTERN

This is a hortatory unit, one of the two most prominent in the epistle. This unit consists of an *APPEAL* and two *bases* for that *APPEAL*.

BOUNDARIES AND COHERENCE

A boundary at 7:1 is indicated by a switch from a discussion of the old sacrificial system to the sacrifice made by Christ. Cohesion within the 5:1—6:20 unit is provided by the extended metaphor regarding milk, three occurrences of ἀρχιερεύς 'Supreme Priest' and several occurrences of terms for 'oath' and 'promise'.

PROMINENCE AND THEME

The theme for this unit is drawn from condensations of the most naturally prominent propositions in the *APPEAL*.

SUB-SECTION CONSTITUENT 5:1–14 (Paragraph Cluster: Basis₁ of 5:1—6:20)

THEME: The Israelites had Supreme Priests, but now God has installed Christ as our Supreme Priest who resembled Melchizedek in many ways, but it is hard for me to explain that to you.

MACROSTRUCTURE	CONTENTS
CLAIM	5:1–10 Every Israelite Supreme Priest was chosen from among humans. Each of them dealt gently with those who ignorantly sinned. Similarly, God installed Christ as our Supreme Priest. Since he resembled Melchizedek in many ways, he is fully qualified to be Supreme Priest; thus we can certainly know that he is able to eternally forgive us who obey him.
complication	5:11–14 Although there is much that I might teach you about how Christ resembles Melchizedek, such teaching is hard for me to explain to you, since you continue to need that someone teach you again the basic truths about Christ. You are not yet able to learn any more profound teaching.

INTENT AND PARAGRAPH PATTERN

This paragraph is deemed to consist of a *CLAIM* and a *complication*. The author is making a claim about Christ being our Supreme Priest, superior to the previous Jewish priests, with resemblances to Melchizedek; but then he realizes it will be hard to explain those resemblances because his audience is still spiritually immature.

The unit begins with γάρ 'since' which is represented by this unit being *basis*₁ of this section.

BOUNDARIES AND COHERENCE

Cohesion within this unit is provided by two occurrences of ἀρχιερεύς 'Supreme Priest', and an extended metaphor regarding milk. A new paragraph at 6:1 is shown by the conjunction διό 'therefore' and an imperative verb.

PROMINENCE AND THEME

The theme is a condensation of the most naturally prominent propositions of the CLAIM in 5:1–10, plus the two naturally prominent propositions of the contraexpectation of the *complication* in 5:11–14.

PARAGRAPH CLUSTER CONSTITUENT 5:1–10 (Paragraph: Claim of 5:1–14)

THEME: *Every Israelite Supreme Priest was chosen from among humans. Each of them dealt gently with those who ignorantly sinned. Similarly, God installed Christ as our Supreme Priest. Since he resembled Melchizedek in many ways, he is fully qualified to be Supreme Priest; thus we can certainly know that he is able to eternally forgive us who obey him.*

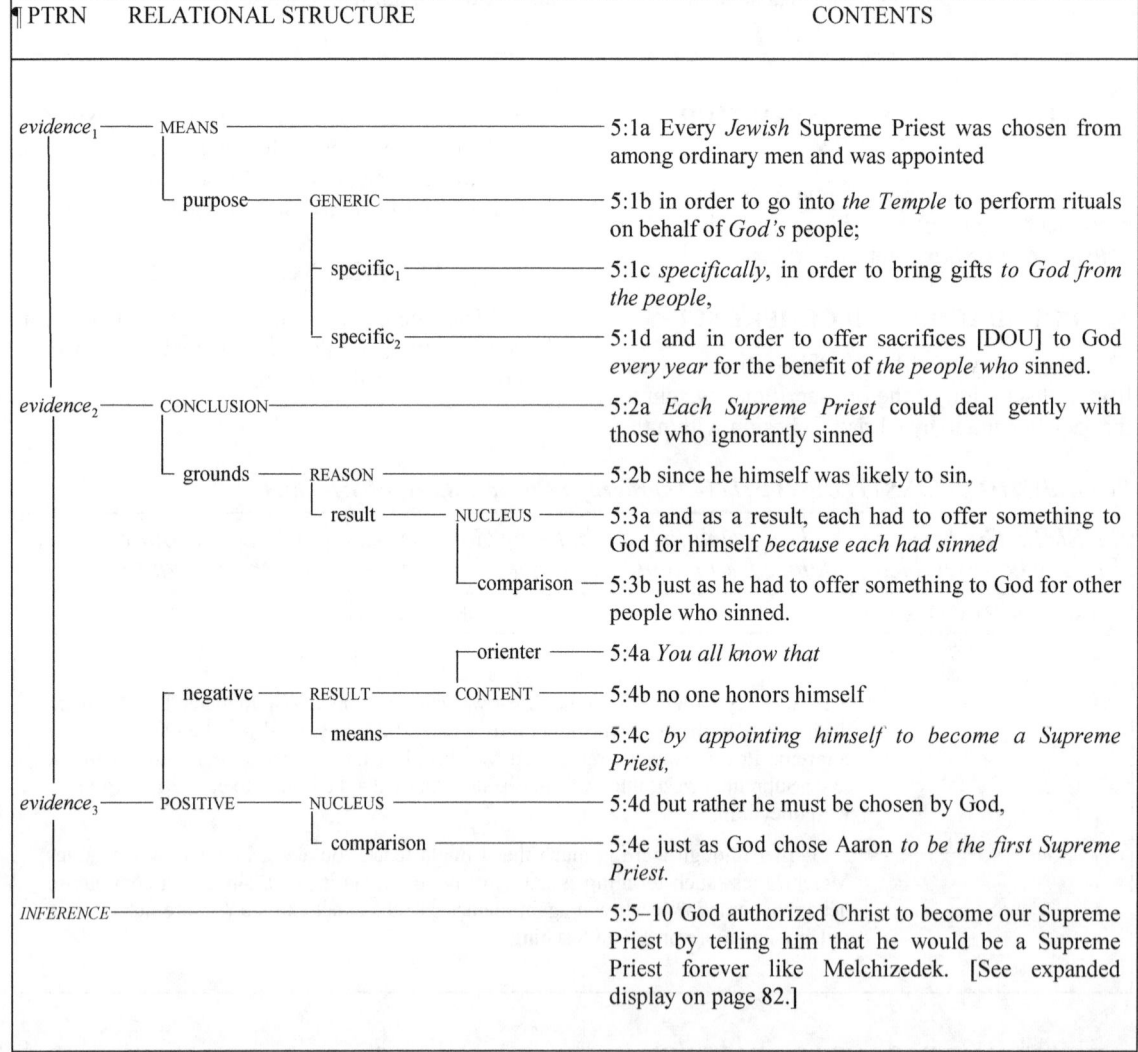

INTENT AND PARAGRAPH PATTERN

The writer returns in the 5:1–10 paragraph to the expository mode. Here he expounds on the reason Christ is superior to all the Supreme Priests who officiated under the Old Agreement. To do so, the writer produced three statements of *evidence* regarding those former Supreme Priests, and then made an INFERENCE about Christ.

NOTES

5:1a *Jewish* **Supreme Priest** The display text makes clear that the writer was referring to the Israelite Supreme Priests (cf. LB).

ordinary men The reason the writer includes the phrase ἐξ ἀνθρώπων 'out of men' seems to be, as Westcott (p. 118) puts it, "The human origin of the High-priest is marked as a ground of the fitness of his appointment."

5:1b go into *the Temple* **to perform rituals** The adverbial accusative phrase τὰ πρὸς τὸν θεόν 'the things toward God' has been taken to mean either 'as a mediator between God and people' or 'in things pertaining to God'. The majority of commentators prefer the latter, which is undoubtedly correct, but that phrase does not seem to communicate much. Since the matters are specified in v. 1c–d, the display simply focuses on the Supreme Priest doing the proper rituals (cf. NCV's "He is given the work of going before God for them").

on behalf of *God's* **people** The phrase ὑπὲρ ἀνθρώπων 'on behalf of men' is parallel lexically to 'out of men' in v. 1a, but 'men' here means generically humans, and more specifically it means God's people.

5:1d sacrifices [DOU] to God *every year* In the clause προφέρῃ δῶρά τε καὶ θυσίας 'to offer gifts and sacrifices,' the two nouns are considered a near synonymous doublet by Moore (p. 57), and the majority of commentators agree that the phrase is a general term describing all kinds of offerings. But Ellingworth notes that there is a question whether the two words denote generic or more specific offerings, whether they denote animal sacrifices vs. cereal offerings, or whether the terms are indeed synonymous. The display attempts to preserve some of the uncertainty by using the word 'gifts' in v. 1c and 'sacrifices' here.

for the benefit of *the people who* **sinned** Making the abstract noun ἁμαρτία 'sin' a verb requires specifying 'people' as the agent.

5:2a *Each Supreme Priest* The GNT continues the singular pronoun from v. 1a, but the sense is generic. The display tries to capture both of these nuances with the words 'each Supreme Priest' in vv. 2–3.

those who ignorantly sinned The GNT phrase τοῖς ἀγνοοῦσιν καὶ πλανωμένοις 'to those unknowing and being led astray' has two participles, but the display follows Miller who suggests (p. 138) "the one article with the two participles makes the phrase a hendiadys. If so, the sense would be: 'those who err through ignorance.'" The great majority of commentators agree.

5:2b he himself was likely to sin The sense of 'weakness' in the clause περίκειται ἀσθένειαν 'is subject to weakness' is the same as it was in 4:15b, as is evidenced by the immediately following context.

5:3a–b The GNT has περὶ ἁμαρτιῶν 'concerning sins' only once, but the display text makes clear that there is an ellipsis: the sins were his own as well as those of other people. Most versions do likewise.

5:4a *You all know that* The display supplies an orienter to indicate that the author was reminding his people of information they knew.

5:4c *by appointing himself to become a* **Supreme Priest** The display makes clear what is referred to by the words τὴν τιμήν 'the honor' (cf. NCV, "did not choose himself to have the honor of being a Supreme Priest").

5:4e God chose Aaron *to be the first Supreme Priest* The verb καλέω means 'call', but the display uses 'God chose Aaron', since God did not speak audibly to Aaron nor to any of the subsequent Supreme Priests. The author wanted the readers to understand that God authenticated verbally both the Aaronic priesthood (albeit indirectly) and Jesus' priesthood. CEV's rendering, "Only God can choose a priest, and God is the one who chose Aaron" is a good alternative.

The display fills in the ellipsis and makes clear what the original audience would have known: viz., that Aaron is mentioned because he was the first Jewish Supreme Priest. (NCV puts this information in a footnote; NLT has "for this work.")

EXPANSION OF THE *INFERENCE* IN THE 5:1–10 DISPLAY

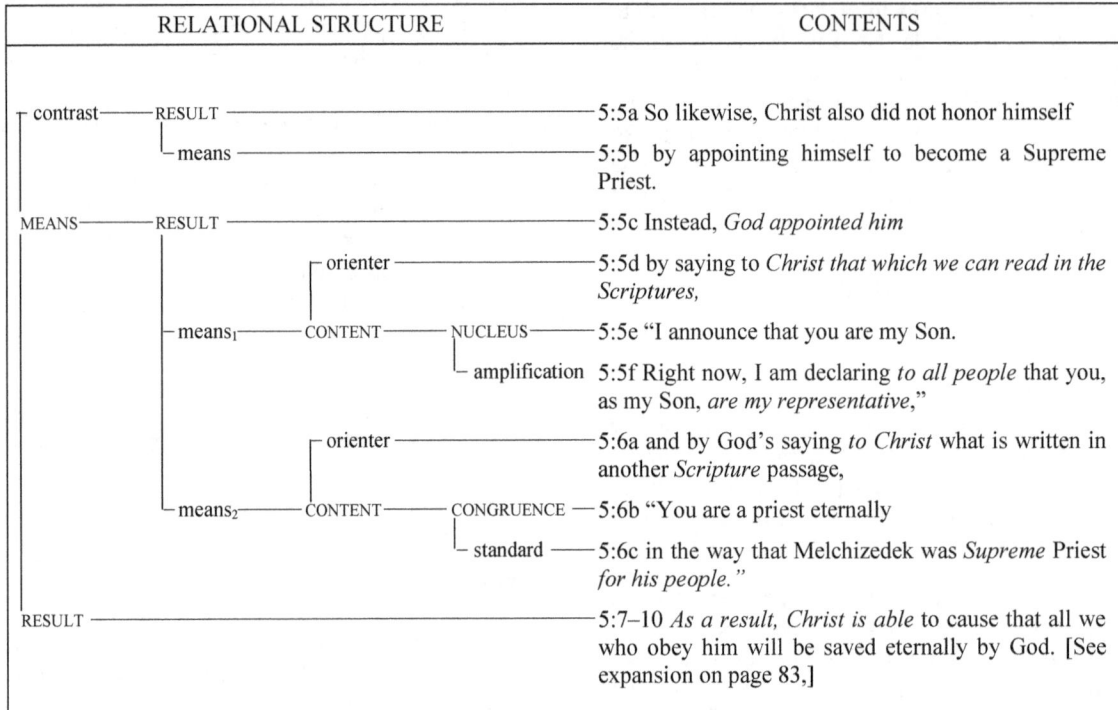

NOTES

5:5c *God appointed him* The GNT has an ellipsis of a main verb. Most commentators suggest repeating the first part of v. 4 as 'God glorified him in the process of making him a Supreme Priest'. But this does not cohere well at all. Other commentators suggest the interpretation followed in the display, which does cohere very well with what follows.

5:5d saying to *Christ* The word 'Christ' is identifying the pronoun αὐτόν 'him'.

that which we can read in the Scriptures This makes clear what the writer assumed his readers would know; what follows is again cited from Ps. 2:7.

5:5e–f See notes on 1:5b–c.

5:6a God's saying *to Christ* what is written in another *Scripture* passage The display text fills in ellipses and makes clear that what follows is another Scripture quote. This citation is from Ps. 110:4.

5:6c in the way that Melchizedek was *Supreme* Priest *for his people* The GNT has κατὰ τὴν τάξιν Μελχισέδεκ 'according to the order of Melchizedek'. but the display is similar to NIV's "just like Melchizedek." As Morris notes (p. 49), "There was no succession of priests from Melchizedek and thus no 'order'. " An acceptable alternative would be 'of the same kind as' or "with the same rank as Melchizedek" (LB). It is true that in this verse the word is 'priest', not 'Supreme Priest', but it clearly means 'Supreme Priest', as is clear from similar wording using ἀρχιερούς 'Supreme Priest' in v. 10.

EXPANSION OF THE RESULT IN THE 5:5–10 DISPLAY

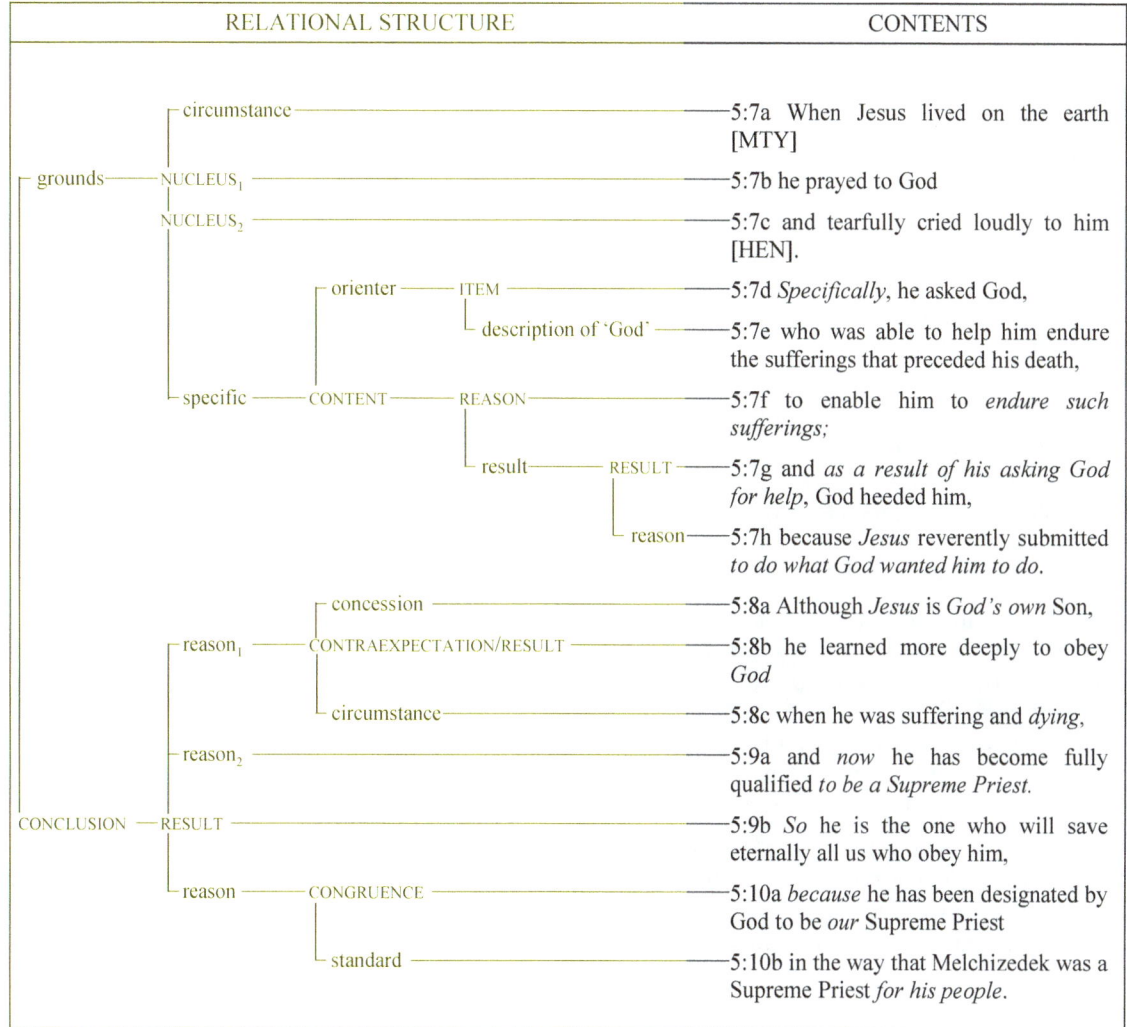

NOTES

5:7a When Jesus lived on the earth The words ἐν ταῖς ἡμέραις τῆς σαρκὸς αὐτοῦ 'in the days of his flesh' are a figurative expression involving metonymy; the sense is as in NCV, "While Jesus lived on earth." There is no name given in the Greek, but since the author was focusing on Jesus' life, not his title, the display follows several English translations (RSV, NIV, TEV, and NLT) in supplying 'Jesus'.

5:7b–c he prayed to God and tearfully cried loudly to him The display text replaces the abstract nouns in the clause δεήσεις τε καὶ ἱκετρίας... προσενέγκας 'offering petitions and entreaties' with clauses. CEV uses only one verb, "begged God," agreeing with Moore who classifies this as a synonymous doublet (p. 57).

5:7c and tearfully cried loudly This represents μετὰ κραυγῆς ἰσχυρᾶς καὶ δακρύων 'with strong crying and tears'. The first term refers more to vocal expression, 'wailing', than just crying. Since 'tears' is a manner of 'crying', the terms are considered a hendiadys.

5:7f to enable *him to endure such suffering* There are several interpretations of the words τὸν δυνάμενον σῴζειν αὐτὸν ἐκ θανάτου 'the one able to save him out of death':

1. It refers to his resurrection. But inasmuch as Christ had already predicted his resurrection several times and told his disciples to meet him in Galilee afterwards, it doesn't make much sense to see him as pleading in Gethsemane for his resurrection.

2. It is a request to be spared from death itself. But inasmuch as Christ knew that "man's only hope of salvation lay in His death on the cross" (Hewitt), such an interpretation is not acceptable. Besides, Christ did die and yet the text here (7g) says his prayer was answered.
3. He was praying to be spared from dying there in Gethsemane. But there is no hint in this context or elsewhere that there was any danger of his anguish in the Garden proving to be fatal.
4. There is another view, suggested by Bruce and Miller. Miller notes (p. 148) that in this context, "The focus is on Jesus' godly fear or reverence which resulted in His prayer being heard…. The point to be emphasized is that Jesus *needed* heavenly aid to drink the appointed cup…. Jesus was praying for strength for deliverance *in* the trial rather than deliverance *from* it."

5:7h reverently submitted *to do what God wanted him to do* Nearly all commentators agree with Bruce, who says (p. 102) regarding the phrase ἀπὸ τῆς εὐλαβείας 'because of awe', "what is in view here is… our Lord's devotion and submission to the will of God." Nearly all the versions render this in a similar way.

5:8b he learned more deeply to obey *God* The display makes clear that Jesus did not begin one day on earth to learn to obey. The author was indicating here that Jesus continued a deepening process.

5:8c when he was suffering and *dying* Lane (p. 121) suggests regarding the meaning of ἔπαθεν 'he suffered'. "The crucial consideration is that in Hebrews the verb πάσχειν, which ordinarily means 'to suffer', is used only of the passion of Jesus and takes on the nuance 'to die.'"

5:9a he has become fully qualified *to be a Supreme Priest* See the note on 2:10a. The verb τελειόω means 'bring to its goal' (BAGD p. 809.2), and the goal is the goal God intended. As Morris notes (p. 50), "This does not mean that he was imperfect and that out of his imperfection he became perfect." Some suggest it includes his exaltation after his resurrection; some say it refers to his consecration as Supreme Priest, but the majority say it refers to the moral discipline by which Christ was qualified to be Supreme Priest.

5:9b *So* **he is the one who will save eternally** The Greek σωτηρίας αἰωνίου 'salvation eternal' refers to the main function of the rituals that our Supreme Priest performed—to save us.

all us who obey him The display makes clear that the writer of Hebrews is included among those who obey God.

5:10a *because* Although some versions (e.g., NIV,) render the relationship signaled by the participle προσαγορευθεὶς 'being designated' by 'and', the display agrees with CEV and with Miller who says (p. 152) "The causal participle προσαγορευθείς serves to indicate a reason for the result expressed in verse 9."

5:10b See note on 6c.

BOUNDARIES AND COHERENCE

A boundary following 5:10 is indicated by the fact that in the following paragraph the author switches from a discussion about Christ using only third person pronouns to a more personal discussion using first person and second person pronouns. All modern translations make a paragraph break here.

PROMINENCE AND THEME

The theme of 5:1–10 is drawn from the most prominent propositions of the three *evidences* and the concluding INFERENCE.

PARAGRAPH CLUSTER CONSTITUENT 5:11–14 (Paragraph: Complication of 5:1–14)

THEME: Although there is much that I might teach you about how Christ resembles Melchizedek, such teaching is hard for me to explain to you, since you continue to need that someone teach you again the basic truths about Christ. You are not yet able to learn any more profound teaching.

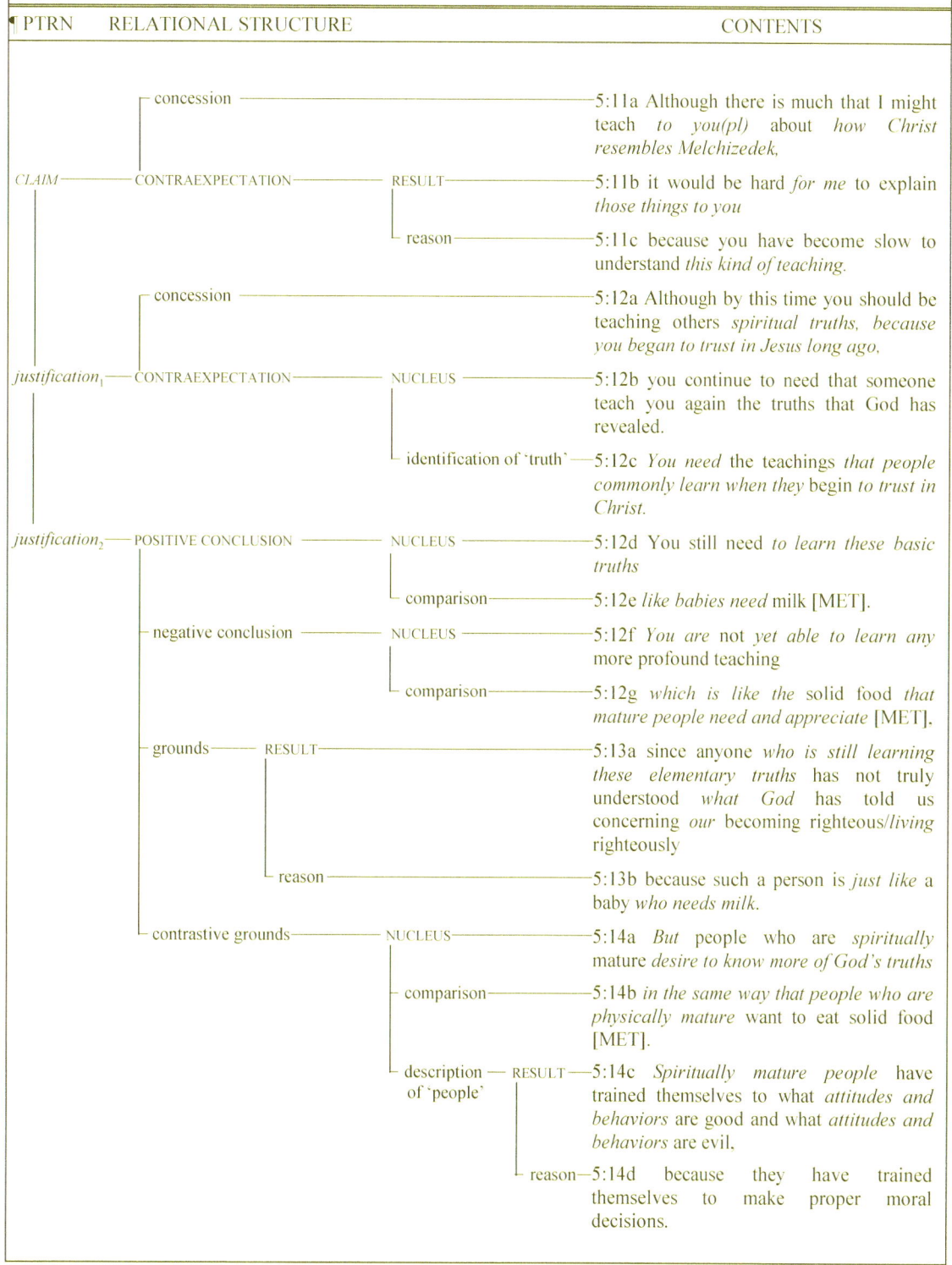

INTENT AND PARAGRAPH PATTERN

The writer continues in the expository mode, making a CLAIM about his readers' inability to understand teaching about Melchizedek, and then giving two *justifications* as to why he feels that people cannot understand such teaching. This is an indirect reprimand.

NOTES

5:11a much that I might teach *to you(pl)* The expression πολὺς ἡμῖν ὁ λόγος 'much to us the word' is very idiomatic. Most versions translate as "we have much to say" (NIV) or something similar. The display fills out the case role by supplying an indirect object as well as indicating the desire of the author. It uses 'teach' instead of 'say' because the author is writing a document, not speaking to people. The writer is clearly using an editorial 'we' (cf. NLT, "there is much more I would like to say").

about *how Christ resembles Melchizedek* The display makes clear the referent of περὶ οὗ 'concerning which/whom'. REB has "About Melchizedek."

5:11c have become slow to understand *this kind of teaching* The clause νωθροὶ γεγόνατε ταῖς ἀκοαῖς 'you have become dull in the hearings' is also idiomatic. The author is not insulting here, but rather urging each reader and listener to continue trying to understand. TEV has "you are so slow to understand" which similarly carries the sense in a somewhat idiomatic way, but the perfect tense indicates that they had become unable to understand that kind of teaching as much as they were able to previously.

5:12a Although by this time you should be teaching others *spiritual truths* The display text fills in the case roles and makes clear what type of teaching is meant. Lane (p. 137) says it refers to "an ability to communicate the faith to others."

because you began to trust in Jesus long ago The Greek has only διὰ τὸν χρόνον 'on account of the time', which is rather nebulous. This clause states the implied logical explanation; cf. Bruce (p. 107), "You have been Christians for such a long time" (NLT's wording is almost identical).

5:12b the truths that God has revealed Nearly all commentators agree that the phrase τῶν λογίων τοῦ θεοῦ 'of the sayings/oracles of God' refers to divine revelation in general, or to divine revelation of Christian doctrine specifically.

5:12c *You need* the teachings *that people commonly learn when they* begin *to trust in* Christ This represents the phrase τὰ στοιχεῖα τῆς ἀρχῆς 'the rudiments of the beginning'. In connection with the above phrase in v. 12b, the display follows Dods who says, "The meaning of 'beginning' would seem to be determined by 'the elementary doctrines of Christ' in 6:1 where it apparently denotes the initial stages of a Christian profession... Here, then, 'the beginning of the oracles of God' would mean the oracles of God as taught in the beginning of one's education of these oracles." Miller has similar comments.

5:12d–e The display spells out the topic of the metaphor. Both NCV and NLT make parts of the topic specific. Also (NLT does it as the paragraph heading, not in the text).

5:12f *You are* not *yet able to learn any* more profound teaching Again the display spells out the topic of the metaphor 'solid food'. NCV also has "You are not ready for."

5:13a-b Again the display text makes clear the topic of the metaphor.

5:13a not truly understood *what God* has told us concerning *our* becoming righteous/*living righteously* The adjective in the phrase ἄπειρος λόγου δικαιοσύνης 'unskilled of word of righteousness' means "unacquainted with" (BAGD p. 83) but commentators have very varied ideas of what the genitive phrase 'word of righteousness' means. Morris (p. 52) states the problem and the basic alternatives quite well: "The problem is that both 'word' and 'righteousness' may be taken in more ways than one. 'Word' may mean the Christian message, in which case we may wish to see 'righteousness' in terms of 'the righteousness of God' that is made known and available in Christ. Or we may see 'righteousness' as the right conduct God expects believers to follow. Or the author may be following up the previous metaphor and thinking of the prattling speech of the child." The third alternative is rejected here as being a very strange way of referring to such. The original readers would certainly have understood one of the first two alternatives. The context in v. 14 (distinguishing good and evil) would favor the second alternative, but the context of v. 12 (the elemental truths of the faith) could favor the first alternative. Both of these are therefore listed as possibilities in the display text. There does not seem enough evidence to choose between them.

5:14a–b Again the display makes explicit the topic of this further metaphor about the kinds of food that people of different ages appreciate. Among the versions, only LB makes any similar attempt to indicate the topic.

5:14a *But people who are spiritually* **mature** *desire to know more of God's truths* It seems important to make clear the concept to which the author referred by ἡ στερεὰ τροφή 'solid food'. The commentaries have not treated the problem. The display tries to indicate the sense.

5:14b *in the same way that people who are physically* **mature** *want to eat solid food* The display fills out the meaning of the Greek ἐστιν 'is'. The author focuses on the type of food that mature people appreciate.

5:14c what *attitudes and behaviors* **are good** and what *attitudes and behaviors* **are evil** The display attempts to show specifically to what the author is referring by the generic Greek καλοῦ τε καὶ κακοῦ 'good both and evil'.

5:14d they have trained themselves to make proper moral decisions The GNT has the phrase διὰ τὴν ἕξιν τὰ αἰσθητήρια γεγυμνασμένα ἐχόντων 'because of practice having the faculties trained' The word 'faculties' which means "ability to make moral decisions" (BAGD p. 25) is taken as a synecdoche; training one's moral faculties is training oneself. It is so taken by NIV, NCV, and CEV. The verb 'trained' literally refers to physical training, but is here used figuratively. The word 'practice' is conveyed by 'to continually determine', as Montefiore says, "It is not practice or habit as such that enables grown men to have moral discrimination, but rather their state or condition which is the result of previous habit or practice."

BOUNDARIES AND COHERENCE

A new paragraph unit at 6:1 is signaled by the conjunction διό 'therefore', a return to hortatory discourse, and a change in topic to a listing of some of the basic elements of Christian teaching and experience. Coherence within the 5:11–14 paragraph is maintained by two references each to 'solid food' and 'milk' and by the contrasting lexemes νήπιος 'infant' and τέλειος 'mature'.

PROMINENCE AND THEME

The theme for the 5:11–14 paragraph is formed from the naturally prominent propositions of the CLAIM and its two *justifications*. Within the CLAIM, although the *concession* and the CONTRAEXPECTATION propositions are not usually considered to be of equal prominence; the latter would be incomplete without at least a good bit of the former. It is, therefore, included in the theme.

SUB-SECTION CONSTITUENT 6:1–12 (Paragraph Cluster: Appeal of 5:1—6:20)

THEME: *You should request that we(exc.) teach you how to become spiritually mature, but it may not be possible that anyone can persuade to repent again those who have renounced the message that they believed about Christ.*

MACROSTRUCTURE	CONTENTS
APPEAL	6:1–8 You should request that we teach you how to become spiritually mature. But it may be impossible for some of you to become spiritually mature because those who have experienced the blessings of a relationship with Christ and who have said that they no longer believe the message about Christ cannot be persuaded by anyone to repent again.
basis	6:9–12 I am certain concerning you that most of you are doing better than those who have rejected God's message. Therefore, I strongly desire that each one of you continue to expect with certainty that you will receive what God has promised you until you finally receive it all.

INTENT AND PARAGRAPH PATTERN

This paragraph is considered to be a hortatory one because of the verb, φερώμεθα, 'let us be carried forward' being a first person plural subjunctive. The writer uses διό 'therefore' to point to the *APPEAL*, from what he has said thus far about the superiority of Christ, urging his readers to be more mature in their understanding of Christian truth, and warning them of the dire consequences if they turn their backs on the message about Christ.

BOUNDARIES AND COHERENCE

A boundary at 6:13 is indicated by a switch from 1st plural to a mention of Abraham and six occurrences of θεός 'God'.

PROMINENCE AND THEME

The theme for this unit is derived from the positive nucleus of the *APPEAL* and the *summary statement* of the *basis* for the *APPEAL*.

PARAGRAPH CLUSTER CONSTITUENT 6:1–8 (Paragraph: Appeal of 6:1–12)

THEME: You should request that we teach you how to become spiritually mature. But it may be impossible for some of you to become spiritually mature because those who have experienced the blessings of a relationship with Christ and who have said that they no longer believe the message about Christ cannot be persuaded by anyone to repent again.

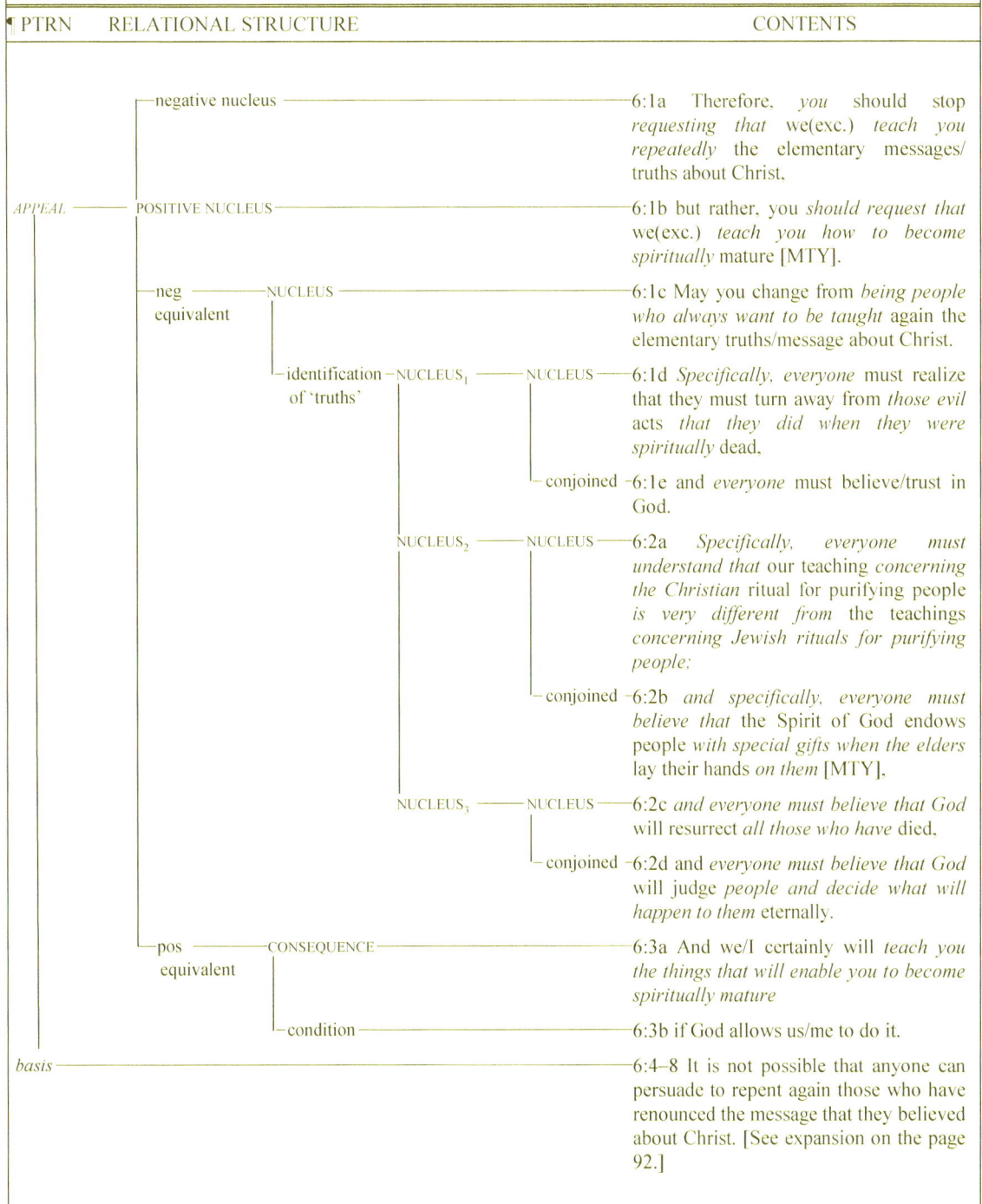

INTENT AND PARAGRAPH PATTERN

The first person plural subjunctive verb φερώμεθα 'let us go on' signals a return to hortatory discourse at 6:1. The paragraph consists of an appeal in vv. 1–3 and its basis in vv. 4–8.

NOTES

6.1a *you* **should stop** *requesting that* **we(exc.)** *teach you repeatedly* A few commentators take the first person plural verbal ending as an editorial 'we', but it seems best to take the verse as referring to the immediately preceding context (5:12) in which the writer refers to his audience; hence the pronoun 'you' in the display. As Moffatt says (p. 72), "The writer wishes to carry his readers along with him." There is, as Davidson suggests, an implied exhortation (OR, in Semantic Analysis terms, a mitigated appeal) here. In languages without first person plural imperatives it might be acceptable to translate 'I urge you(pl) to'. The author was urging the readers and listeners to want to learn the deeper teachings. In some languages, such an appeal might be translated 'I want you(pl) to learn…' It is true that the pronoun 'you(pl)' does not occur in this verse, but a literal translation of φερώμεθα 'let us be carried forward' could easily imply that the writer considered that he himself urgently needed this exhortation.

you **should stop** *requesting* The participle ἀφέντες 'leaving' refers not to abandoning completely but "as applied to those who pass to a new subject" (Westcott, p.142).

the elementary messages/ truths about Christ In the phrase τὸν τῆς ἀρχῆς τοῦ Χριστοῦ λόγον 'the word of the beginning of Christ', λόγος means doctrine, teaching, message, and the genitive 'of Christ' is an objective genitive meaning 'about'. CEV renders the phrase well with "the basic things we were taught about Christ."

6:1b you *should request that* **we(exc.)** *teach you how to become spiritually* **mature** The GNT has only ἐπὶ τὴν τελειότητα φερώμεθα 'let us be borne towards maturity' but in the context it is referring to teaching. However, it is a collocational clash to refer to "grown-up teaching" (NCV), and therefore it is assumed the sense here is 'teaching which will help you to become mature'.

6:1c *always want to be taught* **again** The words θεμέλιον καταβαλλόμενοι 'laying a foundation' are metaphorical. The display text states the topic of the metaphor. Some versions also omit the figure entirely; e.g., NCV's "we should not again start teaching" and NLT's "start all over again."

6:1d *Specifically,* **everyone** *must realize that they must turn away from* **those evil acts** *that they did when they were spiritually* **dead** The first in the writer's list of teachings to be 'left behind' is μετανοίας ἀπὸ νεκρῶν ἔργων 'repentance from dead works'. Commentators are about equally divided as to whether the last two words in the phrase mean 'useless deeds' or 'sinful works resulting in spiritual death', or as Montefiore puts it, "all the activities of anyone who is out of relationship with the living God." No commentator states a reason for preferring one interpretation over the other. Many commentators suggest it means 'evil deeds that result in spiritual death', but that goes against the teaching of Scripture that evil deeds are the result of spiritual death, not the cause of it. The wording chosen here follows Montefiore (and others) because the focus in the first two items in the writer's list is on "aspects of conditions for becoming a Christian" (Miller, p. 163), which necessarily deals with things that characterized our pre-Christian state. If a language has no good expression for 'repent', one could say 'turn away from their sinful behavior/stop doing those evil actions'.

6:1e and *everyone* **must believe/trust** The Greek has μὴ πάλιν θεμέλιον καταβαλλόμενοι 'not again laying a foundation'. Some commentators seem to suggest that this is a live metaphor; but since it is used widely by other pre-Christian Greek writers in a metaphorical sense, it is best taken as a dead metaphor, i.e., an idiom. But even taking its figurative sense, just as a foundation is something which must be laid down, so the basic truths of Christianity are what everyone must believe. See CEV, likewise NLT.

6:2a *Specifically,* **everyone** *must understand that* **our teaching** *concerning the Christian* **ritual for purifying people** *is very different from* **the teachings** *concerning Jewish rituals for purifying people* The second set of two items in the writer's list has to do with a believer's present life. Commentators give two interpretations to the phrase βαπτισμῶν διδαχῆς 'teaching of baptisms'. The occurrence of the plural 'baptisms' "makes it unlikely that Christian baptism alone is being referred to" (Miller, p. 164). But does it then refer only to Jewish ceremonial washings, or Jewish baptism of proselytes, or does it include Christian baptism (and perhaps reference to the baptisms done by John)? The great majority of commentators assume the reference is to both Jewish and Christian ceremonies, and therefore 'Jewish and Christian' is made specific in the display. Beasley-Murray (cited by Kistemaker, p. 154) could well be right in saying it probably expresses a "contrast between Christian baptism and all other religious washings." But since it is not likely believers needed to be taught about Jewish cleansing rites, the rendering in the display assumes that meaning is excluded.

6:2b Spirit of God endows people *with special gifts when the elders* lay their hands *on them* Commentators are also divided as to what ἐπιθέσεώς τε χειρῶν 'laying on of hands' means. In the New Testament the practice is associated with (1) imparting healing, (2) commissioning people, (3) imparting spiritual gifts, and (4) imparting the Holy Spirit to new believers. It is difficult to know which of these the writer may have had in mind. The majority of commentators favor interpretation (4), but theologically that would seem to go against the clear teaching of the New Testament that the Spirit is given to believers at conversion, not by some subsequent act. In the light of references in the epistles to the impartation of gifts of the Spirit by the laying on of hands (1Tim. 4:14, 5:22, 2 Tim. 1:6) interpretation (3) is chosen for the display; but one cannot be dogmatic here.

6:2c *everyone must believe that God* will resurrect *all those who have* died The third set of two items refers to events that will happen in the future. The word 'God' simply completes the case frame.

6:2d *everyone must believe that God* will judge *people and decide what will happen to them* eternally The display makes clear what is meant by κρίματος αἰωνίου 'eternal judgment.' Taken literally the phrase would suggest the process of judging will go on forever, but the sense is more as Bruce (p. 117) suggests: "it is the judgment which is valid for the whole age (αἰών) to come."

6:3a-b we/I…us/me Since the author is here talking about what he intends to convey in this epistle, it is not likely that the first person plural here refers to the author and other apostles. Therefore if the meaning is 'we', the question remains, to whom else is he referring? For that reason, the display suggests that it is very likely an 'editorial we' referring only to the author.

6:3a And we/I certainly will *teach you the things that will enable you to become spiritually mature* The GNT is very cryptic with τοῦτο ποιήσομεν 'we will do this', but nearly all commentators agree with the sense given by Bruce (p. 118): "it would be better to press on to those teachings which belonged to spiritual maturity, in the hope that the maturity would come with the teachings."

There is somewhat of a textual problem here. A number of manuscripts have ποιήσωμεν 'let us do' instead of the indicative. The GNT, which is followed here, gives the indicative a B "almost certain" rating because of much better manuscript support and because the subjunctive 'let us' would be semantically incongruent with the next clause 'if God permits'. It is likely that the author used the indicative to make his urging more friendly to the people.

BOUNDARIES AND COHERENCE

A new paragraph at 6:9 is indicated by a change from hortatory to expressive discourse, by a vocative, and by pronominal devices: a switch from 'they' to a couple occurrences of an editorial 'we' and of 'you (pl.)' in the 6:9–12 unit.

PROMINENCE AND THEME

The theme of the 6:1–8 paragraph is drawn from the most prominent proposition (the positive nucleus) of the APPEAL, and the most naturally prominent (the consequence) proposition of the thesis within the *basis*. The extended illustration in 6:7–8 adds prominence to the appeal. Since the thesis consists of consequence and a series of conditions, and those conditions all involve the blessings that believers experience, those conditions have been condensed semantically into 'those who have experienced the blessings of a relationship with Christ'.

EXPANSION OF THE *BASIS* IN THE 6:1–8 DISPLAY

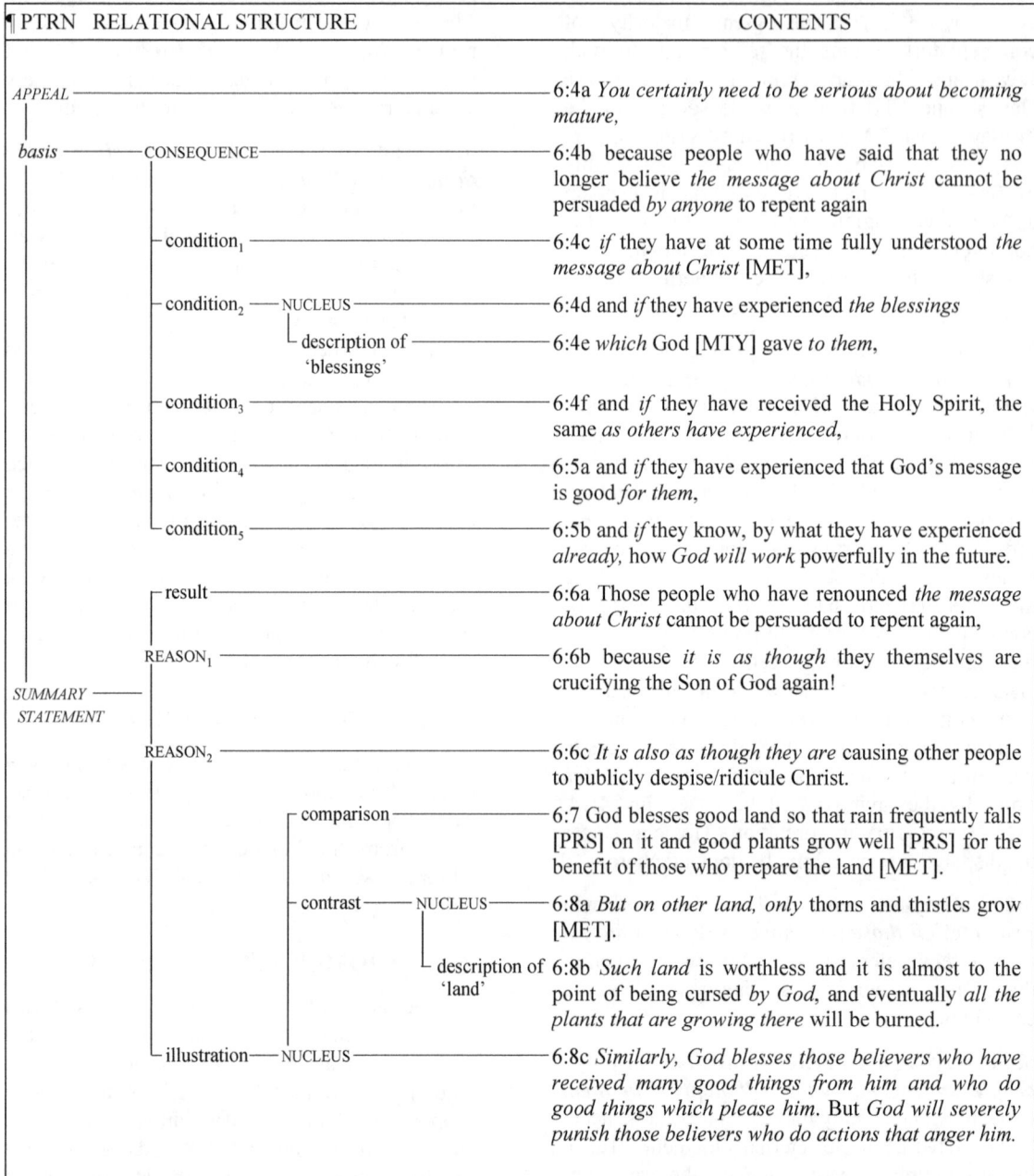

NOTES

6:4a Commentaries differ on whether the γάρ 'for' that introduces this verse is referring to v. 3 or to 6:1b. But the first part of the display is based on 6:1b, in which the writer was saying that they needed to be taught about spiritual maturity. The main clause of the sentence, 'can be persuaded to repent again', is brought up from v. 6 to form a complete sentence; the intervening material in the Greek is simply a series of qualifying participial phrases. (This main clause appears again in 6:6a.)

You certainly need to be serious about becoming mature This entire proposition represents the γάρ 'for'. It is important to keep in mind that the author wrote this paragraph to indicate the seriousness of his appeal that the people should learn the doctrines by which they could become spiritually mature.

6:4b–5b because This represents the γάρ 'since' which introduces this verse.

The clauses here are listed as conditions. The alternative is to follow the Greek forms and make them all relative clauses modifying 'people' in 4a. The structure given here makes the sense and the chronological sequence clearer.

6:4b because people who have said that they no longer *believe the message about Christ* This represents the participle παραπεσόντας 'having fallen away' which occurs at the beginning of v. 6. The verb means 'stop obeying the set of beliefs that the person previously obeyed'. Other alternatives suggested include "commit apostasy" (BAGD p. 621), which is not much help to translators. Louw and Nida suggest (34.26), "forsake," and 'turn away', which leave the problem of supplying an object of the verb. The display text is an attempt to help the translator with the meaning (cf. NCV's "fell away from Christ"). To renounce something means to declare that one no longer believes it.

be persuaded *by anyone* to repent again LB renders this by "no use trying to bring you back to the Lord again" but the words ἀνακαινίζειν εἰς μετάνοιαν 'to restore to repentance' implies someone else acting as the agent.

6:4c fully understood *the message about Christ* The expression φωτισθέντας 'enlightened' is figurative. The nonfigurative sense of the word is given as "to make known" by Louw and Nida (28.36). It is translated as "understood the Good News" in LB.

6:4d-e experienced *the blessings which* God [MTY] gave *to them* The GNT wording γευσαμένους τε τῆς δωρεᾶς τῆς ἐπουρανίου 'having tasted of the heavenly gift' is obviously figurative. 'Heavenly' is taken as a metonymy, the place standing for God. Commentators do agree that 'tasted' is quite metaphorical meaning 'to experience', but there is much speculation as to which heavenly gift the writer refers to. Suggestions vary from "the Eucharist" (Bruce), "salvation" (Moffatt), "forgiveness of sin" (Davidson), "the Gospel" (Brown), "Jesus Christ" (Hewitt), "the redemptive work of Christ" (Miller, p. 170). The display attempts to be neutral here by simply supplying the word 'blessings'.

6:4f received the Holy Spirit, the same *as others have experienced* The phrase μετόχους γενηθέντας πνεύματος ἁγίου 'becoming sharers of the Holy Spirit' is also subject to differences in interpretation, which largely seem to be doctrinally motivated. It is possible, as many commentators suggest, that there is a connection between this phrase and the 'laying on of hands' in v. 2, but this is by no means certain. Even if there were a connection, there seems to be no good justification for saying that 'Holy Spirit' is to be taken as a metonymy standing for the gifts of the Spirit. The term 'Holy Spirit' seldom has that sense elsewhere. Miller notes (p. 171) also that the aorist form of the participle "points toward a spiritual experience." To 'become 'sharers of' something means to receive something just as others have. Thus 'as others have' is clearly implied. Ellingworth and Nida (p. 114) suggest the sense is "that believers receive the Holy Spirit together, in common with one another." Lenski's (p. 183) comments on the meaning and its clear implications are right on the mark: he says the Spirit is a person, and "those are partakers of him who with others receive him in their hearts with all that this saving, sanctifying presence means."

6:5a experienced that God's message is good *for them* The word 'tasted' is exactly the same as the main verb in 4c, and is rendered here the same way, as it has the same figurative meaning. Commentators differ as to exactly what the writer intends by θεοῦ ῥῆμα 'word of God', but in this context it is hard to believe it means something different from "the message of salvation which they had believed" (Hagner, p. 71).

6:5b they know, by what they have experienced *already*, how *God will work powerfully in the future* The participle γευσαμένους 'having tasted' is assumed to carry over from the preceding phrase. Commentators are agreed that δυνάμεις 'powers of the coming age' refers to miraculous deeds; it is rendered here as 'work powerfully' but could be rendered 'perform miraculous deeds'. But they are divided as to whether μέλλοντος αἰῶνος 'of the coming age' in v. 5 refers to signs and wonders which began at Christ's first coming and which will be consummated upon his return, or whether it refers to things which will happen starting with his second coming. The display tries to be neutral, rending 'coming' by 'in the future'. Many commentators suggest that the phrase 'the coming age' refers to the Messianic age which began with Christ. The phrase could well refer to miraculous powers to be in evidence both prior to and subsequent to the return of Christ, but it could hardly be confined to the latter. Since the notion of 'have experienced (past event) the coming (future events) miraculous deeds' does not make sense semantically, the display makes the time distinction clear by 'they know, by what they have experienced already, how God will work in the future'.

6:6a renounced *the message about Christ* This fills out the meaning of the idiom παραπεσόντας 'fallen away'.

6:6b because Commentators are almost unanimous in stating that the participle ἀνασταυροῦντας 'having crucified' states the reason.

it is as though **they themselves are crucifying** The verb cannot be taken literally (cf. Ellingworth and Nida p. 116), "it is just as if they were"). If one wishes to make the metaphor clearer, NLT's rendering "by rejecting him" could be followed. However, it does not seem that it would be useful to try to spell out the metaphor, other than saying 'what they are doing is as though…' The present tense of the participle gives the sense 'they are continuing to'

they themselves Ellingworth and Nida suggest that the dative pronoun ἑαυτοῖς 'to themselves' can be taken various ways:

1. it can be ignored, as in TEV and CEV.
2. as in JBP's "in their own souls;"
3. as a dative of means as in JB's "willfully" or NEB's "with their own hands;" or
4. as meaning 'to their own harm' (cf. NIV's "to their loss").

Solution #1 is not very adequate; #2 distorts the focus, which here is on the effects of their act on others; #3 is suggesting that the 3rd person plural pronoun is being emphasized; #4 is supported by many commentators, but 'to their own disadvantage' seems to be very trite, and is not followed by any versions. Thus the display does not follow any of these interpretations. Instead, it simply has 'they themselves', meaning they are repeating what the original crucifixion team did.

6:6c causing other people to publicly despise/ridicule Christ The verb παραδειγματίζω means 'to disgrace publicly', but this may be hard to render in a passive sense, 'cause him to be disgraced publicly'. It could possibly be rendered as 'cause people to publicly insult/despise/ridicule him'. It probably refers to the fact that crucifixion was the strongest way of humiliating and shaming a criminal.

6:7 The γάρ that introduces this verse is simply introducing a metaphorical illustration, not giving a reason for the preceding statement. It is not represented in any of the modern English translations.

Verses 7–8 are each metaphors. In each case, only the image part of the figure is given in the GNT. Therefore the display presents for each the topic of the metaphor, and makes clear that a comparison is being made.

God blesses The display removes the verb and the abstract noun seen in μεταλαμβάνει εὐλογίας 'receives a blessing'. In some languages a term for 'bless' may not exist or may only apply to humans. In such cases something like 'causes good things to grow from' may be suitable.

good land so that rain frequently falls [PRS] on it and good plants grow well [PRS] The Greek text here has two personifications in which γῆ 'earth' is the subject of a transitive participle πιοῦσα 'having drunk'.. The figures are removed in the display (cf. LB's "land has had many showers upon it"). The only difficulty with removing the figures is that the verb πίνω 'drink' implies that the rain has soaked into the soil. The display uses 'frequently' to try to convey this (cf. NCV's "plenty of rain"). Ellingworth and Nida (p. 117) suggest "soil into which the rain sinks" as a possible translation. Similarly, instead of saying the ground 'produces vegetation' the display has 'good plants grow well' to again avoid the personification.

6:8a *only* **thorns** *and* **thistles grow** The word 'only' is an implicature of the argument (cf. JBP's "nothing but thorns and thistles"). If a translator does not have two terms to correspond with 'thorns and thistles' one would be sufficient; Moore (p. 57) considers them a near-synonymous doublet, but this analyst considers the meaning to be simply 'all kinds of thorny plants' (cf. CEV's "only thornbushes").

6:8b is almost to the point of being cursed *by God* The display attempts to show an implied threat to anyone who might want to abandon his or her following Jesus.

eventually *all the plants that are growing there* **will be burned** The display makes clear that it is not soil which can be burned, but only the vegetation growing on it. In areas where people practice a slash-and-burn type of agriculture, the people will likely understand that the author referred to their burning all the rubbish and bad vegetation while getting the land ready for growing food crops. However, the author referred to pulling out the weeds and burning them completely. "It is to be understood as referring to God's judgment here" (Miller, p. 178); it is possible that in some cases it will be necessary to specify the topic of this part of the metaphor: God will similarly destroy believers who reject his message of salvation.

6:8c *Similarly, God blesses those believers who have received many good things from him and who do good things which please him* In this metaphor there are potentially three different entities that represent human and divine beings. The ground represents believers; the cultivators represent believers, if the agents of 'it is cultivated' are meant to be seen as metaphorical. 'Those for whom it is cultivated' may represent God/Christ or believers or both. Lünemann in Meyer's Commentary on the New Testament understands 'those for whom the land is cultivated' to be God and Christ. As noted above, this proposition is the implied topic of the extended metaphor in the first half of the verse. NCV makes part of this specific by translating as "Some people are like." Commentators agree that the productive soil represents believers, but they say nothing about the significance of 'bearing useful vegetation' or about 'receives a blessing from God'. Brown even suggests (p. 299) that instead of pointing to a reward for being fertile, that the field "shows by its fertility that it is blessed of God." But such a meaning does not seem likely.

The greater part of this proposition spells out the topic of the extended metaphor in the first part of this verse. Bruce says (p. 125) the topic is "those in whose lives the fruits of righteousness do not appear."

PARAGRAPH CLUSTER CONSTITUENT 6:9–12 (Paragraph: Basis of 6:1–12)

THEME: I am certain concerning you that most of you are doing better than those who have rejected God's message. Therefore, I strongly desire that each one of you continue to expect with certainty that you will receive what God has promised you until you finally receive it all.

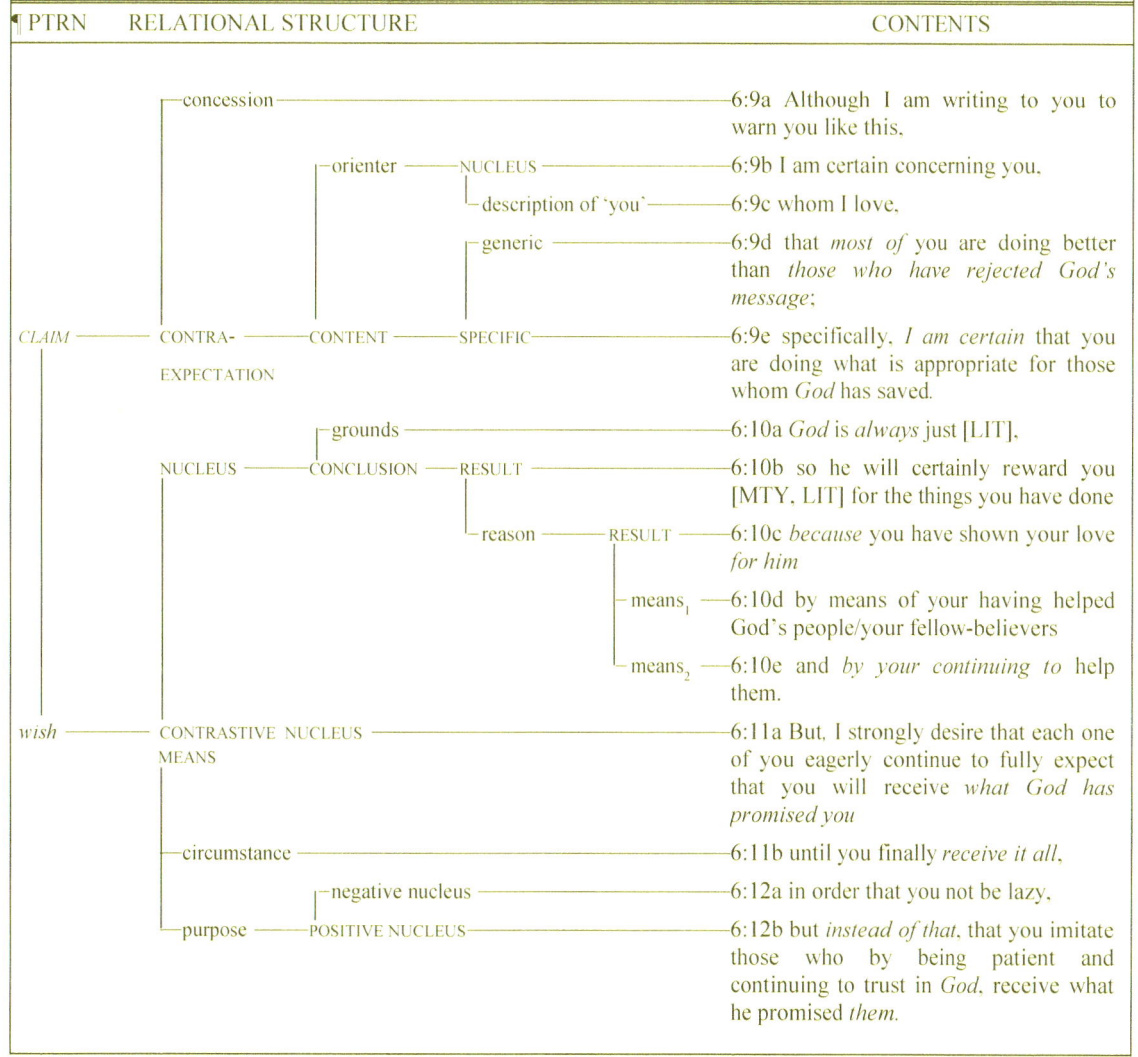

INTENT AND PARAGRAPH PATTERN

It is difficult at first glance to assign a paragraph pattern to the 6:9–12 paragraph. But there are certain elements, such as the first person singular pronominal references and expressions of the author's confident feelings toward most of his audience, that clearly suggest it is an expressive paragraph, giving a statement of the situation (the CLAIM) followed by his reaction. His reaction is a *wish* regarding his readers.

NOTES

6:9a Although I am writing to you to warn you Further, the author was writing, not speaking. The purpose is clearly a warning (so Bruce, Hughes, Kistemaker (p. 165–166), Lane; (cf. JBP), "although we give these words of warning.").

like this The word οὕτως 'thus' implies his intended purpose in what has preceded.

6:9b I am certain concerning you The Greek text has the first person plural verbal pronoun Πεπείσμεθα...περὶ ὑμῶν 'we are certain concerning you'. The verb is Πεπείσμεθα 'we are persuaded' but as several commentators note, this is an editorial 'we' (cf. NLT).

6:9d that *most of* you The Greek text simply has 'you,' but taken literally that would infer that all of them were being referred to. But in the light of the very severe warnings in this epistle, it seems certain that the writer thought that some of his readers were turning or had turned away from faith in Christ. Therefore the pronoun is taken as expressing somewhat of a euphemism, and is rendered as 'most of you'.

are doing better than *those who have rejected God's message* We cannot know certainly to what the author was referring, since there is no verb with the words τὰ κρείσσονα 'the better things'. It is clear there is a reference to the group of people described in v. 8, but we cannot know whether he is saying the present condition of his audience is better, or whether their future destiny will be better, or whether he is referring to both. Since a better present condition would imply a better final destiny, and since the letter is a warning, not a condemnation, the display takes the interpretation that their present state is meant, and supplies 'are doing'.

6:9e you are doing what is appropriate for those whom *God* has saved Again there is an abstract noun in the expression καὶ ἐχόμενα σωτηρίας 'and having salvation'. BAGD (p. 334.III1) says the force of the middle form of the verb here is "close association," and gives the meaning "things that belong to salvation" to the phrase. But that leaves the same uncertainty as in 9d: whether he is talking about their salvation as a present reality or a future possibility. Again Delitzsch suggests "the expression is intentionally ambiguous," but in the light of what immediately follows, the interpretation chosen here is preferred. As Miller notes, (p. 178–179), what he mentions about them in v. 10 "is evidence of the presence of salvation." CEV's "we are sure that you are doing those really good things that people do when they are being saved" and LB's "you are producing the good fruit that comes along with your salvation" are much better than NCV's "better things from you that will lead to your salvation."

6:10a God is *always* just The γάρ 'since' at this point is introducing a very positive evaluation of his hearers, not providing a reason for what precedes. This spells out a litotes. NCV and CEV have removed the figure that was in the words οὐ ἄδικος ὁ θεός 'God is not unjust' by rendering "God is (always) just." In some cases it may be necessary to use an adverb, 'God always acts/treats people justly'. It is important to recognize that the negative concept applies to both 'unrighteous' and 'to forget'. The author is emphasizing the certainty by using two litotes.

6:10b he will certainly reward you The Greek οὐ ἄδικος ὁ θεός 'not unrighteous is God to forget' is a litotes that the author used to emphasize that God would reward the believers for their faithfulness. Morris (p. 57) calls this "a masterly understatement." 'Not overlook' means more than 'remember'. Davidson says this passage should be compared with 11:6 which says that God rewards those that seek him.

This is the continuation of the litotes of 6:10a; 'he will not forget' is a backhanded way of saying 'he will reward you for it'.

he will certainly reward you The expression τοῦ ἔργου ὑμῶν 'your work' refers not to the things they do for a living but "the general Christian activity of their life" (Davidson). But since Christian activity signifies things done 'for God', the words 'for him' are clearly implied. NLT has "how hard you have worked for him."

6:10c you have shown your love *for him* BAGD (p. 262:1) comments on the phrase τῆς ἀγάπης ἧς ἐνεδείξασθε εἰς τὸ ὄνομα αὐτοῦ 'show love for his name' that this is "either the love that you have shown with regard to him, i.e., for his sake, or we have here the frequently attested formula of Hellenistic legal and commercial language: εἰς (τὸ) ὄνομά τινος to the name to the account (over which the name stands). Then the deeds of love, although shown to men, are dedicated to God." Several commentators say the expression is another way of saying 'love for God' (i.e., a metonymy), and it is so taken by NCV, TEV, NIV, NLT.

6:10d by means of your having helped The participle διακονήσαντες 'having ministered' is taken as expressing means, as is done expressly by NCV and NLT and probably how constructions in several versions using 'in' and 'as' (e.g., RSV's "in serving the saints") are to be understood.

God's people/your fellow-believers Both are good alternatives for τοῖς ἁγίοις 'to the saints', or it could be rendered as in TEV and JBP, "fellow Christians."

6:11a I strongly desire The verb ἐπιθυμοῦμεν 'we desire' is another editorial 'we', and it is a word "of strong personal" even passionate "desire" (Westcott, p. 156).

continue to fully expect that you will receive *what God has promised you* The words τὴν αὐτὴν ἐνδείκνυσθαι σπουδὴν πρὸς τὴν πληροφορίαν τῆς ἐλπίδος 'to show the same eagerness to the certainty of the hope' show great semantic skewing and are variously interpreted. Some say it means a full assurance concerning their hope; others, that it means a full development of their hope; and others that it means both, because the one entails the other. But most of the problems are solved by unskewing: 'certainty' is rendered 'fully' and 'eagerness' is rendered 'eagerly continue to' and 'hope' is rendered as '(confidently) expect that you will receive'. And since hope is a cognitive event, it requires an object, which is almost always 'what God desires for you' or 'what God has promised you.' So Brown, p. 311: "'The assurance of hope' is a full expectation of obtaining what God has promised."

6:11b until you finally *receive it all* A few commentators take the phrase ἄχρι τέλους 'until the end' to mean 'to the end of present trials in this life' but the vast majority say it refers to the final realization of their hope when Christ returns. There is little actual difference between the two; for each individual, although he will not receive all he has hoped for until Christ comes, he can only be asked to continue his hope to the end of his life. So in the final analysis, the sense is exactly as NLT puts it, "as long as life lasts."

6:12b The display text follows the Greek closely except for rendering the abstract nouns by clauses.

BOUNDARIES AND COHERENCE

The start of a new paragraph at v. 12 is clearly marked by two references to Abraham (the first one of which is forefronted for topicalization) and several references to swearing, promises, and oaths. In the 6:9–12 unit there is pronominal coherence through several occurrences of (editorial) first plural pronominal forms and second plural forms.

PROMINENCE AND THEME

The theme of the 6:9–12 paragraph is taken from the most naturally prominent propositions of the CLAIM plus the most naturally prominent propositions of the *wish*. A condensed form of the circumstance proposition supporting the nucleus of the *wish* is also included in a very condensed form, because the need of the believers for continuance in the faith to the end of their lives is the main theme of the whole epistle.

SUB-SECTION CONSTITUENT 6:13–20 (Paragraph: Basis₂ of 5:1—6:20)

> **THEME:** *God promised that he would bless Abraham. God also guaranteed his promise to us by saying that he would punish himself if he did not fulfill his promise.*

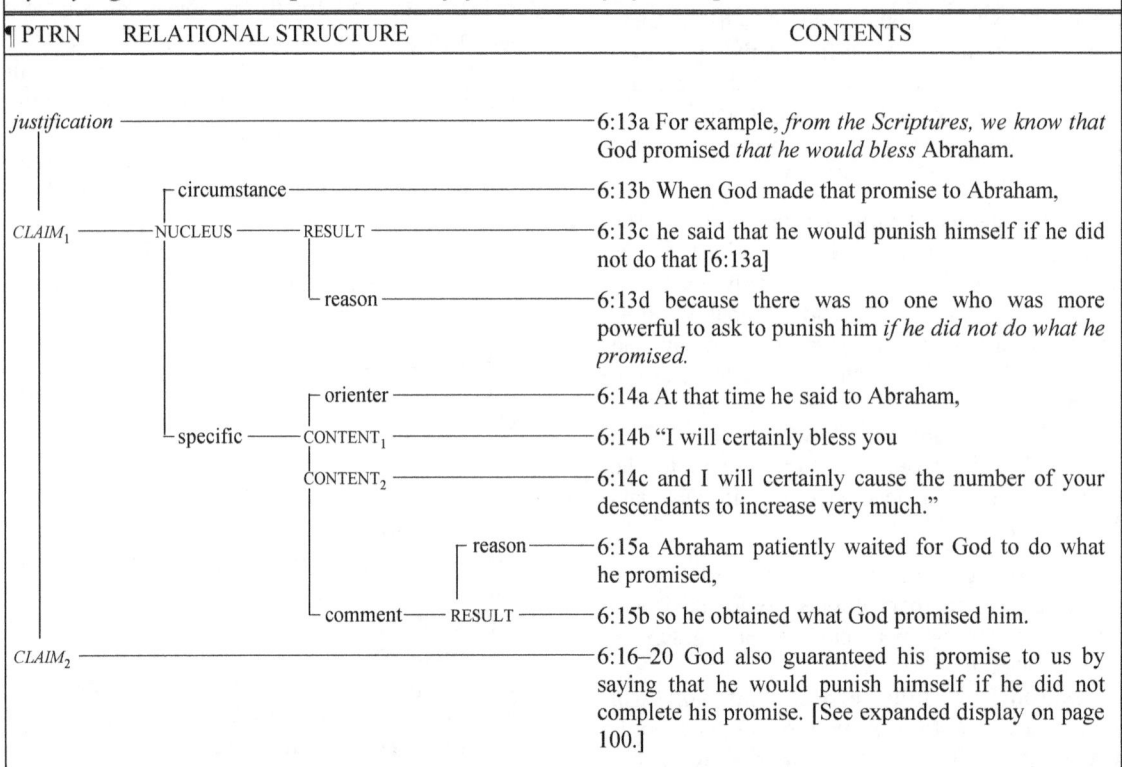

INTENT AND PARAGRAPH PATTERN

In the 6:13–20 paragraph there is a return to expository discourse. Here the writer made two CLAIMS about the certainty of what God has guaranteed that he will give believers, and he introduced it with a scriptural *justification* referring to the guarantee he made along with his promise to Abraham.

NOTES

6:13a For example The γάρ here introduces what follows as an example illustrating and supporting what the writer has just said. The display thus follows NLT in rendering it as 'for example'.

from the Scriptures, we know that This clause makes clear the source-record of the event to which the writer referred. The translator might put it at the beginning of v. 14 as an alternative. This citation is from Gen. 22:17.

that he would bless **Abraham** Since the concept 'promise' always implied some content of what is promised, the words 'that he would bless' are included.

6:13c said that he would punish himself if he did not do that This follows as the meaning of ὤμοσεν καθ' ἑαυτοῦ 'he swore by himself' from the definition given in 13a (though it may seem strange to us). When someone swears in a courtroom to tell the truth, he is saying 'may God punish me if I am not telling the truth'.

6:13d no one who was more powerful to ask to punish him *if he did not do what he promised* The comparative adjective in the phrase μείζονος ὀμόσαι 'greater to swear' means 'greater in ability to enforce'. The verb 'swear' means "to make a solemn declaration, invoking a deity or some person or thing held sacred, in confirmation of the honesty or truth of such a declaration" (American Heritage Dictionary).

6:14a At that time he said to Abraham The present participle λέγων is taken as introducing the specific content of the promise mentioned in v. 13a.

6:14b I will certainly bless you The clause εἰ μὴν εὐλογῶν εὐλογήσω, literally 'surely blessing I will bless', reflects a couple of Hebrew constructions, but its force is that it "conveys the ideas of emphasis and certainty" (Morris, p. 59). Most versions convey this sense with something like "I will surely bless" (NIV, NCV).

6:14c I will certainly cause the number of your descendants to increase very much The clause πληθύνων πληθυνῶ σε 'multiplying I will multiply thee' has the same Hebraism as v. 14a. But the words 'multiply thee' cannot be taken literally. Thus, most English versions remove the figurative language and translate as 'your descendants' or something similar.

6:15a patiently waited for God to do what he promised The verb μακροθυμέω means 'have patience, wait' which then requires a content of what is being waited for to fill out the case frame. NCV has "waited patiently for this to happen."

EXPANSION OF CLAIM₂ IN THE 6:13-20 DISPLAY

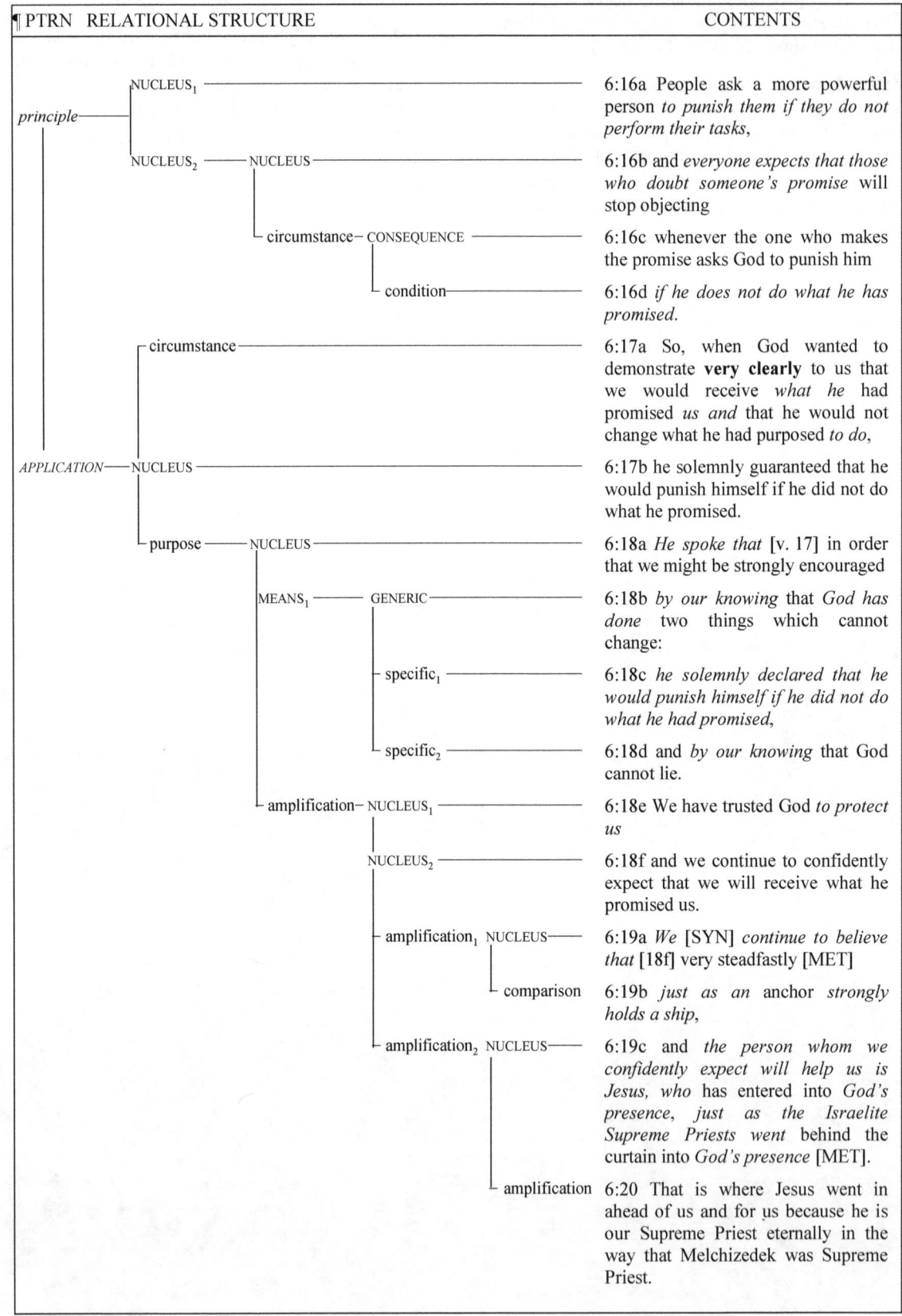

NOTES

6:16 See 13c for discussions of 'greater' and 'swear'.

6:16a The γάρ here introduces an illustration and is not represented in the proposition.

People The word ἄνθρωποι means "people" (NCV), "anyone" (CEV).

ask a more powerful person to *punish them if they do not perform their tasks* The wording in the display represents the GNT κατὰ τοῦ μείζονος ὀμνύουσιν 'swear by the greater' by conveying what the word 'swear' means in this context.

6:16b *everyone expects that those who doubt someone's promise* This makes clear the Greek ἀντιλογίας πέρας 'the stopping of people arguing'. The author referred to those occasions when a person does not accept the validity of someone's promise. He implied that if the promiser swore, then the doubter was obligated to stop demanding some other guarantee.

The phrase πάσης αὐτοῖς ἀντιλογίας πέρας εἰς βεβαίωσιν '(is) an end of all dispute to them for confirmation' is very skewed semantically. JB's "puts an end to all dispute" states the sense well.

6:16c whenever the one who makes the promise asks God to punish him Since the word 'swear' in English often refers to cursing, the display has shown the meaning intended by the author.

6:17a So The Greek construction ἐν ᾧ 'in which' implies a logical relationship.

very clearly The word περισσότερος which means "even more clearly" (BAGD p. 651.3) or 'very emphatically' is forefronted for emphasis. This is indicated in the display by bolding.

to us that we would receive *what he* had promised *us* The phrase τοῖς κληρονόμοις τῆς ἐπαγγελίας 'to the heirs of the promise' uses a dead metaphor; among the versions which treat the metaphor (and the genitive construction) almost exactly as done here are TEV and NCV. The display supplies 'us' as an alternative for those languages in which a third person noun phrase would indicate the writer was not including himself.

6:17b he solemnly guaranteed The GNT has ἐμεσίτευσεν ὅρκῳ 'he put into effect/brought-about-an-agreement with an oath' Louw and Nida (31.21) say of ἐμεσίτευσεν, "one may understand this as implying not only the agreement but the guarantee of its validity." Morris (p. 60) cites Oepke who says, "The only possible translation is 'to guarantee.'" This fits the context well. See v. 13d for a discussion of 'oath.'

6:18b *by our knowing* This verb removes the personification: it is not the things that enable us to be encouraged, but our knowing them (cf. LB, "can take new courage when they hear such assurance").

6:18c-d The display makes clear what two things cannot change. The versions NLT, JBP, NCV, CEV also give abbreviated forms in this manner.

6:18e *to protect us* The Greek ἔχωμεν οἱ καταφυγόντες 'we who have fled for refuge' is a metaphor that focuses on our trusting God. The display attempts to show the meaning. CEV has "we have run to God for safety." The problem with the verb 'flee' is that it requires a statement not only of where one is running to but what one is running from. The text does not say to whom we are fleeing, but God or Christ would both be possible. Morris (p. 60) notes, "The writer does not specify what we have 'fled' from, but the context makes it clear that he is thinking of some aspect of life in a sinful world" (also Lünemann).

6:18f confidently expect that we will receive what he promised us The noun ἐλπίσ 'hope' represents an event and is thus represented in the display by 'confidently expect (to receive) what God has promised'. But the expression κρατῆσαι τῆς προκειμένης ἐλπίδος 'to lay hold of the hope set before (us)' is semantically very skewed. (Kistemaker, p. 175), recognizes the metonymy.) Instead of laying hold of the confident expectation set before us, we actually confidently expect to lay hold of what God has promised to set before us.

6:19a *We* [SYN] *continue to believe that* [18f] very steadfastly The text has a vivid metaphor, ἔχομεν τῆς ψυχῆς ἀσφαλῆ τε καὶ βεβαίαν 'we have a safe and firm anchor of the soul'. As an anchor holds a boat strongly to the rocks where the anchor hooks under the water, so our hope holds us strongly to God and Christ. Lane (p. 153) says "As a ship is held fast when at anchor, the life of the Christian is secured by hope that binds that life to Christ." The word 'soul' is taken as a synecdoche, the soul representing the whole person. Our hope is an anchor for us.

***to believe that* [18f] very steadfastly** The Greek has only the relative pronoun ἥν 'which', referring to 'hope'. In order to avoid nominalizing this whole concept, the display starts a new sentence here and refers to the concept 'hope' by the word 'that', and states the relationship with 'because', but it may be possible to nominalize the concept in some translations.

6:19b Most of this proposition spells out the rest of the image of the metaphor.

6:19c and *the person whom we confidently expect will help us is Jesus, who* has entered into *God's presence* In the Greek phrase εἰσερχομένην εἰς τὸ ἐσώτερον τοῦ καταπετάσματος 'entering into what is inside the curtain' the antecedent of the participle is still 'hope', but this is very skewed: hope is an abstract noun, producing a personification. Jesus is the one who entered God's presence; (cf. Ellingworth and Nida.) Since the word 'hope' in English often is understood to refer to a desire, the Greek is rendered here as 'confidently expect'. The display text makes clear that Jesus is the one we confidently expect to help us.

entered into *God's presence* As Miller notes, (p. 189), the picture is of "Jesus Himself…going on ahead into the presence of God." Jesus did not literally enter the Temple; therefore it is clear that there is a metaphor here. The writer knew that his audience was Jewish and he expected that his phrase 'behind the curtain' would at once call to their minds the curtain in the tent that Moses directed to be built and in the Temple that was later built in Jerusalem. The readers would know that that curtain covered the entrance to the very holy place, which symbolized the most sacred sanctuary. LB makes some of this clear by rendering "connecting us with God himself behind the sacred curtains of heaven."

6:20 because he is our Supreme Priest The participle γενόμενος 'having become' "is causal, stating the reason for the result seen in the verb" (Miller, p. 190). Here it seems that the author implied that Jesus entered the sanctuary because he is our Supreme Priest.

in the way that Melchizedek was Supreme Priest See the note on 5:6c.

BOUNDARIES AND COHERENCE

A new paragraph at 7:1 is indicated by a very extended discussion of Melchizedek, whose name the writer has mentioned at the end of the previous paragraph. Lexical coherence in the 6:13–20 paragraph is provided by several words in the semantic domain of taking oaths: ἐπαγγέλομαι 'promise', ὀμνύω 'swear', ἐπαγγελία 'promise', and ὅρκος 'oath'.

PROMINENCE AND THEME

The theme of the 6:13–20 paragraph is derived from the most naturally prominent propositions of the *justification* and the two CLAIMS. The first CLAIM is not included since it says almost the same thing as the first part of the second CLAIM. The theme uses the word 'oath' for brevity rather than 'said he would punish himself if he did not do this'. In each half of the theme statement, the content of what God promised with the oath is supplied from the context or from the circumstance proposition which immediately precedes the prominent NUCLEUS.

SECTION CONSTITUENT 7:1—9:22 (Sub-Section: Basis of 5:1—9:28)

THEME: Just as Melchizedek was greater than the priests descended from Aaron, and the new agreement is better than the old one, we needed to be consecrated by better sacrifices.

MACROSTRUCTURE	CONTENTS
CLAIM₁	7:1–19 We may deduce that Melchizedek was greater than Abraham and the priests descended from Aaron, and now we have God's Son who is a perpetual Supreme Priest who was like Melchizedek.
CLAIM₂	7:20—9:22 Since Jesus guarantees us a better agreement than the old one, and since the rituals set up by Moses did not allow ordinary people to enter God's presence, Jesus went into that holy place only once to put into effect the new agreement to allow us to have those benefits.
CONCLUSION	9:23–28 Since those who would enter heaven had to be consecrated by better sacrifices than those of the old agreement, Christ has appeared once to cause people to be no longer guilty for sin.

INTENT AND PARAGRAPH PATTERN

This unit consists of two *CLAIMS* plus a *CONCLUSION*. It is all expository: there are no imperative verbs in this unit. Here the author continues his exposition of the superiority of Christ, specifically of his priesthood and of the sacrifice he offered.

BOUNDARIES AND COHERENCE

A boundary at 10:1 is indicated by the switch from a discussion of Christ's adequate sacrifice to the beginning of a discussion of reasons for the insufficiency of the former sacrifices.

PROMINENCE AND THEME

The theme is drawn from what are considered to be the most thematic parts of all the two *CLAIMS* and the *CONCLUSION*.

SUB-SECTION CONSTITUENT 7:1–19 (Paragraph Cluster: Claim₁ of 5:1—9:28)

THEME: We may deduce that Melchizedek was greater than Abraham and the priests descended from Aaron, and now we have God's Son who is a perpetual Supreme Priest who was like Melchizedek.

MACROSTRUCTURE	CONTENTS
basis₁	7:1–3 For several reasons, we may properly consider that God's Son is like Melchizedek, and that it is as though he continues to serve as a priest perpetually.
basis₂	7:4–10 We may deduce that Melchizedek was greater than Abraham. It is as if God wanted us to understand that Melchizedek is still living. Also it was as though Levi himself, and all the Supreme Priests who descended from him, gave gifts to Melchizedek.
CONCLUSION	7:11–19 Some people might suppose that those Supreme Priests who were descendants of Levi's descendant Aaron had completely helped the people. However, those Supreme Priests were not adequate to help us. Instead, God has appointed a new type of Supreme Priest, like Melchizedek. Thus we know that the regulations concerning how God appoints priests also have changed.

INTENT AND PARAGRAPH PATTERN

This unit consists of two *BASES* plus a *CONCLUSION*. It is all expository: there are no imperative verbs in this unit. Here the author continues his exposition of the superiority of Christ, specifically of his priesthood and of the sacrifice he offered.

BOUNDARIES AND COHERENCE

A boundary at 7:20 is indicated by the conjunction καί 'and' and a switch from the subject of Melchizedek to the topic of oaths.

PROMINENCE AND THEME

The theme is drawn from the condensations of the two *bases* and the *CONCLUSION*.

PARAGRAPH CLUSTER CONSTITUENT 7:1–3 (Paragraph: Basis₁ of 7:1—9:22)

THEME: For several reasons, we may properly consider that God's Son is like Melchizedek, and that it is as though he continues to serve as a priest perpetually.

¶ PTRN	RELATIONAL STRUCTURE	CONTENTS
	discourse orienter for 7:1-19	7:1a *Now I will say more about* that *man* Melchizedek.
	justification₁	7:1b He was the King of Salem *city and he was* priest for God, who is supreme.
	occasion	7:1c He met Abraham when Abraham was returning *home* after defeating *the armies of four* kings [SYN].
	justification₂ — OUTCOME — NUCLEUS₁	7:1d Melchizedek *asked God to* bless Abraham,
	NUCLEUS₂	7:2a and Abraham apportioned to him a tenth part of all *the spoils his fighters had gathered after the battle.*
	justification₃ — NUCLEUS₁	7:2b *Melchizedek's name* means 'A King *who rules* righteously'.
	grounds	7:2c And *since* 'Salem' means 'peace',
	NUCLEUS₂ — CONCLUSION	7:2d he was also the king *who rules* peacefully.
	justification₄ — NUCLEUS₁	7:3a *There is* no *record of who* his father *was*
	NUCLEUS₂	7:3b nor *who was* his mother
	NUCLEUS₃	7:3c nor *who were any of* his ancestors.
	NUCLEUS₄	7:3d *There is* no *record of when he was* born,
	NUCLEUS₅	7:3e nor *when he* died.
	CLAIM	7:3f *For these reasons, we may conclude that* it is as though he continues to *serve* as a priest perpetually, like God's Son does.

INTENT AND PARAGRAPH PATTERN

In the 7:1–3 paragraph, the author continues to show the superiority of Christ over the Jewish priests by virtue of his being a priest forever. It consists of one CLAIM about Christ preceded by a series of four *justifications*.

The mention of Melchizedek in 6:20 suddenly comes out of nowhere, which provides the topic which is carried through 7:17. This paragraph is introduced by γάρ 'for' simply to provide a tail-head construction linking chapter 7 with 6:20; recent English versions do not represent γάρ.

NOTES

7:1a *Now I will say more about* that *man* Melchizedek The portions in italics amplify the words οὗτος ὁ Μελχισέδεκ 'this Melchizedek' and provide more of an orienter for what follows. It also serves to show the function of γάρ 'for' which introduces a long amplification of the statement in 6:20.

7:1b King of Salem *city* Attridge says (p. 188), "By the first century CE the identification of Salem with Jerusalem was already traditional," and is supported by Psalm 76:2. A few think it is to be identified with Salim (John 3:23) in the Jordan valley. At any rate, it was a town or city, not a larger geographical area."

priest for God In some cases it may be necessary to clarify the genitive phrase ἱερεὺς τοῦ θεοῦ 'priest of God' to say 'priest appointed by God'.

who is supreme Many translations use the meaning 'the Most High' for ὕψιστος. Louw and Nida (12.4) gives "one who is supreme." Davidson and Westcott both say the title is not used to compare God with other gods, but simply to mark God as being supreme.

7:1c after defeating *the armies of four* kings The GNT has ἀπὸ τῆς κοπῆς τῶν βασιλέων 'from the defeat of the kings'. The word κοπή usually means 'slaughter', but as Westcott notes (p. 171), the word "may mean only 'the smiting', 'the defeat' "; see also BAGD p. 443. Most versions render by 'defeat' or something equivalent. The display text also makes clear what is stated in Gen. 4:11 that 'kings' is a synecdoche standing for the kings and their armies, and that there were four kings defeated. Of course also to be understood (but probably not essential to the passage) is the fact that Abraham did this because they had captured his nephew Lot.

7:1d Melchizedek *asked God to* bless In many languages it will be necessary to make clear that God is doing the actual blessing (cf. BAGD, "call down God's gracious power…on persons" p. 322.2).

7:2a tenth part of all *the spoils his fighters had gathered after the battle* The display supplies the implicit information the readers would be expected to know from Gen. 14:20 (cf. NCV's "a tenth of everything he had brought back from the battle").

7:2b-c means…means The author used the grammatical construction μὲν…δέ to indicate that Melchizedek's personal name and his title had separate meanings. The construction is a means of listing a set of two phrases describing Melchizedek.

7:2b *Melchizedek's name* means This is the sense of the participle ἑρμηνευόμενος 'being interpreted', as nearly all versions make clear.

A King *who rules* righteously The display text supplies the event denoted by the genitive phrase βασιλεὺς δικαιοσύνης 'king of righteousness'. CEV renders it as "King of Justice;" Morris says (p. 63) "it might be more accurate to render it 'my king is righteous' " but Lenski (p. 211) is a bit closer, saying righteousness "is the personal quality which shows itself in righteous ruling;, cf. TFT "king who rules righteously."

7:2c *since* 'Salem' means 'peace' The force of the writer's statement depends on knowing the meaning of 'Salem' in Hebrew. (cf. LB/NLT and CEV.)

7:2d the king *who rules* peacefully As in 2b, the genitive is spelled out the same way. Davidson says, "The immediate consequence of the righteousness of the Messiah and His kingdom is stated to be peace."

7:3a-b *There is* no record *of who* his father was…*who was* his mother The GNT has only two words, ἀπάτωρ ἀμήτωρ 'without father without mother'. But as Kistemaker notes (p. 185), "we ought not take this verse literally, for the author, reasoning from silence…is comparing Melchizedek with the priests who descended from Aaron. The writer expected a priest to establish and prove his "priestly descent." TEV has "There is no record of Melchizedek's father or mother," very similar to what is in the display. An alternative would be to follow NCV, which has "No one knows who Melchizedek's father or mother was." The author was saying that no one knew the names of his father or of his mother or any of his ancestors.

7:3c nor *who were any of* his ancestors See preceding note. CEV has "We are not told that he had…ancestors."

7:3d-e There is no record of when he was born, nor when he died See note on 3a-b. The Greek phrase μήτε ἀρχὴν ἡμερῶν μήτε ζωῆς τέλος ἔχων 'having neither beginning of days nor end of life' is rendered excellently by TFT: "There is no record of when he was born, nor is there any record of when he died."

7:3f *For these reasons, we may conclude that* The display text makes clear the force of the succession of participial phrases leading up to the one fully inflected non-subordinated verb μένει 'he remains' in this paragraph. Lane's comment (p. 146), "Melchizedek's sudden appearance and equally sudden disappearance from recorded history evoked the notion of eternity, which was only prefigured in Melchizedek but was realized in Christ," is a good one.

it is as though Since Christ is not literally a priest in the way the Jewish priests were (the author is comparing and contrasting them throughout this chapter), the fact that a comparison is being made is made specific.

BOUNDARIES AND COHERENCE

The coherence in the 7:1–3 paragraph is seen mainly in its consisting of a series of descriptive phrases and only one fully inflected non-subordinated verb at the end. A new paragraph at v. 4 is indicated by the imperative θεωρεῖτε 'see, consider' and the beginning of a lengthy discussion about tithes.

PROMINENCE AND THEME

The theme statement here is taken from the *CLAIM* in 3f. The four *justifications* that precede the claim are simply a long list of basically individual propositions. They are summarized in the theme in order to maintain the clarity of the theme.

PARAGRAPH CLUSTER CONSTITUENT 7:4–10 (Paragraph: Basis₂ of 7:1—9:22)

THEME: We may deduce that Melchizedek was greater than Abraham. It is as if God wanted us to understand that Melchizedek is still living. Also it was as though Levi himself, and all the Supreme Priests who descended from him, gave gifts to Melchizedek.

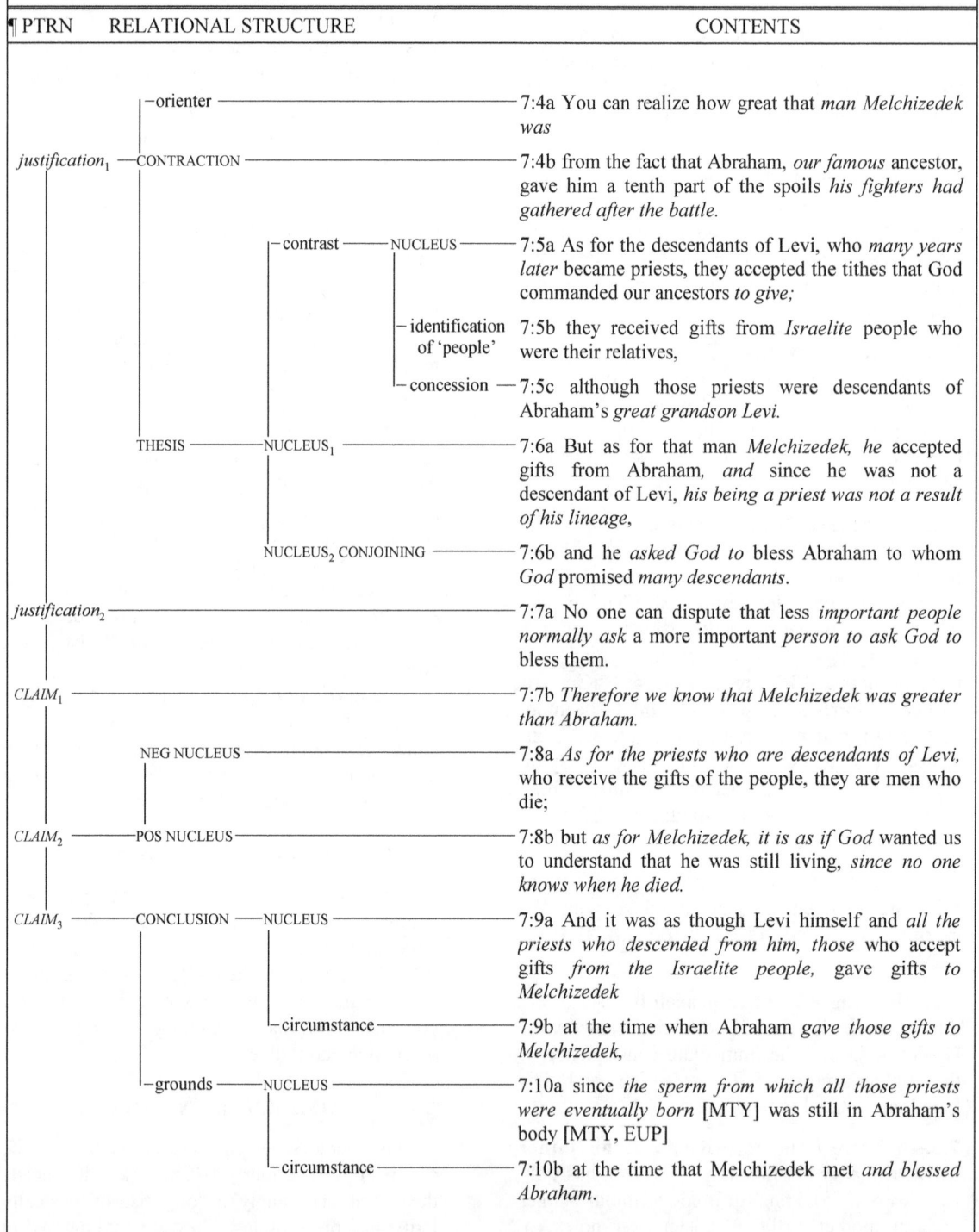

INTENT AND PARAGRAPH PATTERN

The 7:4–10 paragraph is again expository, stating more of the reasons for the superiority of Melchizedek and the way he acted as a priest to Abraham. It is of the volitionality subtype, with three CLAIMS and two supporting *justifications*.

NOTES

7:4a You can realize Hewitt calls the word θεωρεῖτε 'see' an "oratorical imperative." It is an orienter; and it is rendered as an indicative verb by NCV ("You can see") and TEV ("You see, then,").

that *man Melchizedek was* The display text specifies the referent of οὗτος 'the person to whom I have been referring'.

7:4b *our famous* ancestor This captures the sense of ὁ πατριάρχης 'the patriarch'. The word 'our' means 'of us Jews'.

gave him a tenth part of the spoils his *fighters had gathered after the battle* The display makes clear what is meant by ἐκ τῶν ἀκροθινίων 'from the spoils'.

7:5–7 There is a great deal of implicit information in these verses that the writer expected his audience to understand, either from their knowledge of the Old Testament or from deductions from his argument. The main force of the implicit information is to show the superiority of Melchizedek over Abraham, the ancestor whom the Jews revered.

7:5a *many years later* The display indicates explicitly that generations lived and died after Abraham gave the tithe to Melchizedek, until the time when the priests who served in the Tabernacle began to accept gifts for that sanctuary.

that God commanded our ancestors *to give* The Greek has ἐντολὴν ἔχουσιν...κατὰ τὸν νόμον 'commandment having...according to the regulation'. The display text specifies what regulations the author meant. An alternative is 'the regulations God gave Moses concerning the people giving tithes'.

7:5b *Israelite* people Miller (p. 198) notes the word λαός 'people' "is the term used for Israel as the people of God." LB has "God's people." NLT has "the people of Israel."

7:5c those priests were descendants of Abraham's *great grandson Levi* There is some ambiguity as to the referent of the third person plural subject of the participle ἐξεληλυθότας 'having come forth'. Does it refer to the priests or the people? Most versions are ambiguous, but those who make the reference clear choose 'priests,' and that is the interpretation taken here.

Abraham's *great grandson Levi* The argument depends on the readers knowing that Levi was directly descended from Abraham. The display specifies exactly what that relationship was.

7:6a *his being a priest was not a result of his lineage* The phrase μὴ γενεαλογούμενος ἐξ αὐτῶν 'not having his descent from them' requires that the pronominal referent, 'the sons of Levi' (v. 5) be clear.

7:6b *asked God to* bless See note on 1d. Morris (p. 64) says it means "an inferior prays that God will prosper some superior."

Abraham to whom *God* promised *many descendants* The GNT has only τὸν ἔχοντα τὰς ἐπαγγελίας 'the (one) having the promises'. The display text makes the referent clear (cf. CEV, "Melchizedek blessed Abraham, who had been given God's promise"). The author does not specify what promises were in mind; those mentioned in Gen. 12:2–3, 13:14–17 include many descendants, being a blessing to all nations, and possessing the land of Canaan. But in this context, it is clearly Abraham's descendants that the author had in mind.

7:7a less *important people normally ask* a more important *person to ask God to* bless them See again notes on v. 1d and v. 6b. The word κρείττων means 'more prominent, higher in rank' (BAGD p. 449.1). The referent here is made plural because the singular is used in a generic sense; he is not referring to one specific individual. The display includes the words 'ask God to' because semantically, when one human 'blesses' another, it means he is asking God to act favorably toward and do kind things for that person.

7:7b This proposition is the implied conclusion of the argument; as Miller says, (p. 199), "Since the one who blesses is greater, therefore Melchizedek is greater than Abraham." See also Attridge, Brown, Kistemaker, Hewitt. The argument in its entirety is:

1. It is more important people who bless the less important people;
2. Melchizedek blessed Abraham;
3. Therefore Melchizedek was greater than Abraham.

Brown says (p. 333), "There can be no reasonable doubt that the words before us are the statement of an argument for the superiority of Melchizedek to the Aaronical priesthood;" Hewitt, Lane, and Miller have similar comments. And of course in the larger context of the rest of the chapter Morris's comment (p. 65) is also true: "The author wants his readers to be in no doubt about the superiority of Christ to any other priests and sees the mysterious figure of Melchizedek as powerfully illustrating that superiority."

7:8a *As for the priests who are descendants of Levi* The GNT has only the word ὧδε 'here'. Hewitt says, "Here refers to the Levitical system which was in use at the time of writing." Hughes says (p. 253) "Here, that is, in the case of the descendants of Levi." TEV has "In the case of the priests." The fuller identification used in the display text, incorporating the comments of both Hewitt and Hughes, simply repeats their description given in v. 5.

they are men who die The present participle is ἀποθνῄσκοντες, literally 'dying'. REB renders it "men who must die;" NCV's rendering "men who live and then die" captures the sense very well. Westcott's note (p. 178) is very good: they are "men who were not only liable to death, mortal, but men who were actually seen to die from generation to generation."

7:8b *as for Melchizedek* This represents the word ἐκεῖ 'there'. Hewitt says, "There refers to the time of the Melchizedek priesthood which preceded the institution of the Aaronic priesthood." TEV has "as for Melchizedek."

it is as if God* wanted us to understand that he was still living, *since no one knows when he died The words μαρτυρούμενος ὅτι ζῇ 'being testified that lives' present several problems. First, we must decide who is the implied agent of the passive 'testified'. Lane says (p. 170) the verb "almost certainly has reference to Scripture." Westcott, Miller, and Kistemaker agree. CEV translates it "the Scriptures teach" and thus 'in Scriptures' is implied, and God is the implied agent of the verb. Second, how does Scripture record that he is still living? It doesn't; as Morris notes (p. 65), "The writer does not say that Melchizedek lives on but that the testimony about him is that he lives." Kistemaker says (p. 189), "Although Scripture is silent about the death of Melchizedek, we nonetheless conclude that he died." But what the writer is doing here is making an argument from silence. Since nothing is recorded about Melchizedek's death, "The silence of Scripture is here given the force of an assertion: 'The Scripture testifies that he (Melchizedek) lives on'" (Miller, p. 200). The 'argument from silence' is conveyed by 'it is as though', and the part about nothing being recorded about his death, the grounds for the conclusion about his still being alive, is repeated from 3d–e.

7:9 As in vv. 5–7, there is a lot of implicit information in this verse from either the Old Testament or in logical reasoning that the writer expected that the readers would understand.

7:9a And it was as though Levi himself and *all the priests who descended from him, those* who accept gifts *from the Israelite people,* gave gifts to Melchizedek It is a crucial part of the argument to recognize, as Miller notes, that Levi "is regarded as the head and representative of the tithe-taking tribe of Israel" (i.e., a synecdoche). CEV recognizes this by translating "Levi's descendants are now the ones who receive a tenth from people."

7:9b at the time when Abraham *gave those gifts to Melchizedek* This information supplies the sense of δι' Ἀβραάμ 'through Abraham'.

7:10a *the sperm* The Greek has a singular 'he' but it really refers to Levi and his descendants.

***the sperm*…was still in Abraham's body** The Greek expression ἔτι ἐν τῇ ὀσφύι τοῦ πατρὸς ἦν 'he was still in the loins of his father' is rather enigmatic as well as possibly being rather indelicate in a literal translation. The word 'loins' is a metonymy because it stands for the sperm located in the loins; the word means "the place of the reproductive organs" (BAGD p. 587.2); which is why many translations say, more euphemistically, "body" (e.g., NIV, TEV, NCV). CEV, like the display text, makes the sense clearer by avoiding any mention of the reproductive organs of the body, translating as "Levi was born later into the family of Abraham." For languages in which it is not necessary to be euphemistic here, the word 'testicles' could be used instead of 'body'. For an insightful comment on 'still', see Ellingworth.

Hughes and Lane state here that the writer is arguing on the basis of a concept of the corporate solidarity of the nation of Israel. Hughes says "Paul's [sic] reasoning is of the same kind when he teaches, on the basis of the solidarity of the human race in Adam, that when Adam sinned all sinned (Rom. 5:12)."

from which all those priests were eventually born The GNT says ἐν τῇ ὀσφύϊ τοῦ πατρός 'he was in the loins of (his) father'. This is taken as a metonymy, 'he' standing for the sperm that engendered successively Abraham's descendants, including Levi and specifically his descendants who became Supreme Priests.

BOUNDARIES AND COHERENCE

Though the next paragraph, beginning with v. 11, continues the subject of Melchizedek, its focus changes, in that it discusses priesthood, the imperfection of the Levitical priesthood, and 'another priest' Jesus. Coherence within the 7:4–10 paragraph is seen in three occurrences of the noun δέκατος 'tithe' and one each of the cognate verbs δεκατόω and ἀποδεκατόω, both meaning 'to collect tithe from'. There is also somewhat of a sandwich structure with references to 'Abraham the patriarch' in v. 4 and 'the father (Abraham)' in v. 10.

PROMINENCE AND THEME

The theme for the 7:4–10 paragraph is drawn from the most naturally prominent propositions of the first two *justifications*, with some adjustment in order to maintain the focus on Melchizedek, and the three CLAIMS. It is interesting to note that most of the information in the three CLAIMS is implicit; they are implicatures of the arguments.

PARAGRAPH CLUSTER CONSTITUENT 7:11–19 (Paragraph: Conclusion of 7:1—9:22)

THEME: Some people might suppose that those Supreme Priests who were descendants of Levi's descendant Aaron had completely helped the people. However, those Supreme Priests were not adequate to help us. Instead, God has appointed a new type of Supreme Priest, like Melchizedek. Thus we know that the regulations concerning how God appoints priests also have changed.

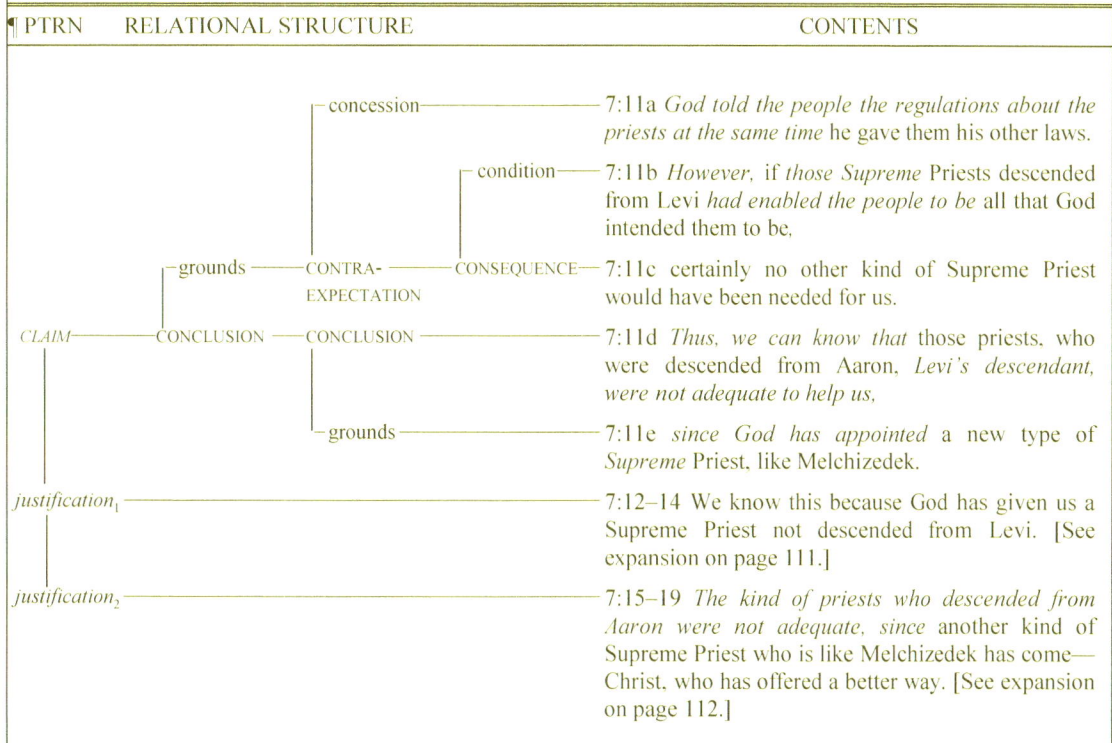

INTENT AND PARAGRAPH PATTERN

In the 7:11–19 paragraph the author continues trying to influence the ideas of his audience with a further expository paragraph of the volitionality subtype, giving one CLAIM that the priests descended from Aaron were not adequate to help us and the superiority of a priesthood resembling that of Melchizedek, and two supporting *justifications* stating that we have been given a new Supreme Priest, one like Melchizedek.

NOTES

7:11 The author used μέν to introduce a construction that links to a following contrastive proposition that is usually introduced by δέ. Miller suggests (p. 202–203) that although there is no δέ here, the last half of the verse contains an implied contrast: "…perfection…will be possible through a different kind of priest."

The display tries to show the implication of the rhetorical question, by which the author implied that no one should evaluate the Aaronic Supreme Priesthood as being adequate.

7:11a *God told the people the regulations about the priests at the same time* **he gave them his other laws** This represents the clause ὁ λαὸς γὰρ ἐπ' αὐτῆς νενομοθέτηται 'for the people were furnished with law along with it'. According to BAGD (p. 542.1) the passive form of the verb gives the sense "the people received the law." Since 'receive' is the reciprocal of 'give', the display has used 'give' here, has indicated God as the agent, and has identified the law as the Mosaic laws. The real problem here is the sense of the preposition ἐπί. Most versions follow BAGD (p. 286.II b β) translating it as "on the basis of it." But no one seems to explain satisfactorily in what way the Mosaic laws were the basis of the priesthood. The rendering here follows Hughes and Lane, who suggest the meaning 'in association with'. Hughes' comments here are excellent: he suggests (p. 256) this clause "is a reminder of the close interdependence between the priestly and the [Israelite] legal systems; for the Levitical priesthood and its ministrations were instituted by Moses simultaneously with his communication of the law of God to the people of Israel…since the law… was universally broken (cf. Rom. 3:9–23), there was a continuous necessity for the ministry of expiation and reconciliation which the Levitical priesthood provided." With that in mind the sense of 'in association with' is rendered as 'at the same time', and 'told the people the regulations about the priests' is both necessary to complete the case frame and is contextually correct.

7:11b *However* This is an unskewed representation of τῆς Λενιτικῆς ἱερωσύνης 'the Levitical priesthood'; NCV has "a system of priests from the tribe of Levi." 'Priesthood' is taken as a metonymy standing not for the system but the work they did (cf. Morris, p. 66), "the work of the priests in the line of Levi."

We must decide the best meaning for τελείωσις 'perfection'. The commentaries offer "providing access to" or "a right relationship with God" (Hewitt, Lane), "bringing people to God" (Miller, Brown), and "providing expiation of the guilt for sin" (Attridge, Lünemann, Montefiore). There is merit in all of these, but the rendering in the display is generic enough to include these and other specifics.

We must also decide what is the relationship between 'perfection' and the Aaronic priesthood. It would seem that the primary function of those priests was to perform the ritual sacrifices for sin. However, "the Levitical priesthood could not provide cleansing of the conscience" (Miller, p. 203). This is further made clear in 10:2: "If the law could make them perfect, the sacrifices would have already stopped. The worshipers would be made clean, and they would no longer feel guilty for their sins" (NCV).

7:11b *However* This introduces the implication of the rhetorical question.

would *have been needed* The author implied this as the condition for the grounds statement that follows.

7:11c certainly no other…would have been needed The rhetorical question τίς ἔτι χρεία 'why yet a need'? is rendered by an emphatic statement which expresses its function in a straightforward way, as is done in TEV, NCV, CEV.

7:11d those priests…*were not adequate to help us* This is supplied to form a complete clause following the connection 'thus, we can know'. It may not be necessary to translate 'to help us' in some languages.

who were descended from Aaron This states simply the sense of κατὰ τὴν τάξιν Ἀαρών 'according to the order of Aaron'. CEV's rendering, "one from the priestly family of Aaron," is similar.

Levi's descendant The author counted on his Jewish audience to know this fact, which is essential to the argument. CEV has a footnote here: "Levi was the ancestor of the tribe from which priests…were chosen. Aaron was the first Supreme Priest."

7:11e *since God has appointed* a new type of *Supreme* Priest, like Melchizedek This proposition makes clear the missing step in the writer's argument:

- If priests … had been adequate
- no other type of priest … needed
- but since God appointed … new type
- we know the first type … not adequate

EXPANSION OF *JUSTIFICATION*₁ IN THE 7:11–19 DISPLAY

RELATIONAL STRUCTURE	CONTENTS
RESULT — NUCLEUS — reason	7:12a *We know this* because *God* has appointed a new kind of priest,
	7:12b *so God* also had to change the regulation *by which he has appointed priests.*
amplification — CONCLUSION — ITEM	7:13a *Jesus,* the one about whom I have been telling you these things, is *not* a descendant of *Levi, but rather* of *Judah,*
description of 'Judah'	7:13b none of whose descendants served as priests [MTY].
grounds — NUCLEUS	7:14a *We know this* since it is from *the tribe of* Judah that our Lord *Jesus* is descended.
amplification	7:14b Moses never authorized any of Judah's descendants to *serve as* priests.

NOTES

7:12a ***We know this*** **because** The author uses γάρ 'for' to introduce a *justification* of his CLAIM that God had appointed a new kind of Supreme Priest. The words 'we know this' are included simply to introduce a new unit while maintaining the grounds relationship.

God **has appointed a new kind of priest** This simply summarizes the argument of v. 11

7:12b ***God*** **also had to change the regulation** ***by which he has appointed priests*** Most commentators take the genitive absolute participial phrase μετατιθεμένης τῆς ἱερωσύνης 'the priesthood being changed' as expressing condition, 'if here there is a change', whereas most versions translate it in a temporal sense, 'whenever there is a change'. But there is nothing conditional about the author's statement here and nothing temporal in the sense of 'whenever': the priesthood was changed, and it was changed only once. Therefore the display connects 12a-b with a reason-result relationship.

The question here is, what does νόμος 'law' refer to? Most commentators say it refers to the Mosaic law in general. But the writer was not talking about changing the Mosaic law in v. 13, which amplifies v. 12. Rather, he discussed a new tribe from which a new priest has been appointed. The analysis here follows Brown, who says (p. 339), "The law he is speaking of throughout the whole of this paragraph, is the law of the priesthood to which the Israelitish people had been subjected."

7:13a ***Jesus*** This is supplied to provide identification for the relative pronoun in the GNT. Several versions supply "our Lord;" NCV has "Christ."

The γάρ here introduces the amplification.

about whom I have been telling you The agent of the verb in the phrase ἐφ᾽ ὅν λέγεται ταῦτα 'about whom these things are said' could be taken to be the writer of this epistle, e.g., 'about whom *I* am writing' (cf. CEV's "The person we are talking about" and NCV's "We are saying these things about"), or to refer to the passage he is talking about. Nearly all commentators choose the second interpretation and take the word 'said' to refer to the *passage* (Psalm 110:4) in which the Psalmist says "You are a priest forever, in the order of Melchizedek" (NIV), the passage which the writer is expounding. The display takes the former interpretation. An alternative would be 'about whom the Psalmist wrote'.

not **a descendant of** ***Levi, but rather*** **of** ***Judah*** The clause φυλῆς ἑτέρας μετέσχηκεν 'belonged to another tribe' demands that the reader know which tribe Jesus was *not* from. The display has made a more specific statement. LB's rendering "Christ did not belong to the priest-tribe of Levi" is good.

7:13b served as priests The clause προσέσχηκεν τῷ θυσιαστηρίῳ "officiated at the altar" (BAGD p. 714.1c) is a metonymy, the place and work standing for the office of the person doing it. Lünemann says "attends at the altar, i.e., performs the priestly functions." TEV has both: "served as a priest at the altar" (also CEV).

7:14a *We know this* **since** The γάρ here introduces the grounds for knowing the statement in v. 13a is true. See also v. 15a.

it is from *the tribe of* Judah...is descended The phrase ἐξ Ἰούδα 'out of Judah' implies a group, not an individual; it can be considered a synecdoche. NCV, TEV, CEV and LB/NLT all have "tribe of Judah." This phrase is emphasized by being forefronted, and that emphasis is shown by a cleft construction in the display.

7:14b **to** *serve as* **priests** The GNT has περὶ ἱερέων 'about priests'. Some verb is implied: Alford says "i.e., nothing to imply that any priest should be consecrated out of it." NCV has "priests belonging to that tribe," LB has "Moses had never given them that work," CEV has "priests would [never] come from that tribe."

EXPANSION OF *JUSTIFICATION*₂ IN THE 7:11–19 DISPLAY

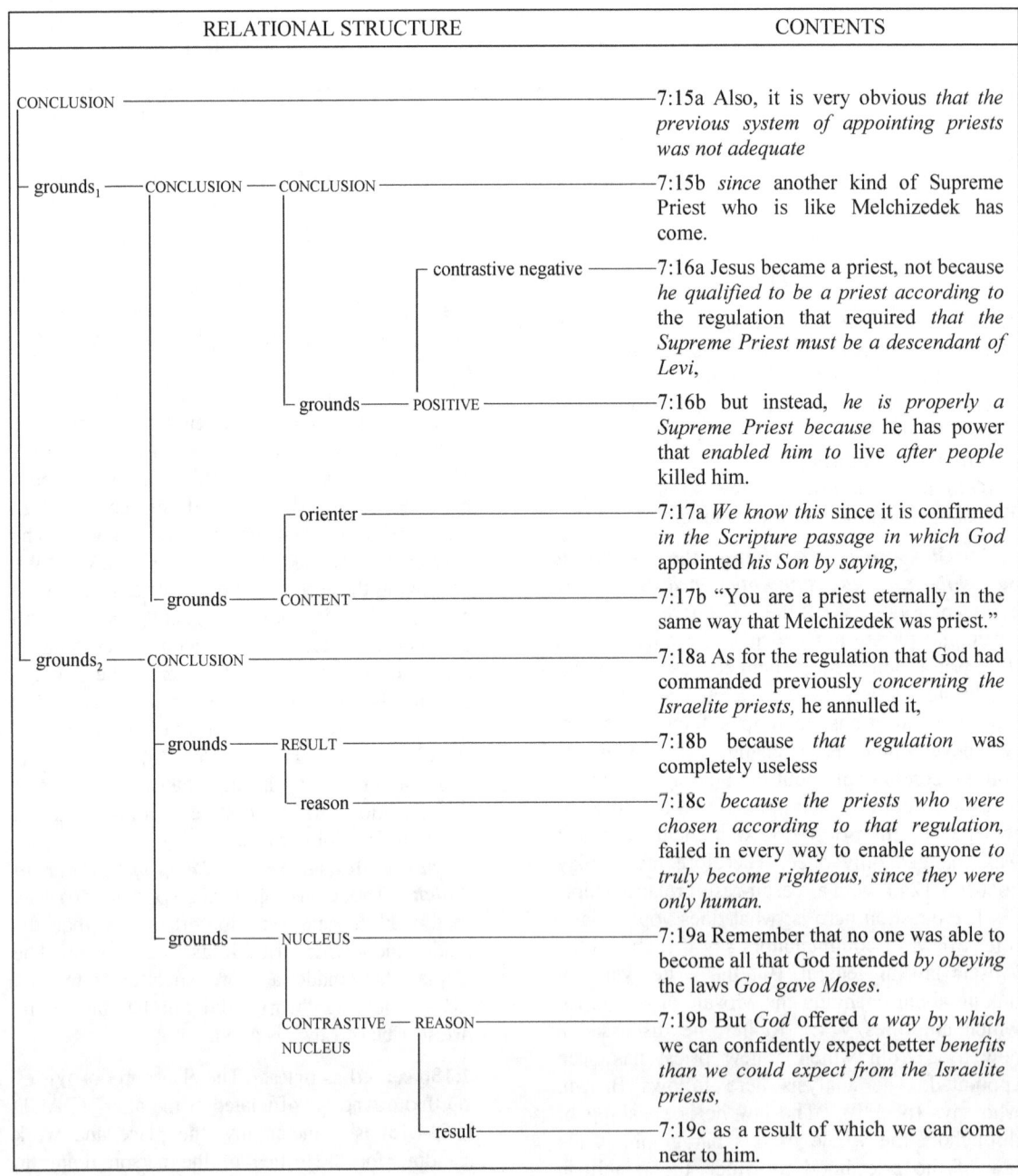

NOTES

7:15a-b it is very obvious that *the previous system of appointing priests was not adequate since* Miller (p. 207) agrees that the καί 'and' here "coordinates additional grounds as proof of the inadequacy of the Levitical priesthood." Although several commentators think this verse supplies the grounds for the changing of the law regarding priests (11b), it coheres much better as the grounds of v. 12a, and the majority of commentators agree. The part in italics is simply a repeat of v. 11e to specify what is 'very obvious'.

7:15b another kind of Supreme Priest who is like Melchizedek has come The Greek ἀνίσταται ἱερεὺς ἕτερος 'arises a different priest' is somewhat figurative; the modern English idiom would be 'has come upon the scene'.

7:16a not because *he qualified to be a priest according to* the regulation that required *that* The phrase οὐ κατὰ νόμον 'not according to law' is an abbreviated way of saying 'not by complying with the law'; BAGD (p. 407.II5aδ) says regarding κατά here "in accordance with and because of are merged" and so 'because' is appropriate here. NLT has "by meeting the old requirement."

the Supreme Priest must be a descendant of Levi Louw and Nida suggest the phrase ἐντολῆς σαρκίνος 'of a fleshly commandment' can mean "regulations made by people" (9.13) or "human rules and regulations" (26.8) but commentators are very divided as to what is meant. The majority take it as referring to regulations concerning physical descent of the Levitical priesthood (and so do NIV, RSV, CEV, JB, NLT, and REB) but some of the older commentaries say it refers to outward observances of the Mosaic law. A few say it refers generally to all external features of the Mosaic law. But the context indicates the first interpretation is the correct one; as Attridge says (p. 202), "In the immediate context, where the qualifications for priesthood have been discussed, it obviously refers to the genealogical, hence 'fleshy', requirements of Levitical legitimacy."

7:16b *he is properly a Supreme Priest because* This implied information defines Jesus' validity of being a Supreme Priest.

he has power that *enabled him to* live *after people* killed him The display text unravels both the genitive construction δύναμιν ζωῆς ἀκαταλύτου 'power of an indestructible life' and the abstract noun within it. Many commentators agree essentially with Westcott who says (p. 185) that 'indestructible' means that although "in the earthly sense He died, yet His life endured unchanged even through earthly dissolution.". It might be even clearer to say 'he has power which enabled him to live after people thought they had destroyed him' but of course the agents necessary for full clauses are not in focus at all.

7:17a *We know this* since See note on v. 14a.

it is confirmed *in the Scripture passage in which God* appointed *his Son by saying* The parts in italics specify where it is confirmed and identify the speaker and addressee within the quote which follows. NCV has "in the scripture passage in which he said to his son," and NLT has "the Psalmist pointed this out when he said of Christ." The quote is again from Psalm 110:4.

7:17b See notes on 5:6c.

7:18a As for The author uses γάρ here and δε in 19b to introduce two contrastive propositions.

the regulation that God had commanded previously *concerning the Israelite priests*, he annulled it The display specifies what commandment is meant. Lane (p. 185) says, "The 'former commandment' has primary reference to the particular ordinance regulating the priesthood mentioned in v. 16," and nearly all other commentators agree.

7:18b was completely useless The expression τὸ αὐτῆς ἀσθενὲς καὶ ἀνωθελές 'its weakness and uselessness' was analyzed by Moore (p. 58) as a near-synonymous doublet: both parts mean 'unable to help anyone'.

7:18c *because the priests who were chosen according to that regulation*, failed in every way The Greek text suggests that the regulation failed, which is a personification and a metonymy. The display makes clear that the author was accusing the system of selecting priests as failing.

to enable anyone *to truly become righteous* The concept of 'enabled people' semantically requires specification of what the enabling is for. That which is supplied here is generic and repeated from v. 19a. Commentators suggest "forgiveness of sins…communion between man and God" (Moffatt, p. 98), "to save man" (Barnes), "cleanse the conscience from sin" (Hewitt), "effect the justification of sinners before God" (Hughes, p. 265).).

since they were only human The author implied that the humanness of those priests was the main reason for their inadequacy.

7:19a The author used γάρ 'for' to indicate that he was commenting on, but also supplying the reason for, calling the regulation regarding priests ἀνωφελές 'useless'. Some interpreters suggest that the author shifted his focus and he commented on the uselessness of the Mosaic law, accusing it that the people did not attain 'perfection' by obeying it. However, it seems more logical to assume that the author commented on the regulation by which the Israelite Supreme Priests were installed, which has just been mentioned in v. 18a-b. Note that the author contrasted the regulation with God's new way of appointing the different kind of Supreme Priest. RSV and NIV put this sentence in parentheses, but v. 19a is not just a comment; it is logically related to what precedes.

become all that God intended See note on 5:9a.

by obeying the **laws** *God* **gave Moses** Supplying the verb 'obey' in the display text removes the personification.

7:19b *God* **offered** *a way by which* **we can confidently expect better** *benefits* The clause ἐπεισαγωγὴ δὲ κρείττονος ἐλπίδος 'but an introduction of a better hope' has two abstract nouns but no verb; the display text renders these nouns as clauses and supplies 'God' as the agent. Miller says (p. 210), "The sense is, 'God introduced a better hope.'" For 'hope' see note on 3:6.

than we could expect from the Israelite priests Most commentators do not comment on the meaning of the concept 'better'. But Morris says (p. 69), "Notice that the hope is said to be better than the regulation or commandment, not better than the hope associated with the commandment."

a way by which This represents the prepositional phrase δι' ἧς 'through which'. It is by means of Christ performing his work as our Supreme Priest that we are confident enough to suppose that we can come near to God.

7:19c we can come near to him It is recognized that the wording in the display of the Greek ἐγγίζομεν τῷ θεῷ 'we come close to God' is somewhat figurative, but there does not seem to be any way to avoid it.

BOUNDARIES AND COHERENCE

Cohesion within the 7:11–19 paragraph is seen in three occurrences of the name Melchizedek (and none in the following paragraph) and several references to laws: three occurrences of νόμος 'law' and two of ἐντολή 'commandment'. and also in a sandwich structure involving the noun τελείωσις 'perfection' in verses v. 11 and the cognate verb form ἐτελείωσεν 'perfected' in v. 19. The new paragraph at v. 22 begins with καί 'and' which "introduces an additional proof of the superiority of the New Covenant" (Miller, p. 211) centering on a discussion of ὁρκωμοσία 'oath-taking'.

PROMINENCE AND THEME

The theme of the 7:11–19 paragraph is drawn from the most naturally prominent statement of the CONCLUSION in v. 11e (plus enough of the contrast proposition in 11d to provide pronominal identification) and the most naturally prominent propositions of the two *justifications*, somewhat rearranged to avoid reduplication.

SUB-SECTION CONSTITUENT 7:20—9:22 (Paragraph Cluster: Claim₂ of 5:1—9:28)

THEME: Since Jesus guarantees us a better agreement than the old one, and since the rituals set up by Moses did not allow ordinary people to enter God's presence, Jesus went into that holy place only once to put into effect the new agreement to allow us to have those benefits.	
MACROSTRUCTURE	CONTENTS
basis₁	7:20—8:13 Since Jesus guarantees us a better agreement than the old one and will be a Supreme Priest forever, he can completely and eternally save those who come to God because of what Christ has done.
basis₂	9:1–10 God told Moses what rituals were to be performed and about the Sacred Tent for those rituals, but those rituals indicated that the way for ordinary people to enter God's presence was not yet revealed.
INFERENCE	9:11–22 It was as though Christ went into that very holy place only once, taking his own blood with him, thus putting into effect a new agreement.

INTENT AND PARAGRAPH PATTERN

This unit consists of two *bases* plus an *INFERENCE*. It is all expository: there are no imperative verbs in this unit. Here the author continues his exposition of the superiority of Christ, specifically of his priesthood and of the sacrifice he offered.

BOUNDARIES AND COHERENCE

A boundary at 9:23 is indicated by the conjunction οὖν 'therefore' and a switch from a discussion of the sacrifices under the old agreement to the sacrifice of Christ.

PROMINENCE AND THEME

The theme is drawn from the first part of the first *basis*, the second part of the second *basis*, and a condensation of the *INFERENCE*.

PARAGRAPH CLUSTER CONSTITUENT 7:20—8:13 (Sub-Paragraph Cluster: Basis₁ of 7:20—9:22)

THEME: Since Jesus guarantees us a better agreement than the old one and will be a Supreme Priest forever, he can completely and eternally save those who come to God because of what Christ has done.

MACROSTRUCTURE	CONTENTS
CLAIM₁	7:20-25 Since Jesus guarantees us a better agreement than the old one and will be a Supreme Priest forever, he can completely and eternally save those who come to God because of what Christ has done.
CLAIM₂	7:26—8:6 Jesus is the Supreme Priest, since God solemnly declared that Jesus is the one whom he has appointed as the eternal Supreme Priest. Jesus is the kind of Supreme Priest that we need and he ministers in the true place of worship in heaven. If he were now living on the earth, he would not be a Supreme Priest. But where he is now, Christ ministers in a more excellent way than the Jewish priests do, and the agreement he has validated is better than the former agreement.
CLAIM₃	8:7–13 A new agreement was needed, as is supported by what the Scriptures say about God making a new agreement.

INTENT AND PARAGRAPH PATTERN

This unit consists of three *CLAIMS*. It is all expository: there are no imperative verbs in this unit. Here the author continues his exposition of the superiority of Christ, specifically of his priesthood and of the sacrifice he offered.

BOUNDARIES AND COHERENCE

A boundary at 9:1 is indicated by the beginning of a description of the objects involved in the Sacred Tent and its very holy room. Coherence is provided by four occurrences of ἱερεύς 'priest' and five occurrences of ἀρχιερεύς 'Supreme Priest'.

PROMINENCE AND THEME

The theme is drawn from what are considered to be the most thematic parts of the three *CLAIMS* in this unit.

SUB-PARAGRAPH CLUSTER CONSTITUENT 7:20–25 (Paragraph: Claim₁ of 7:20—8:13)

THEME: Since Jesus guarantees us a better agreement than the old one and will be a Supreme Priest forever, he can completely and eternally save those who come to God because of what Christ has done.

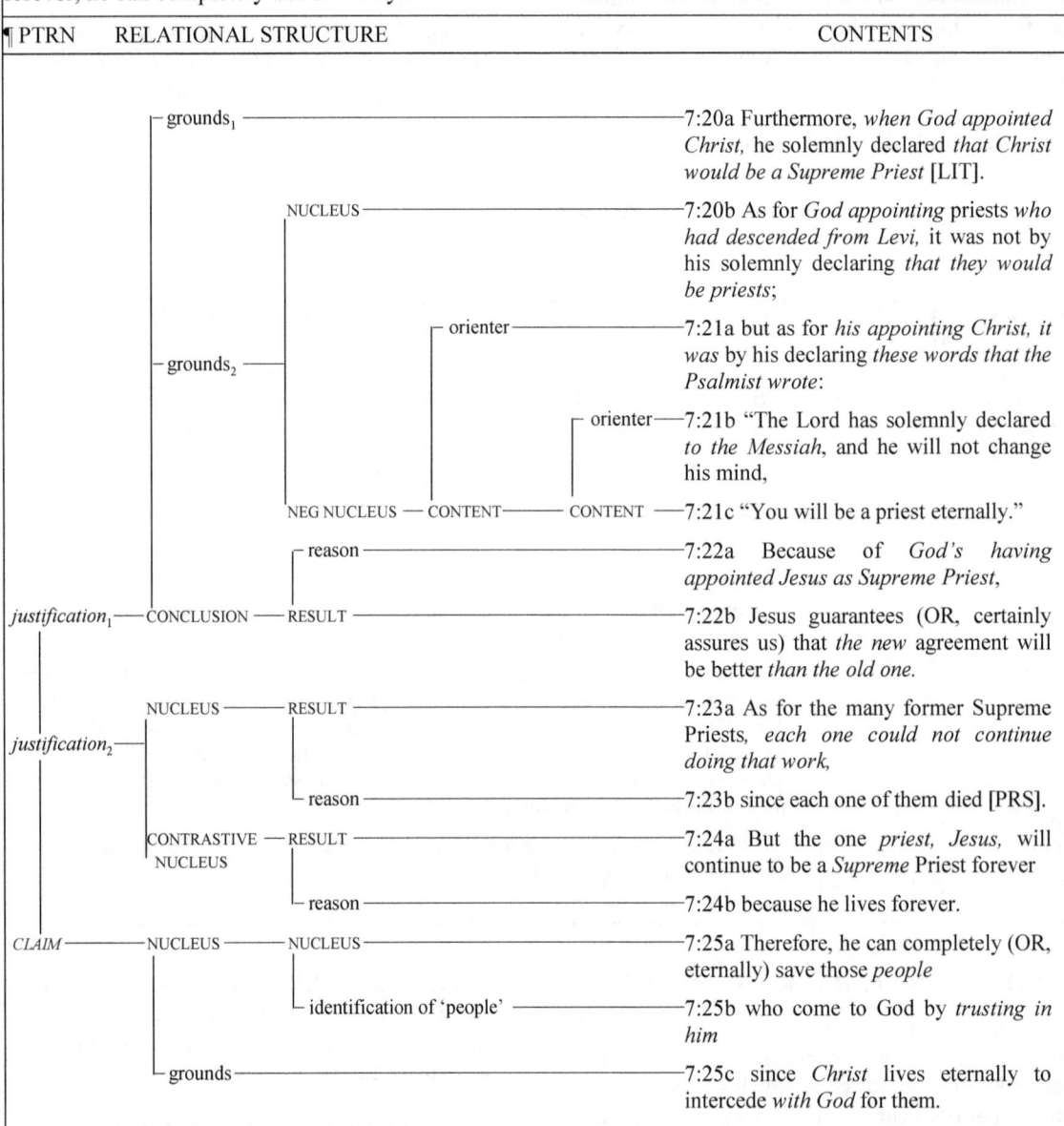

INTENT AND PARAGRAPH PATTERN

The 7:20–25 paragraph is again an expository one of the volitionality subtype, in which the writer is trying to influence his audience's ideas about the superiority of Christ over the former Jewish priests. It consists of two *justifications* and one CLAIM.

NOTES

7:20–22 The phrase καθ᾿ ὅσον 'in proportion' introduces the first part of a comparison which is completed by κατὰ τοσοῦτο 'by so much' at the beginning of v. 22. But the sense is carried much better by combining the two to form a grounds-conclusion pair signaled as such in the Relational Structure and by the phrase 'because of God having appointed Jesus as Supreme Priest' at the beginning of v. 22. Nearly all the versions do likewise (cf. NIV, "Because of this oath").

The Greek construction μεν...δε has the idiomatic sense 'on the one hand...on the other hand' and is rendered here as 'as for...as for.'

7:20a *when God appointed Christ* The display supplies an active verb; there is no verb in the Greek text. The Greek text, οὐ χωρὶς ὁρκωμοσίας 'not without oath-taking' is brief but complex semantically. It is an ellipsis. Most commentators supply something like "Jesus has become our priest" (JBP) to fill in the ellipsis. A few suggest 'Christ was made a surety', supplying the ellipsis from v. 22, but this gives no improvement in sense, fits the context no better, and is just contrary to how ellipses are made in Greek. Furthermore, the phrase "is a litotes, stating in negative form what is intended positively in a decided way" (Lenski, p. 233).

7:20b As for *God appointing* priests *who had descended from Levi,* it was not by his solemnly declaring *that they would be priests* The GNT οἱ ἀχωρὶς ὁρκωμοσίας εἰσὶν ἱερεῖς γεγονότες 'the ones having become priests without oath-taking' is also elliptical: the display text makes clear who 'the ones' are (cf. RSV, "Those who formerly became priests").

As for *God appointing* priests *who had descended from Levi* These words are supplied to make clear the referent of the Greek pronoun οἱ 'they'.

7:21a but as for *his appointing Christ, it was by his declaring these words that the Psalmist wrote* There is a great deal of implicit information in the words ὁ δὲ μετὰ ὁρκωμοσίας διὰ τοῦ λέγοντος πρὸς αὐτόν 'but the (other) with oath-taking through the one saying to him'. Since there is no verb, 'became priests' is assumed to be repeated in singular form from 20b with reference now to Christ. God is the assumed agent of 'saying' (cf. NIV, TEV) and 'God' is needed to clarify to whom 'Lord' in the following quote refers. The display also specifies that the sentence that follows is from Scripture (cf. NEB's "as Scripture says of him"). The words 'to Jesus' are needed to specify the referent of 'you' (v. 21c) in the quote from Psalm 110:4.

these words that the Psalmist wrote The display makes clear that the author cited from Psalms (Psalm 110:4).

7:21b declared *to the Messiah* The implied words specify the referent of the pronoun 'you' in the quote.

he will not change his mind The words 'he will not change his mind' convey the sense of οὐ μεταμεληθήσεται 'he will not repent' in a more natural way in current English (cf. RSV, NIV, TEV).

7:21c The words 'after the order of Melchizedek' are found at the end of the quotation in the Textus Receptus. This was obviously added by some later scribe(s) to make it conform to the previous references to or citations of the verse in 6:20 and 7:17. The GNT omits these words, with an A "certain" rating.

7:22b Jesus guarantees (OR, certainly assures us) that *the new* agreement will be better *than the old one* The word ἔγγυοσ in the phrase γέγονεν ἔγγυος 'has become a guarantor' means "one who guarantees the reality of something – '..., guarantor' (Louw and Nida 70.8). It does not refer to a mediator. Morris says (p. 70) that, with the Aaronic priesthood, there was "no one to guarantee that the people would fulfill their undertaking. But Jesus…guarantees to men that God will fulfill his covenant of forgiveness." The word 'better' requires an understanding of 'better than what?' and therefore 'than the old one' is included.

better The author affirmed and emphasized the better quality with κατὰ τοσοῦτο 'according to such'.

7:23a *each one could not continue doing that work* The verb παραμένω means "continue in an occupation or office" (BAGD p. 620.2). In some languages it may be necessary to include the words *'who served in the temple and tabernacles'*.

7:23b **each one of them died** The display removes the personification of θανάτῳ κωλύεσθαι 'be prevented by death' (cf. TEV, "because they died and could not continue their work").

7:24a *Jesus* The display text specifies the referent of the relative pronoun as Jesus, as do NIV, TEV, REB, LB/NLT, and NCV.

7:25a **he can completely (OR, eternally) save** BAGD (p. 608.3) say that the phrase εἰς τὸ παντελές means 'forever, for all time' but Louw and Nida (78.47) give that sense and 'completely, totally, entirely, wholly' as alternate possibilities for the meaning. Commentators are about equally divided, and some (e.g., Attridge, Hughes) suggest the writer is deliberately ambiguous. The display follows this suggestion, and supplies both alternatives.

7:25b **who come to God by** *trusting in him* Here GNT has only the phrase δι᾿ αὐτοῦ 'through him'. The 'him' refers to Christ. The 'through' indicates an abbreviated means proposition requiring some verb, and 'trusting in him' seems the most appropriate. The words 'trusting in what Christ has done for them' could be included in languages that semantically require a full clause following the word 'trust' to complete the case frame.

7:25c since There is no conjunction in the Greek, only a participle. But in contexts like these, participles often indicate grounds, and a host of commentators support a grounds relationship here.

to intercede *with* God for them Semantically 'intercede' requires an explication of the individual with whom one is interceding (cf. TEV, "plead with God for them"). The word 'intercede' means "to speak to someone on behalf of someone else" (Louw and Nida 33.347).

BOUNDARIES AND COHERENCE

Coherence within the 7:20–25 paragraph is supplied by two sets of μὲν...δέ 'on the one hand...on the other hand' sets of clauses referring to contrasts between the former priests and Jesus. The boundary of a new paragraph at v. 26 is marked by γάρ which "introduces all that is meant in 'just such' a high priest, as grounds for a summary that will be given in verses 26 to 28" (Miller, p. 216).

PROMINENCE AND THEME

The theme of the 7:20–25 paragraph is taken from the most naturally prominent propositions of the two *justifications* and the CLAIM. It also of necessity includes in abbreviated form the identification proposition in 25b.

SUB-PARAGRAPH CLUSTER CONSTITUENT 7:26—8:6 (Paragraph: Claim₂ of 7:20—8:13)

THEME: Jesus is the Supreme Priest, since God solemnly declared that Jesus is the one whom he has appointed as the eternal Supreme Priest. Jesus is the kind of Supreme Priest that we need and he ministers in the true place of worship in heaven. If he were now living on the earth, he would not be a Supreme Priest. But where he is now, Christ ministers in a more excellent way than the Jewish priests do, and the agreement he has validated is better than the former agreement.

¶PTRN   RELATIONAL STRUCTURE   CONTENTS

CLAIM — 7:26a *Jesus is* the kind of Supreme Priest that we need.

justification₁:
- NUCLEUS₁ — 7:26b He was set apart *for God*;
- NUCLEUS₂ — 7:26c he never did wrong actions,
- NUCLEUS₃ — 7:26d and he was innocent of any evil attitude.
- NUCLEUS₄ — 7:26e He has *now* been separated *by God* from living among sinners,
- NUCLEUS₅ — 7:26f and he has ascended to the highest heaven, *close to God.*

justification₂:
- negative — NONCONGRUENCE — 7:27a *Because he never sinned,* he does not need to sacrifice *many animals* day by day *as well as year by year,* firstly, *to atone for* his own sins, and also *to sacrifice animals for other* people *who have sinned,*
- standard — 7:27b as the *Jewish* Supreme Priest needs to do.
- POSITIVE — 7:27c Instead, he offered his own self only once as a sacrifice.

justification₃:
- NUCLEUS — 7:28a *Remember that the men who became* Supreme Priests according to the regulation God gave Moses *were men who* easily tended to sin.
- CONTRASTIVE NUCLEUS — CONTENT:
  - orienter — NUCLEUS — 7:28b But *God* solemnly declared,
  - circumstance — 7:28c *after he had told the people* his laws,
  - ITEM — 7:28d that *he would appoint* his Son *to be a Supreme Priest,*
  - description of 'Son' — 7:28e who has eternally become all that God intends him to be.

PRIMARY CLAIM:
- orienter — 8:1a The main point *of all that I have* written *is*
- NUCLEUS₁ — ITEM — 8:1b that *Jesus is that kind of* Supreme Priest.
- description of 'priest' — 8:1c He has sat down to rule [MTY] with God [EUP] at the place of greatest honor in heaven.
- NUCLEUS₂ — ITEM — 8:2a He ministers in the Most Holy Place, that is, *in the* true *place of worship in heaven,*
- description of 'place' — 8:2b *which Moses'* tent *represented,*
- positive description — 8:2c and which was made by *the Lord God.*
- negative description — 8:2d *It was* not *made by* any human.

justification:
- NUCLEUS₁:
  - grounds — 8:3a Since every Supreme Priest is appointed to offer gifts *to God* and sacrifices *for the people who sinned,*
  - CONCLUSION — 8:3b *Jesus would* also have had to offer something *as our Supreme Priest.*
- NUCLEUS₂ — 8:4–6 If he were *now* living on the earth, he would not be a Supreme Priest. But where he is now, *Christ* ministers in a more excellent way *than the Jewish priests do and* the agreement he has validated is better than the former agreement. [See expansion on page 122.]

INTENT AND PARAGRAPH PATTERN

This is another expository paragraph in which the writer expounds more on the superiority of Christ as our Supreme Priest. The unit consists of one CLAIM and four *justifications*.

The 7:26—8:6 paragraph is again an expository one. It develops the main point of the expository paragraphs about Melchizedek in chapter 7.

Again it seems best to be a volitionality subtype with a primary CLAIM in 8:1–2 and a *justification* in 8:3–6. Miller (p. 223) says the γάρ in v. 3 "gives *grounds* for the *conclusion* in verses 1 and 2."

NOTES

7:26a *Jesus is* the kind of Supreme Priest that we need Several versions are similar to the display text here (e.g., NCV's "Jesus is the kind of high priest we need") in specifying who is referred to by τοιοῦτος 'such' and making it sound natural in English. The γάρ here is resumptive of the previous topic; thus it is not represented in the display nor in most English versions.

7:26b set apart *for God* Morris says (p. 72) that "There are two Greek words for 'holy', one (hagios) refers to the quality of separateness, of belonging to God, and the other (hosios) signifies rather the character involved in that separation." But Louw and Nida say (88.24) for definitions of both words "pertaining to being holy in the sense of superior moral qualities and possessing certain essentially divine qualities in contrast with what is human—'holy, pure, divine' " and add in a footnote, "There may be certain subtle distinctions in these two sets of meaning, those with the stem ἀγ- and those with the stem ὁσ-, but this cannot be determined with any degree of certainty from existing contexts."

7:26c he never did wrong actions The word ἄκακος means "innocent, guileless" (BAGD p. 29), "without fault, guileless, innocent" (Louw and Nida 88.2), "entirely free from all that is evil and harmful" (Hughes, p. 272, "he has no fault or sin in him" (TEV).

7:26e He has *now* been separated *by God* from living among sinners BAGD (p. 890.2c) gives a useful discussion on the phrase κεχωρισμένος ἀπὸ τῶν ἁμαρτωλῶν 'separated from sinners': "the meaning can include not only that Christ has been separated from sinful men by being exalted to the heavenly world (s[ee] what follows in the context of Heb. 7:26) but also that because of his attributes (s[ee] what precedes in the context:...) he is different from sinful men."

There are two issues that the translator must then decide:

1. Was the author intending to refer to both Jesus being in heaven and his being very different from us sinful humans?
2. It is not likely that he had two meanings in mind.

If the author meant only one of those meanings, which one did he intend?

The commentaries give arguments for both interpretations, but Lane's comment (p. 192) points to a right decision. He says, "...when χωρίζειν implies mere difference or 'distinction', it is rarely, if ever, followed by the preposition ἀπό.... The evidence suggests that the idiom...denotes local separation and that the perfect tense of the verb is used to express the state of having been separated."

7:26f he has ascended to the highest heaven, close to God The phrase ὑψηλότερος τῶν οὐρανῶν γενόμενος 'having become higher than the heavens' "has specific reference to the place of God's throne" (Lane) and follows the Jewish concept of three heavens, the highest of which is God's dwelling (see note on 4:14). The verb γίνομαι, being intransitive, does not in itself mean "exalted" (RSV, NIV) or "raised high above" (REB).

7:27a Because he never sinned This provides the logical explanation for the statement which follows. As Lane puts it (p. 193), "because he was the sinless priest described in v. 26."

many animals day by day *as well as year by year* There is a lot of discussion by commentators on the phrase καθ' ἡμέραν 'daily'. Some say it says 'daily', so he must be referring specifically to such daily sacrifices. Others note that the two offerings mentioned here are those of the Day of Atonement "which, as the author knows (9:7), was a once-yearly observance" (Attridge). The majority agree with Attridge (p. 213) who says "it seems likely that our author has somehow conflated the daily sacrifices with that of the Day of Atonement." The analysis here assumes the writer would expect his readers to know the sacrifices he mentions are annual; he therefore mentions the daily ones which the priests have to make 'as well'.

to atone for The display supplies this verb to make clear the sense of the preposition ὑπέρ 'concerning'. LB supplies "to cover over."

for other* people *who have sinned The GNT is very elliptical, having only τῶν τοῦ λαοῦ 'of the people' (cf. TEV, "for the sins of the people"). The display makes clear that the Supreme Priest was a person, too.

7:27c Instead, he offered his own self only once as a sacrifice Many versions (e.g., CEV, REB, NCV, NIV, RSV) ignore the causal relation here. Miller says, (p. 218), the γάρ "introduces grounds for a conclusion made in the first part of the verse." But 'he sacrificed himself once' does not cohere semantically as the reason for 'he doesn't need to make sacrifices'. This statement is a contrast to the one made in v. 27a.

7:28a *Remember that* The display uses an orienter to remind the readers of known information. It communicates the relationship of the Greek connector γάρ that introduced this sentence. This analysis assumes that the γάρ is introducing a prominent *justification* of the CLAIM in v. 26a.

the men This communicates the meaning of the personification of ὁ νόμος...καθίστησιν ἀρχιερεῖς 'the law appoints...Supreme Priests' by indicating the actual persons who became the replacements for dead Supreme Priests.

according to the regulation God gave Moses This completes the personification of 'the law appoints Supreme Priests'.

***were men who* easily tended to sin** The GNT has ἔχοντας ἀσθένειαν 'having weakness'. Some commentators suggest that 'weakness' refers to a tendency to sin on the part of the men who became Supreme Priests. In the light of 7:27a, this seems to be the best interpretation. As Kistemaker says (p. 208), "The term *weak* does not refer to physical ailments, for Jesus shared our weaknesses when he was on earth (4:15). Rather, it relates to our sinful condition and is therefore synonymous with sin" (cf. also Lane, Westcott, Davidson).

7:28c after *he had told the people* his laws This rendering supplies a verb for choosing a new Supreme Priest; none occurs in the phrase μετὰ τὸν νόμον 'after the law'.

7:28d that *he would appoint* his Son *to be a* Supreme Priest Nearly all versions supply 'appoint' to fill in the ellipsis of the Greek, and NCV includes "to be the high priest."

7:28e eternally become all that God intends him to be The word τετελειωμένον 'having been perfected' has a different meaning than in 5:9a. A literal translation would imply that the author supposed that Jesus, at some time, was not perfect.

8:1a The main point The vast majority of commentators as well as BAGD (p. 429.1) take κεφάλαιον to mean 'main point', not 'summary'. As Miller notes (p. 222), here "the author reaches the main point of his argument."

***of all that I have* written** The GNT ἐπὶ τοῖς λεγομένοις literally means 'about the things said' but the author is writing, not speaking (cf. 2:5). He is introducing his amplification of the topic that he began in 7:1.

8:1b *Jesus is that kind of* Supreme Priest The author focused on Jesus as the Supreme Priest for the benefit of the believers. The Greek words ἔχομεν ἀρχιερέα 'we have a Supreme Priest of that kind' are not meant to convey that we possess him.

8:1c sat down to rule [MTY] with God [EUP] at the place of greatest honor The clause ἐκάθισεν ἐν δεξιᾷ τοῦ θρόνου 'sat at the right (hand) of the throne' involves a double metonymy: 'sat down at the throne' consists of an event and a location standing for the event of ruling associated with it (cf. Miller, p. 221) "The sense is: at the right side of the throne where the Majesty sits"). Then 'right hand' stands for the very high honor associated with that position (cf. NLT, "in the place of highest honor").

with God The word μεγαλωσύνη 'greatness' is "a periphrasis for God himself" (BAGD p. 497), a euphemism to avoid the name of God. It is rendered as 'God' in NCV, CEV, and NLT.

8:2a *true place of worship in heaven* Commentators and versions agree that τῶν ἁγίων λειτουργός 'a minister of the holy (things)' refers to "'the Sanctuary', and especially what is elsewhere... called 'the Holy of Holies'" (Westcott, p. 214).

(cf. LB/ NLT's "he ministers...in heaven, the true place of worship.")

that is The conjunction καί here is taken as introducing a "further description of the heavenly sanctuary" (Lane, p. 205), not a different entity (cf. also NIV, TEV, CEV, NCV, and REV). The great majority of commentators agree.

8:2b *which Moses'* tent *represented* The words τῆς σκηνῆς τῆς ἀληθινῆς 'of the true tent' is taken as a metaphor. Jesus ministers in "The real tabernacle in heaven, of which that among the Hebrews was but a type" (Barnes); Hughes says

(p. 281–282), "It is described as 'the true tent' because, in contrast with the perishable tent or tabernacle which accompanied the Israelites in their wilderness wanderings, the heavenly reality into which the Lord has entered is the genuine sanctuary, the imperishable holy of holies." (cf. also Lünemann, Brown, Attridge, and Davidson).

8:2c made When we refer to God's *actions*, we must be careful that we do not imply human limitations. God did not assemble the ritual space from materials that he had prepared before he started construction.

the Lord God Again 'Lord' refers to God the Father.

8:3a offer gifts *to God* and sacrifices *for the people who sinned* The recipient is included to complete the case frame (cf. TEV, NCV). The notion 'for sins' is implied (it was stated specifically in 5:1).

8:3b *Jesus* would also have had to offer something *as our Supreme Priest* The referent of τοῦτνον 'this' is specified by name as in LB and CEV. The words 'as our Supreme Priest' are an implicature of the argument. An alternative is TEV's "our high priest;" another would be an appositional phrase, 'this Supreme Priest, Christ'.

EXPANSION OF NUCLEUS₂ OF THE *JUSTIFICATION* IN THE 7:26—8:6 DISPLAY

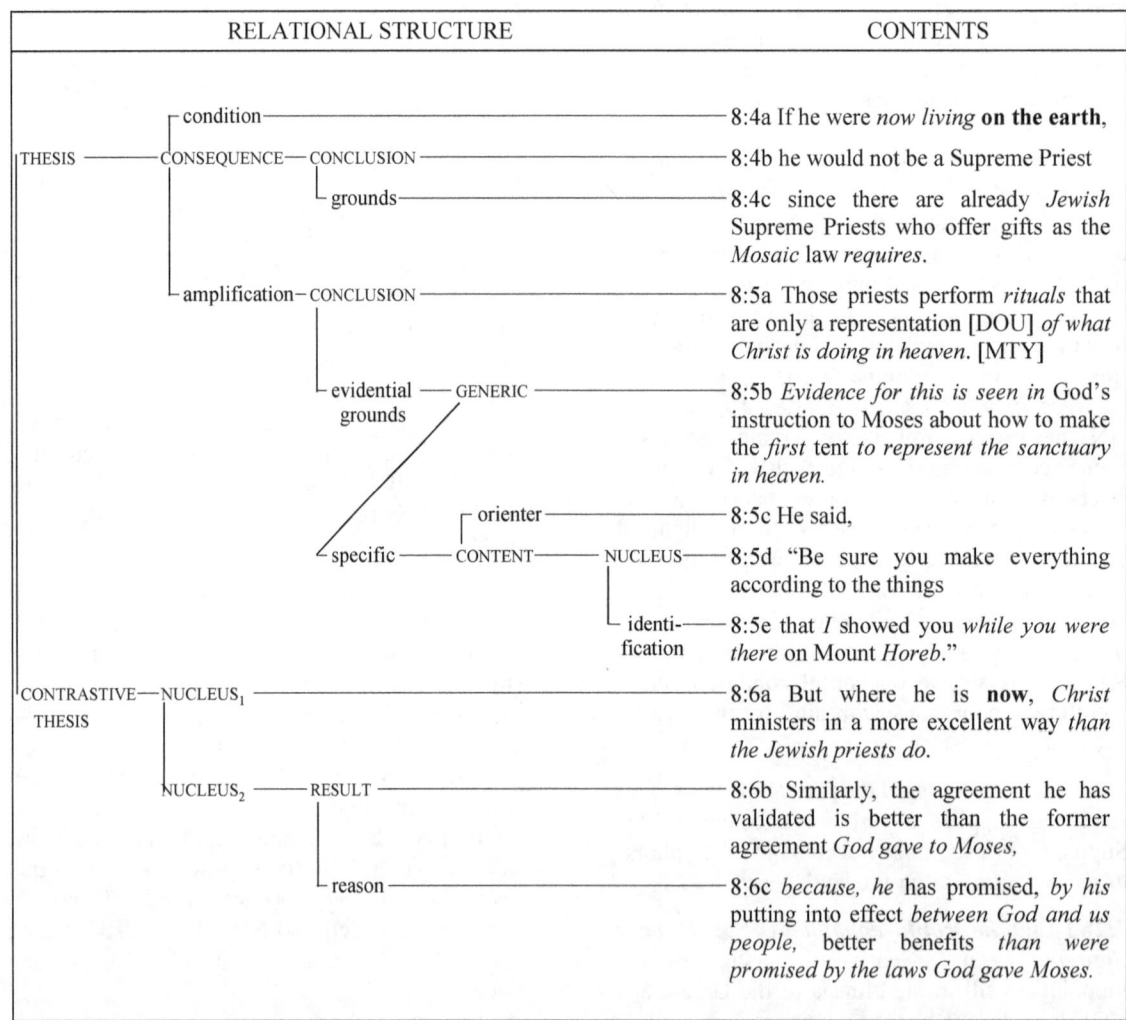

NOTES

8:4–6 The Greek grammatical construction μὲν...δὲ contrasts the unreal situation of Christ with his real situation. The bolding in v. 4a and v. 6a highlights the contrast.

8:4a If he were *now living* <u>on the earth</u> The display indicates with bold letters (underscored here) the unreal situation signaled by the construction that μὲν introduces.

were *now living* The GNT has only ἦν 'were': the rendering here follows NCV. Lünemann says, "if He were now on earth, had His dwelling-place on earth…"

8:4c *Jewish* Supreme Priests…*Mosaic* law The rendering here makes clear the writer is referring to Judaism.

requires This verb makes clear what is meant by the preposition in the phrase κατὰ νόμον 'according to law': JBP has "prescribed by."

8:5a perform *rituals* BAGD (p. 467) say the verb λατρεύω refers to "the carrying out of religious duties, especially of a cultic nature." Louw and Nida (53.14) give the sense as "perform religious rites as part of one's religious duties." NCV has "the work they do as priests." The present tense in the display, following the Greek, is an indication that this book was written before the destruction of Jerusalem in 70 AD.

that are only a representation Many commentators agree with the analysis here that the phrase ὑποδείγματι καὶ σκιᾷ 'example and foreshadowing' is a hendiadys. Moore (p. 58) classifies it as a figurative doublet.

of what Christ is doing in heaven The phrase τῶν ἐπουρανίων 'of the heavenly (things)' is taken as a metonymy, the place standing for the event that Christ performs there. What the earthly priests *do* is a model of what someone else *does*, not of a place. Bruce says (p. 166), "Jesus exercises His high-priestly ministry in the heavenly sanctuary, of which the earthly one was but a replica."

8:5b *Evidence for this is seen* The word καθώς 'as' introduces the Scriptural evidential grounds for the statement in 8:5a. The writer expected his audience to know about the quote.

God's instruction to Moses about how to make the *first* tent NCV has "the Holy Tent." In some cases it might be necessary to specify 'in the desert'.

8:5c He said The passage which follows is cited from Exodus 25:40.

8:5e *I* showed you The display supplies the agent of the passive phrase δειχθέντα σοι 'shown to you', which is probably used euphemistically to avoid using God's name more than necessary.

***while you were there* on Mount** The display text specifies the mountain, as does LB. LB has "Mount Sinai." But the Greek does not specify the location, and all the O.T. references to this Mount are to Mt. Horeb in Arabia.

8:6a But where he is <u>now</u> The author used νυν[ὶ] δὲ 'now and' to introduce his contrastive declaration.

more excellent way *than the Jewish priests do* The word κρείττων 'better' implies that the translator must decide what other ritual is not as good. NCV has "than the work that was given to the other priests."

8:6b the agreement he has validated is better than the former agreement *God gave to Moses* The words μεσίτης '(of which he is) mediator' semantically demands an understanding of the parties being put into effect between. NCV has "the new agreement that Jesus brought from God to his people," which is excellent. The word νενομοθέτηται 'has been established' indicates that the mediation has been completed.

8:6c *because*, he has promised, *by his* putting into effect *between God and us people*, better benefits *than were promised by the laws God gave Moses* This explicates the phrase ἐπὶ κρείττοσιν ἐπαγγελίαις 'upon better promises'. The word κρείττων again requires a resolution of what is 'better'. The author used the abstract phrase καὶ κρείττονός ἐστιν διαθήκης 'and the agreement is better' to indicate that Jesus offers to his followers better benefits than the old Israelite system offered. The whole thrust of this epistle suggests the information that is supplied in italics and is supported in commentaries; e.g., Hewitt, "The Mosaic covenant was a covenant of law." An alternative is 'than the old agreement did'. (It is recognized that both wordings are somewhat of a personification.)

BOUNDARIES AND COHESION

A new paragraph at 8:7 is indicated by a switch from the discussion of Jesus as Supreme Priest to a discussion of the inadequacy of the old agreement. The γάρ which introduces this paragraph is simply indicating this transition; it is not represented in recent versions such as CEV and NLT. Cohesion in this paragraph is provided by five occurrences of ἀρχιερεύς 'Supreme Priest' and three occurrences of οὐρανός 'heaven'.

PROMINENCE AND THEME

The theme for this paragraph is taken from the *PRIMARY CLAIM* and its following *justification*.

SUB-PARAGRAPH CLUSTER CONSTITUENT 8:7–13 (Paragraph: Claim₃ of 7:20—8:13)

THEME: A new agreement was needed, as is supported by what the Scriptures say about God making a new agreement.

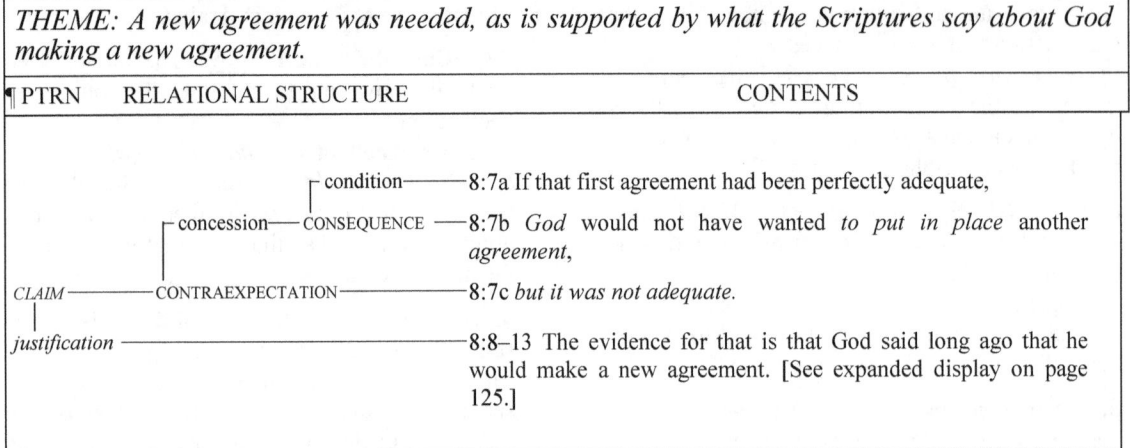

INTENT AND PARAGRAPH PATTERN

The 8:7–13 paragraph continues the writer's attempt to persuade his audience of the superiority of Christ as the enactor of a better agreement. It is thus an expository paragraph of the volitionality subtype, containing a CLAIM in v. 7 and its *justification* in vv. 8–13.

NOTES

8:7a If that first agreement had been perfectly adequate The rendering here removes the double negative conveyed by ἄμεμπτος 'faultless'. JBP translates "had proved satisfactory," CEV puts "had been all right." The γάρ here is resumptive referring to the word 'agreement' in the previous verse.

8:7b God would not have wanted *to put in place* another *agreement* The display text specifies the agent of the passive construction οὐκ ἂν δευτέρας ἐζητεῖτο τόπος 'a place of a second would not have been sought'. Attridge (p. 226) says the expression "involves a common Hellenistic metaphorical use of 'place'." The concept has a rather skewed sense of 'seek', with the meaning that God, as the 'seeker', would desire to offer a new agreement as a substitute. The author implied that God was offering the replacement and annulling the first one at the same time. TEV renders it as "there would have been no need for a second one."

***to put in place* another** This is an implicature of the argument, and makes clear what the author means by 'second'. Lünemann says, "it would not have been expressed by God himself, that a second agreement is to come in beside the first, and replace it."

8:7c *but it was not adequate* This is an implicature of the argument. What follows in vv. 8–13 is not the justification for the contrafactual statement of v. 7 about why the first agreement was inadequate, but the explanation of why a new one was necessary. Morris says here, "The writer proceeds to show that a place was indeed sought for a new agreement."

EXPANSION OF THE *JUSTIFICATION* IN THE 8:7–13 DISPLAY

RELATIONAL STRUCTURE	CONTENTS
CONTENT₁ — CONTENT — orienter — NUCLEUS	8:8a *This is supported by what was written in the Scriptures* that the Lord God said
circumstance	8:8b *after he had* declared *that our ancestors* were guilty *of not obeying the first agreement;*
ITEM — orienter	8:8c "Listen!
ITEM	8:8d There will be a time when I will make a new agreement with all the Israelite people.
description₁ of 'agreement' — NUCLEUS	8:9a That agreement will not be like the agreement I made with their ancestors
circumstance	8:9b when I led them out of Egypt *like a father leads a child to safety* by the hand.
description₂ — RESULT	8:9c I rejected them
reason	8:9d because they did not continue to *obey* my agreement.
CONTENT₂ description of agreement — CONTENT — orienter — NUCLEUS	8:10a This is the agreement that I will make with *all* the Israelites
circumstance	8:10b at the time *when I offer* them a new agreement:
OUTCOME — occasion	8:10c I will cause that they understand the laws *that I want them to obey* [MTY]
OUTCOME	8:10d then I will cause that they sincerely want to obey them (OR: truly know them) [MTY].
amplification — NUCLEUS₁ — NUCLEUS — CONJOINED₁	8:10e I will be the God they will *worship*,
CONJOINED₂	8:10f and they all will belong to me.
RESULT — orienter	8:11a And *as a result,* no one will *need to* teach a fellow citizen or his fellow kinsman,
RESULT — CONTENT	8:11b 'You should know what the Lord God desires for all people!
reason — NUCLEUS	8:11c because all *my people* will know what I *want:*
reason — equivalent	8:11d *My people of every status* will know *what I want,* whether very young or very old.
NUCLEUS₂ — NUCLEUS	8:12a I will mercifully *forgive them concerning* their having sinned;
restatement	8:12b I will no longer *consider* that *they are guilty for having* sinned.'"
amplification — CONCLUSION — grounds	8:13a Since *God* spoke about a new *agreement,*
CONCLUSION — NUCLEUS 'obsolete'	8:13b *he implied that* he considered the first *agreement* to be getting obsolete,
comment — comparison	8:13c and *just as* old things disappear when they [MET] [DOU] become very obsolete,
comment — NUCLEUS	8:13d *it* will soon disappear.

NOTES

8:8a *This is supported by what was written in the Scriptures* **that the Lord** *God* **said** The author used γάρ 'for' here to connect the citation to v. 7. He cited God's speech from Jer. 31:31–34.

the Lord *God* **said** The Greek present tense of the word λέγει 'he says' is a transliteration of the Hebrew aspect. However, the author was citing a speech event that happened in the distant past. The speech introducer occurs prior to the quote, at the end of v. 9 and the middle of v. 10. However, what God continued to instruct Jeremiah continues up to the end of v. 12. A translator should use the natural quotation markers for the language of the translation. Here 'he said' is rendered 'was written' to avoid saying 'he/the Lord says' two times in a row. The word 'God' is included to make clear which member of the Trinity is being referred to.

8:8b *after he had* **declared** *that our ancestors were guilty* **of not obeying the first agreement** Louw and Nida (33.431) say the verb μέμφομαι means "to bring accusations against someone on the basis that the person in question is clearly to blame." In the context (v. 9c) the cause of the blame is stated to be the failure to obey the agreement.

The GNT has only μεμφόμενος αὐτούς 'finding fault with them'. But there is a textual variant here: the dative αὐτοῖς 'to them' which would most naturally be connected with the verb λέγει that follows, to give the sense 'he says to them' (although the verb μέμφομαι can take either the accusative or dative). It is perhaps for that reason that some commentators say that God declared the old agreement as being guilty, instead of the Israelites. However, it is likely that a copyist who saw the verb λέγει would write αὐτοῖς instead of αὐτούς. It is not likely that he would have written αὐτούς after seeing αὐτοῖς. Furthermore, the context (v. 9c) supports 'them' as the object of 'find fault with'. The GNT gives the accusative form, followed here, a C "almost certain" rating, and the great majority of versions translate it as 'them' or 'his people'.

8:8c Listen! This is the sense of ἰδού, literally 'behold'. It is a word calling special attention to what follows; most versions do not translate it at all.

8:8d There will be a time when This is a Hebrew idiom, represented in the GNT as ἡμέραι ἔρχονται 'days are coming', for referring to a future event, but in many languages 'time' cannot be the agent of a verb of motion.

the Israelite people The phrases οἶκον Ἰσραήλ 'house of Israel' and οἶκον Ἰούδα 'house of Judah' are dead figures of metonymy, 'house' standing for the people (cf. TEV, LB/NLT, NCV, CEV). God was referring to all the Israelites. His mentioning the two groups is a doublet for the whole ethnic group, which is listed as 'Israelites' here, lest naming them both here conflict with just the one group being mentioned in v. 10a.

8:9a ancestors The word πατέρες means ancestors, forefathers.

8:9b *like a father leads a child to safety* **by the hand** The rendering here spells out the metaphor. Morris says (p.78), "The metaphor is that of a father or mother taking a little child by the hand to lead him safely to the place where he is going."

8:9c I rejected them As Miller notes (p. 230), "The καί here introduces a result."

rejected The verb ἀμελέω means "neglect, be unconcerned about" (BAGD p. 44) or "pay no attention to" (Louw and Nida 30.50) but here it must have more of an active sense (cf. "turned away from" (NIV), "abandoned" (REB), "deserted" (JB). Barnes uses "reject".

8:9d not continue to *obey* **my agreement** This spells out the sense of the preposition in the clause οὐκ ἐμένειναν ἐν τῇ διαθήκῃ μου 'not continue in my agreement' (cf. TEV, "not remain faithful to"). Another alternative is "broke their agreement with me" (CEV).

8:10a *all* **the Israelites** See note on 8:8c.

8:10b at the time *when I offer* **them a new agreement** It is difficult to determine the meaning implied by 'those days' in the expression μετὰ τὰς ἡμέρας ἐκείνας 'after those days'. Several commentators say it means after the time period mentioned in v. 8 has been completed. But v. 8 refers to making a new agreement; therefore this cannot refer to an agreement made after the new one is made. Alford is much closer in saying it means "after the end of that dispensation." One way of expressing this would be "after the end of the time during which [the] first agreement was in effect." Another alternative would be to ignore the word 'after' and translate the phrase as 'in the future'.

The Greek text includes the words 'says the Lord' which is simply a repetition of the speech frame expressed in v. 8a. Translators may include this repetition where it is natural in the target language.

8:10c cause that they understand the laws *that I want them to obey* The words διδοὺς νόμους μου εἰς τὴν διάνοιαν αὐτῶν 'putting my laws into their mind' is figurative: 'mind' is a metonymy standing for the mental activity associated with it.

8:10d cause that they sincerely want to obey them (OR: truly know them) The clause ἐπὶ καρδίας αὐτῶν ἐπιγράψω αὐτούς 'on their hearts I will inscribe them' is also very figurative. But the question is, in addition to the metonymy involving 'heart' and the metaphorical sense of 'write', is this clause a semantic doublet with 'putting my laws into their minds'? Moore (p. 58) classifies it as a figurative doublet. Further evidence supporting that conclusion is seen in the fact that 'laws' is not repeated in the second expression, that the first one is introduced by a participle and not a fully inflected verb, and that 'heart' was the "center and source of the whole inner life, with its thinking, feeling, and volition" (BAGD p. 403.1b), and the second half of the verse can be considered a doublet. But since neither commentaries nor versions seem to support that interpretation, the display gives two alternatives. If they are not a doublet, the sense of the second figure is taken following Barnes: "the obedience rendered will be internal" (cf. also Bruce). An alternative to what is given in the display would be to consider this an occasion-outcome hendiadys, with v. 10d being expressed as 'and then they will sincerely want to obey them'.

8:10e-f I will be the God they will *worship* and they all will belong to me This is a mutual action couplet. God promised that both conditions would happen simultaneously and continually. He described the two sides of a mutual relationship.

The display supplies the word 'worship' to indicate the relationship implied by the possessive construction. An alternative would be to say 'I will be the God they serve'.

8:11a And *as a result* Although this verse begins with καί 'and', semantically it seems to be the result of v. 10, not coordinate with it.

no one will *need to* teach The GNT says οὐ μὴ διδάξωσιν 'by no means may they teach', which sounds like a prohibition, which it clearly is not. The sense is clearly, as in NCV, "will no longer have to" (cf. also CEV, TEV, JB, LB/NLT, Attridge, Morris, and Kistemaker).

fellow citizen The Textus Receptus follows the reading πλησίον 'neighbor' instead of πολίτης 'fellow-citizen'. The latter has much stronger manuscript support (given an A "certain" rating in the GNT). Some scribe evidently wanted to substitute a much better known word.

8:11b You should know what the Lord *God desires for all people* The Greek text says "Know the Lord" but it is not natural to command someone to know someone else. Therefore, this is taken as a metonymy, the person standing for what that person desires.

Lord *God* It is important that the readers recognize that the reference here is to God the Father (not to Jesus), and that God is referring to himself.

8:11c all *my people* The Greek says πάντες 'all', but this is taken as hyperbole (which is probably true of the word ἕκαστος 'each' in 11a also). Morris (p. 79) says "all those in the new covenant;" see also Barnes. Calvin says it means "all kinds," but the context favors the interpretation taken here.

will know what I *want* The GNT εἰδήσουσίν με 'shall know me,' is somewhat idiomatic, with the meaning that every person will know what God wants for him or her.

8:11d *of every status*...whether very young or very old The phrase ἀπὸ μικροῦ ἕως μεγάλου αὐτῶν 'from small to great of them' is a Hebrew idiom that refers to every person regardless of age or social status classification. God was promising to interact with every one of his people. Barnes has "among all classes from the highest to the lowest;" CEV has "no matter who they are;" NCV has "from the least to the most important."

8:12a The verse begins with ὅτι which could mean 'because' or it could simply introduce part of the content of the new agreement (10a). Although commentators take the causal sense, many versions (NIV, TEV, REB, LB/NLT, NCV) do not include any causal conjunction. Semantically, it fits better as the crucial content of the agreement, much better than just as the "grounds of the preceding statement 'all shall know me'" (Miller, p. 234).

I will mercifully *forgive them concerning their having sinned* The words ἵλεως ἔσομαι ταῖς ἀδικίαις αὐτῶν 'I will be merciful to their unrighteousnesses' is not clear in what way God will be merciful. NCV omits the 'merciful' altogether saying "I will 'forgive them;" and NIV and JB do likewise.

8:12b I will no longer *consider* that *they are guilty for having* sinned The καί here is taken as introducing a restatement of the preceding proposition, not something different. The words τῶν ἁμαρτιῶν οὐ μὴ μνησθῶ ἔτι 'their sins by no means will I remember more' is poetic and is an understatement for emphasis. As Barnes says, "It cannot mean literally that God forgets that men are sinners, but it means that he treats them as if this were forgotten." Some interpreters have considered that v. 12a and v. 12b form a doublet, but the form in the Hebrew text of Jeremiah seems to have greater emphasis as a statement-restatement propositional pair.

8:13b he considered the first *agreement* to be getting obsolete The GNT says πεπαλαίωκεν τὴν πρώτον 'he has made the first old' but in BAGD (p. 606.1) the clause is given the meaning "treat the first agreement as obsolete."

8:13c *just as* old things disappear when they [MET] [DOU] become very obsolete This is a comment on 'obsolete' of 8:13b. It contains two figures of speech: the verb γηράσκω means 'grow old' but people, not agreements, grow old. Hence a comparison is intended. Secondly, the two participles παλαιούμενον καὶ γηράσκον 'being made old and growing old' are considered a doublet (Moore, p. 58, considers it a near-synonymous doublet) and rendered here by one term. The force is indicated by the word 'very' in the display. If one wants to retain the poetic form, "old and worn-out" (TEV, CEV) is a good alternative.

BOUNDARIES AND COHERENCE

Cohesion within the 8:7–13 paragraph is provided by references to the first and/or the new agreements in vv. 7, 8, 9 (2X), 10, and 13. The boundary of a new paragraph at 9:1 is marked by a resumptive οὖν (returning to the thought of 8:5) followed by a complete change of topic: the items within the tent in the desert.

PROMINENCE AND THEME

The theme of the 8:7–13 paragraph is derived from the result portion of the most naturally prominent proposition of the CLAIM in v. 7b and a brief condensation of the orienter proposition of the *justification*. Usually content propositions are perceived as being more prominent, but in this case to include both contents would make an extremely long theme statement, and furthermore the fact that the writer is able to support his claim by a lengthy OT quotation is probably more prominent than the content of the quote itself.

PARAGRAPH CLUSTER CONSTITUENT 9:1–10 (Sub-Paragraph Cluster: Basis₁ of 7:20—9:22)

¶ PTRN	RELATIONAL STRUCTURE	CONTENTS
THEME: God told Moses what rituals were to be performed and about the Sacred Tent for those rituals, but those rituals indicated that the way for ordinary people to enter God's presence was not yet revealed.		
	┌ concession	9:1–5 When God gave Moses the first agreement, he told Moses exactly how the priests should do the rituals and exactly how to build the tent for those rituals. The tent had two rooms—the outer room, which they called the Holy Place, with its furniture, and the inner room, which they called the Very Holy Place, with its furniture.
CLAIM └ CONTRAEXPECTATION		9:6–10 These rituals indicated that the way for ordinary people to enter God's presence was not yet revealed; people who brought the sacrifices still sensed that they were guilty for their sins. The Holy Spirit has shown that the ordinary people could not enter the presence of God as long as the Jewish system of offering sacrifices was in effect.

INTENT AND PARAGRAPH PATTERN

This unit is a *CLAIM* which consists of a *concession* and a CONTRAEXPECTATION. It is all expository: there are no imperative verbs in this unit. Here the author continues his exposition of the superiority of Christ, specifically of his priesthood and of the sacrifice he offered.

BOUNDARIES AND COHERENCE

A boundary at 9:11 is indicated by a switch from a discussion of the ministry of the Supreme Priest at the Sacred Tent to a discussion of Christ 'entering'. Coherence is provided by three occurrences of terms referring to the very holy place inside the Sacred Tent.

THEME AND PROMINENCE

The theme for this unit is basically a condensation, eliminating repetition, of the CONTRAEXPECTATION. The *concession* is always less thematic.

SUB-PARAGRAPH CLUSTER CONSTITUENT 9:1–5 (Descriptive Paragraph: Concession of 9:1–10)

THEME: When God gave Moses the first agreement, he told Moses exactly how the priests should do the rituals and exactly how to build the tent for those rituals. The tent had two rooms—the outer room, which they called the Holy Place, with its furniture, and the inner room, which they called the Very Holy Place, with its furniture.

¶ PTRN	RELATIONAL STRUCTURE	CONTENTS
	discourse orienter for 9:1-28	9:1a *I will say something about how wonderful was the Sacred Tent and its furnishings.*
DECLARATION	NUCLEUS	9:1b *When God gave the first agreement* to Moses, he told Moses exactly how *the priests* should perform the rituals in the Sacred Tent here on earth.
	description of 'tent'	9:2a *This place for rituals* was a tent that the Israelites set up.
description of 'first room'	NUCLEUS	9:2b *There were two rooms.* The priests put in the outer room the lamp stand and the table *on which they put the loaves of bread that were presented to God* (OR, that symbolized *God's* presence).
	identification of 'first room'	9:2c That *outer room* they called 'The Holy Place'.
description of 'second room'	NUCLEUS	9:3a Behind the curtain inside *that room* there was *another* room,
	identification of 'second room'	9:3b which they called 'The Very Holy Place'.
	description of 'entrance to second room'	9:4a *Near the entrance of the second room* they put an altar *covered with* gold, *on which they burned* incense.
	description of 'chest' — NUCLEUS	9:4b Inside *the second room* was *the chest which was called* the sacred chest *containing the tablets on which were written God's* agreement.
	description₁	9:4c It had sheets of gold put on all its sides;
	description₂ — NUCLEUS₁	9:4d and inside was the golden pot which contained *some of the food called* manna *with which God miraculously fed the people.*
	NUCLEUS₂	9:4e Inside *the chest* was also Aaron's walking stick that *God caused to* bud.
	NUCLEUS₃	9:4f Inside the chest were also the stone tablets *on which Moses had written* the ten commandments.
	description₃ — NUCLEUS	9:5a On top of *the chest* were *figures of* winged creatures *which symbolized God's* glory,

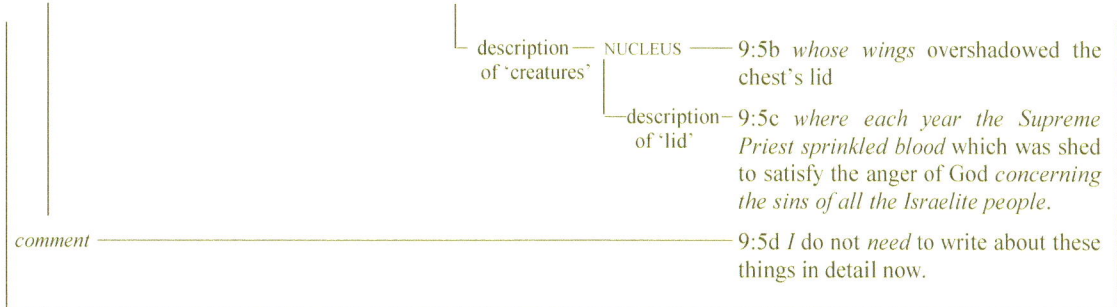

INTENT AND PARAGRAPH PATTERN

The 9:1–5 paragraph is very clearly a descriptive one. The writer is building rapport with his Jewish Christian audience by listing some of the delightful features of the Sacred Tent set up by Moses, before reminding them of the vastly superior and more wonderful work of Christ as our Supreme Priest (v.11 ff). The paragraph consists of a general *DECLARATION* followed by *descriptions* of the outer and inner rooms of that tent.

NOTES

9:1a *I will say something about how* This attempts to carry the sense of the οὖν which, in Miller's words, (p. 236), "serves to resume a subject after it has been interrupted." More specifically the writer means to continue on the subject of the Sacred Tent, which had been mentioned in 8:5.

9:1b *When God gave the* **first** *agreement* **to Moses, he told Moses exactly how** *the priests* **should perform the rituals in the Sacred Tent** This unskews the Greek clause εἶχε ἡ πρώτη δικαιώματα 'the first had ordinances', supplying the ellipsis of 'agreement' and making God the agent of the action.

   how *the priests* **should perform the rituals** The abstract noun λατρεία 'worship' refers to the various rituals which were involved in worship.

   here on earth The phrase ἅγιον κοσμικόν 'earthly holy (place)' has been taken in two ways: to refer to the tent in the desert as being temporary, or as being here on earth (as contrasted to one in heaven). The context which follows (v. 11) suggests the second interpretation is correct, and is followed by the great majority of commentators as well as in this analysis.

9:2a The γάρ here introduces a series of descriptions of the Sacred Tent mentioned in the previous verse.

9:2b *There were two rooms* This statement is implied in ἡ πρώτη 'the first'. The display inserts it in order to clarify that the author was referring to the tent, not to the first agreement.

   in the outer room The word πρώτη 'first' means the first one you come to as you enter; hence "outer, anterior" (BAGD p. 726.1d).

   on which they put The Greek simply has καί 'and' but the rendering here specifies what the table was for, as well as the relationship between the loaves and the table. NLT has "loaves of holy bread on the table." Morris (p. 81) calls it a hendiadys meaning "the table of the consecrated bread" (see also Bruce and Hughes).

   loaves of bread that were presented *to God* **(OR, that symbolized** *God's* **presence)** The phrase ἡ πρόθεσις τῶν ἄρτων means literally 'the presentation of the loaves'. A few commentators and versions take the phrase to mean "bread of the Presence [of God]" (RSV, REB) but it seems best to follow Attridge who suggests it is just another variation of phrases referring to this bread that was presented to God. TEV has "the bread offered to God." But both alternatives are supplied. If a translator chooses the first alternative, it might be necessary to make clear that God was the observer of the bread, not the receiver.

9:2c *That outer room they called 'The Holy Place'* Attridge gives a lot of discussion to problems associated with the relative clause ἥτις λέγεται Ἅγια 'which is called holy'. The basic problem, in Attridge's words (p. 233), is that "the author apparently uses a term (ἅγια) that he regularly reserves for the inner tabernacle." But it seems the problem is easily resolved by recognizing that here, in Attridge's words, the author "simply took over the standard designations of the tabernacle without worrying about consistency" and is making a distinction between the outer room which he called the holy place and the inner one called the ἅγια ἁγίων 'the holy of holies' (v. 3b).

9:3a *another* room The GNT says σκηνή 'tent', but this was not a separate tent, just a portion curtained off from the rest of the tent. Lane says (p. 219) "These terms do not designate two separate tents but rather one tent that was divided into a 'front' sanctuary and a 'rear' sanctuary."

9:3b The Very Holy Place The phrase 'holy of holies' is a Hebraism to indicate a superlative meaning the holiest place of all, but the rendering here uses the adjective 'very' because many languages do not have a superlative degree construction.

9:4a *Near the entrance of the second room* they put The problem here is that the author did not explicitly tell the location of either the gold-covered altar or the gold-covered chest. According to Ex. 3:6 this altar was in front of the curtain leading to the Most Holy Place, not inside the room with the chest. It is not likely that the author made a mistake, since he has shown that he knew the Temple and its sacrificial system very well. It is not likely that the author omitted referring to the altar but referred to a portable incense pot that the Supreme Priest used inside the room, since that would imply that he took coals of fire into the room along with the container of blood. Kistemaker notes, "The altar of incense was much more significant than a censer." Miller solves the problem by suggesting that the participle 'having' could be translated "to which belonged" and not 'in which was located'. The display makes clear the location of each item.

altar *covered with* gold By the phrase χρυσοῦν ἔχουσα θυμιατήριον 'having a golden altar' seems to refer to the altar for burning incense described in Ex. 30:1–6, which was covered with gold, not made of pure gold.

***on which they burned* incense** The GNT has only χρυσοῦν ἔχουσα θυμιατήριον 'having a golden incense-burner'. We know from Exodus that every afternoon they ritually burned incense on the altar.

9:4b Inside *the second room* was *the chest which was called* the sacred chest *containing the tablets on which were written God's* agreement It is difficult to decide the best way to render the genitive construction τὴν κιβωτὸν τῆς διαθήκη 'the box/chest of the agreement'. One can say it simply is an abbreviation for 'chest which contained the two tablets of stone on which God had inscribed the "ten commandments, the sum of the terms to which the people swore on entering the covenant" (Dods)'. The chest came to be known for the most prominent thing it contained.

9:4d *some of the food called* manna *with which God miraculously fed the people* The Jews comprising the writer's audience were very familiar with the term μάννα 'manna', but for those for whom a transliteration will have no meaning, the information given in italics here will be crucial. CEV has a long footnote here; NCV has a reference to a glossary entry.

9:4e *God caused to* bud Some translations may need to supply more information about Aaron's rod budding, so that those who have not yet read Numbers 16 will be able to understand why the people kept such a rod in the chest. In such a case, one might want to supply something like 'miraculously, to prove that he was God's true priest'.

9:4f stone tablets *on which Moses had written* the ten commandments The word πλάξ means 'flat stone'. The display text spells out what is implied in the genitive phrase πλάκες τῆς διαθήκης 'flat stones of the agreement' and the fact that 'agreement' here refers to the ten commandments; CEV has "the flat stones with the Ten Commandments written on them" (cf. also LB).

9:5a *figures of* winged creatures *which symbolized God's* glory The phrase Ξερουβὶν δόξης 'cherubim of glory' presents several problems. First, what are cherubim and how do you translate the term? BAGD says (p. 881) they were "winged figures over the ark of the covenant" and the display text states only that. Versions which try to do this instead of transliterating cherubim are NCV, CEV, TEV; LB includes both. But most of these do not make clear they were just statues, not real winged creatures. A few commentators think that the glory refers to that of the carved creatures themselves. But the vast majority would agree with Hughes who notes (p. 316), "it was between them that the glory of God's presence appeared above the mercy seat, as promised in Exodus 25:22: 'There I will meet with you, and from above the mercy seat, from between the two cherubim that are upon the ark of the testimony, I will speak to you'. The glory in the holy of holies is thus the shekinah glory of God's presence in the midst of his people." The rendering here also spells out the genitive by supplying 'symbolized'; an alternative would be 'represented' (as in TEV) or even 'showed' (as in CEV).

9:5b *whose wings* **overshadowed** Among versions which make clear it was the wings which overshadowed the chest are TEV, NLT, CEV, and NCV.

9:5c *each year the Supreme Priest sprinkled blood* **which was shed to satisfy the anger of God** *concerning the sins of all the Israelite people* This represents the word ἱλαστήριον. BAGD (p. 375) notes that some say the term means 'place of propitiation' but that the Septuagint "uses ἱλαστήριον of the lid of the ark of the covenant, which was sprinkled with the blood of the sin-offering on the Day of Atonement" (cf. also Miller, Morris, Kistemaker, Brown, Dods, and Bruce). The display tries to spell out in non-technical words the sense of 'atone for'. The phrase 'mercy seat' used in many versions is not very instructive. Louw and Nida (40.13) say the sense is "the location or place where sins are forgiven" but that is a metonymy, the effect standing for the cause.

9:5d *I* **do not** *need* **to** The Greek here, οὐκ ἔστιν νῦν λέγειν 'there is not now to speak' is somewhat elliptical: some word such as 'time' or 'necessity' or 'possibility' or even 'desire' is needed to complete the thought. CEV's rendering, "Now is not the time to go into detail about these things" is excellent. The rendering here follows Barnes, Hughes, and Bruce.

BOUNDARIES AND COHERENCE

The main thing that sets off the 9:1–5 paragraph is the fact that it is a descriptive one between two expository paragraphs. The paragraph consists of a list of items found in the tent of worship in the desert. The new unit at v. 6 is indicated by a genitive absolute phrase introducing a series of action verbs concerning the actual work of the priests.

PROMINENCE AND THEME

The theme for the 9:1–5 paragraph is taken from somewhat abbreviated statements of the DECLARATION in v. 1b and of the most prominent propositions of the two *descriptions* (including the identification propositions).

SUB-PARAGRAPH CLUSTER CONSTITUENT 9:6–10 (Paragraph: Contraexpectation of 9:1–10)

THEME: These rituals indicated that the way for ordinary people to enter God's presence was not yet revealed; people who brought the sacrifices still sensed that they were guilty for their sins. The Holy Spirit has shown that the ordinary people could not enter the presence of God as long as the Jewish system of offering sacrifices was in effect.

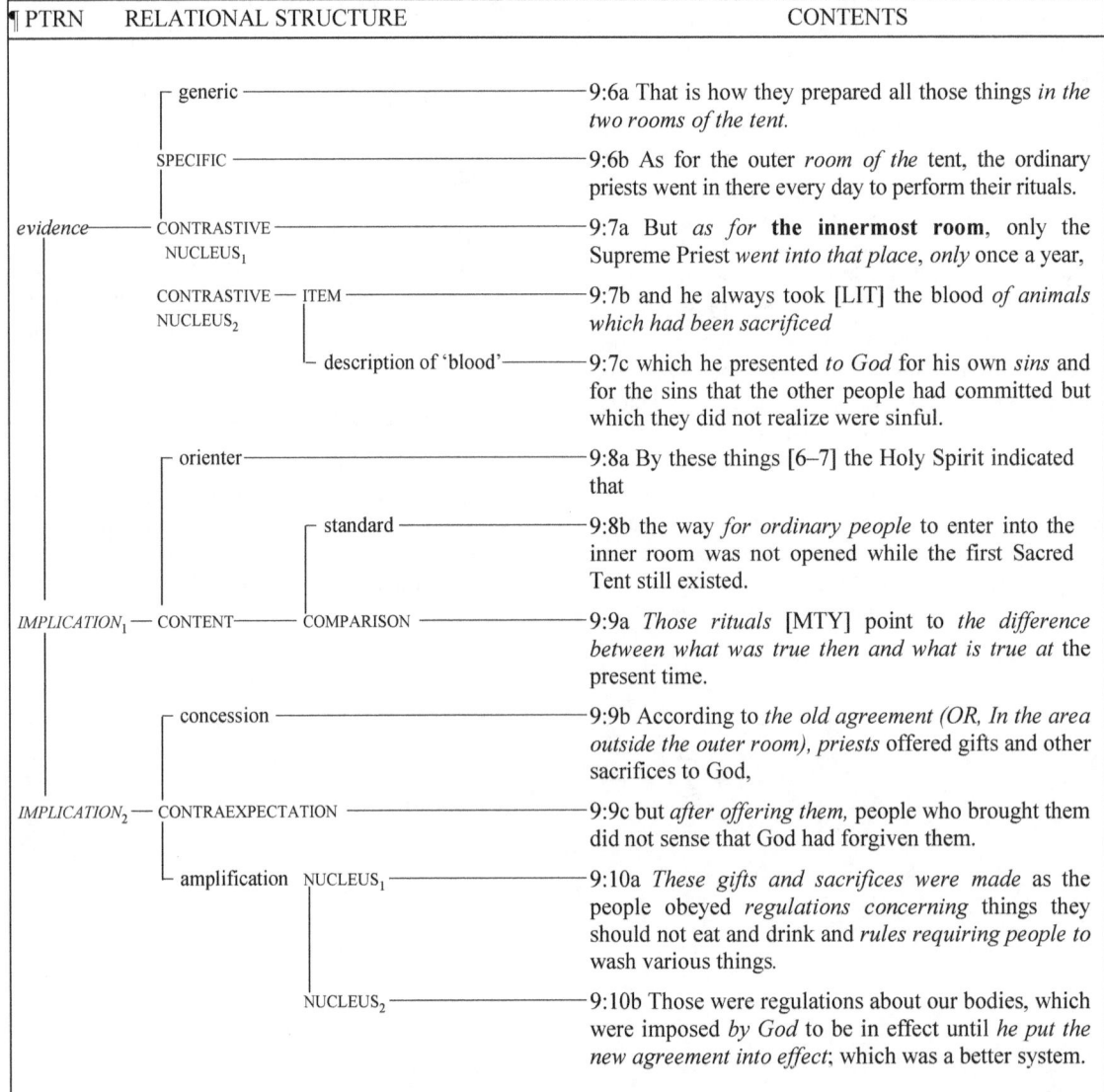

INTENT AND PARAGRAPH PATTERN

The writer continues in the expository mode discussing the inadequacy of the old sacrificial system. Since he makes certain statements about the work of the Jewish priests and then draws inferences from them, the paragraph is listed as being of the causality subtype, consisting of one *evidence* followed by two IMPLICATIONS.

NOTES

9:6–10 As Lenski (p. 280) says, "The description is worded in the present tenses, which, referring, as they do, to the Tabernacle that is now long lost, are nothing but historical narration and contain no reference to what was done in Herod's Temple at the writer's time." The display uses past tense, as do NIV, CEV, NCV, LB/NLT, and JBP.

9:6a That is how they prepared all those things *in the two rooms of the tent* This rendering specifies to what 'these things' refer.

9:6b As for the outer *room of the* tent, the ordinary priests went in there every day to

perform their rituals The author used the words εἰς μὲν τὴν πρώτην σκηνὴν διὰ παντὸς εἰσίασιν οἱ ἱερεῖς 'in regard to the first tent at all times enter the priests'. He indicated that the often repeated rituals in the outermost room contrasted with the single ritual that the Supreme Priest did each year.

outer *room of the* **tent** The phrase τῇ πρώτῃ σκηνῇ 'the first tent' refers again to the outer room or compartment (cf. 2b).

9:7a But *as for* **the innermost room, only the Supreme Priest** *went into that place, only* **once a year** The author completed his contrast of the rituals that the priests did in the outermost room with those performed in the innermost room in the Tabernacle and the Temple. He wrote here εἰς δὲ τὴν δευτέραν ἅπαξ τοῦ ἐνιαυτοῦ μόνος ὁ ἀρχιερεύς 'but in regard to the second room once each year alone the Supreme Priest'.

the innermost room This phrase is forefronted in the Greek; the emphasis indicated thereby is shown in the display by bold type.

only the Supreme Priest *went* There is no verb in the Greek.

9:7b The display translates the litotes of οὐ χωρίς 'not without' with the emphatic positive expression 'always' (cf. NLT). NEB maintains the emphasis with "he must take." Other versions which remove the litotes are CEV, TEV, JBP, REB, and JB.

blood *of animals which had been sacrificed* The rendering here indicates what blood is meant.

9:7c for his own *sins* The rendering here clarifies what is meant by ὑπὲρ ἑαυτοῦ 'for himself' (cf. CEV, NLT, and JB).

for the sins that the other people had committed but which they did not realize were sinful Commentators suggest different opinions about the meaning of the phrase τῶν τοῦ λαοῦ ἀγνοημάτων 'of the (sins) of the people committed in ignorance'. Some say that it refers to all sins; others suggest that the expression should be interpreted literally. It is true that all sin needed atonement, and, as Calvin says, "No sin is free from error or ignorance"; but it is also true, as Kistemaker says (p. 243), that "The Old Testament makes a clear distinction between sins committed unintentionally (that is, in ignorance) and those sins man committed defiantly." Therefore it seems best to choose the latter interpretation. But we must decide what sins were people ignorant of. We may choose to interpret that the author implied that the people always tried to make sacrifices for the sins they knew they had done, and the Supreme Priest performed this ritual for the sins that the people had overlooked. It does not seem likely that the author meant that the people supposed that some sins were less serious but still needed an annual atonement. TEV has "sins which the people have committed without knowing they were sinning" and that seems to convey quite well the sense.

9:8–9 The author introduced an allegory in v. 8 and stated clearly the meaning of the allegory in v. 9.

9:8a-b By these things [6–7]… *the way for ordinary people to* **enter into the inner room was not opened while the first Sacred Tent still existed** The words παραβολὴ εἰς τὸν καιρόν '(is) a parable for the time' are somewhat of a metonymy: 'time' standing for the situation that existed during that time. The display makes clear what that situation was.

9:8a the Holy Spirit indicated Translations should not imply that the Holy Spirit did an action in the past. Translations should indicate that the author affirmed that the Holy Spirit told him to compare that situation of long ago with the situation of the believers in the author's time

9:8b the way *for ordinary people* **to enter into the inner room was not opened while the first Sacred Tent still existed** Commentators agree that this is a metaphor, but disagree as to what the topic of the metaphor is. Some say it refers to the earthly tent as a symbol of the first agreement, which needed to be replaced. Others say it refers to the first tent as a symbol of blocking the people's access to God. While it is true that in chapter 8 the writer has shown the inadequacy of the old agreement, that is not what the first half of this chapter is about. Here the context is about entering into God's presence in the Most Holy Place. The great majority of commentators agree with this second interpretation.

The GNT has μήπω πεφανερῶσθαι τὴν τῶν ἁγίων ὁδὸν 'not yet revealed into the holies a way'. The author was focusing on the people not being permitted to enter the presence of God to ask for forgiveness.

while the first Sacred Tent still existed The words ἔτι τῆς πρώτης σκηνῆς ἐχούσης στάσιν 'while yet the first tent was having standing (validity)' could be taken as a metonymy, the place standing for the events that happened there—the continued functioning of the old

Israelite ritual system (cf. NLT, "the first room and the entire system it represents were still in use").

9:9a *Those rituals* We must make a decision as to the referent of the relative pronoun ἥτις 'which/that is'. A few interpreters say it refers to the following word 'parable'. Such an interpretation is grammatically possible, because there is no verb in the Greek. A few others say it refers to the whole situation described in vv. 6–8. The majority suggest that it refers to the outer room in the tent. Lane (p. 224) points out that elsewhere the author "consistently uses ἥτις to refer to a specific antecedent, and the gender and number are modified accordingly." The nearest such antecedent is 'the outer room' in v. 8. Thus, the display text assumes a metonymy: the outer room standing for the rituals that the priest did there and in the courtyard in front of it. The display also makes clear that the gifts and slaughtered animals were burnt on the altar outside the first room.

point to The words παραβολὴ εἰς τὸν καιρόν '(was) a parable for the time' are again taken as somewhat of a metonymy: 'time' standing for the situation that existed during that time.

The phrase τὸν καιρὸν τὸν ἐνεστηκότα 'the present time' has been understood in two ways: either the Old Testament period, or the Christian era. This analysis assumes that the author is referring to both eras. The clause 'which is a parable for the present time' is very difficult to understand. The previous verses have been talking about the inadequacy of the old system, not the new system. Therefore, this analysis assumes that the writer points to the differences between the old system and the new system.

9:9b According to *the old agreement* (OR, *In the area outside the outer room*) The phrase καθ᾽ ἥν 'according to which' has been interpreted several ways. Many think it means 'according to this parable' but that is not much help: the image in the parable is only representing what he is really talking about, which was the impossibility of entering God's presence under the old system. Therefore the majority of commentators who suggest the reference is to the tent in the desert and perhaps the offerings associated with it have a better interpretation. The display text gives two alternatives, both of which take up concepts mentioned in 9a.

9:9c did not sense that God had forgiven them The subject of the clause μὴ δυνάμεναι κατὰ συνείδησιν τελειῶσαι τὸν λατρεύοντα 'are not able to perfect the one worshiping with respect to conscience' is 'gifts and sacrifices', which is a personification. This is stated in a contra-expectation proposition. (The subject is made plural because the singular carries a generic sense.) Miller says (p. 249) it refers to "a conscience not freed from guilt and a sense of uncleanness." But to translate this as 'not able to make them feel that they were not guilty' involves a double negative, which is removed by translating it as 'not feel that God had forgiven them.'

9:10a *regulations concerning* things they should not eat and drink The phrase βρώμασιν καὶ πόμασιν 'foods and drinks' is a metonymy, the objects standing for the prohibitions concerning them (cf. CEV's "these rules are merely about," also JB, JBP).

and *rules requiring people to* wash various things The phrase καὶ διαφόροις βαπτισμοῖς 'and various washings' refers to "laws concerning washing rites of various kinds" (Montefiore). The author recognized that the people completed properly all the ritual washings but he implied that they always felt that they had failed in some way.

9:10b Those were regulations The Greek is very elliptical, having only the words μόνον ἐπί 'only concerning', but all modern commentaries agree that the subject is 'gifts and sacrifices', and supply some verb.

The Textus Receptus follows the reading καὶ δικαιώμασιν 'and with regulations'. The GNT reading omitting the 'and', given a B 'almost certain' rating, is to be preferred because there is a much greater likelihood that a scribe would change the nominative δικαιώματα to the dative to agree with the preceding datives (and then someone later added a connecting καί) than that the opposite could somehow have happened.

which were imposed *by God* The display shows the agent and object of the passive ἐπικείμενα 'imposed' explicitly and the verb related to 'regulations'.

until *he put the new agreement into effect*; which was a better system The phrase μέχρι καιροῦ διορθώσεως means literally 'until a time of reformation'; but we must decide what the author meant by 'reformation'. Morris says (p. 84), "Though he does not explain this, the drift of his argument shows that he has in mind the new covenant Christ brought." This is supported by Dods, Hewitt, Bruce, and Miller.

BOUNDARIES AND COHERENCE

The main feature of cohesion within the 9:6–10 paragraph is the references to activities of the various priests, with three references to the first or second rooms of the tent. The start of a new paragraph at v. 11 with the forefronted words δέ Ξριστός 'but Christ' starts a discussion of what Christ did as our Supreme Priest.

PROMINENCE AND THEME

The theme of the 9:6–10 paragraph is drawn from the most naturally prominent propositions of the *evidence* and the two IMPLICATIONS. But in each case they are greatly abbreviated: the material in the two nuclei in the evidence are summarized by the words 'these rituals', and only the topic of the metaphor in the first implication is included; the topic of a metaphor is always more prominent than the illustrative part.

PARAGRAPH CLUSTER CONSTITUENT 9:11–22 (Sub-Paragraph Cluster: Inference of 7:20—9:22)

THEME: It was as though Christ went into that very holy place only once, taking his own blood with him, thus putting into effect a new agreement.

¶ PTRN	RELATIONAL STRUCTURE		CONTENTS
INFERENCE	grounds		9:11–14 Christ being our Supreme Priest enabled us to have many good benefits. It was as though he went into that very holy place only once, taking his own blood with him.
	CONCLUSION		9:15–22 Forgiveness for sins has, ever since the time of Moses, always required the shedding of blood. Therefore, since Christ by his death redeemed those who did not obey the first agreement, he puts into effect a new agreement by shedding his own blood

INTENT AND PARAGRAPH PATTERN

This unit is one *INFERENCE* which consists of two NUCLEI. It is all expository: there are no imperative verbs in this unit. Here the author continues his exposition of the superiority of Christ, specifically of his priesthood and of the sacrifice he offered.

BOUNDARIES AND COHERENCE

Coherence in this paragraph is provided by nine occurrences of the word αἷμα 'blood'.

PROMINENCE AND THEME

The theme is drawn from what are considered to be the most prominent parts of all the two paragraphs in this unit.

SUB-PARAGRAPH CLUSTER CONSTITUENT 9:11–14 (Expository Paragraph: Grounds of 9:11–22)

THEME: Christ being our Supreme Priest enabled us to have many good benefits. It was as though he went into that very holy place only once, taking his own blood with him.

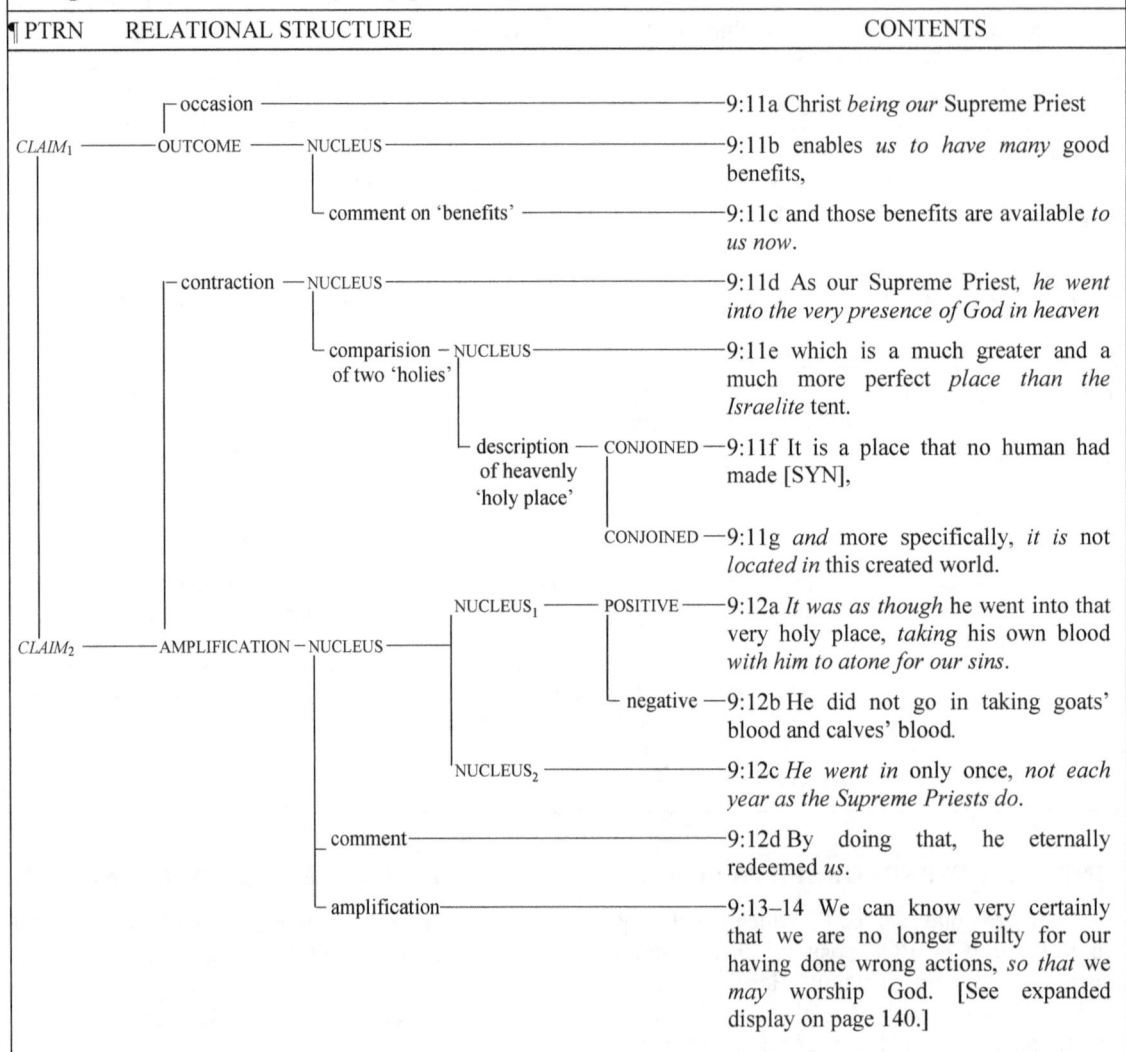

INTENT AND PARAGRAPH PATTERN

It is obvious that the 9:11–14 paragraph continues as another expository paragraph as the writer attempts to influence the understanding of his audience further regarding the Supreme Priestly ministry of Christ. The paragraph consists of two CLAIMS. The γάρ in v. 13 is taken as introducing an *amplification*, not as a *grounds* of the CLAIM made in v. 12. In effect the 11–14 paragraph functions as the *grounds* of the 15–22 paragraph.

NOTES

9:11–14 The Greek text connects this paragraph to the content of 9:1–10 in a way that shows that Jesus was properly a Supreme Priest and his sacrifice was better than all the rituals of the old agreement. The Greek connector δε may be translated as 'and, likewise' or as 'but, differently'. Thus, the display begins this paragraph with 'Christ as Supreme Priest, different from the Israelite priests…'

9:11a Christ *being our* Supreme Priest The clause Χριστὸς δὲ παραγενόμενος ἀρχιερεὺς 'Christ having come Supreme Priest' is figurative. The verb literally means 'having come'; most versions render it as 'appear', but the author was referring to Jesus' status, not to his movement. Another good alternative would be 'having become' (as in NLT).

9:11b enables *us to have many* good benefits The display clarifies with an active verb the relationship implied in the genitive expression ἀγαθῶν of 'the good (things)'. In some translations it may be necessary to specify that the good things are spiritual; and Miller is probably right in saying it primarily refers to the eternal redemption referred to at the end of v. 12.

9:11c and those benefits are available *to us now* The majority of commentators evidently follow a textual reading μελλόντων 'yet to come'. The text here follows the GNT reading of γενομένων 'which have come about', which is given a C "difficulty in deciding" rating. This reading has a greater variety of text type supporting it, and as Kistemaker says (p. 248), "Possibly a scribe copying 9:11 may have been influenced by the reading [τῶν μελλόντων ἀγαθῶν] in 10:1."

9:11d *he went into* In the GNT the verb does not occur until v. 12.

9:11e which is a much greater and a much more perfect *place than the Israelite* tent The phrase διὰ τῆς μείζονος καὶ τελειοτέρας σκηνῆς 'through the greater and more perfect tent' is a metaphor. Kistemaker (p. 248) notes that the words here have a parallel in 8:1–2 and especially in 9:24 where it says "he entered heaven itself, now to appear for us in God's presence" (NIV), and adds, "We ought not take the words went through literally in the sense that Christ passed through the tabernacle to another place." Barnes says "Christ passed through a more perfect tabernacle on his way to the mercy-seat in heaven," but such a literal interpretation has no justification elsewhere in Scripture.

The author indicated that he evaluated the place in heaven as much more desirable and perfect than the Tabernacle or Temple on earth.

9:11f no human had made The phrase οὐ χειροποιήτου 'not made-by-hand' is a synecdoche, meaning 'not made by humans'.

9:11g more specifically, *it is* not *located in* this created *world* The author was careful to indicate that Jesus did his ritual in heaven by adding τοῦτ' ἔστιν οὐ ταύτης τῆς κτίσεως 'specifically, not related to this creation'.

9:12a *It was as though* he went into that very holy place The text says εἰσῆλθεν εἰς τὰ ἅγια 'he entered into the holy (places)'. But there are two interpretations:

1. This is to be taken literally, that Christ took his blood into God's presence.
2. This is a metaphor: he is comparing Christ's blood flowing down with what the Israelite Supreme Priests did in their sanctuary. Since Jesus did not literally enter the holy place in the Sacred Tent, the rendering here makes clear that a comparison was intended; Attridge says (p. 248) "the image should not be pressed here, or through the rest of the chapter, to mean that Christ actually brought his blood into heaven." The full sense might be expressed as 'what Christ did when he shed his blood as a sacrifice was like what the Supreme Priests did when they entered into the Most holy Place'.

The display chooses the second interpretation, for two reasons:

It is supported by the majority of the commentators.

It is never stated elsewhere in the Scriptures that Christ took his blood into heaven.

If the first interpretation is chosen, all that the translator needs to do is omit the words 'it was as though'.

taking *his* own blood with *him* This clarifies the phrase διὰ δὲ τοῦ ἰδίου αἵματος 'but through his own blood'; The verb 'entered' requires supplying some verb such as 'taking' to make sense; (cf. NJB, TEV.)

to atone for our sins This supplies information that would have been very clear to the Jewish readers.

9:12b not...taking goats' blood and calves' blood The Greek text has οὐδὲ δι' αἵματος τράγων καὶ μόσχων 'not through blood of goats and calves'.

9:12c only once, *not each year as the Supreme Priests do* The point here is that the Supreme Priests were obligated to perform the ritual every year, whereas Christ made his sacrifice only once. See v. 7; also the comments by Davidson, Kistemaker, Hughes, and Lane.

9:12d By doing that, he eternally redeemed *us* As Miller says (p. 253), "The participle presents the result obtained by Christ's entry... into the holiest." The pronoun 'us' not only completes the case frame but specifies it is 'us believers' who are redeemed. TEV, LB, NCV, and CEV all supply 'us'.

EXPANSION OF THE AMPLIFICATION OF *CLAIM*₂ IN THE 9:11–14 DISPLAY

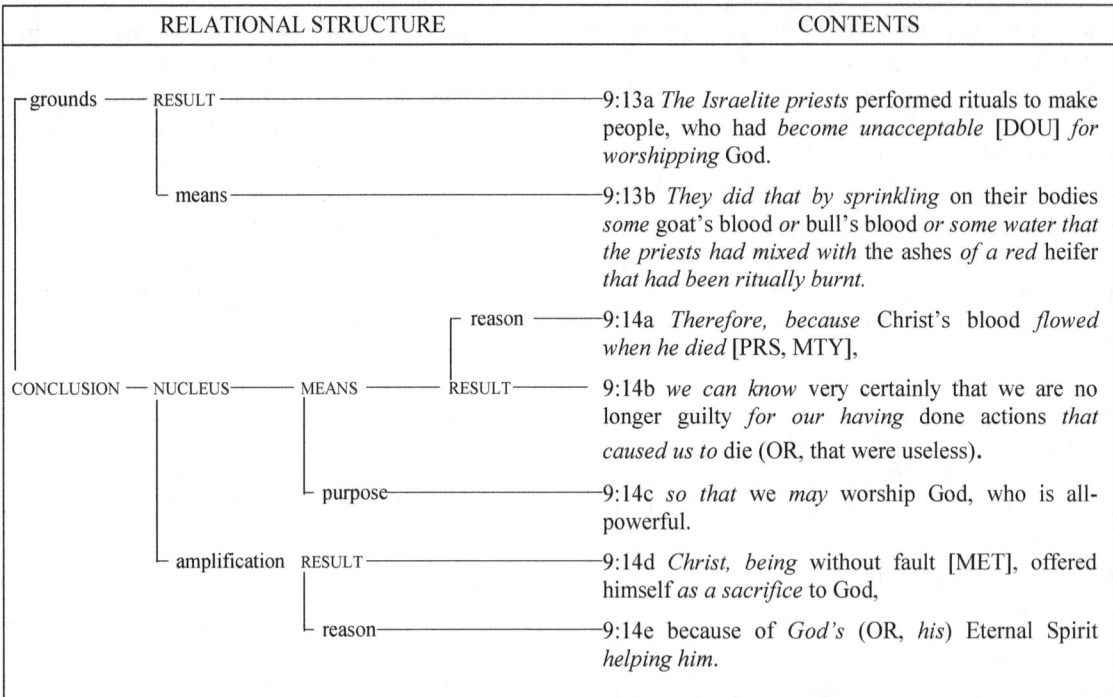

NOTES

9:13a *The Israelite priests* The display supplies the actors of the event 'sprinkling' and removes the personification of 'blood, ashes ... sanctifies'.

performed rituals to make people, who had *become unacceptable* [DOU] *for worshipping* God Commentators are quite agreed that the sense of 'sanctifies' here is that the ritually sprinkled person was then allowed to participate in worship rituals of the Tabernacle (and later the Temple). Bruce says (p. 202), the defiled person "was no longer religiously tabu but could take part once more in the prescribed ordinances of worship." The Greek expression ἁγιάζει πρὸς... καθαρότητα 'sanctify toward purity' is taken as a doublet.

This communicates with a verbal form the meaning of the noun καθαρότητα 'cleanness'.

who had *become unacceptable* [DOU] *for worshipping* The display clarifies τοὺς κεκοινωμένους 'defiled persons', by stating that the author was referring to ceremonially rejected people.

9:13b *by sprinkling* **on their bodies** *some goat's blood or bull's blood* The display clarifies that the priests used goat's blood for some rituals, bull's blood for others, and ash-water for others. It is important that a translation does not imply that a priest might have used all three liquids in the same ritual, or that he used all the blood of each goat or all of the blood of each bull or all of the ash-water from one heifer.

on their bodies The author referred to τῆς σαρκὸς 'flesh', which is a metonymy, a part for the whole person.

or some water that the priests had mixed with* the ashes *of a red* heifer *that had been ritually burnt There seems to be a difference between commentators as to how to interpret the process outlined briefly in Numbers 19:1–10. Kistemaker says (p. 250) "A red heifer in perfect condition...had to be slain and burned...Ashes from the burned heifer were put into a jar; fresh water was poured over them; and with hyssop dipped into the water, an unclean person was sprinkled on the third and seventh days." But Bruce (p. 202) is representative of nearly all other commentators in saying, "Anyone who contracted ceremonial defilement through touching or approaching a dead body was to be cleansed by being sprinkled with water containing some of the ashes of the heifer." Since the ashes of that heifer were preserved and used over and over, it seems more reasonable to interpret that the priests used water that had passed through the ashes. Otherwise, the ashes would soon be used up. At any rate, the author used 'ashes' as a metonymy to refer to the water that had wet them.

9:14a *because* **Christ's blood** *flowed when he died* The display makes clear, as usual, the relationship expressed by the genitive construction 'blood of Christ', referring to his death on the cross.

9:14b *we can know…***that we are no longer guilty** This is the sense of καθαριεῖ τὴν συνείδησιν ἡμῶν 'cleanse our conscience'; Brown says (p. 403), it "relieves his mind from the constraints, and terrors, and jealousies, and pollutions of guilt."

very certainly The author used an unusual idiom here to emphasize the contrast between the rituals of the Israelite priests and the unique ritual that Jesus did. BAGD (p. 489.2b) say the sense of πόσῳ μᾶλλον is "more (surely), more (certainly)."

we The rendering here follows the GNT ἡμῶν 'our' and not ὑμῶν 'your' as in KJV and RSV. Although the GNT rendering is given a C "difficulty in deciding" rating, Metzger points out (p. 599) that "the author uses the direct address only in the hortatory sections of the Epistle." In some languages it would be necessary to use 'our' anyway, lest readers assume the statement did not apply to the writer.

for our having **done actions** *that caused us to* **die (OR, that were useless)** Commentators are divided as to the sense of the phrase ἀπὸ νεκρῶν ἔργων 'from dead works'. Some say the sense is 'useless or ineffectual'; as Lenski (p. 300) puts it, "false legal observances and self-invented works whereby men would seek to stand before God;" see REV, NCV, TEV, GW. Others say the sense is "acts that lead to death" (Miller; p. 257; also Kistemaker, Lane). This later interpretation is the one chosen here; see NLT, NIV, CEV, REB. It seems impossible to determine which interpretation is correct, so both are given here.

9:14c God, who is all-powerful See note on 3:12b.

9:14d *Christ, being* **without fault [MET], offered himself** *as a sacrifice* **to God** The author used the clause ἑαυτὸν προσήνεγκεν ᾶτῷ θεῷ 'offered himself…to God' to refer back to his teaching in v. 12.

himself The pronoun ἑαυτὸν 'himself' is in an emphatic position, which emphasizes the contrast between Christ's blood and the blood of animals.

as a sacrifice to **God** He was without fault/sinless similar to the animals with no defects that were always offered to God. The clause ἑαυτὸν προσήνεγκεν ἄμωμον τῷ θεῷ 'offered himself unblemished to God' is a metaphor referring to the type of animals offered in sacrifice as prescribed in Leviticus. God required that the animals that people sacrificed must not have any defect. So Christ certainly had no defect, neither in his body or his soul or his actions. Thus, his sacrifice accomplished our forgiveness. CEV has "Christ was sinless, and he offered himself as a … sacrifice to God."

9:14e because of *God's* **(OR,** *his***) Eternal Spirit** *helping him* The phrase διὰ πνεύματος αἰωνίου 'through (the) eternal spirit' has been taken various ways (Lünemann says there are ten different interpretations). The interpretation taken here is that διά as elsewhere (e.g., 1:2, 2:10, 3:16, 7:9, 19, 25) introduces an abbreviated means proposition requiring a verb for its completion, and that πνεύμα αἰωνίου refers either to the Spirit of God or to Christ's eternal spirit. In support of the former is the possibility that the writer is thinking of the Servant of the Lord imagery from Isaiah. In proposing this, Morris says (p. 86–87), "Just as the prophet sees the Servant as accomplishing his entire ministry in the power of the divine Spirit, so we should see Christ as winning men's salvation by a mighty act performed in the power of the Spirit of God." Büchsel says "He offers Himself to God as a spotless sacrifice, and the eternal Spirit enables Him to do so." Others, noting that the Holy Spirit is nowhere else referred to in this way, think it refers to the divine nature of Christ. But one can argue as well that references to Christ's divine nature are scarce and certainly never referred to by this phrase. A few other commentators think it refers to Christ's sacrifice as being a spiritual and eternal one. But once again this would seem a very strange expression to use with that meaning, and it doesn't make much sense with διά 'through'.

BOUNDARIES AND COHERENCE

Lexical coherence within the 9:11–14 paragraph is seen primarily in four occurrences of αἷμα 'blood'. The new paragraph at v. 15 is introduced by καὶ διὰ τοῦτο 'and therefore' followed by a discussion of the two agreements, a paragraph which states the CLAIM for which 9:11–14 is the *justification*.

PROMINENCE AND THEME

The theme for the 9:11–14 paragraph is taken from the outcome proposition of $CLAIM_1$ and the naturally prominent *means* and *result* propositions of the conclusion of CLAIM₂ in v. 12. Within the CLAIM₂ the *amplification* is deemed more prominent than the *contraction* because of the reference to blood, which is so focal in the whole context.

SUB-PARAGRAPH CLUSTER CONSTITUENT 9:15–22 (Expository Paragraph: Conclusion of 9:11–22)

THEME: Forgiveness for sins has, ever since the time of Moses, always required the shedding of blood. Therefore, since Christ by his death redeemed those who did not obey the first agreement, he puts into effect a new agreement by shedding his own blood.

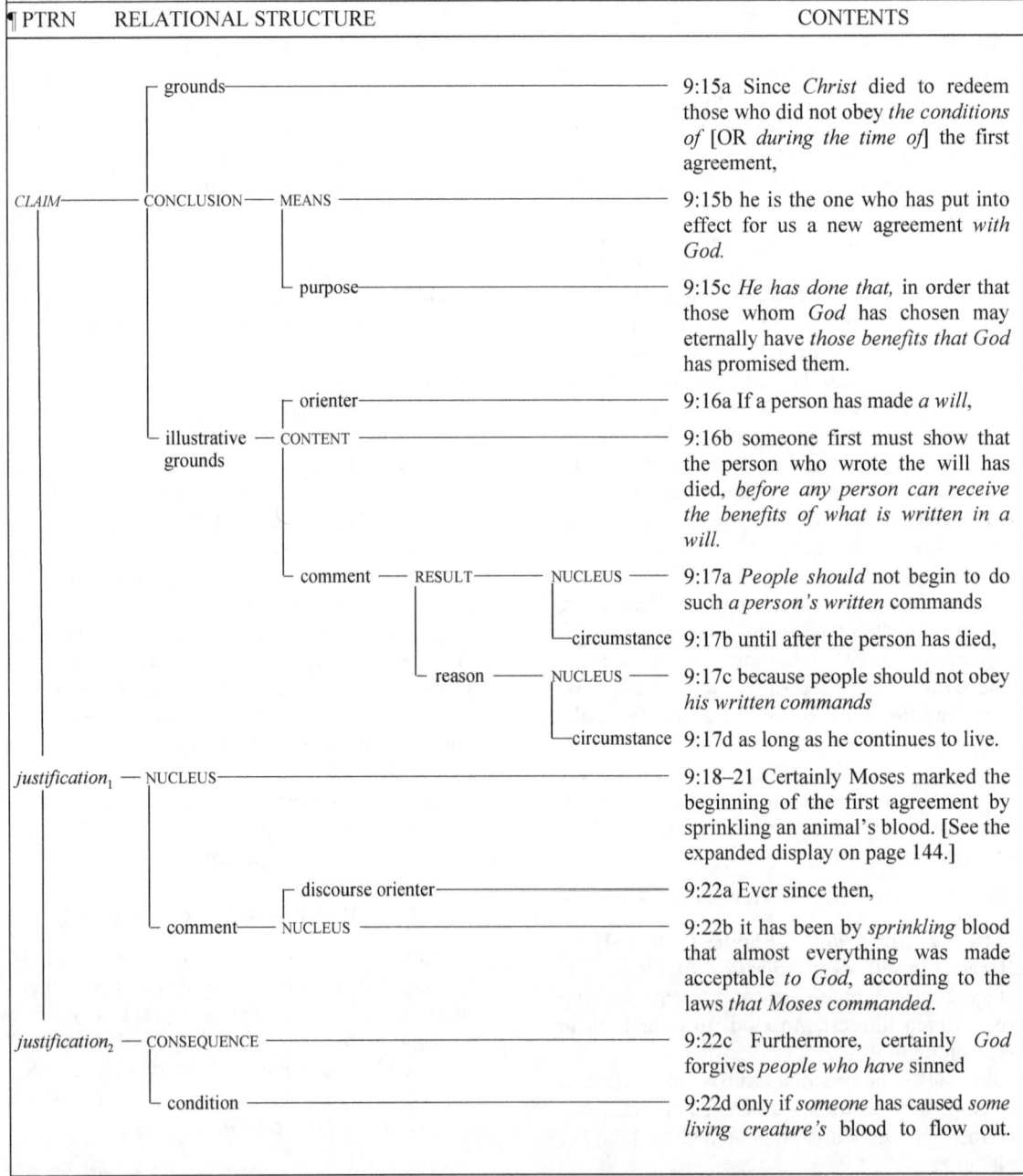

INTENT AND PARAGRAPH PATTERN

The author continues with another expository paragraph to influence his audience's ideas about the superiority of Christ. The paragraph has one CLAIM about Christ establishing a new agreement and two *justifications*.

NOTES

9:15a Since *Christ* died to redeem those who did not obey The GNT has only Καὶ διὰ τοῦτο 'and for this (reason)', with which the author referred back to his CLAIM in 9:12, that Christ had taken his blood into the holy place.

died The genitive absolute phrase θανάτου γενομένου 'a death having occurred' is referring in this context not only to Christ's death but his death as the substitute for sinful people. Montefiore says "A covenant requires a blood sacrifice; and such was Jesus' death."

to redeem The author related his reference to Jesus' death to the expected end/purpose of the process with ὅπως 'so that'.

those who did not obey *the conditions of* [OR *during the time of*] the first agreement There is a problem as to the meaning of the phrase ἐπὶ τῇ πρώτῃ διαθήκῃ 'under the first agreement'. Some agree with Westcott who says (p. 264) "Ἐπί expresses the conditions, the accompanying circumstances, under which anything takes place." Miller (p. 258) represents quite a few others in saying "ἐπί with the dative here denotes *time*." Both make good sense (and there is little semantic difference between them).

9:15b he is the one who has put into effect for us a new agreement *with God* As noted previously (8:6), the concept of μεσίτης 'mediator' requires that we indicate for whom he put into effect and with whom.

9:15c *He has done that* These words are supplied to begin a new sentence which relates Jesus' purpose for beginning the new agreement.

in order that those whom *God* has chosen The display supplies the agent of the action, which is given here as 'chosen' (cf. CEV) because 'called' connotes a vocal action. Some versions have 'invited' but that is avoided because people can refuse an invitation.

eternally The author wrote τῆς αἰωνίου κληρονομίας 'the eternal inheritance', but 'eternal' relates to duration of time and thus is best related to the duration of the believers' possessing the benefits.

***those benefits that God* has promised them** The word κληρονομία 'inheritance' is used in an extended sense (i.e., as a dead metaphor); to inherit is simply to eventually receive those things which have been promised. The rendering here is very similar to that of NCV, TEV, and NLT.

9:16a If a person has made *a will* The γάρ here introduces an amplification of the subject of 'agreement' mentioned in 15a–b. The majority of commentators recognize that the word διαθήκη covers two English words with quite different meanings, agreement and will. The first of these (the sense in v. 15 and implied in v. 18) is basically an agreement between two parties with terms each agrees to fulfill. The second (the sense in vv. 16–17) is an agreement by one individual concerning another, which does not go into effect until the first individual dies.

9:16b someone first must show that the person who wrote the will has died The author specified the legal requirement with θάνατον ἀνάγκη φέρεσθαι τοῦ διαθεμένου 'death, it is necessary that it happen to the writer of the will'. The display has translated this by a clause that describes the normal steps of executing a will.

before any person can receive the benefits of what is written in a will The author focused on a certain requirement very important concerning wills with ὅπου …διαθήκη 'in an occurrence of a will'.

9:17a *People should* not begin to do such *a person's written* commands The Greek has only διαθήκη γὰρ ἐπὶ νεκροῖς βεβαία 'an agreement over the dead is firm'. The display attempts to show clearly the conditions for executing a person's will.

9:17b until after the person has died This is the sense of the very brief phrase ἐπὶ νεκροῖς 'over dead (persons)', which is plural in the Greek so as to refer generically. TEV's rendering is very similar: "it goes into effect only after his death" (cf. also NEB, LB/NLT, NCV).

9:17c because people should not obey *his written commands* The display translates the personification of ἐπεὶ μήποτε ἰσχύει 'certainly not it has ability' as an active statement of the reason.

9:17d as long as he continues to live A durative time clause states the circumstance of ὅτε ζῇ ὁ διαθέμενος 'when is living the writer of the will'.

9:18–21 The notes for these verses follow the expansion on page 144.

9:22a Ever since then The commentaries and translations all interpret that the participle καθαρίζεται 'are ritually cleansed' as present tense, implying that the author shifted focus to the later dedications made by many priests down through the ages. He has stopped referring to Moses doing the first rituals.

The author made this comment in order to generalize about the rituals of purifying things by sprinkling blood on them.

9:22b it has been by *sprinkling* blood The forefronting of the phrase σχεδὸν ἐν αἵματι πάντα 'by blood almost everything' gives it an emphasis which is also maintained in the display by forefronting. The word 'sprinkling' is implied and made specific in LB and CEV. The word 'ritually' is also implied; BAGD (p. 387.2c) say in this reference "ceremonial and moral purification merge." Louw and Nida (53.28) say the sense of καθαρίζω here is "make them ritually acceptable" which might be translated 'made acceptable to God/in God's sight'.

almost everything Commentators are divided as to whether 'almost' modifies 'everything' or the whole clause, giving the sense "one may almost say that according to the law all things" (Lünemann). The former interpretation requires an ellipsis of 'one may say' to be understood and it then sheds doubt as to whether the phrase that follows (22b–c) is to be understood absolutely or as being only partially true. Furthermore, 'one may almost say' seems to clash with the type of forthright statements the author makes in this epistle. Finally, as several commentators point out, "there were exceptions to the rule that atonement for sins needed an animal sacrifice" (Moffatt, p. 130) such as those mentioned in Leviticus 15:10 and Numbers 31:22ff. Nearly all modern versions and the great majority of commentators take 'almost' as modifying 'everything'.

the laws *that Moses commanded* In the New Testament the words 'the law' always have a plural sense; i.e., they refer to the Mosaic laws.

9:22c certainly God forgives *people who have sinned* As Kistemaker (p. 261) notes regarding ἄφεσις, "this noun includes the concept sins. It refers to God's forgiveness of sins."

9:22d only *if someone* has caused *some living creature's* blood to flow out The GNT has χωρὶς αἱματεκχυσίας οὐ γίνεται ἄφεσις 'separately from (someone) pouring blood there can be no forgiveness'. The concepts 'separately' and the negation together communicate an emphatic positive statement. A translation of the double negative might be misleading in some languages. The display has inverted the order of the clauses in order to present the best emphatic statement.

The display makes clear that blood is in focus; NCV tries to indicate this by "blood to show death." The double negative is maintained here using a *condition*-CONSEQUENCE pair of propositions; alternatively one could eliminate the double negative by 'sins can be forgiven only if blood of some sacrifice is poured out'.

BOUNDARIES AND COHERENCE

Cohesion in this paragraph is provided by four occurrences of διαθήκη 'agreement' and two occurrences of ῥαντίζω 'sprinkle'

PROMINENCE AND THEME

The theme is drawn from the *grounds* and CONCLUSION propositions of the CLAIM, and brief condensations of the two *justifications*.

EXPANSION OF NUCLEUS OF *JUSTIFICATION*₁ IN THE 9:15–22 DISPLAY

RELATIONAL STRUCTURE	CONTENTS
NUCLEUS	9:18 And so, the first agreement was confirmed only [LIT] *by having some animal's* blood *being sprinkled*.
amplification NUCLEUS₁	9:19-20 Then Moses told them, "*Your accepting the sprinkling of* this blood *means that you promise to obey* the agreement that God commanded you." [See the expanded display on page 145.]
NUCLEUS₂	9:21a Likewise, he sprinkled the tent with the mixture in the same way,
NUCLEUS₃	9:21b and *he sprinkled* everything that the priests would use in performing *the new* rituals.
	9:22 [See main display on page 142.]

NOTES

9:18 the first agreement was confirmed The display uses 'confirmed' to express the Greek ἐγκεκαίνισται 'began a ritual'. An alternative would be 'ratified'.

only The translation in the display eliminates the double negative οὐδὲ...χωρίς 'not without'. Other versions which do this are TEV, JB, NLT.

only [LIT] *by having some animal's blood being sprinkled* The display makes clear the significance that the author meant by αἷμα 'blood'.

9:21b everything that the priests would use in performing *the new* **rituals** The author indicated that Moses sprinkled every tool, every container and every piece of furniture.

EXPANSION OF NUCLEUS₁ OF THE AMPLIFICATION IN THE 9:18–21 DISPLAY

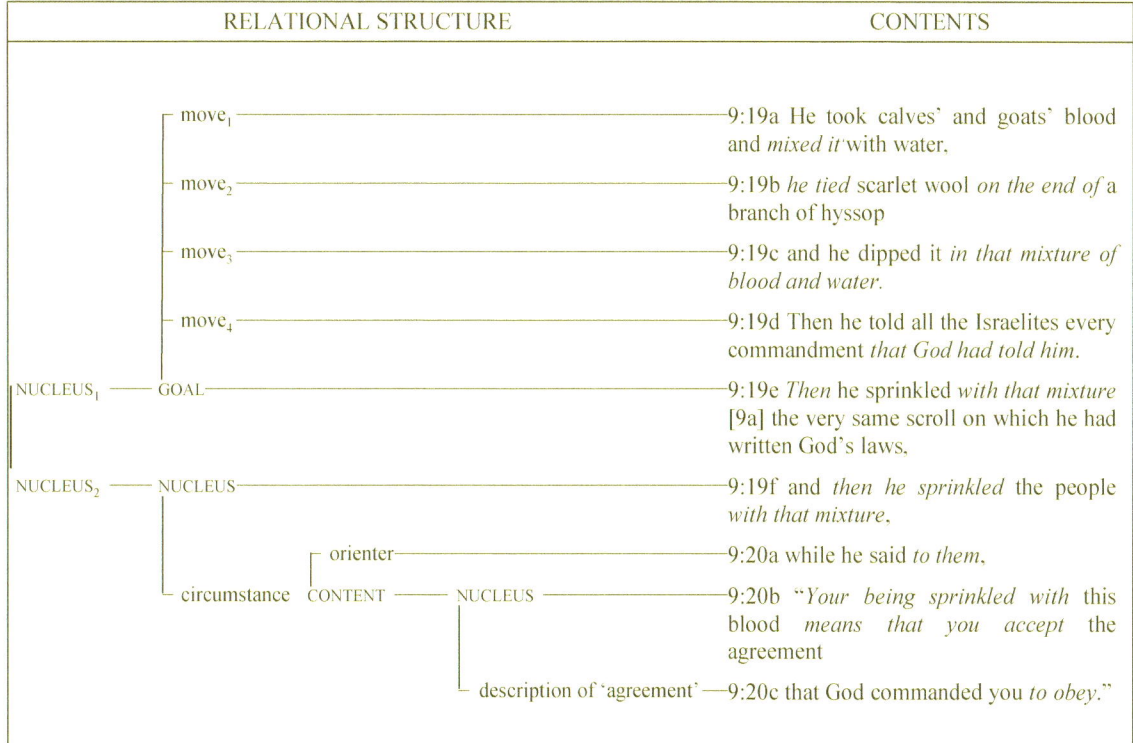

NOTES

9:19a The γάρ here is more an "explanation of the assertion in the last verse" (Barnes) than the grounds for it (Miller). Thus, 9:19–20 are an amplification of 9:18.

He took calves' and goats' blood There is a textual problem as to whether the words καὶ τῶν τράγων 'and of goats' should be in the text or not. It is omitted in TEV, NEB, NIV, and REB. It is included in the GNT with a C "difficulty in deciding" rating. Although it is possible that copyists might have expanded the shorter expression to make it more like v. 12, it is more likely that it was accidentally omitted, or deliberately omitted by a copyist "to make what is said here conform to what is read in Exodus 24:5" (Hughes).

9:19b *he tied* **scarlet wool** *on the end of* **a branch of hyssop** The display makes clear the next step in the process for sprinkling the blood.

9:19c and he dipped it *in that mixture of blood and water* This is the next step of the process. The GNT has only μετὰ ὕδατος καὶ ἐργίου κοκκίνου καὶ ὑσσώπου 'with water and scarlet wool and hyssop'. The display supplies the culturally understood information of how these concepts are related to each other. NCV is not quite so clear with "Then he used red wool and a branch of a hyssop plant to sprinkle..." (also CEV, NLT).

9:19d Israelites This specifies who is meant by παντὶ τῷ λαῷ 'to all the people'.

9:19e he sprinkled *with that mixture* [9a] the very same scroll on which he had written God's laws The word βιβλίον means 'scroll' not book as we know it today, and the display specifies what the original audience would have known as to its contents.

the very same scroll The author inserted an identifying Greek idiom αὐτό τε 'itself' to indicate that Moses sprinkled the exact scroll on which he had written the commandments.

9:20b-c *Your being sprinkled with* this blood *means that you accept* the agreement that God commanded you *to obey* The display makes clear that Moses was indicating to the people that they were promising to obey the laws written in the agreement. This Scripture citation is from Exodus 24:8.

The display spells out the genitive phrase 'blood of the agreement'. NLT has "confirms." TEV has "which seals;" Brown also suggests the verb 'confirms' and Lane suggests 'ratifies'.

The verb 'obey' or its equivalent is implied and stated in TEV, NCV, and NIV.

BOUNDARIES AND COHERENCE

Lexical coherence within the 9:15–22 paragraph is seen in five occurrences of διαθήκη 'agreement/will' and one of the cognate verb διατίθημι 'make a will', five occurrences of αἷμα 'blood' and one of the cognate noun αἱματεκχυσία 'pouring of blood', and two occurrences of θάνατος 'death' and one of νεκρός 'dead (body)'.

A new paragraph at 9:23 is indicated by use of the conjunction οὖν 'therefore' and a switch from a discussion of the activities of the Supreme Priest to a discussion of the sacrifice of Christ. Coherence within this paragraph is provided by three occurrences of διαθήκης 'agreement' and six occurrences of αἷμα 'blood'.

PROMINENCE AND THEME

The theme of the 9:15–22 paragraph consists of the naturally prominent proposition of the CLAIM in 15b, but it also includes bits of the important *justifications* in 21–22.

SECTION CONSTITUENT 9:23–28 (Expository Paragraph: Basis$_2$ of 5:1—9:28)

THEME: Since those who would enter heaven had to be consecrated by better sacrifices than those of the old agreement, Christ has appeared once to cause people to be no longer guilty for sin.

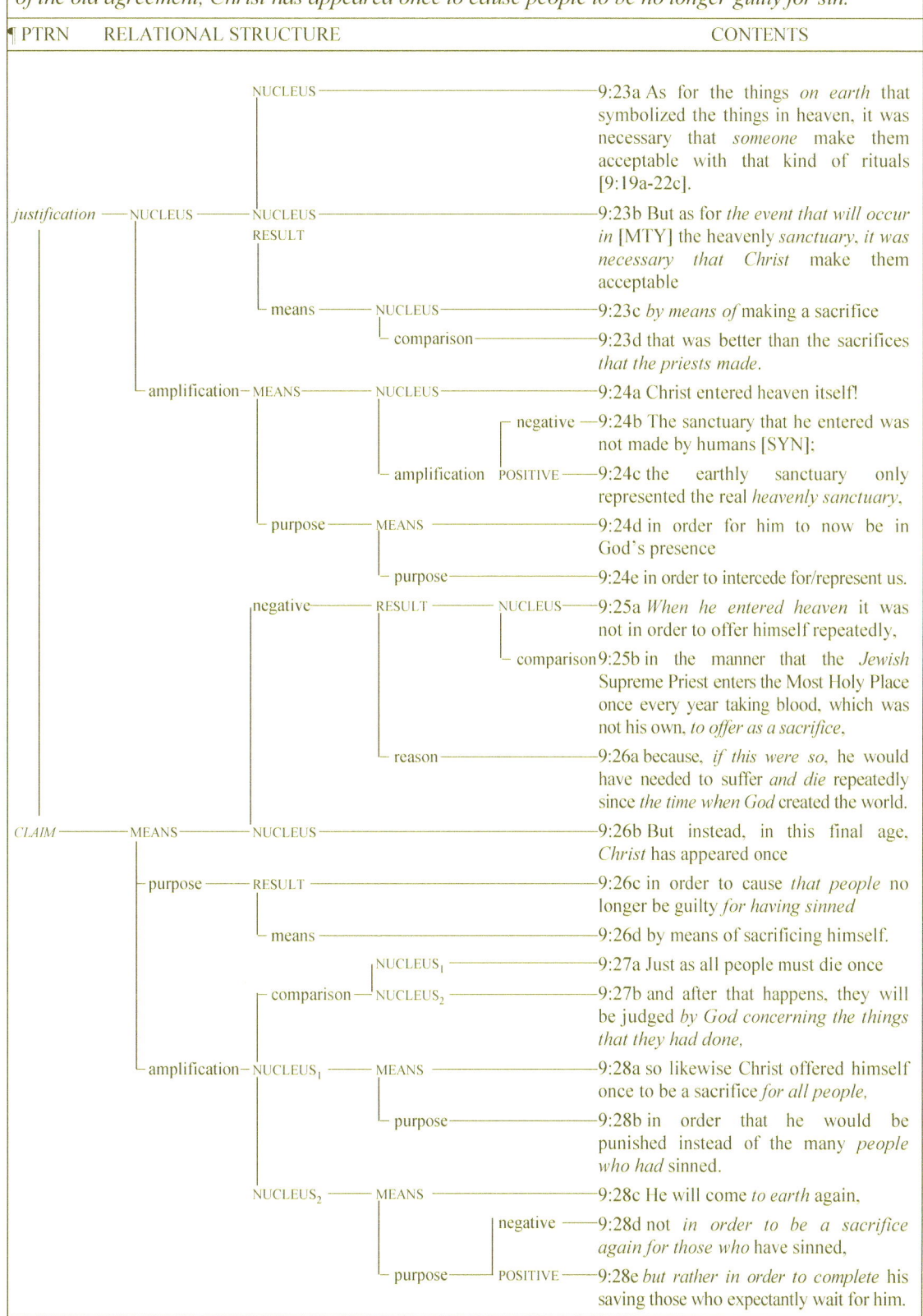

INTENT AND PARAGRAPH PATTERN

The 9:23–28 paragraph continues in a long chain of expository units in which the writer is attempting to influence his audience's ideas about the superiority of the ministry of Christ. It consists of one *justification* in vv. 23–24 followed by a CLAIM in vv. 25–28.

NOTES

9:23a As for the things *on earth* that symbolized the things in heaven The author introduces the first clause of the μὲν...δὲ construction with τὰ μὲν ὑποδείγματα τῶν ἐν τοῖς οὐρανοῖς 'in regard to the things that represent the things in the heavens', He compared the purifying of the things in the Tabernacle and Temple with the purifying of Jesus' people in order that they might enter heaven.

the things *on earth* that symbolized The word ὑπόδειγμα means 'copy, imitation' (BAGD p. 844.2); it was rendered as 'model' in 8:5. But since it can be argued that the rituals of the earthly priests occurred before Christ's heavenly ministry began, 'copies' is not a very appropriate word here.

the things in heaven Commentators do not discuss what is meant by the phrase τῶν ἐν τοῖς οὐρανοῖς 'of the (things) in the heavens'. Apparently, the author wanted the audience to remember the sentence that he wrote in 8:5, that God had told Moses to carefully build the Tabernacle according to the visions that Moses had seen.

with that kind of rituals This translates τούτοις 'with these', a back-reference to the rituals that the author described in 9:12a–22c.

9:23b But as for *the event that will occur in* [MTY] the heavenly *sanctuary* Here the author competed μὲν...δὲ construction with αὐτὰ δὲ τὰ ἐπουράνια κρείττοσιν θυσίαις παρ ἀ ταύτας 'as for themselves of the heavenlies with better sacrifices than these'. The word ἐπουράνια is considered a metonymy, the place standing for the events that will occur there. The author indicated that it was also necessary to purify the followers of Jesus.

***the event that will occur* in [MTY] the *heavenly* sanctuary** The author related the previous statement to this with αὐτὰ δὲ 'themselves also'. The word αὐτὰ refers to the people that Christ intended to bring into the heavenly sanctuary.

***Christ* make them acceptable** There is considerable difference of opinion by commentators as to the sense of the phrase τὰ ἐπουράνια 'the heavenly things'. A few have suggested it be taken literally, but as Kistemaker says (p.262), "The heavenly sanctuary is not man-made and therefore untainted by sin. It does not need to be cleansed." Other commentators say the phrase refers to a sphere of worship, not a locality and still others that it means heaven is now made accessible to sinners by the sacrifice of Christ. But these explanations all have problems in showing how the phrase relates to the elided verb 'cleansed'. Such solutions are not nearly as reasonable as assuming a metonymy here: heaven standing for the people who would eventually enter it.

The Greek verb here is passive; the display supplies 'Christ' as the agent of the event.

9:24b The sanctuary that he entered was not made The display puts the negative with the verb with which it belongs (cf. RSV, JB, NEB).

not made by humans The word χειροποίητα 'made by hand' is a synecdoche, the body part standing for the skills of those humans.

9:24c only represented the real *heavenly sanctuary* The word ἀντίτυπα means 'antitype'. But, the display uses 'represented' because 'antitype' is a very difficult concept to express in most languages. The word 'only' is implied by contrast and expressed in most versions.

9:24d in order for him to now be in God's presence The Greek νῦν ἐμφανισθῆναι τῷ προσώπῳ τοῦ θεοῦ 'now to appear before the face of God' is a restatement of Jesus entering heaven, communicating his purpose for entering.

9:24e in order to intercede for/represent us Commentators suggest both of these verbs as possibilities to express the meaning of ὑπὲρ ἡμῶν 'on our behalf'.

9:25a *When he entered heaven* These words are repeated from 24a (cf. NIV, TEV, NLT). There is no main verb here in Greek, only a negative purpose clause, but semantically the negative does indeed go with the purpose clause, not with 'enter'.

not in order to offer himself repeatedly The Greek οὐδ'... πολλάκις προσφέρῃ ἑαυτόν 'not often he might offer himself' refutes the concept that people might suppose that Jesus needed to repeat his ritual.

9:25b the Most Holy Place See discussion of ἅγια in v. 12a.

which was not his own The GNT has ἀλλότριος which means 'belonging to another' but the alternate gloss (BAGD p. 40.1) "not one's own" fits much better here.

to offer as a sacrifice See comment on v. 12b.

9:26a *if this were so* This clarifies the reason no one should suppose that Jesus repeated his ritual.

he would have needed to suffer *and die* repeatedly The verb παθεῖν means 'suffer', but in this context it is talking about Jesus' sacrificial death. NLT has "die again and again" and JBP has "suffer death."

since *the time when God* created the world The Greek ἀπὸ καταβολῆς κόσμου 'since the founding of the world' is displayed in an active clause.

9:26b But instead BAGD (p. 546:2b) makes clear that νυνί here is "introducing a real situation after an unreal conditional clause or sentence" and does not have the temporal sense of 'now'.

in this final age It seems best to follow Westcott who says (p. 275) the phrase ἐπὶ συντελείᾳ τῶν αἰώνων 'upon completion of the ages' "marks a point of termination of a series (so to speak) of preparatory ages."

once The sense of ἅπαξ is, as Barnes says, "once in the sense that it is not to be repeated again."

9:26c to cause *that people* no longer be guilty *for having sinned* The phrase εἰς ἀθέτησιν τῆσ ἁμαρτίας means 'unto removal of sin'; but in what sense is sin removed? Brown (p. 428) makes it very clear: "'Sin' here plainly means guilt."

9:27a all people The display makes clear that ἄνθρωποι 'men' intends people of both sexes (cf. TEV's "everyone" and CEV's "we").

9:27b judged *by God concerning the things that they had done* The display specifies the agent and the sphere of the judgment.

9:28b in order that he would be punished instead of the many *people who had* sinned Commentators do not agree as to the meaning of the phrase εἰς τὸ πολλῶν ἀνενεγκεῖν ἁμαρτίας 'unto the bearing of the sins of many'. The division centers on whether the verb means 'to take away' (the minority view) or 'to bear' (the majority view). Both those interpretations seem inaccurate. BAGD (p. 63.3) suggests the clear sense of the verb ἀναφέρω is 'take upon oneself'. Thus, the meaning of 'to take upon oneself another's sin' is to allow oneself to be punished instead of some other person.

9:28c He will come *to earth* again The verb is ὀφθήσεται 'he will appear', but since the reference is to his second coming, the verb 'come' is used here (as in NCV, CEV, NLT).

9:28d not *in order to be a sacrifice again for those who* have sinned The phrase χωρὶς ἁματρίας means literally 'without sin' but commentators are agreed that the sense is "not to deal with sin" (TEV) or, as Barnes puts it more clearly, "he will not make himself a sin offering."

9:28e *rather in order to complete* his saving The GNT has εἰς σωτηρίαν 'unto salvation', but what does this mean if, as other Scripture indicates, Christ has already removed our guilt by his sacrificial death? We Christians affirm that Christ began our salvation by his sacrifice, but our salvation will be complete only when we arrive in heaven as God's children. As Attridge notes (p. 266), "While 'salvation' has been inaugurated by the activity of Christ, it has yet to be consummated;" see also Hughes, Morris, Brown, and Westcott.

BOUNDARIES AND COHERENCE

Lexical coherence within the 9:23–28 paragraph is seen in two occurrences of οὐρανός 'heaven' and one of the cognate word ἐπουράνιος 'heavenly', two of εἰσέρχομαι 'enter', three of ἁμαρτία 'sin', and two of θυσίας 'sacrifice'. A new paragraph at 10:1 is marked by the forefronted phrase ὁ νόμος 'the law' and a discussion of how the Mosaic law was unable to make perfect those who continually made the sacrifices stipulated in the law.

PROMINENCE AND THEME

The theme for the 9:23–28 paragraph is taken from the naturally prominent nucleus of the *justification* and the three naturally prominent propositions of the CLAIM.

PART CONSTITUENT 10:1–39 (Section: Appeal₄ of 1:4—12:29)

THEME: Since Christ offered one sacrifice which is eternally adequate, and since there is no other sacrifice to appease God but only judgment facing us, let us not become discouraged when we are persecuted. Let us come to God sincerely, keep firmly professing the truth, incite one another to love and good deeds, and encourage each other.

MACROSTRUCTURE	CONTENTS
APPEAL₁	10:1–25 Since Christ offered one sacrifice which is eternally adequate, and since Christ is our great Supreme Priest, let us come to God sincerely, keep firmly professing the truth, incite one another to love and good deeds, and encourage each other.
APPEAL₂	10:26–39 Since there is no sacrifice to appease God if we keep sinning, but only judgment facing us, let us not become discouraged when we are persecuted.

INTENT AND MACROSTRUCTURE PATTERN

This is a hortatory unit; it ends with imperatives in vv. 32 and 35, and a mitigated exhortation in v. 36. The unit consists of two *APPEALS*.

BOUNDARIES AND COHERENCE

A new unit at 11:1 is clearly shown by the beginning of a long list of individuals who exhibited faith. Cohesion in this paragraph is seen in four occurrences of θυσία 'sacrifice' and four occurrences of the noun προσφορά 'offering' and cognate words.

PROMINENCE AND THEME

The theme for this unit is drawn from condensations of the most naturally prominent propositions in the two *APPEALS*.

SECTION CONSTITUENT 10:1–25 (Sub-Section: Appeal₁ of 10:1–39)

THEME: Since Christ offered one sacrifice which is eternally adequate, and since Christ is our great Supreme Priest, let us come to God sincerely, keep firmly professing the truth, incite one another to love and good deeds, and encourage each other.

MACROSTRUCTURE	CONTENTS
basis	10:1–18 In fulfillment of the Scriptures which state that Christ indicated these sacrifices were inadequate and that he had come to do what was truly needed, God abolished the first way of atonement to establish the second way, that of Christ offering his body as a sacrifice.
MITIGATED APPEAL	10:19–25 Since we can confidently enter God's presence and since Christ is our great Supreme Priest, let us come to God sincerely, keep firmly professing the truth, incite one another to love and good deeds, and encourage each other.

INTENT AND PARAGRAPH PATTERN

This unit is a hortatory one, being signaled as such by a series of 1st person plural subjunctive verbs, 'let us approach', 'let us hold fast', 'let us consider', and two participles which have hortatory force. The sub-section consists of one *basis* and a final mitigated *APPEAL* (it is considered mitigated because the appeals are expressed as subjunctives, not imperatives).

BOUNDARIES AND COHERENCE

A new unit at 10:26 is indicated by a switch from a set of exhortations to an expository unit. Coherence is given by three occurrences of νόμος 'law', five occurrences of ἁμαρτία 'sin', and seven occurrences of θυσία 'sacrifice.'

PROMINENCE AND THEME

The theme is taken from the second CONCLUSION of the *basis*, and the mitigated APPEAL. The material in the first CONCLUSION of the *basis* is not considered to be as thematic as that in the second CONCLUSION.

SUB-SECTION CONSTITUENT 10:1–18 (Paragraph Cluster: basis of 10:1–25)

THEME: In fulfillment of the Scripture, God abolished the first way of atonement to establish the second way, that of Christ offering his body as a sacrifice.	
MACROSTRUCTURE	CONTENTS
grounds	10:1–4 These yearly sacrifices can never make those who offer them perfect, otherwise they would have ceased. Instead they remind people that their guilt remains.
CONCLUSION₁	10:5–10 In fulfillment of the Scriptures which state that Christ indicated these sacrifices were inadequate and that he had come to do what was truly needed, God abolished the first way of atonement to establish the second way, that of Christ offering his body as a sacrifice.
CONCLUSION₂	10:11–18 Christ offered one sacrifice, and now is ruling with God until all his enemies are completely subdued. We know his sacrifice is eternally adequate since we, by trusting in that sacrifice, are eternally made perfect, and since the Scriptures support this claim.

INTENT AND PARAGRAPH PATTERN

This unit is an expository one, being signaled as such by indicative verbs. The sub-section consists of one *grounds* and two CONCLUSIONS. The author's purpose is to compare and contrast the sacrifices made under the old agreement with the sacrifice made by Christ.

BOUNDARIES AND COHERENCE

A new unit at 10:19 is indicated by a switch from this exposition to a hortatory unit. Coherence is given by three occurrences of νόμος 'law', two occurrences of ἁμαρτία 'sin', and two occurrences of θυσία 'sacrifice.'

PROMINENCE AND THEME

The theme is taken from the two CONCLUSIONS.

PARAGRAPH CLUSTER CONSTITUENT 10:1–4 (Expository Paragraph: Grounds of 10:1–18)

THEME: These yearly sacrifices can never make those who offer them perfect, otherwise they would have ceased. Instead they remind people that their guilt remains.

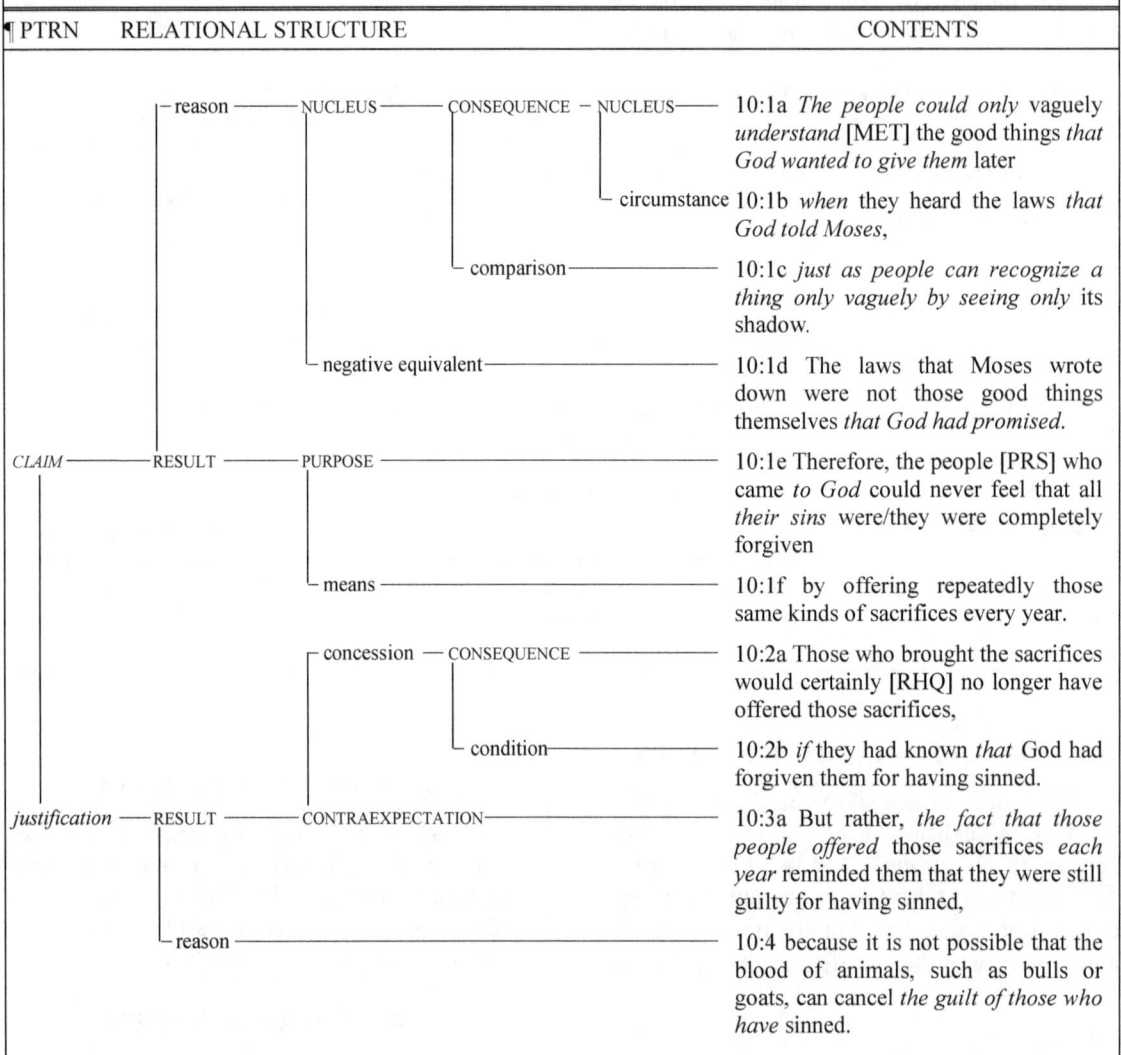

INTENT AND PARAGRAPH PATTERN

This paragraph is an expository one, consisting of one CLAIM in v. 1 that the Jews could never be assured that their sins were really forgiven, and one *justification* in vv. 2–4 that their yearly sacrifices just reminded them that their guilt still remained. In effect, this paragraph serves as the *grounds* for the first CONCLUSION in 10:5–10.

NOTES

10:1a The γάρ here introduces a further discussion of the Mosaic law.

The people could only vaguely understand** [MET] **the good things that God wanted to give them later The GNT wording, Σκιὰν ἔχων ὁ νόμος 'the law having a shadow' is clearly expressing a metaphor. But what is the point of comparison between the Mosaic law and a shadow? Barnes says the word 'shadow' "refers to a rough outline," Hewitt suggests "a shadowy outline," Brown (p. 433) says "a rude sketch," Miller (p. 277) suggests "a dim outline," Kistemaker (p. 272) "dim representation," NCV has "an unclear picture." Stated non-figuratively, the focus is on vagueness of the cognitive process, not the vagueness of God's communication.

10:1b *when* they heard This continues the reference to 'vagueness.' It would seem that even the experts in the laws did not understand the good things that God wanted to give them.

the laws *that God told Moses* As usual, the display tries to make clear what laws are being referred to, and it follows CEV. An alternative would be 'the laws God gave Moses', or as in TEV, "the Jewish Law."

10:1d The laws that Moses wrote down were not those good things themselves *that God had promised* The GNT has οὐκ αὐτὴν τὴν εἰκόνα τῶν πραγμάτων 'not the image itself of the matters'. The word 'image', in plain words, means 'the thing that the shadow is a shadow of', which here is simply the 'good things that God had promised' referred to in v. 1a. The words 'God had promised' also further define what the writer meant by 'good things'; NLT has "good things Christ would do for us."

10:1e the people [PRS] who came *to God* Since the Greek word μελλόντων 'coming' is a motion verb, in some languages it may be necessary to include the concept 'to the sacred place' (cf. NIV "to worship"). The word 'God' is supplied to complete the case frame.

could never feel that all their *sins* were/they were completely forgiven The subject of 'is able to make perfect' in the Greek is 'law' which is a personification. The display replaces this with passive construction 'could never feel that they were forgiven' with 'people' as the subject. For languages with no passives it may be necessary to say something like 'people can never become all that God intended them to be' (see note on 5:9a).

10:1f by offering repeatedly those same kinds of sacrifices every year The Greek phrase κατ' ἐνιαυτὸν ταῖς αὐταῖς θυσίαις ἃς προσφέρουσιν εἰς τὸ διηνεκὲς 'year by year with the same ritual sacrifices they offer in perpetuity' emphasize the Supreme Priests doing the ritual on the Day of Atonement each year.

10:2a would certainly [RHQ] no longer have offered those sacrifices The rendering here changes the rhetorical question into an emphatic statement. It is handled similarly in several versions (cf. NEB's "would surely have ceased").

10:2b *if* they had known *that* God had forgiven them for having sinned The Greek clause ἔχειν ἔτι συνείδησιν ἁμαρτιῶν 'still to have a consciousness of sins' is referring to the guilt of sin. It could be considered a metonymy, the cause standing for the effect (cf. NLT "their feelings of guilt would have disappeared").

The verb κεκαθαρισμένους 'having been cleansed' is a dead metaphor, the removal of guilt being compared with the removal of filth by washing. CEV has "have their sins washed away."

10:3a But rather, *the fact that those people offered* those sacrifices *each year* reminded them that they were still guilty for having sinned The wording here spells out the ellipsis expressed in the words ἐν αὐταῖς 'in them'. To avoid the awkward 'the fact that' construction it may be necessary in some cases to say 'because the people must offer those sacrifices every year, they remember…'

The word 'sin' in the phrase ἀνάμνησις ἁμαρτιῶν 'a remembrance of sins' is again standing for the guilt of sin (also in v. 4). The context is not talking about reminding people of specific sins, as TEV's "remind people of their sins" would seem to suggest. Barnes' comment, "they…were therefore constantly reminded of their guilt" is excellent.

10:4 because it is not possible that the blood of animals, such as bulls or goats The words 'animals, such as…' are included because other creatures such as sheep and doves were often sacrificed; 'bulls and goats' is a synecdoche, two kinds of sacrifices representing all the kinds of sacrifices. An alternative might be something like 'no blood of creatures'.

can cancel *the guilt of those who have sinned* The word ἁμαρτίας is a metonymy, 'sins' standing for the guilt for having sinned.

BOUNDARIES AND COHERENCE

A boundary at 10:5 is indicated by the conjunction οὖν 'therefore' which introduces the CONCLUSION for the *grounds* in 10:1–4. Coherence in the paragraph is shown by two occurrences of the expression 'year after year', two occurrences (one being by ellipsis) of 'sacrifices', and two occurrences of the expression 'sins'.

THEME AND PROMINENCE

The theme for this paragraph is drawn from the most naturally prominent propositions in the CLAIM and the *justification*.

PARAGRAPH CLUSTER CONSTITUENT 10:5–10 (Expository Paragraph: Conclusion₁ of 10:1–18)

THEME: In fulfillment of the Scriptures which state that Christ indicated these sacrifices were inadequate and that he had come to do what was truly needed, God abolished the first way of atonement to establish the second way, that of Christ offering his body as a sacrifice.

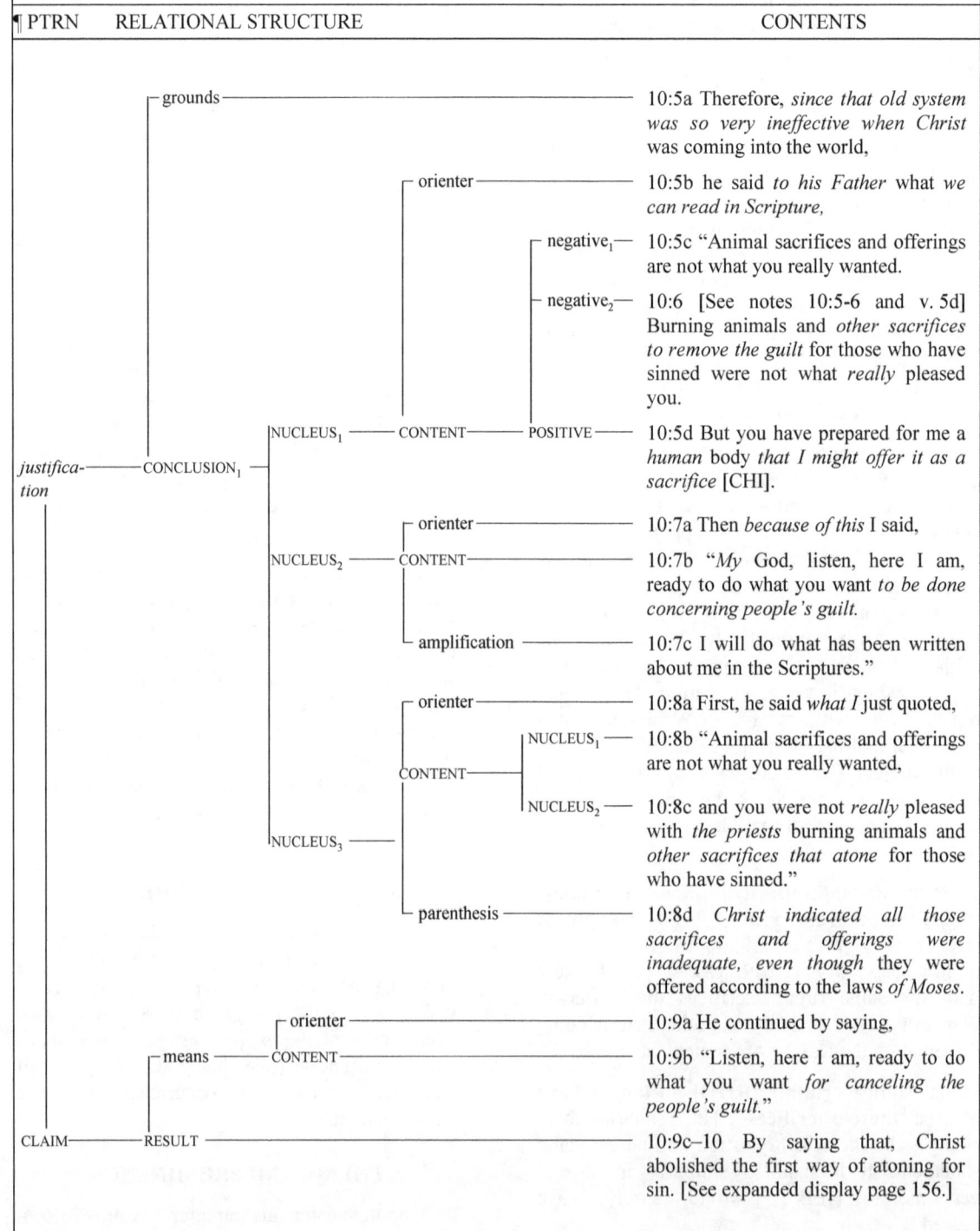

INTENT AND PARAGRAPH PATTERN

The verbs in this unit being all indicative, it is an expository paragraph containing a *justification* and a CLAIM. It continues a long set of units showing the superiority of Christ to the old Jewish system.

NOTES

10:5a Therefore This word introduces the whole paragraph, not just the first sentence. It indicates that this paragraph is the CONCLUSION of the *grounds* in 10:1–4. In languages where the word διό 'therefore' by itself may not convey clearly how this paragraph relates to the previous one, it may be necessary to include something like 'Since that old system was so very weak…'

when Since the participial clause refers to the circumstance of the event, the display clearly marks that relationship.

Christ The GNT has only a participle here, but most versions specify the pronominal referent.

10:5b said *to his Father* **what** *we can read in Scripture* The first part of what is in italics is supplied to identify the referent of 'you' in the quotation. TEV and CEV have "said to God." The last part is to make specific that this is an OT quotation; most versions indicate such by orthographic devices. The passage that the author cited here is Psalm 40:6–8 from the Septuagint. The MT Hebrew text has a very different text in the middle of the chiasmus.

10:5–6 There is a chiasmus here that focuses on the statement 'a body you have prepared for me'. The display has labeled that proposition as a conclusion. It is followed by the focusing pair as 'grounds,' which is formed as a single proposition.

10:5d But you have prepared for me a *human body* *that I might offer it as a sacrifice* The purpose of the giving of a body to Christ is an implicature of the argument. LB has "you have made ready this body of mine to lay as a sacrifice upon your altar" (cf. also Davidson, Hughes, and Ellingworth). The Hebrew text of Psalm 40:7 has a very different meaning from the Septuagint text. It is clear here that the author is using the Septuagint text, which implies that the Psalmist volunteered himself as a living faithful servant. The Psalmist implied that he was dedicating himself as if he was an animal that was killed and burnt on the brazen altar. The author of this document took this statement to mean that Christ volunteered his body as a killed sacrifice.

The propositions 10:5c, 6a, and 5d are considered a chiasmus. 10:5d is almost a repetition of 6a, and 5d, being in the middle, is in focus. For that reason, the display has shown 5d to follow the other two, to keep together the two statements about not desiring sacrifices.

10:5c, 6 Animal sacrifices and offerings are not what you really wanted. Burning animals and *other sacrifices to remove the guilt* **for those who have sinned were not what** *really pleased* **you** You were not really pleased with the priests burning animals and other sacrifices to remove the guilt for those who have sinned. The statements 'Sacrifice and offering you did not desire' and 'with burnt offerings and sin offerings you were not pleased' are understatements that arise out of the Greek translation of the Hebrew text. These understatements should not be translated in a way that implies that the Psalmist supposed that God was rejecting the regular Tabernacle/ Temple rituals.

The rendering here attempts to make sense of the rather elliptical Greek phrases Θυσίαν καὶ προσφορὰν 'sacrifices and offerings' and ὁλοκαυτώματα καὶ περὶ ἁμαρτίας 'burnt offerings and for sins'. The author is referring to a thank offering and two types of animal sacrifice. Louw and Nida say the first term refers to "offering of animals burned whole," and NLT has "other offerings for sin" for the third expression. Moore (p. 58) calls the two references to animal sacrifice a near-synonymous doublet; the sense is really 'any kind of animal sacrifice'.

10:7a Then *because of this* **I said** The great majority of commentators say that the Greek conjunction τότε 'then' is temporal, but the context indicates it means much more than just 'at a later time.' Dods suggests it means "when it was evident that animal sacrifices were not sufficient;" Morris also suggests the sense is more 'in those circumstances'.

10:7b *My* **God** The expression ὁ θεός 'the God' is what is known as an articular vocative; God is being addressed directly. Most versions render it as 'O God'.

listen It is always difficult to determine the force of the particle ἰδού, which in most English versions is either rendered as 'Lo' or omitted. NCV has "Look" but though that follows the etymology of the word, the writer is not suggesting something God is to look at. None of the commentators examined even mentions it. Its function is to call the audience (here, God) to take special note of what the writer is about to say.

here I am The verb ἥκω 'I am come' is taken as a Hebrew idiom for communicating willingness. Louw and Nida suggest it could be rendered "I am here" but such a rendering would suggest the speaker is answering someone who is searching for him. NIV, TEV, and JB have the same rendering as the display has.

you want *to be done concerning people's guilt* The GNT has only ποιῆσαι τὸ θέλημά σου 'to do thy will' but in the context the specific aspect of God's will involves making atonement for sin. LB boldly states "to do your will, to lay down my life." Brown (p. 442) says it refers to the "will of God respecting the salvation of mankind."

10:7c written about me in the Scriptures The GNT expression is ἐν κεφαλίδι βιβλίου 'in the roll of a scroll'. It indicates the actual form used, but even if one were to translate literally, the reader needs to know the scroll in question is one containing Scriptures; Miller says the meaning is "The O.T. Scriptures." NLT also renders it as "in the Scriptures" and CEV has "as the Scriptures say." For languages with no passives, it will be necessary to state an agent such as 'someone' or 'the prophets.'

10:8d *Christ indicated all those sacrifices and offerings were inadequate* This is a crucial implicature of the argument. LB has "Christ said this, about not being satisfied with the various sacrifices."

even though **they were offered according to the laws** *of Moses* Miller says (p. 283) the phrase αἵτινες κατὰ νόμον προσφέρονται 'which according to law are offered' is parenthetical, and a number of versions put their renderings of the phrase in parentheses, e.g., NEB, TEV, and NLT. But the force of the argument would strongly suggest that a concessive relationship is meant (cf. Lenski, p. 332–333). The writer is making the point that even though such offerings were part of the Mosaic law, they were really insufficient to handle guilt for sin.

EXPANSION OF THE RESULT OF *CLAIM*₂ IN THE 10:5–10 DISPLAY

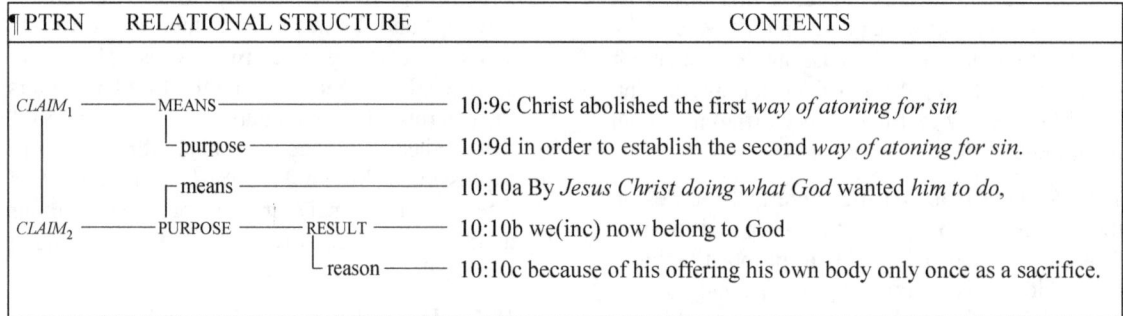

NOTES

10:9c-d the first *way of atoning for sin*...**second** *way of atoning for sin* The question here is, what do the words πρῶτον 'first' and δεύτερον 'second' refer to? Miller suggests 'agreements', but the two agreements per se are not in focus in this context. Many commentators say they refer to the old sacrifices and Christ's sacrifice. TEV tries to capture the sense with "God does away with all the old sacrifices and puts the sacrifice of Christ in their place," but that doesn't do justice to 'first' and 'second'. Others suggest 'first' refers to sacrifices and the second to Christ doing the will of God; but again the latter does not collocate at all with 'second'. NCV handles it quite well with "the first system of sacrifices," but the rendering in the display also fits very well.

10:10a By *Jesus Christ doing what God wanted* *him to do* The GNT phrase ἐν ᾧ θελήματι 'by which will' is a very elliptical way (involving personification) of saying "Because Jesus Christ did what God wanted him to do" (TEV).

10:10c offering his own body only once as a sacrifice The word ἐφάπαξ means 'once and never again'. The words 'as a sacrifice' define more clearly what is meant by 'offer'. NIV and NLT replace 'offer' with "sacrifice;" LB has "dying."

BOUNDARIES AND COHERENCE

The start of a new paragraph at 10:11 is indicated by the conjunction καί and a switch from discussing Christ to talking about the Jewish priests. Coherence is shown by two occurrences each of three different words for sacrifices or offerings.

PROMINENCE AND THEME

The initial phrases in verses 5–6 exhibit prominence by being forefronted. This prominence is expressed in the display by cleft constructions. The theme is drawn from the two naturally prominent CONCLUSIONS of the first CLAIM and the RESULT of the second CLAIM.

PARAGRAPH CLUSTER CONSTITUENT 10:11–18 (Expository Paragraph: Conclusion₂ of 10:1–18)

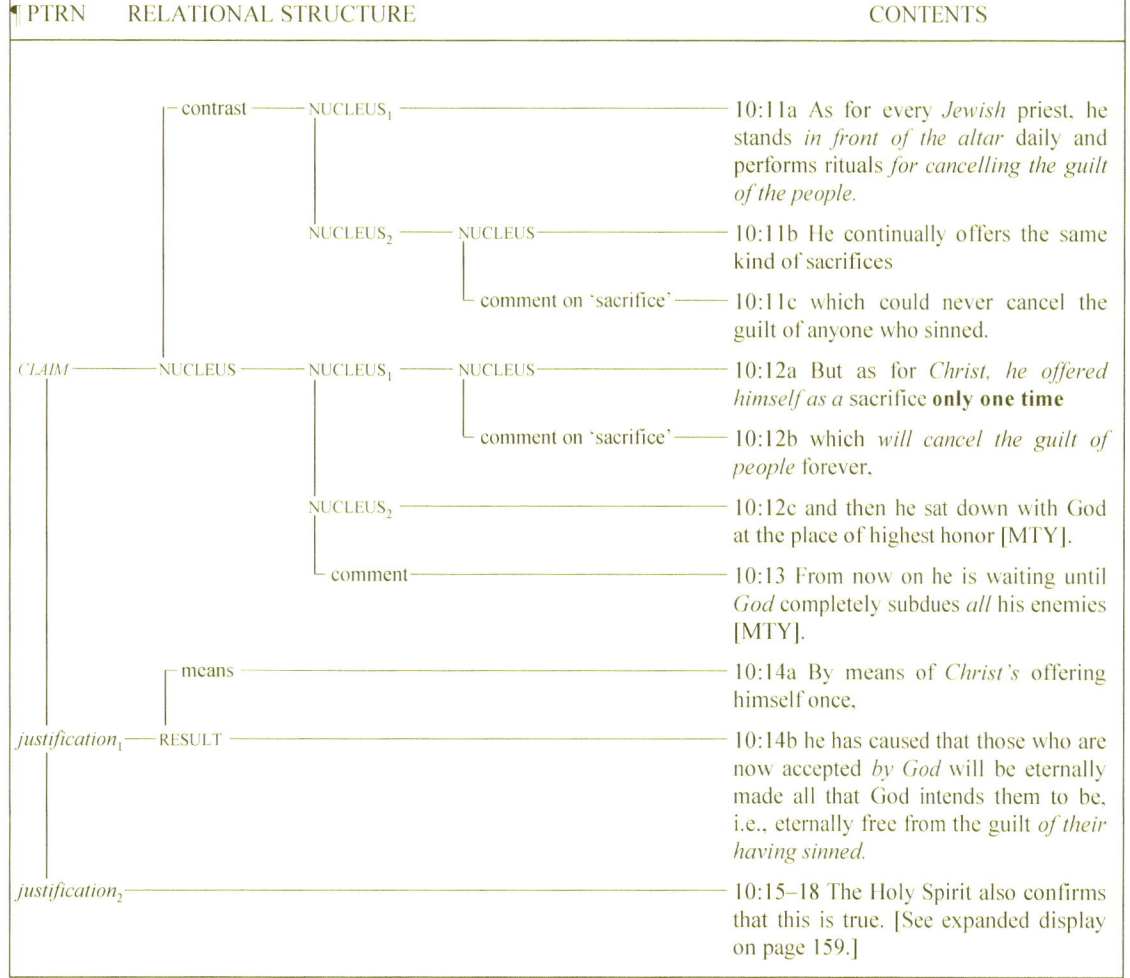

INTENT AND PARAGRAPH PATTERN

This is an expository paragraph consisting of one CLAIM and two justifications. The author is trying to persuade his audience that Jesus is the eternal Supreme Priest, greatly superior to the Jewish priests.

NOTES

10:11a As for every *Jewish* priest The word 'Jewish' is supplied to convey to the reader what the writer assumed his audience would infer (cf. TEV). The author again uses the μέν...δέ construction, beginning here with πᾶς μέν ἱερεὺς 'in the case of every priest', then follows in verse 12 with οὗτος δὲ 'but in regard to this one'. He was indicating that actions of the priests in the first clause contrasted to the actions of the person in the second clause. He implied that Jesus made once a sacrifice that was similar to the repeated sacrifices that the priests performed in the Tabernacle and Temple.

There is a variant text here. Some old manuscripts have πᾶς...ἀρχιερεὺς 'every Supreme Priest'. Instead of πᾶς...ἱερεὺς 'every priest'. The editors of the GNT list the variant with an 'A' 'certain' rating, and it is likely that the author wrote 'every priest'. Metzger says (p. 600) that "the reading ἀρχιερεὺς... appears to be a correction introduced by copyists who recalled 5:1 or 8:3."

stands *in front of the altar* The words in italics supply the implied location. At least one commentator suggests the verb makes clear that the priests were required to stand to do their work, which seems irrelevant to the argument. Most others suggest it implies their task was never finished, in contrast to the statement in v. 12 that after Christ made his one sacrifice he sat down. Thus there is a contrast between the incomplete nature of the work of the priests versus the once-for-all nature of Christ's sacrifice. This contrast is carried by the word 'daily' in v. 11a and the word 'permanently' in v. 12c.

daily The author wrote καθ' ἡμέραν 'each time unit'. Most commentators interpret this as referring to 'each day/on a daily basis'.

performs rituals The verb λειτουργέω means "perform service at the altar of God" (BAGD p. 470.1) and more specifically "perform religious rites" (Louw and Nida 53.13). A couple of commentators suggest that the use of the present tense here suggests that the Jewish sacrificial system was still in operation at the time he wrote.

for cancelling the guilt of the people These words in italics complete the purpose of the ritual. This information comes from v. 11c. It is restated in the comment in 10:12b.

10:11c cancel the guilt of anyone who sinned All versions examined translate ἁμαρτίας as 'sins', but this is a metonymy; what Christ takes away is the result of sin, (i.e., of the guilt.) Miller alone comments on the word, saying (p. 287) it suggests "all the moral aspects of sin: its guilt, power, presence, deceitfulness, entangling persistency, etc." but in this context none but the first of these, (i.e., guilt), is in focus.

10:12a But as for *Christ* Here the author completes the construction that he began in v. 11, introducing the clause with οὗτος δὲ 'but in regard to the other'.

Christ The GNT has οὗτος 'this', but the reference is to Christ. JBP has "this man" and NIV has "this priest" but all other versions examined have 'Christ'.

only one time The forefronting of the word μίαν 'one' gives it emphasis which is shown by bolding in the display.

10:12b *will cancel the guilt of people* **forever** The phrase εἰς τὸ διηνεκές means 'forever', but commentators are equally divided as to whether it modifies the verb 'sat down' which follows, or whether it modifies what precedes it. Although the clause 'he sat down permanently' is listed as an alternative, the 'will cancel the guilt of people forever' is chosen for the display (cf. CEV's "a sacrifice that is good forever"). In this context, the fact that Christ's sitting to rule was permanent is completely out of focus. On the other hand, the fact that his one sacrifice was adequate forever is very much in focus. Furthermore, as Miller notes (p. 288), the use of this phrase meaning 'forever' "is according to the usage of this epistle which elsewhere [always] places the phrase after what it qualifies."

10:12c sat down...at the place of highest honor See notes on 1:3e and 8:1c. In the gospels Christ's sitting down always implies 'to teach', and in the other epistles his sitting at the right hand of the Father usually implies 'to rule'. But here, as several commentators note, the mention of sitting down seems to emphasize that the sacrifice was complete; there was nothing more to do.

10:13 *God* **completely subdues** *all* **his enemies** See note on 1:13c. 'Put one's enemies as a footstool' (Psalm 110:1) is considered a dead metaphor. Both NCV and CEV recognize this by translating as "put under his power."

10:14a *Christ's* **offering himself once** The display makes clear that the words μιᾷ προσφορᾷ 'by one offering' refer to Christ himself being that offering.

10:14b made all that God intends them to be, i.e., eternally free from the guilt *of their having sinned* See note on 5:9a

EXPANSION OF *JUSTIFICATION₂* IN THE 10:11–18 DISPLAY

¶ PTRN	RELATIONAL STRUCTURE	CONTENTS
	CLAIM	10:15a The Holy Spirit also informs us *that this* [v. 12] *is true.*
	┌ orienter	10:15b *Remember the* Lord *God's promise that* I mentioned before [8:10, 12], *in which he said,*
	│ ┌ orienter	10:16a 'This is the *new* agreement that I will make with my people in the future:
	NUCLEUS₁ ─ CONTENT ─ CONTENT₁	10:16b I will enable them to understand my laws,
	│ └ CONTENT₂	10:16c and I will enable them to sincerely obey them, [MTY] [OR: truly know them]."
justification₁	┌ orienter	10:17a *Remember that he* also *said,*
	NUCLEUS₂ ─ CONTENT₁	10:17b "I will forgive them concerning their having sinned [DOU]
	└ CONTENT₂	10:17c and I will *consider* they are no longer *guilty for* having sinned."
	┌ circumstance	10:18a *When God* has forgiven people's sins,
justification₂ ─ NUCLEUS ─ NEGATIVE MEANS		10:18b *there is* no need *for people to make more* offerings
	└ purpose	10:18c in order to atone for their sins.

NOTES

10:15a also By this word, the writer means 'in addition to the passage that I just cited from the Psalms'.

informs us *that this* [v. 12] *is true* The words in italics simply complete the case frame (cf. NLT's "testifies that this is so"). The author claimed that the Holy Spirit shows to the believers that Jesus' sacrifice properly cancelled the guilt of people's sins.

If the readers are unable to supply the referent for 'this', it may be necessary to include 'Jesus completed the cancelling of peoples' sins'.

10:15b *Remember the* Lord *God's promise that* I mentioned before [8:10, 12], *in which he said* The words in italics again make clear that the sentence that follows is an OT quote (from Jeremiah 31:33). Most English versions simply indicate such by quotation marks.

The GNT has λέγει κύριος 'says the Lord' in v. 16, but the display shows it here so as not to break up the quote (cf. CEV). The word 'God' is included to make clear that the speaker is God, not Christ.

10:16a with my people The GNT has πρὸς αὐτούς 'to them'; the identification of the pronoun comes from the OT passage, which says 'the house of Israel', LB has "the people of Israel" and NLT has "my people."

in the future The GNT says μετὰ τὰς ἡμέρας ἐκείνας 'after those days'. But to what days was God referring? Several versions translate the phrase very generically, such as "in the days to come" (TEV), "when the time comes" (CEV). In 8:8 and 8:10, God also referred generically to the future.

10:16c The wording in the display is a clear statement of the Greek, which is very figurative. See the notes on 8:10. As was done in chapter 8, two alternatives are given. If the second one is chosen, then the two propositions (10c and 10d) become a figurative doublet. It is so classified by Moore (p. 58).

10:17a *Remember that he* also *said* The author continued citing the passage that he first cited in chapter 8, with some different words than he cited in 8:12. Most versions also begin this verse with a similar orienter.

10:17b-c forgive them concerning their having sinned and I will *consider* they are no longer *guilty for* having sinned The GNT has τῶν ἁμαρτιῶν αὐτῶν καὶ τῶν ἀνομιῶν αὐτῶν οὐ μὴ μνησθήσομαι ἔτι 'Their sins and their iniquities I will by no means still remember'.

These two terms are listed by Moore (p. 58) as a near-synonymous doublet. They are retained in the display as two full propositions because the passage from which it is quoted (Jer. 31:34) is a poetic one. CEV does something similar, with "I will forget about their sins and no longer remember their evil deeds." That rendering also points to the fact that 'no longer remember' can be consider a litotes meaning 'forget about'. For the wording given here, see the note on 8:12b.

10:18a When God has forgiven The display states the agent, as is done in JBP and supported by several commentators.

10:18b there is no need for people to make more offerings The GNT simply has οὐκέτι προσφορά 'no longer offering', which requires some verb to be supplied to make a full proposition. Many versions supply 'need'. A translation supplying the verb 'be' (e.g., JB's "there can be no more sin offerings") could give a totally wrong meaning.

BOUNDARIES AND COHERENCE

A new paragraph at 10:19 is signaled by the conjunction noun 'therefore' plus a vocative αδελφοι 'brothers'.

PROMINENCE AND THEME

The theme of this paragraph is drawn from a condensation of the two nuclei in the first nucleus of the CLAIM, the result proposition of the 1st *justification*, and the NUCLEUS of the 2nd *justification*. Coherence is provided by the three 1st person plural subjunctives.

SUB-SECTION CONSTITUENT 10:19–25 (Paragraph: Mitigated Appeal of 10:1–25)

THEME: *Since we can confidently enter God's presence and since Christ is our great Supreme Priest, let us come to God sincerely, keep firmly professing the truth, incite one another to love and good deeds, and encourage each other.*

¶ PTRN	RELATIONAL STRUCTURE	CONTENTS
basis₁ — NUCLEUS — RESULT — NUCLEUS		10:19a Therefore, my fellow-believers, *since* we can confidently approach God *when we worship and pray*,
— comparison		10:19b *it is as if we are entering* the Most Holy Place *in the Temple* [MTY],
— reason		10:19c because of *what* Jesus *accomplished* when he bled *for us*;
equivalent — GENERIC — PURPOSE		10:20a that is, he opened a way for us to approach God,
— means		10:20b by means of his making a new and effective way.
— means		10:20c Specifically, he offered himself as a sacrifice for us
specific — RESULT — NUCLEUS		10:20d *with the result that nothing can* prevent us from approaching God,
— comparison		10:20e in the manner that the curtain *in front* of the Most Holy Place *prevented people from approaching God* [MET].
basis₂		10:21 And Christ is a Supreme Priest *who cares for us*, who are God's people. [MTY].
APPEAL		10:22–25 Therefore, let us come to God and keep professing the truth. [See expanded display on page 162.]

INTENT AND PARAGRAPH PATTERN

This can be considered a hortatory paragraph, inasmuch as it consists of two *bases* and an APPEAL. It is the positive exhortation toward which the whole epistle has been leading.

NOTES

10:19–25 There is one sentence in the GNT comprising vv. 19–25. The main verb does not come until v. 22. The display breaks this into several sentences. The οὖν here introduces this paragraph as being the MITIGATED APPEAL following the *basis* in the unit 10:1–18.

10:19a *since* we can confidently approach *God when we worship and pray* The words τὴν εἴσοδον τῶν ἁγίων 'the entering of the holies' are figurative. So, 'when we worship and pray' indicates how we approach God.

10:19b *it is as if we are entering* the Most Holy Place *in the Temple* The phrase τὰ ἅγια basically means the Most Holy Place in the Temple, but it is a metonymy, the place standing for the Person who was worshipped there. Guthrie (p. 211) says "understood symbolically of the presence of God" (cf. also Bruce, Ellingworth, and LB's "where God is"). NLT's "heaven's Most Holy Place" is unwarranted.

in the Temple These words specify what holy place was being referred to. There was a 'Most Holy Place' in both the sacred tent in the desert and in the Temple; but most likely the author is referring to the latter (cf. Barnes).

10:19c because of *what* Jesus *accomplished* when he bled *for us* The preposition in the phrase ἐν τῷ αἵματι Ἰησοῦ 'by the blood of Jesus' is taken as expressing reason— the reason for our confidence. Miller takes it as expressing means, but in a means proposition the agent must be the same as that of the verb in the result clause. The author affirmed that we are confident as we trust that his sacrifice was effective. Ellingworth and Nida (p. 228) suggest the word 'blood' can be translated by 'death', but since blood has such a high symbolic value here and throughout the rest of Scripture, this is not advisable. TEV had "death" but CEV now retains "blood."

10:20a that is The relative pronominal adjective ἥν 'which' refers to the noun 'entrance' in 19a, but with a full proposition here, the equivalence relationship seems the most appropriate. This is the way NLT handles it also.

he opened a way for us to approach God The verb ἐγκαινίζω means 'to put into effect', but collocated with the word ὁδός 'way, road' it means to open. It is recognized that 'open a road' is figurative; the sense is 'it is as if he created an opening for us into heaven'.

10:20b new...way The GNT has πρόσφατον ἃ 'newly made' to indicate that Jesus accomplished a condition that did not exist before.

effective way The participle ζῶσαν 'living' could mean "life-giving" (NLT) or "that leads to life" (CEV), but that would much more likely be the meaning if the participle were from the verb ζῳοποιέω 'give life to'. The meaning ascribed here follows that given to the same participle in 3:12, 4:12, and 10:31. Miller also gives the meaning as 'effective' here.

10:20c he offered himself as a sacrifice for us Commentators agree that the phrase τῆς σαρκὸς αὐτοῦ 'of his flesh' refers to Christ's body, and in this context it means "by offering himself as a sacrifice" (Louw and Nida).

10:20d *with the result that nothing can* prevent us from approaching *God* There has been a lot of debate by commentators on the significance of the phrase διὰ τοῦ καταπετάσματος 'through the curtain'. All interpreters consider that 'curtain' refers to the curtain in front of the Most Holy Place inside the tent in the wilderness or inside the Temple. The issues that a translator must examine are:
1. Should 'of his flesh' in 20b be related to 'curtain' or to 'way'?

Ellingworth says that the choice will be theologically motivated and that the decision is related to the decision about the next issue.
2. Is the curtain to be understood as an obstacle or a means of access?

Although the death of Christ and the tearing of the curtain (Mark 15:38) were obviously related, it is not warranted to try to derive the meaning of this passage from Mark's record alone. However, it seems clear that the tearing of the curtain symbolized both the removing of the obstacle and that access was now available.
3. Does διά mean 'through' or 'by means of'?

In conjunction with the word 'curtain,' the preposition clearly means 'through' (cf. Ellingworth).

10:21 Christ is The Greek is an ellipsis, the participle 'our having' being assumed to be repeated from v. 19a, with the meaning here of 'since Jesus is…'

a Supreme Priest *who cares for us* The author seems to be referring back to his claim in 3:6, that Christ cares for his siblings. An alternative might be 'who rules over us' (as in LB/NLT; cf. Miller, Lane). Another alternative that might be useful in reference to the work of a priest would be 'who serves for our benefit'.

***who are* God's people** The GNT has ἐπὶ τὸν οἶκον τοῦ θεοῦ 'over the house of God'. The word 'house' is a metonymy, the place standing for the people. A couple versions (JBP, LB) have 'household' and NLT makes it very clear with "rules over God's people."

EXPANSION OF THE *APPEAL* IN THE 10:19–25 DISPLAY

RELATIONAL STRUCTURE	CONTENTS
EXHORTATION₁–RESULT	10:22a Therefore, *as we come to God,* we(incl) should approach *him* sincerely,
└ means	10:22b by confidently trusting *that he will heed us.*
– grounds₁–NUCLEUS	10:22c *It is as if Jesus had* sprinkled his blood *on our hearts* [MET] to make us no longer *guilty for having sinned,*
└ comparison	10:22d *just as* the priests were sprinkled with blood [MET].
– grounds₂–NUCLEUS	10:22e And, *it is as though* we have allowed Christ to make us pure,
└ comparison	10:22f *just as the priests'* bodies *were ceremonially* washed by pure water.
EXHORTATION₂–GENERIC	10:23a Therefore, we should also unwaveringly keep telling others *what we believe;*
└ specific — CONCLUSION	10:23b that is, we should confidently expect that God *will do for us all that he has promised,*
└ grounds	10:23c since *God* faithfully *does all that* he promised *to do.*
EXHORTATION₃–MEANS	10:24a We should consider how each of us can stimulate the others
├ purpose₁	10:24b in order that *each one* loves the others,
└ purpose₂	10:24c and in order that each one does good actions *to help others*.
negative	10:25a Some people are habitually not attending [LIT] the meetings of the believers. We should not be like them.
EXHORTATION₄–POSITIVE	10:25b Rather, each one of us should encourage/exhort the others.
└ amplification–EXHORTATION	10:25c *We should do this* (10:25c) all the more *urgently*
└ grounds	10:25d since we know that Jesus will *certainly* return soon [PER, MTY].

NOTES

10:22a Therefore The word οὖν occurs at the beginning of verse 19, but the conclusion that it introduces begins here.

as we come to God,* we(incl) should approach *him The GNT has προσερχώμεθα 'we should approach/let us approach', which is figurative for coming to God in prayer, worship, etc..

The words 'to God' complete the case frame, as is done in versions such as NIV, CEV, and NCV.

we(incl) should In verses 22–25 there is a series of clauses using first person plural subjunctive forms, usually translated in English by 'let us'. But since the primary sense of 'let' is 'permit', and since many languages do not have 1st person plural exhortation, the display here uses 'we should'.

sincerely The words μετά ἀληθινῆς καρδίας 'with a true heart' are an idiom. Every version examined uses the word 'heart'. Hewitt says the phrase means "with perfect sincerity."

10:22b by confidently trusting *that he will heed us* The phrase ἐν πληροφορίᾳ πίστεως 'in full assurance of faith' contains two abstract nouns which are unskewed in the display (cf. NLT's "fully trusting him"). In some languages a fuller content of 'believe' will be necessary, such as 'in the perfection of His sacrificial work on the cross' (Hewitt).

10:22d *just as* the priests were sprinkled with blood The phrase ῥεραντισμένοι τὰς καρδίας ἀπὸ συνειδήσεως πονηρᾶς 'hearts sprinkled from an evil conscience' seems to be an implied reference to Ex. 29:20–21, and/or Lev. 8:30 when Moses sprinkled Aaron and his sons, making them priests. It is a metaphor, with the topic given in 22c and the image in 22d-e. The sprinkled blood symbolized that blood had been sprinkled to atone for their sins; hence 'we are no longer guilty for having done evil' is that which is symbolized. The perfect passive participle ῥεραντισμένοι 'sprinkled' introduces the first grounds for the exhortation in 22a (so Miller, p. 299.) In some languages it might be necessary to include the words '*to consecrate them for their sacred work*' to make clear the purpose of 'sprinkling the blood'.

10:22e we have allowed Christ to make us pure Nearly all the commentators suggest that the author was referring to baptism. However, such an interpretation could imply baptismal regeneration, which is contrary to New Testament teaching. Therefore, the display supplies an alternative that does not mention baptism.

The author used another metaphor to imply our purification by our Supreme Priest.

10:22f *just as the priests'* bodies *were ceremonially* washed by pure water Commentators also agree that the phrase λελουσμένοι τὸ σῶμα ὕδατι καθαρῷ 'the body washed in pure water' is a reference to passages such as Ex. 29:4, 30:20, 40:30–31, and Ezek. 36:25. This is another metaphor very much parallel to that in 10:22c-d. The washing of the priests' bodies symbolized that they had been purified from sin. Similarly, Christ washes our inner beings; hence the display has 'we are allowing Christ to continually make us pure'. Taken this way, the first part (10:22c-d) symbolizes what Christ has already done for believers, and the second part (f) symbolizes what he continues to do as a Supreme Priest. The alternative is to take the two symbols as a doublet (Moore does not mention this verse) and translate the verb in 22e in the past tense: 'we have allowed…'

10:23a-b we should also unwaveringly keep telling others *what we believe*; that is, we should confidently expect that God *will do for us all that he has promised* By removing the mismatch involving the abstract nouns in the phrase κατέχωμεν τὴν ὁμολογίαν τῆς ἐλπίδος ἀκλινῆ 'let us hold fast the profession of hope without wavering' we must first answer the question: does 'profession' refer to telling something to others, or does it refer to something we profess? BAGD (p. 568) says the sense of the verb is "confession, acknowledgment;" therefore 'keep telling others' expresses the sense. We must also supply some object for 'profess', so 'what we believe' is supplied generically and 'hope' is made a second proposition supplying the specific content of what we believe. Then as before, making 'hope' a clause using the more meaningful words 'confidently expect' we need to supply something generic as the content (see 3:6, 6:11, 6:18, 7:19).

10:23c *God* faithfully *does all that* he promised *to do* Commentators agree that the phrase πιστὸς ὁ ἐπαγγειλάμενος 'faithful the one who promises' is describing God. But in the context of promise, the quality 'faithful' is seen more as modifying the action of carrying out the promises (hence 'does') than just an attribute of God himself (cf. NCV's "we can trust God to do what he promised").

10:24a stimulate The noun παροξυσμός usually means 'provoking' with a negative connotation, but here it is used in a positive way. NIV's "spur one another on" is very good.

10:25a Some people are habitually not attending [LIT] *the meetings* The negative clause is somewhat of a litotes meaning 'let us be sure to meet as God's people regularly'. The words in italics identify who is meant by 'some'. CEV has "meeting for worship." Several versions have "church meetings" which is all right for English but probably not suitable for many other languages.

We should not be like them The words καθὼς ἔθος τισίν 'as (is) a custom with some' is an ellipsis. The problem here is that the writer is comparing what believers should do with what some do *not* do. If one removed the litotes in

25a, the verse could be translated 'some believers have habitually not met together with others for worship; don't you do like they do'.

10:25b encourage/exhort The verb παρακαλέω can have either of these meanings, and it is very difficult to tell whether the writer had one meaning in mind, or the other, or both. Nearly all versions have 'encourage' but commentators are equally divided. Westcott (p. 326) seems to suggest both, and NLT translates it as "encourage and warn."

10:25d since The relative pronominal adjective ὅσῳ is given the meaning 'as' by BAGD (p. 586.3) but is rendered 'since' by CEV and TEV and 'because' by REB. Here it has much more a logical force than simply circumstance.

we know The GNT has βλέπετε 'you(pl) see', which is figurative, referring to a cognitive process of feeling an urgency.

that Jesus will *certainly* return soon The Greek has only ἐγγίζουσαν τὴν ἡμέραν 'coming near the day' which is personification— an occasion behaving as a person, and a metonymy— the occasion standing for the event associated with it. NLT has "the day of his coming back again."

BOUNDARIES AND COHERENCE

A new paragraph at 10:26 is signaled by a new topic: a severe negative warning to the audience following a paragraph listing several positive exhortations. Coherence is provided by the three exhortations signaled by 1st person plural subjunctives, plus two participles which have hortatory force.

PROMINENCE AND THEME

The theme of this paragraph is drawn from a set of naturally prominent propositions: the nucleus of the first *basis* and the second *basis*, the result of the first EXHORTATION, the generic proposition of the second EXHORTATION, and the means proposition of the third EXHORTATION.

SECTION CONSTITUENT 10:26–39 (Sub-Section: Appeal₂ of 10:1–39)

\multicolumn{2}{l}{*THEME: Since there is no sacrifice to appease God if we keep sinning, but only judgment facing us, let us not become discouraged when we are persecuted.*}	
MACROSTRUCTURE	CONTENTS
warning basis	10:26–31 If we deliberately keep sinning, no other sacrifice is available that can appease God for our sinning; instead we will face God's judgment, since anyone who thus despises Christ and his shed blood deserves to be greatly punished by God.
APPEAL	10:32–39 You recall how previously you continued to believe when you suffered for your faith. So do not become discouraged now when you are persecuted, since God will greatly reward you if you keep believing, and since we are ones who will be saved because of our faith.

INTENT AND PARAGRAPH PATTERN

This is a hortatory unit with two imperative verbs. The unit consists of a *warning basis* and an APPEAL. This unit would seem to serve as the central unit of the epistle; it provides the conclusion for all the expository units leading up to it which state the excellence of Christ. And as such it gives a very strong warning to the readers.

BOUNDARIES AND COHERENCE

A new unit at 11:1 is indicated by a tail-head linkage with πίστεως 'believe' in 10:35 and πίστις 'faith' in 11:1. Cohesion in 10:26–39 is shown by a series of terms referring to punishment by God: judgment, raging fire, punish, avenge, repay, judge, fall into the hands of.

PROMINENCE AND THEME

The theme for this unit is drawn from a condensation of the most prominent propositions of the *warning basis* in 26–31 and the APPEAL in 32–39.

SUB-SECTION CONSTITUENT 10:26–31 (Paragraph: Warning basis of 10:26–39)

THEME: If we deliberately keep sinning, no other sacrifice is available that can appease God for our sinning; instead we will face God's judgment, since anyone who thus despises Christ and his shed blood deserves to be greatly punished by God.

¶ PTRN	RELATIONAL STRUCTURE	CONTENTS
CLAIM	NEGATIVE CONSEQUENCE — condition — NUCLEUS	10:26a *We(incl) must do these things* [22–25 or 23–25 or 25] because if we deliberately sin habitually
	circumstance	10:26b after we have known the true message about Christ,
	NEGATIVE CONSEQUENCE	10:26c no sacrifice is available that can appease God for our having sinned *deliberately.*
	POSITIVE CONSEQUENCE — sequence	10:27a Instead we must fearfully expect that God will judge us,
	NUCLEUS — NUCLEUS	10:27b and then he will angrily destroy us whom *he will consider* to be his enemies,
	comparison	10:27c just as a fierce fire destroys things [MET].
justification	grounds — NUCLEUS	10:28a *You all know that* anyone who rejected the laws given to Moses was mercilessly killed
	circumstance	10:28b whenever at least two or three people testified that the person *had refused to obey those laws.*
	CONSEQUENCE	10:29a You certainly can be sure that [RHQ] anyone will deserve a punishment even worse than *being killed*
	CONDITION₁	10:29b if that person shows much contempt for [MTY] God's Son,
	CONDITION₂ — NUCLEUS	10:29c and *if that person* rejects the truth that Christ's blood is worthy of much respect/is valuable/important,
	description of 'blood'	10:29d the blood *with which he enacted* the new agreement
	CONDITION₃	10:29e *and if that person rejects the truth that* Christ freed that person from his guilt,
	CONDITION₄	10:29f and *if that person* insults the Spirit *of God, the one who acts* graciously *toward him.*
	evidential grounds₁ — orienter	10:30a *You can be sure that God will severely punish that person, since* we know that God said *in Scripture*
	CONTENT — NUCLEUS₁	10:30b "I myself will get revenge on those who sinned
	NUCLEUS₂	10:30c and I will punish them severely, as they deserve [HEN].
	evidential grounds₂ — orienter	10:30d And in another *Scripture passage we can read,*
	CONTENT	10:30e "The Lord will judge his people."
CONCLUSION		10:31 It will be terrible to at last be punished by the all-powerful God [MTY]!

INTENT AND PARAGRAPH PATTERN

This is an expository paragraph; all the fully-inflected verbs are indicative. It is probably the central paragraph of the epistle: it is the conclusion of all the preceding paragraphs that state the excellence of Christ over various aspects of the Jewish system. And as such it serves as a strong warning to the readers.

NOTES

10:26a We(incl) must do these things [22–25 or 23–25 or 25] because By using the conjunction γὰρ, the author is introducing the 'reason' for the previous sentence, but it is difficult to decide whether he is referring to the exhortations in vv. 22–25, or only those in vv. 23–25 or only those in v. 25.

if we deliberately sin Almost all commentators and all versions agree that the participle ἁμαρτανάντων 'sinning' indicates a condition. In some languages it may be necessary to say 'anyone' or 'any of us' instead of 'we'.

The adverb ἑκουσίως means "deliberately, intentionally" (BAGD p. 243). Several commentators suggest that the wording here indicates deliberate apostasy.

habitually Many commentators note that the present tense of the participle refers to continuous sinning; TEV has "go on sinning."

10:26b we have known the true message about Christ Kistemaker says the phrase τῆς ἀληθείας 'of the truth' means "God's revelation in general and the gospel in particular." Some commentators say that the word ἐπίγνωσις means more than γνῶσις–a thorough or clear or full understanding, a "dynamic assimilation of the truth of the gospel" (Lane, p. 292), but neither versions nor lexicons support this notion.

10:26c no sacrifice is available that can appease God for our having sinned deliberately The GNT has only οὐκέτι περὶ ἁμαρτῶν ἀπολείπεται θυσία 'there no longer (remains) a sacrifice concerning sins'. The phrase 'sacrifice for sins' implies sacrifice to atone for, or as here, to remove the guilt of. TEV has "sacrifice that will take away sins" but as usual in Hebrews (and elsewhere in the N.T.), 'sin' stands for the guilt and consequent punishment for sin.

The author uses first person plural pronouns all through this clause; but in some languages it may be more natural to use 'anyone' when referring generically to an accused offender (cf. LB).

deliberately The word 'deliberately' is included as an implicature of the argument; the writer is not talking about the sins of anyone else. As Westcott says, "The writer does not set limits to the efficacy of Christ's work for the penitent."

10:27a Instead Although the writer uses δέ and not αλλά, the sense of the verse clearly gives the sense of 'instead' (so TEV, although several versions carry this force with 'but only').

we The author continued to use first person plural pronouns. As in 10:26c, the first person plural is the natural pronoun for a speaker to refer generically to anyone whom that speaker is admonishing. (cf. CEV.) Lane uses "the person who, those who" which we can cite if we want to change the pronoun to exclude the writer. In some languages it would be more natural to use the second person 'you'.

must fearfully expect that God will judge us The display translates the nouns in the phrase ἐκδοχὴ κρίσεως 'expectation of judgment' as full clauses.

10:27b-c he will angrily destroy us whom *he will consider* to be his enemies, just as a fierce fire destroys things The GNT expression πυρος ζῆλος εσθίειν μέλλοντος τοὺς ὑπεναντίους 'a zeal of fire about to consume the adversaries' (Isa. 26:11) is a metaphor and also a personification, as many commentators suggest. The topic of the metaphor— that God will do the destroying— is stated in 27b. The image, of a raging fire destroying things, is stated in 27c. The majority of commentators say that 'zeal' modifies 'fire' in a figurative sense. BAGD (p. 337.1) says the word here is describing "the fire of judgment which, with its blazing flames, appears like a living being intent on devouring God's adversaries." If 'fierce fire' is a collocational clash, 'raging' or 'roaring' may be more suitable.

10:28a *You all know that* These words indicate that the author was reminding the audience of the regulations contained in the instruction God told to Moses.

laws given to Moses The phrase τις νόμον Μωϋσέως 'law of Moses' is consistently used to refer to what was a set of laws, not one law (cf. LB "laws given by Moses"). A good alternative is 'laws God gave to Moses'.

was mercilessly killed The GNT has ἀποθνῄσκει 'dies' but this is a polite way of saying 'executed, put to death' (cf. NCV, CEV, TEV, JB, REB, and NLT).

10:28b at least two or three This is an implicature of the argument; CEV says "two or more."

testified that the person *had refused to obey those laws* The words in italics complete the case frame; LB has "witnesses to his sin." (See Deut. 17:6.)

10:29a Though there is no conjunction here in the Greek, v. 29 is the conclusion of a fortiori argument (so Attridge), for which v. 28 is the grounds.

You certainly can be sure This changes the rhetorical question introduced by πόσῳ δοκεῖτε 'by how much do you think?' into an emphatic positive statement; JB likewise has "you may be sure."

even worse than *being killed* For languages which do not have a natural way for indicating that a condition is more undesirable than another, it may be necessary to say something like 'such punishment was very harsh, but…will be very much more harsh'.

10:29b if that person shows much contempt for The participle καταπατήσας 'having trampled on' comes to mean 'treat with disdain' (BAGD p. 415.2) by metonymy, the effect standing for the cause; the basic sense of the word is 'trample underfoot'.

10:29c and *if that person* rejects the truth that Christ's blood is worthy of much respect The GNT has τὸ αἷμα…κοινὸν ἡγησάμενος 'having considered the blood common'. The term 'common' means 'not worthy of respect'; (cf. Louw and Nida "being of little value/worthless,") TNT "of no account," JBP "treated like dirt." The display treats the words as a sort of litotes: 'consider worthless' = 'not consider worthy of respect'.

10:29d blood *with which he enacted* the new agreement The words in italics spell out the relationships in the genitive construction αἷμα τῆς διαθήκης 'blood of the agreement' in a way which is suggested by many commentators (see Miller, Barnes, Calvin, and Lünemann).

10:29e *if that person rejects the truth that* Christ freed that person from his guilt The Greek word is ἡγιάσθε 'made holy' but the writer here in this epistle is not talking about sanctification but about cleansing from the guilt of sin. Louw and Nida, Hughes, and Hewitt support this interpretation. Weymouth has "he was set free from sin;" Norlie has "he had his sins forgiven."

10:29f *if that person* insults the Spirit *of God, the one who acts* graciously *toward him* The words πνεῦμα χάριτος 'spirit of grace' are taken by the great majority of commentators as meaning 'Spirit who gives grace' or 'Spirit who is gracious', with probably little difference in meaning. In the light of the whole context of the book, the author is here clearly talking about those who rejected the whole way of salvation through the undeserved gracious substitutionary death of Christ.

10:30a *You can be sure that God will severely punish that person* The γάρ which introduces this verse relates back to the 'you can be sure' in v. 29a, which is repeated here to maintain the flow and still start a new sentence.

since* we know that God said *in Scripture The passage which follows is from Deut. 32:35–36. The display makes specific that Scripture is being cited, and states God as the speaker; NCV and CEV do likewise. The GNT has only τόν εἰπόντα 'the [one] having said'.

10:31 It will be terrible The author was warning the believers of the consequences of no longer following Jesus.

to at last be punished by the all-powerful God [MTY]! The GNT has τὸ ἐμπεσεῖν εἰς χεῖρας θεοῦ ζῶντος 'to fall into the hands of the living God'. This Hebrew idiom was once a metonymy (a part of a person representing the ability that the person to do with that part.) The idiom is also a dead metaphor that implies that eventually God will certainly punish the evil person.

BOUNDARIES AND COHERENCE

A new paragraph at 10:31 is signaled by an initial imperative verb plus a switch to a new topic —a discussion of their persecution. Coherence in the paragraph is exhibited by several words in the semantic domain of punishment: judge, fire, punish, avenge, and the idiom 'fall into the hands of'.

PROMINENCE AND THEME

The theme of the paragraph is drawn from the naturally prominent propositions of the negative and positive CONSEQUENCES plus the *condition* in the CLAIM, plus the *consequence* of the *justification*.

SUB-SECTION CONSTITUENT 10:32–39 (Paragraph: Appeal of 10:26–39)

> THEME: *You recall how previously you continued to believe when you suffered for your faith. So do not become discouraged now when you are persecuted, since God will greatly reward you if you keep believing, and since we are ones who will be saved because of our faith.*

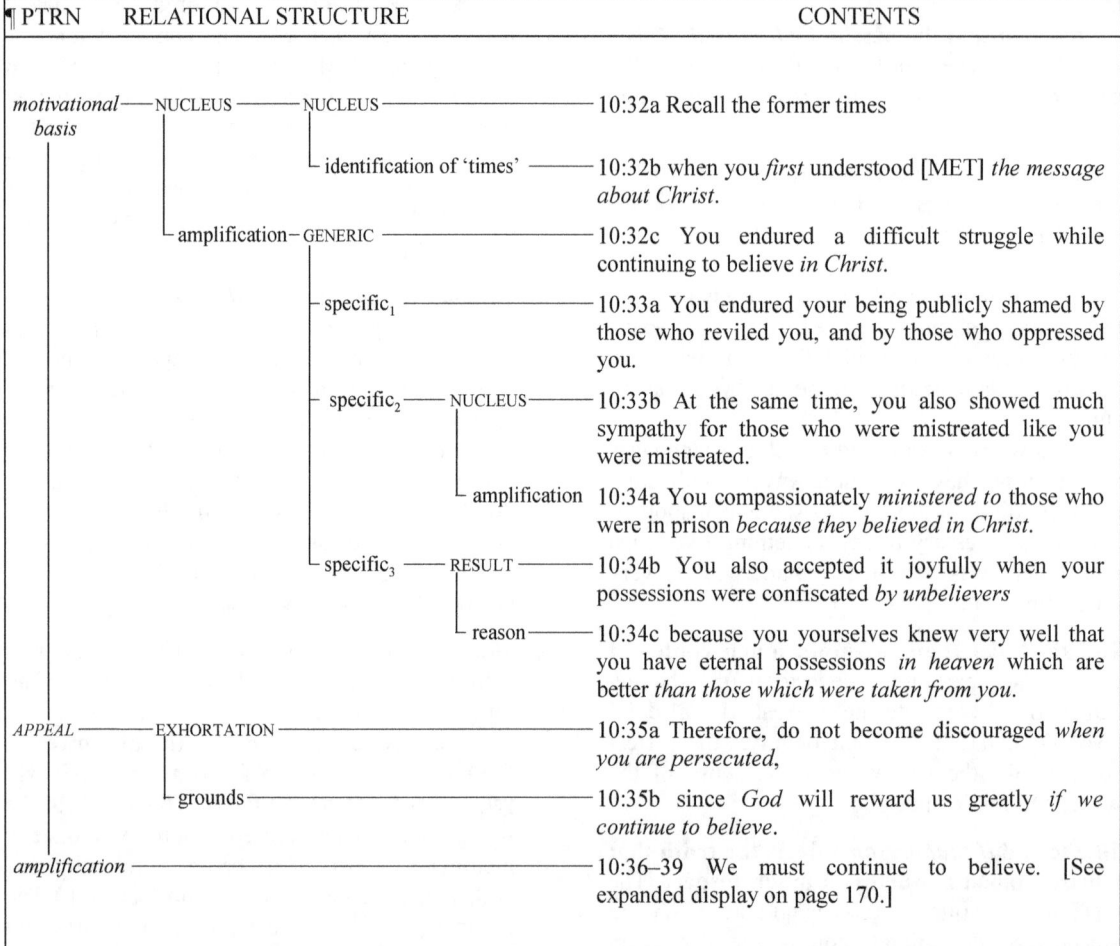

INTENT AND PARAGRAPH PATTERN

The 10:32–39 paragraph is a hortatory one as evidenced by the negative imperative in v. 35. That imperative comprises the one *APPEAL* of the paragraph, which is supported by a *motivational basis*. Although v. 32a also begins with an imperative Ἀναμιμνῄσκεσθε 'remember', this imperative is not listed as an *APPEAL* for two reasons: (1) the imperative in v. 35 is accompanied by the conjunction οὖν 'therefore', suggesting that what precedes is the grounds for the *EXHORTATION* in v. 35, and (2) because 32a-b really only forms an orienter to the main part of the *basis* in vv. 32c–34. The author was implying here 'as a result of remembering what you have endured as believers, do not become discouraged.'

NOTES

10:32a *times* The word ἡμέρας means 'days', but the author is referring to an unspecified time or times which was not necessarily 'days'; CEV has "all the hard times."

10:32b *first understood* **[MET]** *the message about Christ* The participle φωτισθέντες 'having been enlightened' is a dead metaphor, and therefore, the sense is here given non-metaphorically. The form is almost identical to that found in 6:4b and is rendered here in almost the same way. NLT has "first learned about Christ;" NCV similarly removes the metaphor and has "first learned the truth." The words 'the message about Christ' are supplied to complete the case frame. For those who prefer a more literal translation, 'enlightened about the way of salvation' would be a good possibility.

10:32c You endured a difficult struggle The phrase πολλὴν ἄθλησιν ὑπεμείνατε 'you endured a great struggle' is a metaphor involving "an athlete engaged in some kind of hard competition" (Louw and Nida). NIV makes the figure more explicit with "you stood your ground in a great contest" but this is very idiomatic. To avoid the abstract noun 'struggle' used in the display, it might be necessary to say something like 'when people persecuted you severely'. It is admitted that the rendering here uses an abstract noun and is translated very literally, but it seems hard to avoid doing so.

continuing to believe The verb 'you endured' means more than 'you underwent'; BAGD (p. 602) give the meaning here as "stand one's ground, hold out" (cf. NIV); hence 'continuing to believe'. TEV has "were not defeated," NLT has "you remained faithful."

in Christ The words in italics are a situational implicature. Commentators agree that the writer is talking about persecution, and Webster defines 'persecute' as "to cause to suffer because of belief." Commentators are quite divided as to how the genitive 'of sufferings' relates to the word 'struggle'. Most of these are irrelevant when the abstract nouns are made full clauses; the struggle was obviously simultaneous with the sufferings. What is clearly implied and not made clear in the versions is that the sufferings were the result of their faith in Christ.

10:33a-b You endured…At the same time, you also The author uses the μέν…δέ construction to indicate that the two participial clauses represent events that happened at the same time, τοῦτο, μέν…τοῦτο, δέ 'this as well as that'. The display shows this as "You endured… At the same time, you also…'

Miller (p. 317) says the two participles in v. 33 express the means of 'you endured', but if they did express means, it would be the means of 'suffered' which is represented in the Greek by a noun, not a verb. While they could be taken as expressing means, the display follows Lane (p. 298) who says they "clarify the character of the sufferings endured," (i.e., they are specifics.)

10:33a You endured your being publicly shamed by those who reviled you The display supplies a verb to represent the noun ὀνειδισμοῖς 'reproaches' and an adverb to represent the passive participle θεατριζόμενοι 'being exposed publicly' and a relative clauses to represent the noun θλίψεσιν 'afflictions'.

10:33b At the same time The author indicated that he recognized that the believers had endured suffering and had sympathized with other believers in their troubles.

you also showed much sympathy The phrase κπινωνοὶ γενηθέντες 'having become sharers' means they were "sharing their perils by the active avowal of sympathy" (Westcott, p. 334).

10:34a The γάρ here cannot be taken as introducing the grounds of the exhortation in v. 32a (so Miller) because it does not cohere as a grounds. Lenski (p. 366) says it "explains and at the same time adds the limit of what the readers suffered;" (i.e., it is an amplification.) But the items referred to in v. 33 are now treated in reverse order; it is thus a chiastic structure.

You compassionately *ministered to* those who were in prison *because they believed in Christ* This proposition clarifies the clause τοῖς δεσμίοις συνεπαθήσατε 'you sympathized with the prisoners'. To 'sympathize with' means more than just feel pity towards; as several commentators note, the sense is that "Christians in prison had to be fed and visited by their fellow-members" (Moffatt, p. 154). TEV has "were kind to," NCV has "you helped." The phrase 'because they believed in Christ' is basically repeated from v. 32c to avoid wrong meaning.

There is a textual problem here. Quite a few manuscripts have 'in my bonds', and this reading found its way into the KJV. But the reading without 'my' is supported in the GNT with only a B "almost certain" rating. The 'my' was undoubtedly added either due to such a phraseology being found in Phil. 1:7, 13, 14, 17 and Col. 4:8, or, as Bruce explains it, due to a belief especially in the Alexandrian area that Paul was the author of the book.

10:34b when your possessions were confiscated by unbelievers The display supplies an appropriate agent for the verb representing the abstract noun 'seizure'. Louw and Nida have "when the authorities seized all that you owned;" it is implied that those who made the seizures were not believers.

10:34c you yourselves knew There is another slight textual problem here. The GNT, which is followed here, accepts 'yourselves' with an A "certain" rating, but a very few manuscripts follow what was probably an accidental change to the dative form of the pronoun, whose meaning was later strengthened by adding the pronoun ἐν 'in'. These texts with the sense of 'in' were the basis of the KJV translation.

eternal possessions *in heaven* which are better *than those which were taken from you* The phrase κρείττονα ὕπαρξιν καὶ μένουσαν 'a better and remaining possession' has several problems: first, is the writer referring to only one possession in using the singular, or should it be taken as plural (as in NIV and NLT)? Either is acceptable; one could use the singular as long as the readers do not assume there is only one blessing awaiting believers in heaven. A second problem is the comparative degree construction; the display fills out the ellipsis, but in languages with no comparative construction it may be possible to use a verb such as 'surpass' or even say something like 'what they took from you had some value but what you will receive in heaven has very great value'. A greater problem is the meaning of the word 'remaining': does it mean 'something they still have, even when other goods were confiscated' or should 'in heaven' be understood? The former is possible (cf. TEV's "you still had…something much better") but the majority of commentators support the interpretation taken here (cf. NLT's "waiting for you in eternity;" LB and KJV have "in heaven").

There is little difference in meaning: since the former interpretation would have to be taken as meaning 'which you still have now and which you will still have in heaven', the latter, being implied anyway, seems preferable.

10:35a do not become discouraged The clause μὴ ἀποβάλητε τὴν παρρησίαν ὑμῶν 'do not throw away your confidence' could be perceived as a litotes, emphasizing the positive 'be very confident' (cf. JB or CEV's "keep on being brave") or simply a somewhat idiomatic way of saying "don't give up!" (Louw and Nida).

when you are persecuted This is an implicature of the argument, implied in the context. NLT has "no matter what happens."

10:35b *God* **will reward us greatly** *if we continue to believe* The implied part of this proposition is a strong implicature of the argument. The latter part makes a clause out of the noun μισθαποδοσία 'reward'; either Christ or God could be considered the agent.

EXPANSION OF THE *AMPLIFICATION* IN THE 10:32–39 DISPLAY

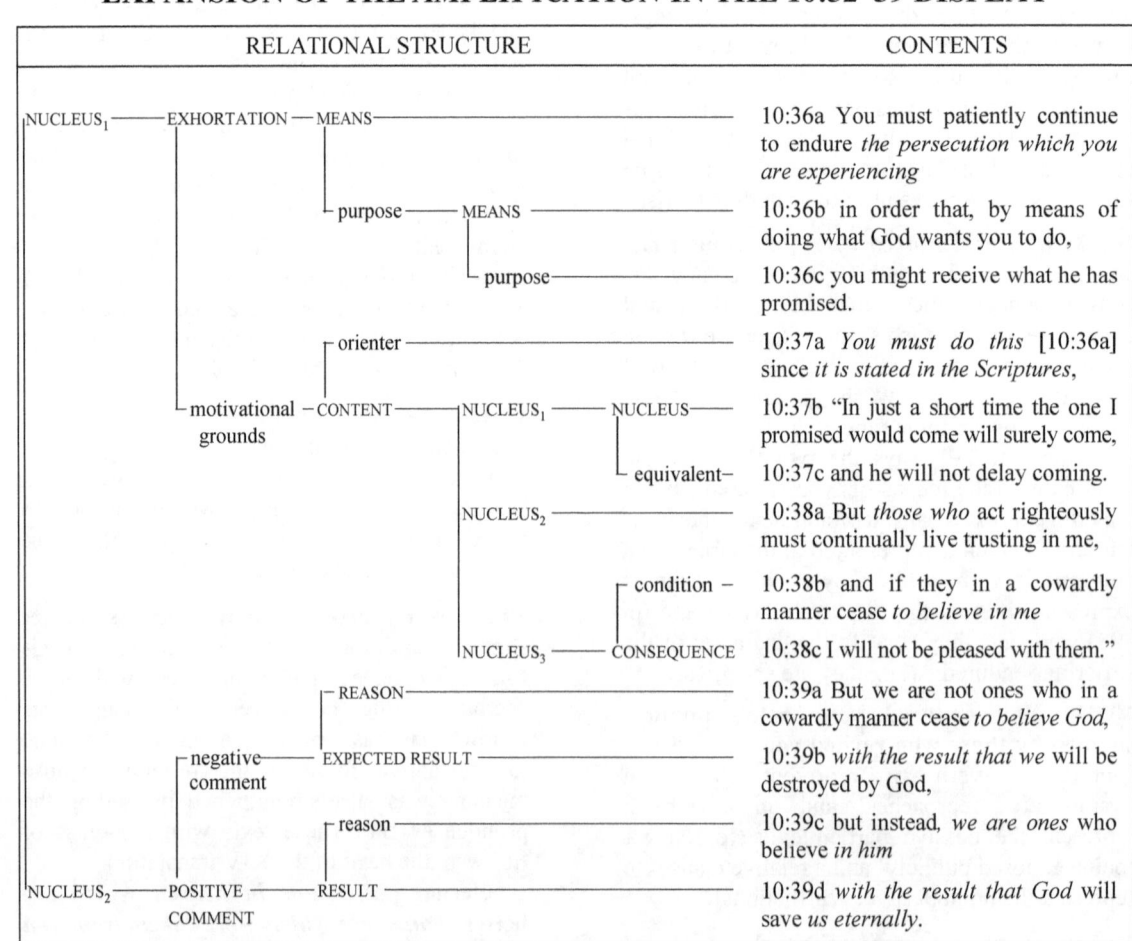

NOTES

10:36a patiently continue to endure *the persecution which you are experiencing* The noun ὑπομονή means 'patience' but semantically patience is adverbial, modifying some event. The situation the readers found themselves in, which led to some of them thinking of returning to Judaism, was the trials which they had been experiencing. LB's alternative "keep on patiently doing God's will" is too generic. JBP and NLT both have "patient endurance." The γάρ here introduces this unit as the *amplification* of the preceding APPEAL.

10:36b *by means of doing* Many commentators say the relationship signaled by the participle ποιήσαντες 'having done' is a temporal one, (i.e., 'after you have done'.) But the receiving of what God has promised is not just something which happens to occur after doing God's will; the one is the result of the other.

10:37a *it is stated in the Scriptures* What follows in vv. 37–38 is from the Septuagint version of Isaiah 26:20 and Habakkuk 2:3–4. Most of the versions indicate by orthographic devices that it is an OT quote; CEV has "as the Scriptures say." The words 'God said' are necessary to supply a referent for the first person singular pronouns in v. 39. In some languages the words '*that God said about the Messiah*' may be necessary to make clear what the commentators are unanimous in saying—that 'the coming one' (v. 38a) refers to the Messiah.

10:37b *In just a short time* This conveys the sense of the rather strange expression ἔτι μικρὸν ὅσον ὅσον 'yet a little how long how long'.

the one I promised would come As Brown (p. 484) so well puts it, "'He that is coming' was an appellation given by the Jews to the Messiah. It is here used plainly in reference to some 'promise of His coming.'"

10:38a *those who* act righteously must continually live trusting in me The first part of this proposition is needed to give the sense of the possessive pronoun in the phrase 'my righteous (person)' and also to make clearer the sense of 'turns back' in v. 38b. Miller says (p. 323) the sense of the phrase can be given as "the righteous one who belongs to me." The sense, however, is plural (cf. TEV's "My righteous people;" cf. also CEV, LB/NLT).

There is a question whether the word δίκαιος 'righteous' is referring to those who are declared righteous in the sense Paul uses in Romans, or whether it is referring to righteous or moral living. The great majority of commentators agree with BAGD (p. 195.1b) in giving the sense here as "conforming to the laws of God and man, and living in accordance with them." This is the sense intended by Habakkuk, and it would be wrong to infer the meaning Paul gives to this passage in Romans 1:17.

must continually live trusting in me Greenlee (p. 424) sums up the view of almost all the commentators in saying this clause "indicates how the righteous person is to live."

10:38b in a cowardly manner cease *to believe in me* The verb ὑποστέλλω means to 'withdraw in fear' (BAGD p. 847.2a). But draw back from what? Lane (p. 305) says that in the context the word "is a denotation for apostasy," or in simpler words it means to "give up one's faith" (Lenski, p. 371).

10:39a *we* The analysis assumes here that the 'we' is inclusive, though one might assume from the emphatic pronoun here plus the rest of the epistle that the sense would be 'we who have held to the faith are not…' or even 'I hope you are not…'. Davidson says the writer "uniting himself with his readers, is confident that they are not of the faint-hearted faithless class who draw back."

10:39b-d *with the result that* This analysis agrees with Miller that the εἰς introduces a result both times, but here the reason and result propositions seem equally prominent.

10:39d save *us eternally* The GNT has περιποίησιν ψυχῆς 'possession of soul' which taken literally does not make much sense. Lünemann says it means "gaining of the soul, i.e., everlasting life and blessedness." A good alternative would be "and are saved" (so TEV, NIV).

BOUNDARIES AND COHERENCE

A new section starting at 11:1 is indicated by a completely new topic, faith, which is discussed at great length. Coherence in the 10:32–39 paragraph is given by several terms describing their suffering: struggle, suffering, reproach, affliction, insult, and imprisonment, and also terms referring to the rewards for faithful believers: reward, receiving what God has promised, and 'possessing of souls' = salvation.

PROMINENCE AND THEME

The theme is drawn from the nucleus of the *motivational basis* plus the generic proposition of the *amplification*, plus the exhortation of the APPEAL and a condensation of the *amplification*.

PART CONSTITUENT 11:1—12:6 (Hortatory Sub-Part: Appeal₅ of 1:4—12:29)

THEME: Since we know about many people who trusted in God during difficult circumstances, we must be like them—we must put aside the things that hinder us spiritually, and try to achieve God's will, imitating Jesus.

MACROSTRUCTURE	CONTENTS
basis	11:1–40 We can confidently expect to receive the good things that God has promised, when we trust him. Whenever we read in the Scriptures about some of our ancestors, we can know that God esteemed their faith. But God did not give them the most important benefit, since he planned that they receive that benefit only as they join together with us who trust God now.
APPEAL	12:1–6 Since we know so many people with faith like that, let us put aside anything, especially sin, which hinders us, and let us strive to achieve God's will and concentrate on Jesus.

INTENT AND PARAGRAPH PATTERN

This is a hortatory unit; the list of people in chapter 11 forms the *basis* of the APPEAL in 12:1–6. Following the strong negative warning in chapter 10, the writer is urging his readers positively to put aside their spiritual hindrances by considering how their ancestors trusted in God.

BOUNDARIES AND COHERENCE

A new unit at 12:7 is indicated by a tail-head linkage involving the word παιδεύει 'discipline' which is found in 12:6 and then becomes the topic of the following paragraph.

PROMINENCE AND THEME

The expression πιστει 'by faith' is prominent in this section, occurring eighteen times, each time exhibiting prominence by occurring first in its clause. The theme is a slightly condensed version of the APPEAL, which has more natural prominence than the *basis*.

SUB-PART CONSTITUENT 11:1–40 (Section: Basis of 11:1—12:6)

THEME: We can confidently expect to receive the good things that God has promised, when we trust him. Whenever we read in the Scriptures about some of our ancestors, we can know that God esteemed their faith. But God did not give them the most important benefit, since he planned that they receive that benefit only as they join together with us who trust God now.

MACROSTRUCTURE	CONTENTS
CLAIM₁	11:1–2 We can confidently expect to receive the good things that God has promised, because we trust him. We can confidently expect to finally see them. It is because our ancestors *trusted in God* that he commended them. [See displays on pages 173 for v. 1 and 176 for v. 2]
CLAIM₂	11:3 It is because we trust God that we know that when he created the world, he did not create it from things that can be seen. [See SECTION CONSTITUENT 11:3 on page 175.]
CLAIM₃	11:4–38 Our Patriarchs were commended for trusting in God. Many more, including the judges and prophets lived trusting in God and doing great things for God, but others suffered for their faith.
SUMMARY	11:39–40 God did not give these people all that he promised them, because he foresaw that what he would later give them and us together would be better.

INTENT AND PARAGRAPH PATTERN

It is very difficult to decide on the pattern of this unit. Clearly it is one unit on some level, since its cohesion is provided by the one word πίστις 'faith'. But should we consider it to be one paragraph or a number of paragraphs? Both the GNT and a number of the versions (e.g., NIV, NEB, TEV, JB, CEV) give the whole chapter one title using the word 'faith' in it. They also break it up into untitled paragraphs. But there is a fair amount of disagreement among them as to how to divide it. JBP gives titles to the smaller units, either a one-word title, giving the name of the individual being discussed, or a fuller section heading. The main difficulty with trying to postulate several paragraphs is that most of them would not have a paragraph pattern even though many of them center around one individual. For that reason the whole unit is considered to be one semantic paragraph.

The next question is, what is the overall paragraph pattern? The first two verses clearly give the theme; most of what follows is illustrative examples of v. 2. Miller says (p. 326) the γάρ 'for' "introduces v. 2 as the author's familiar way as grounds to conclusion." But semantically v. 2 does not cohere as a grounds, and that may be the reason that most of the modern versions do not give any connective between the first two verses.

The material in the rest of the chapter consists of a long list of specifics of v. 2 (i.e., examples of the Jews' ancestors' faith), plus (vv. 13–16) a restatement of v. 2, and a final summary (vv. 39–40).

BOUNDARIES AND COHERENCE

The start of a new paragraph in 12:1 is indicated by a switch from indicative clauses to a hortatory clause introduced by a first person plural subjunctive. Cohesion in the 11:1–40 unit is provided by twenty-three occurrences of the noun πίστις 'faith' or its cognate verb.

PROMINENCE AND THEME

The most naturally prominent propositions are in the three claims and the summary. The theme focuses on the claims and the summary.

SECTION CONSTITUENT 11:1 (Claim₁ of 11:1–40)

THEME: We can confidently expect to receive the good things that God has promised, because we trust him. We can confidently expect to finally see them.

¶ PTRN	RELATIONAL STRUCTURE	CONTENTS
DECLARATION	REASON	11:1a It is because we trust *God*
	└result	11:1b that we confidently expect *to receive the blessings that God has promised.*
description	CONTRAEXPECTATION	11:1c We are sure *that we will finally receive those things,*
	└concession	11:1d even though we do not experience them *yet.*
THESIS		11:2 [See displays on pages 176]

INTENT AND PARAGRAPH PATTERN

This brief unit consists of only one CLAIM. It is the first in four CLAIMS that form the *basis* of the APPEAL in 12:1–6.

NOTES

11:1a It is because we trust *God* There are two problems in propositionalizing the meaning of the Greek word πίστις 'faith'. It is an abstract noun that represents a semantic event (so Louw and Nida 31:104), so thus requires a full clause. We also need to supply an agent and a patient in order to complete the case frame. The agent is not at all in focus. We supply a generic first person plural subject; (cf. CEV, JBP.) An alternative would be 'anyone who trusts God'.

The word πίστις is forefronted before the other nouns in the Greek, giving it prominence. This prominence is shown in the display by a cleft construction, here and seventeen more times in this chapter.

Two questions discussed by the commentators need to be mentioned: first, is this verse a definition of faith or a description of it, and second, are the two halves synonymous? Since hope deals with future things, and faith can have present things as its object, it seems best to agree with most commentators that it is much more a description than a definition. As to the second question, the absence of a καί 'and' to connect the two would tend to suggest they are probably synonymous or nearly so. As Ellingworth says (p. 566), "There are so many unknowns in the equation that it is simplest to take the two statements as synonymous, making the verse as a whole a typical chiasmus." BAGD (p. 249.1) suggests the word ἔλεγχος here means 'inner conviction', which is semantically an event which could be represented by the verbs 'convince', 'assure', or 'persuade'. These are transitive verbs, but the agent is again not in focus; and as commentators note, there is little difference between ὑπόστασις 'substance' and ἔλεγχος 'evidence'. The other problem is the relationship between the clause being expressed by πίστις and the verb ἔστιν 'is'. The meaning that seems to fit best semantically is to supply a reason relationship expressed by 'because'.

11:1b that we confidently expect *to receive* BAGD (p. 847.3) says there are no Greek documents that imply a meaning 'assurance', but it says there are documents that imply the meaning 'realization' in the sense of 'cause to become reality'. However, once again it becomes hard to fit such a meaning to 'faith' when it is made a clause. The notion that 'faith' causes things to become real seems foreign to the teaching of the writer of Hebrews (as Attridge notes). It is also foreign to the teaching of any other writer of Scripture. It is true that faith causes things hoped for to become real in the mind of the believer, but it is a rather weak claim.

Supplying the verb 'receive' makes clear the semantic connection between the noun ὑπόστασις 'assurance' and the participle ἐλπιζομένων '(the things) hoped for', and also shows that several of the interpretations offered for ὑπόστασις are really quite similar. 'It is because we have faith that God assures us we will receive' is not much different from 'it is because we have faith that we are guaranteed we will receive' or 'it is because of our faith that we know what we hope for will be a reality'.

the blessings that God has promised The verb ἐλπίζω and the cognate noun ἐλπίς are consistently rendered by the verb phrase 'to confidently expect' in this study. Case frames require an object to be supplied; the rendering here and an alternative 'what God will give him' are very generic. The rendering here follows very closely that which is suggested by Ellingworth and Nida (p. 251) for the first part of this verse: "Those who trust God are sure that he will give them what they hope for."

11:1c We are sure *that* The word ὑπόστασις has been variously interpreted. Because it meant 'substance' as used by Greek philosophers, it was thus understood by the early Greek fathers and it was so translated in KJV. NEB uses the same word by translating "Faith gives substance to our hopes" but it is difficult to know what that might mean, and becomes even more difficult when 'faith' is rendered by a full clause. There is a second meaning, 'foundation', with the sense of 'faith is the foundation upon which our hopes rest'. That meaning makes good sense, but again it is very difficult to use when we translate 'faith' as a clause. We have rendered a third meaning, 'assurance' in the display text as 'we are sure that', which is how it is taken in most versions. This meaning fits in well when 'faith' is spelled out by a clause. Another interpretation, which is supported by a number of Greek papyri, is 'guarantee'. JB follows that meaning and begins the verse with "Only faith can guarantee."

An alternative to the one in the display would be 'God assures us that', but the sense of both is 'we are absolutely certain'.

11:1c-d *we will finally receive those things* even though we do not experience them *yet* The phrase πραγμάτων...οὐ βλεπομένων 'of things not seen' is taken as an objective genitive phrase which a partial unskewing would represent as "certain of what we cannot see" (Ellingworth and Nida, p. 251). But the word 'certain' semantically requires a full clause as its object. That leaves two possibilities: 'certain that they are real' or 'certain that they will occur'. Several commentators assume that the former is meant (e.g., Hughes, Kistemaker (p. 311), and Montefiore). But in the list of examples of faith which follows, it is certainly true that many of them involve faith that things yet to come would surely happen (e.g., Noah, Abraham, Sarah, Joseph, Moses). It is best to note as Bruce (p. 279 footnote) does that "This 'conviction of things not seen'...embraces things which are invisible because they belong to the spiritual order and things which are invisible because they belong to the future, like the fulfillment of God's promises.' " There does not seem to be any way to express both of these using one verb and therefore the display presents both. The expression 'not seen' is then rendered by a concessive clause. LB similarly uses a concessive clause, "even though we cannot see it up ahead;" (cf. also NCV.) Since 'see' focuses on visible things, and blessings are not always visible, the display has 'receive'.

SECTION CONSTITUENT 11:3 (Claim₂ of 11:1–40)

THEME: It is because we trust God that we know that when he created the world, he did not create it from things that can be seen.

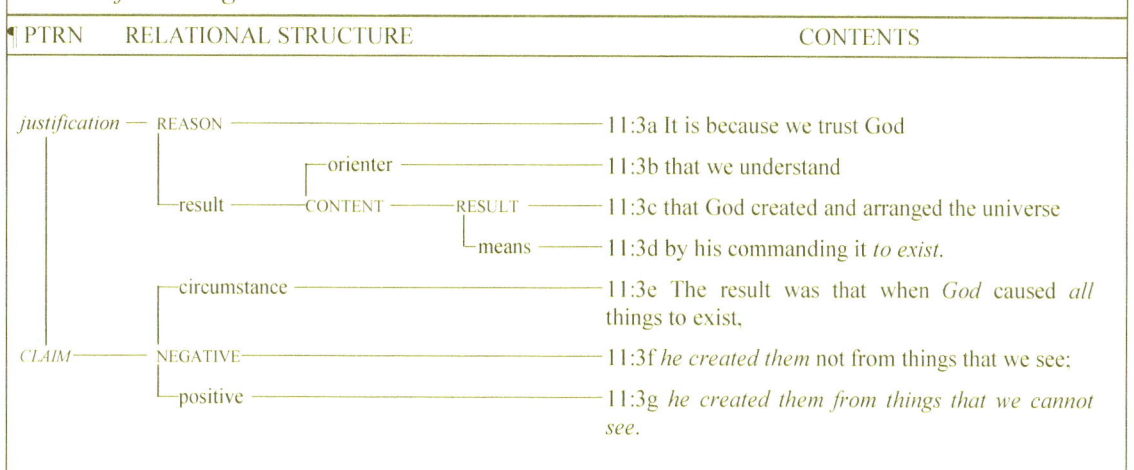

INTENT AND RELATIONAL STRUCTURE

This unit covers only one verse. It consists of only one CLAIM and one *justification*, containing one REASON cluster and one RESULT cluster.

NOTES

11:3c that God created and arranged The verb here is a passive form of καταρτίζω which, as some commentators note, means not just 'created' (BAGD p. 418.a, Louw and Nida 42.36) but in Lünemann's words, "placed in a completed or perfect condition." But since the one concept implies the other, two verbs are used in the display. NEB tries to cover both with the phrase "was fashioned."

the universe Since the expression here is τοὺς αἰῶνας 'the ages', many commentators agree with Bruce (p. 280) that the sense is "the universe of space and time." But that is probably pressing the etymology too far as well as probably being impossible to translate; BAGD does not suggest such a meaning. The display follows Louw and Nida (1.2) and several versions (TEV, NIV, NB, JBP) in rendering it as "universe."

11:3d by his commanding it *to exist* The phrase ῥήματι θεοῦ 'by a word of God' is taken as a metonymy, 'word' standing for the event of 'command'. The words 'it to exist' are required from case frame considerations but would not be necessary where 'command' can be expressed by a noun.

11:3e The result was that As Miller notes (p. 330), εἰς plus an infinitive clause introduced by the article here must signify result, not purpose, because this chapter presents the results of faith, not its purposes.

***God* caused *all* things to exist** The GNT has only the infinitive 'to become' which here has the sense of 'come into existence, be created'. In the context God is the implied agent, though it may be possible to use an intransitive verb such as "has come into being" (JBP), "came forth from" (NEB).

11:3f not from things that we see There is a question of what the negative particle goes with in the phrase μὴ ἐκ φαινομένων τὸ βλεπόμενον γεγονέναι 'not from appearing (things) the (things) being-seen have become'. It could be taken with the infinitive, giving the sense 'it was not created out of things that are seen', as in NIV's "was not made out of what was visible." Or it could be taken with the participle φαινομένων (though this would seem strange with the ἐκ intervening) to give the sense 'it was created out of things not seen', as in TEV's "was made out of what cannot be seen." Lane says that the negative usually occurs before the item that is negated, which suggests that the NIV rendering is correct. There is little semantic difference, but if the former interpretation (it was not created...) is taken, it semantically requires the latter interpretation to be implied anyway.

This verse is the first of many in this chapter that start with the word πίστει 'by faith'.

It is separated from the others because it is only a generic statement and does not contain the name of any individual, as the others do.

BOUNDARIES AND COHERENCE

A new paragraph at v.4 is signaled by the beginning of the list of individuals who exhibited faith in God.

THEME AND PROMINENCE

The theme is drawn from the more naturally prominent REASON clause of the *justification*, the orienter proposition of the RESULT, and the NEGATIVE proposition of the CLAIM.

SECTION CONSTITUENT 11:2, 4–38 (Expository Sub-Section: Claims₃ of 11:1–40)

THEME: It was because our ancestors trusted God that he commended them. Those included Abel, Enoch, Noah, Abraham, Isaac, Jacob, Moses, Rahab, Gideon, Barak, Samson, Jephthah, David, Samuel, and others who suffered torture and death, who, because they trusted in God, each did things that pleased God.

MACROSTRUCTURE	CONTENTS
THESIS	11:2 It is because our ancestors *trusted in God* that he commended them.
basis₁	11:4–31 Our Patriarchs were commended for trusting in God.
basis₂	11:32–38 Many more, including the judges and prophets lived trusting in God and doing great things for God, but others suffered for their faith.

INTENT AND MACROSTRUCTURE

This unit (2, 4-38) consists of a long list of specifics of v. 2 (i.e., examples of the Jews' ancestors' faith) developed until v. 38.

BOUNDARIES AND COHERENCE

The start of a new paragraph in 12:1 is indicated by a switch from indicative clauses to a hortatory clause introduced by a first person plural subjunctive. Cohesion in the 11:2–38 unit is provided by twenty-three occurrences of the noun πίστις 'faith' or its cognate verb.

PROMINENCE AND THEME

The most naturally prominent propositions are in the three claims and the summary. The theme focuses on the THESIS and the two *bases*.

(THESIS: CONSTITUENT 11:2 of Unit 11:2, 4–38)

THEME: It is because our ancestors trusted in God that he commended them.

RELATIONAL STRUCTURE	CONTENTS
justification	11:2a It is because *many of our* ancestors *trusted in God*
CLAIM	11:2b that he commended them.

INTENT AND RELATIONAL STRUCTURE

This very brief paragraph consists of one *justification* and one CLAIM. The author's intent is to introduce a long discussion of those who exhibited faith, as a prelude to urging his readers to do likewise.

NOTES

11:2a It is because *many of our* ancestors *trusted in God* The author referred generically to οἱ πρεσβύτεροι 'the ancestors', but since most of the ancestors were unbelievers, 'many of' is supplied. The words 'trusted in God' simply specifies what the phrase ἐν ταύτῃ 'in this' refers to.

many of our ancestors Commentators agree that the phrase οἱ πρεσβύτεροι 'the elders' means essentially the same as τοῖς πατράσιν 'our ancestors' in 1.1.

trusted in God The author wrote only ἐν ταύτῃ 'in this', with 'this' referring to 'faith'. Because this phrase and its usual equivalent in the rest of the chapter, πίστει 'by faith', are emphasized by being forefronted, the clauses which represent it are also emphasized by being forefronted in a cleft construction in the display. However, such a way to emphasize a concept is awkward in many languages. The translator should choose a natural way to emphasize these concepts. The words 'in God' satisfy the case frame. In some cases the noun πίστις is represented in the display by the verb 'believe' and sometimes by 'trust' but the translator should not feel obliged to find or use two different terms.

11:2b he commended This expresses the meaning of ἐμαρτυρήθησαν 'were approved', which, as Hughes notes (p. 441), is "an instance of a 'divine passive' in which the implication is that the unexpressed agent is God himself."

BOUNDARIES AND COHERENCE

A new paragraph at v.3 is indicated by a switch from a general statement about faith in v. 2 to the first example of faith introduced by πίστει 'by faith' followed by a long list of individuals who had faith in God.

THEME AND PROMINENCE

The theme is taken from the *justification* and the CLAIM.

(BASIS₁: CONSTITUENT 11:4–31 of 11:4–38)

THEME: *Our Patriarchs were commended for trusting in God.*	
RELATIONAL STRUCTURE	CONTENTS
CLAIM₁	11:4 It was because Adam's son Abel trusted in God that he sacrificed something better to God than what his older brother Cain offered to God. [See Expanded Display on page 178]
CLAIM₂	11:5–6 It was because Enoch trusted God that God took him *directly to heaven* with the result that he did not die. [See Expanded Display on page 179.]
CLAIM₃	11:7 It was because Noah trusted in God that Noah showed that he reverently obeyed God with the result that he saved his family and himself by building a huge boat. [See Expanded Display on page 181.]
CLAIM₄	11:8–19 Abraham and these others continued to trust God, but they died without having received the things that God promised. [See Expanded Display on page 182.]
CLAIM₅	11:20 It was because Isaac trusted God that *he prayed that God* would *bless his* sons *Jacob* and Esau in the future. [See Expanded Display on page 190.]
CLAIM₆	11:21 It was because Jacob trusted God that he blessed each of Joseph's sons, and he worshipped God as he leaned on his *walking-stick just* before he died. [See Expanded Display on page 191.]
CLAIM₇	11:22 When Joseph was about to die, it was because he trusted in God that he told his fellow Israelis *that their descendants* would someday leave *Egypt,* and he commanded that *those descendants must* carry his bones *with them when they left Egypt.* [See Expanded Display on page 191.]
CLAIM₈	11:23–30 It was because Moses' parents trusted in God that they hid Moses for 3 months. It was because Moses trusted in God that he refused to accept the privileges of being the son of the king's daughter, he departed from Egypt not fearing the king, he instituted *the feast* called Passover, *the people of* Israel walked *through the water* called the Red *Sea as though they walked* over dry land, marched around the walls for seven days so that the walls around *Jericho* city collapsed. [See Expanded Display on page 192.]
CLAIM₉	11:31 It was because Rahab, who had been a prostitute, trusted God that she did not perish with those within Jericho who disobeyed God. [See Expanded Display on page 198.]

INTENT AND RHETORICAL STRUCTURE

This paragraph consists of a long set of examples of those who had faith in God. The author's purpose is to list the names of various individuals who kept trusting in God throughout their lives.

This long unit consists of a set of *CLAIMS* plus a SUMMARY STATEMENT describing how those who lived in former times had exhibited their faith in God; the whole unit forms the *basis* of the APPEAL in the paragraph 12:1–6 that follows. The author here gives a long series of examples of faith, to encourage his readers to follow their example.

Most modern versions have a separate paragraph for each person listed as an example of faith. But to do so would require discussing not only the themes but boundaries and cohesion and author intent.

PROMINENCE AND THEME

The theme is a very short summary of the deeds of those who exhibited faith. The prominence shown by the forefronting of the word πίστει 'by faith' is maintained in the display by use of cleft constructions.

(CLAIM₁: CONSTITUENT 11:4 of 11:4–31)

THEME: It was because Adam's son Abel trusted in God that he sacrificed something better to God than what his older brother Cain offered to God
RELATIONAL STRUCTURE — CONTENTS

REASON		11:4a It was because *Adam's son* Abel trusted in God
RESULT₁	COMPARISON₁	11:4b that he offered to God a sacrifice that was better
	COMPARISON₂	11:4c than what *his older brother* Cain offered to God.
	reason	11:4d Because he did that,
RESULT₂	RESULT	11:4e God testified *that* Abel was a righteous man.
	amplification	11:4f God testified that [11:4e] because of the gifts that he offered.
RESULT₃	CONTRAEXPECTATION	11:4g And we can still learn from Abel *about* trusting *God*,
	concession	11:4h even though Abel is now dead.

NOTES

11:4a *Adam's son* Abel The designation 'Adam's son' is supplied for situations in which Abel would not be known; otherwise it should not be included.

11:4b a sacrifice As Ellingworth notes (p. 573) concerning the word 'gifts', "the context suggests a number of animal sacrifices"; NIV and JB convey the same sense with "offerings."

11:4b-c better...than For languages which have no comparative construction it will be necessary to use whatever means is available, such as 'he sacrificed something good which surpassed what Cain offered'. A discussion of what made Abel's sacrifice better does not belong here; it is best to presume from the context simply that "it was the quality of Abel's faith which made the difference" (Miller, p. 335).

11:4c *his older brother* This specifies the relationship which the original readers of Hebrews would have been expected to know.

11:4d Because he did that The prepositional phrase δι' ἧς 'through which' introduces a result.

11:4e God testified There is a question of how the genitive absolute phrase ματυροῦντος...τοῦ θεοῦ 'God testifying' relates to what precedes it. Some versions (e.g., TEV and NEB) assume a grounds relationship. Miller (p. 334) says that the genitive absolute "makes it apparent that it is not connected grammatically to the rest of the verse." Other versions (NIV, JB) postulate a temporal relationship. But it fits well as an amplification of v. 4e.

The verb μαρτυρέω means basically to testify, but in conjunction with the words ἐπὶ τοῖς δώροις αὐτοῦ 'concerning his gifts' it must convey another of the senses listed by BAGD

(p. 493.1c), 'testify favorably, speak well (of), approve (of)'. This is the sense taken by NIV, CEV, TEV, NEB, and NCV.

testified *that Abel* **was a righteous man** Here the same verb ἐμαρτυρήθη in a finite form does mean 'testified' or 'declared'. The word 'righteous' here does not mean 'justified' in the Pauline sense, but that his actions were good or righteous; NLT has "a good man."

11:4g we can still learn from Abel *about trusting God* The GNT has δι' αὐτῆς ἔτι λαλεῖ 'through it still he speaks'. The 'it' refers to faith, which is rendered here as a verb plus the object 'God'. The words 'he still speaks' are taken as hyperbole; dead people do not speak to us. The question then is, is this a subtle reference to Gen. 4:10 where God says 'The voice of your brother's blood is crying to me from the ground', and thus the 'speaking' means crying out for vengeance, or does the speaking mean, following Hughes, p. 457, "by his example of faith and righteousness still speaks to us today"? The context clearly is talking about faith, not about vengeance, and thus the latter interpretation is correct. To avoid the hyperbole the display renders 'we still learn about'. LB similarly renders it by "we can still learn lessons from him about trusting God."

11:4h even though Abel is now dead The aorist participle ἀποθανών 'having died' expresses a concession. The verb is used in 9:27 and 11:37 to express a violent death and applies here as well; hence JBP's rendering "though Cain killed him" is well justified and would be a good alternative.

(CLAIM₂: CONSTITUENT 11:5–6 of 11:4–31)

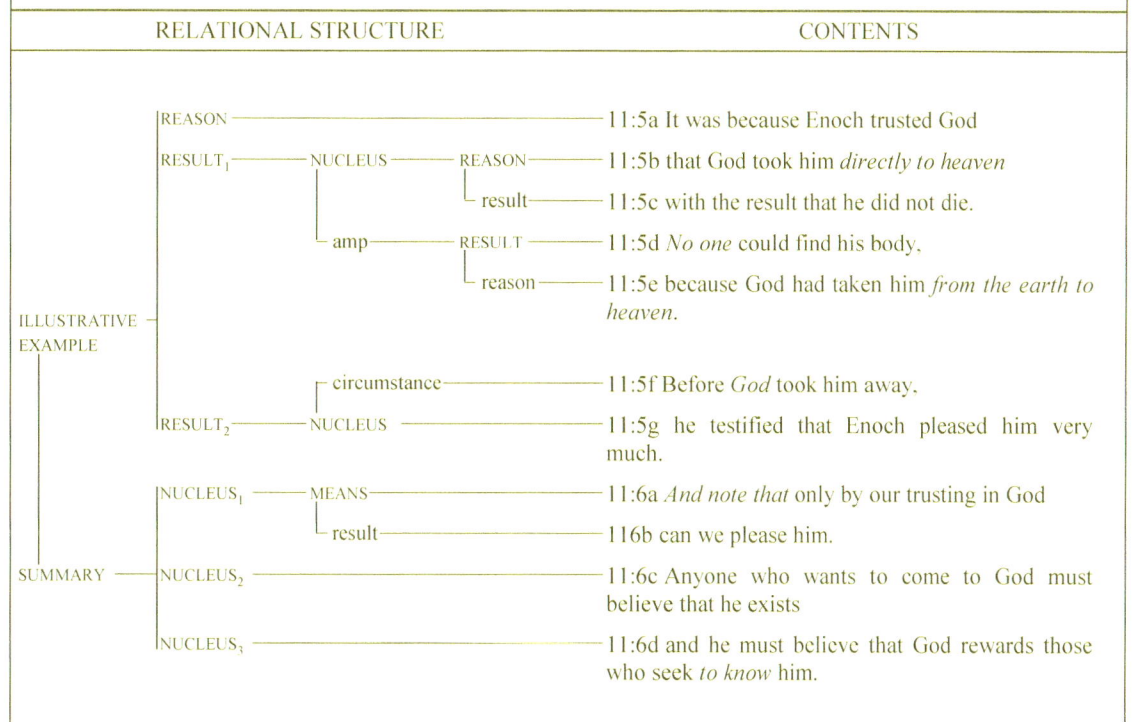

NOTES

11:5b God took him *directly to heaven* The verb μετατίθημι means 'convey to another place' (BAGD p. 513:1). The idea of 'taken <u>up</u>' which is found in many versions may not be technically correct, as Louw and Nida note (15.2), but either way, case considerations demand a specification of location, from where or to where or both. The original reference (Gen. 5:24) does not specify either. NIV specifies the former, "from this life"; most other versions specify the latter with phrases such as "to God" (TEV), "to the eternal world" (JBP), "to another life" (NEB), or "to heaven" (CEV, LB). Miller argues (p. 339) that according to OT terminology the place must be understood as "to the realm of the righteous dead," not to heaven or to God's presence. But Attridge claims (p. 317) that the notion of Enoch's "exaltation into heaven was widespread in intertestamental Judaism"; and on that basis 'to heaven' is supplied in the display also. The word 'directly' is an implicature of v. 5c.

11:5c not die The phrase μὴ ἰδεῖν θάνατον 'not to see death', which occurs several times in both the Old and New Testaments, "is a literal translation of a Hebrew idiom meaning 'experience death' (compare Phillips) or simply 'die'" (Ellingworth and Nida, p. 255). Since 'experience death' is still semantically skewed, the rendering here avoids the abstract noun; NCV renders it similarly. NLT has "so he would not die" and CEV has "and did not die."

11:5d *No one* could find his body The rendering here changes the passive οὐχ ηὑρίσκετο 'he was not found' into an active clause, as also in TEV. The CEV renders this as "his body was never found" which might be clearer in some languages, although it seems to imply that his body was somewhere, but was never located. The author cites Gen. 5:24 here.

11:5e taken him *from the earth to heaven* See note on v. 5b. The display supplies both the locations from which and to which, to satisfy the case frame for 'take away'. In many translations it will be possible to avoid both.

11:5f God took him away The display text renders the noun μετάθεσις 'removal' by a verb and the passive μεμαρτύρηται 'was testified (to)' as an active, and in both cases 'God' is supplied as the implied agent. NCV has "the Scripture says" which is fine for languages which accept such personification.

11:6a *And note that* The δέ introduces what Attridge (p. 318) calls a "general principle," and Miller (p. 337) calls "a *generic summary* of universal application." It is thus given the label "SUMMARY". To indicate that this verse departs from the list of examples of faith, it is introduced in the display by 'And note that'. Ellingworth (p. 576) calls this verse "the major premise of a syllogism of which v. 5c formed the minor premise, while the conclusion, 'therefore, Enoch had faith', is left implicit." He could be right about a syllogism, but considering the main theme of the epistle it would be far better to see v. 6 stand on its own and be considered a mitigated appeal, with the content of the verse forming the grounds for an implied exhortation, 'therefore, continue to trust God'.

only by our trusting in God The words χωρὶς πίστεως ἀδύνατον 'without faith (it is) impossible' is a negative way of saying what is expressed positively in the display text. If one prefers to retain a more literal form, it could be rendered using a conditional clause: 'if someone does not trust God, it is not possible for that person to please him'.

11:6c Anyone who wants to come to God The phrase τὸν προσερχόμενον τῷ θεῷ 'the one approaching to God' is singular but with a generic sense which is expressed by 'anyone'.

Semantically some aspect such as 'wants to' or 'seeks to' is implied; faith in God must precede approaching him. In some languages it may be necessary to say 'come to God to worship him' (see note on v. 6d).

11:6d God rewards The noun μισθαποδότης 'rewarder' is made a verb (as in almost every modern English translation).

those who seek *to know* him The difficulty of translating literally the GNT phrase τοῖς ἐκζητοῦσιν αὐτόν 'those who seek him' (as in JBP's "those who search for him" and JB's "try to find him") is that they imply God is lost somewhere. Ellingworth suggests 'in worship' to be the content of the 'seeking'; the display has 'to know'. The lexicons do not suggest that the verb has the added component of 'diligently' given in KJV.

(CLAIM₃: CONSTITUENT 11:7 of 11:4–31)

THEME: It was because Noah trusted in God that Noah showed that he reverently obeyed God with the result that he saved his family and himself by building a huge boat.

RELATIONAL STRUCTURE	CONTENTS
REASON	11:7a It was because Noah trusted in God,
⸺ circumstance	11:7b *when* God warned him about a *flood* that had not yet occurred
⸺ result	11:7c that Noah showed that he reverently obeyed God
RESULT₁ ⸺ NUCLEUS ⸺ MEANS	11:7d by building a huge boat to save his family,
RESULT	11:7e *with the result that* he saved his family *and himself*.
RESULT₂ ⸺ NUCLEUS	11:7f *It was because of* his faith that God considered him righteous.
⸺ orienter	11:7g *He made clear to* all the people *around him*
AMPLIFICATION – CONTENT	11:7h *that they deserved to be* condemned *by God*.

NOTES

11:7b about a *flood* that had not yet occurred The GNT has only the phrase περὶ τῶν μηδέπω βλεπομένων 'about (things) not yet seen'. Commentators generally agree with Hughes (p. 463) that the reference is to "the destruction of the flood by which the unrepentant would be judged and of the deliverance of himself and of those who would join him in the ark," but that is a lot of implicit information to include. The display supplies only 'a flood' as an alternative; JBP has a more generic "impending disaster" while LB is much more specific with "even though there was then no sign of a flood." The alternative 'had not yet occurred' is supplied because that is the extended sense intended by 'seen' and would avoid the wrong meaning that the reference is to things that had occurred but which Noah hadn't seen.

11:7c he reverently obeyed God There is a question as to whether εὐλαβέομαι here means 'to fear', 'to show reverence for (God)', or 'to obey'. The first of these does not relationally cohere well in a discussion of faith. Louw and Nida (53.7; 36.13) and Dods suggest the latter two are both possible, the latter being an implication of the former. Since this solution fits best both the meaning of the word and the situational context, both are included in the display text. The participle is taken as expressing attendant circumstance.

11:7d huge boat Though nearly all English versions have "ark" (CEV is an exception with "boat"), that word is not in current English. The word 'huge' is included for translations in societies which know only canoes, if they know boats at all. NCV, NLT, and NCV have "large boat" which is quite good.

his family The primary sense of οἶκος is 'house', but by metonymy it first comes to mean 'household' and then, as here more specifically, 'family'.

11:7f God considered him righteous The word 'heir' in the phrase δικαιοσύνης ἐγένετο κληρονόμος 'became an heir of righteousness' is taken as a dead metaphor; to become an heir simply means to receive something. The display drops the sense altogether by making the abstract noun 'righteousness' into a verb phrase 'considered him righteous'. The word is taken here to be the same as the Pauline sense (Rom. 3:21ff); (i.e., God erased the record of his sins.)

11:7f-g *He made clear to* all the people *around him that they deserved to be* condemned *by God* The first question here is, how do v. 7e-g relate to what precedes it? Miller suggests this is an amplification, but it does not cohere semantically as an amplification of 'because of his faith'. It seems best to be taken as another result of v. 7a.

There are two other problems here. First, what is meant by τὸν κόσμον 'the world'? It is first of all a metonymy standing for people, but with a negative connotation here. Moffat gives the sense here as "sinful humanity" and Lünemann says "the unbelieving world of sinful men," but here the sense must be more restricted. Attridge (p. 319) is more to the point in saying, "Because they failed to accept this message, his contemporaries were condemned." Thus the display renders the word by 'those people around him'. Then we must ask, 'In what sense did Noah condemn them?' God is the one who did the actual condemnation. Most commentators take the sense to be that Noah revealed them as condemned or worthy of condemnation and destruction.

(CLAIM₄: CONSTITUENT 11:8–19 of 11:4–31)

THEME: Abraham and these others continued to trust God, but they died without having received the things that God promised.	
RELATIONAL STRUCTURE	CONTENTS
NUCLEUS₁	11:8–10 It was because Abraham trusted God that he went to a place that God would later give him. [See expanded display on page 183.]
NUCLEUS₂	11:11–12 It was because Abraham trusted God that he and Sarah were able to have a son, even though they were both far beyond child-bearing age. [See expanded display on page 184.]
NUCLEUS₃ SUMMARY	11:13–16 It was while those people still trusted *in God* that they all died; even though they had not *yet* received *all the things God* had promised *to give them*. [See expanded display on page 186.]
NUCLEUS₄	11:17–19 It was because Abraham trusted *God* that he *was ready to* kill *his son* Isaac as a sacrifice when *God* tested Abraham's *faith/obedience*. The result was as though he received him back after he died. [See expanded display on page 188.]

INTENT AND RHETORICAL STRUCTURE

This is a very key and focal unit in the entire chapter. More space is given to Abraham than any other individual. This unit has chiasmus, putting in the center and most prominent part of the chiasmus the fact all of these people died without receiving what God had promised. The arrangement of the units seems illogical until it is seen as a chiasmus. Lane is at a loss to explain the ordering of units. The author has used a rhetorical device to bring this unit into focus. Its emphasis is on the patriarchs looking for something better and eternal.

NOTES

The contents of each of the four units in this paragraph are greatly abbreviated statements of the material contained in each of them.

(NUCLEUS₁: NUCLEUS₁ 11:8–10 of 11:8–19)

THEME: It was because Abraham trusted God that he went to a place that God would later give him and he lived in that land as though he was a foreigner.	
RELATIONAL STRUCTURE	CONTENTS
REASON	11:8a It was because Abraham trusted in God
RESULT — NUCLEUS	11:8b that he obeyed God,
circumstance — NUCLEUS	11:8c when God told him to go to a place
identification of 'place'	11:8d that *God* would later give to him.
amplification — CONTRAEXPECTATION	11:8e Abraham went,
concession	11:8f even though he did not know to where he was going.
REASON₁	11:9a It was because he trusted God
RESULT — NUCLEUS — NUCLEUS	11:9b that he lived in that land to which he went
description of 'land'	11:9c which God had promised *to give to him,*
comparison	11:9d as though he was a foreigner.
amplification₁	11:9e He lived there *only* in tents.
concession	11:9f *His son* Isaac and *his grandson* Jacob also lived in tents,
amplification₂ CONTRAEXPECTATION	11:9g but God promised *to give to them* the same things that he promised *to give to Abraham.*
REASON₂ — NUCLEUS	11:10a Abraham *lived like that* because he was looking forward to *living in* the city *in heaven* that would exist forever,
description of 'city'	11:10b the city that God was designing and building.

NOTES

11:8c God told him The present participle καλούμενος 'called' is taken as expressing circumstance. The word means 'summon someone' (BAGD p. 399.1d) but taken literally it would convey the notion that God was in Canaan summoning Abraham to come there. In actuality the summoning was a command to depart for Canaan. Both CEV and LB also use "told."

11:8d that *God* would later give to him The words ὃν ἤμελλεν λαμβάνειν εἰς κληρονομίαν 'which he was about to receive as an inheritance' are, like 'heir' in v. 7, taken as including a dead metaphor; God did not die in order for Abraham to receive anything. The display uses 'God would give' expressing the reciprocal of 'receive'. The renderings in TEV, NCV, and LB are very similar.

11:8f even though The present participle ἐπιστάμενος 'knowing' is given a concessive sense (as in NIV) but it also could be given a circumstantial sense, 'while he did not know'.

11:9b lived in Most versions assume the verb παροικέω means 'live as a stranger in', but followed by the preposition εἰς 'into' (not 'in') it means 'migrate to' (BAGD, p. 628.1c).

11:9c which God had promised *to give to him* The display spells out the sense of the genitive phrase τῆς ἐπαγγελίας 'of promise' and satisfies the case frame of the verb; (cf. also TEV and NCV.)

11:9e Miller (p. 345) says that the function of the aorist participle κατοικήσας 'dwelling' here is to be more specific of 'lived' in v. 9b, but 'amplification' is a better label.

only **in tents** Many commentators state that the phrase ἐν σκηναῖς 'in tents' implies temporariness, compared to living in a house. Thus 'only' is included as implied.

11:9f His son Isaac and his grandson Jacob also lived The kinship designations are supplied for situations in which this information would not be readily understood. The GNT has μετὰ Ἰσαὰκ καὶ Ἰακώβ, literally 'with Isaac and Jacob', but it implies similarity of circumstances, not identity of time.

11:9g God promised to give to them the same things that he promised to give to Abraham This wording simply unskews the Greek wording τῶν συγκληρονόμων τῆς επαγγελίας τῆς αὐτῆς 'the co-heirs of the same promise'. TEV, CEV, NCV, and LB use similar wording. CEV includes the word 'later' which may be helpful in some languages. Since this paragraph is dealing with Abraham, this proposition is considered a thematic comment.

11:10 Abraham lived like that because The γάρ is considered by nearly all commentators to introduce this verse as the reason for v. 9e.

11:10a looking forward to living in the city The verb ἐκδέχομαι means to expect or wait for or look forward to something, hence here to anticipate. But semantically one does not anticipate a city; therefore 'living in' is supplied to complete the sense (so Ellingworth and Nida, p. 260); LB supplies "for God to bring him to."

in heaven Commentators agree that the city referred to is the 'heavenly Jerusalem', as is made clear in 12:22; it is specified as the 'heavenly city' in LB.

that would exist forever The GNT has τοὺς θεμελίους ἔχουσαν 'having the foundations'. The sense of 'permanent' (cf. TEV) is implied in the context as a contrast to the tents he lived in while on earth. CEV's rendering ('the eternal city') is similar to that given here.

11:10b was designing and building The present tense is given to the two verbs to avoid the idea that the city was already completely built in Abraham's time.

(NUCLEUS₂: NUCLEUS₂ 11:11–12 of 11:8–19)

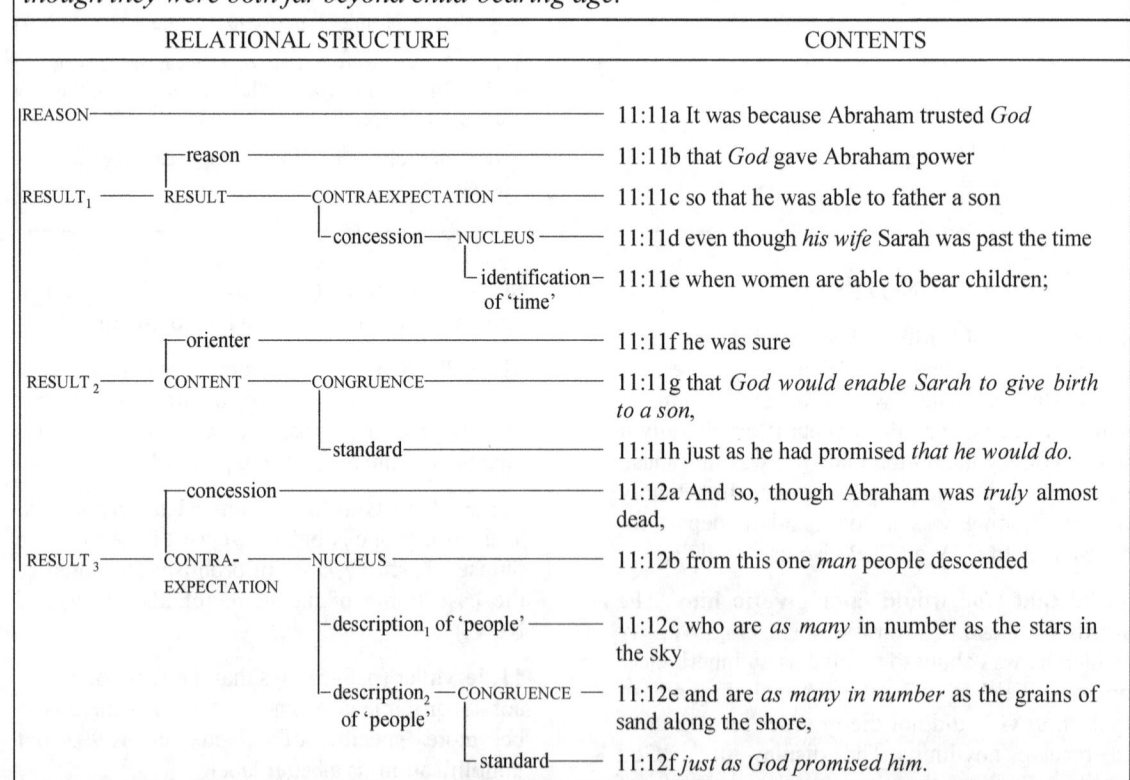

THEME: *It was because Abraham trusted God that he and Sarah were able to have a son, even though they were both far beyond child-bearing age.*

NOTES

11:11a Abraham There are a couple of very difficult problems with this verse, and textual difficulties are also involved. There are five textual variants here, many of which seem to have arisen because of the other difficulties of interpretation. Strictly on the basis of the evidence, it seems best to follow the fourth edition of the UBS text which includes the words αὐτή 'herself' and στεῖρα 'barren' as modifying Sarah (their inclusion is given a C "difficulty in deciding" rating). It is admitted that the word στεῖρα could have been 'added as an interpretative gloss' (Metzger p. 602) to help with the sense, but the UBS committee thought it more likely the word was omitted accidentally because of similarity with the word which precedes it. The next problem is, who is the subject of the words δύναμιν ἔλαβεν 'received power'? If the word στεῖρα were absent, one would expect that αὐτὴ Σάρρα 'Sarah herself' would be the subject. But there are two major difficulties in doing so (in addition to the problem of accounting for στεῖρα if it is original).

The first is that the passage, from v. 8 through v. 14, is about Abraham, not about Sarah (whose faith, from the account in Gen. 18:9–15, is very questionable to say the least). The second difficulty is that the word καταβολή in the phrase δύναμιν εἰς καταβολὴν σπέρματος 'power unto production of sperm' cannot refer to a woman's part in childbearing. BAGD (p. 409.2) comments rather interestingly that "If this meaning is correct for Heb. 11:11, there is probably some error in the text, since this expression could not be used of Sarah, but only of Abraham." But one does not need to presume textual error if one accepts the UBS text: all one needs (p. 323) to do is to take the words αὐτὴ Σάρρα στεῖρα as being 'a Hebraic circumstantial clause' (Metzger p. 602) with no copular verb. This is the interpretation taken here, and it allows 'Abraham' to continue as the subject of the sentence, the one whose faith is being discussed here. An alternate solution suggested by some, one which still retains Abraham as the subject, is to assume the phrase αὐτὴ Σάρρα στεῖρα to express a dative of accompaniment, giving the sense 'he also, together with Sarah (who was) barren, received power' (cf. NLT). As Kistemaker (p. 323) notes, this is a plausible explanation but without manuscript support. Of the versions, only NIV, NCV, NLT and TEV make Abraham the subject, but most modern commentators do also.

11:11c to father a son This is a more euphemistic expression of 'produce sperm' (see note on 11a). There is not a good English word to express this; 'procreate' and 'beget' are possible but cumbersome or archaic. An alternative is "made able to become a father" (NCV) except that in many languages kinship terms obligatorily indicate possession.

11:11d-e even though *his wife* Sarah was past the time when women are able to bear children This interpretation still keeps Abraham as the subject of the sentence. The words καὶ παρὰ καιρὸν ἡλικίας 'even beyond time of age' seem somewhat strange and can be taken as a metonymy and/or a euphemism, 'age' standing for the age during which people bear children. JBP has "far beyond the normal years of child-bearing" and CEV "too old to have children." As noted above, στεῖρα means 'barren' but since this word has a different primary sense in English, the display text uses a longer but clearer expression.

11:11f-h he was sure that *God would enable Sarah to give birth to a son,* just as he had promised *that he would do* The GNT has only the words πιστὸν ἡγήσατο 'he considered faithful'; but since 'faithful' has several meanings, its meaning in this context is spelled out clearly (cf. also CEV and LB). Other words in English would be "reliable," "trustworthy," "dependable." 'God' is supplied as the referent (as in TEV, CEV, and LB) even though it is left unspecified in the Greek text.

11:11g just as he had promised *that he would do* Commentators agree this was the promise being referred to (Gen. 17:19, 18:14, 21:2); the content of the promise is supplied here as an implicature of OT knowledge and from case frame considerations.

11:12a though Abraham was *truly* almost dead The phrase καὶ ταῦτα in the phrase καὶ ταῦτα νενεκρωμένου 'and that having died' is emphatic, pointing to something unexpected (see Ellingworth); hence 'truly'. The word 'dead', as Attridge notes (p. 326), is hyperbole. Even the rendering here is somewhat hyperbolic. Several versions have "as good as dead" which is an English idiom. The real sense is perhaps carried best by LB's rendering, "who was too old to have even one child;" in other words, being almost dead was the reason for the unexpressed result: presumed inability to have a child.

11:12b from this one *man* The numeral εἷς 'one' by itself here stands for one person, namely Abraham.

11:12c *as many* in number as The words 'as many' are implied by the comparison and the words τῷ πλήθει 'in multitude'. For languages which do not have such a comparative construction, it will be necessary to use an equivalent, 'many, at the same level as the stars' for example. All versions, even KJV, make the point of comparison clear.

11:12f *just as God promised him* These words are not in the Greek text, but the writer would expect his audience to know this information; he is in effect citing Gen. 22:17 (JBP and JB make clear by orthographical devices that there is an OT citation here).

(NUCLEUS₃: SUMMARY 11:13–16 of 11:8–19)

THEME: It was while those people still trusted in God that they all died; even though they had not yet received all the things God had promised to give them.

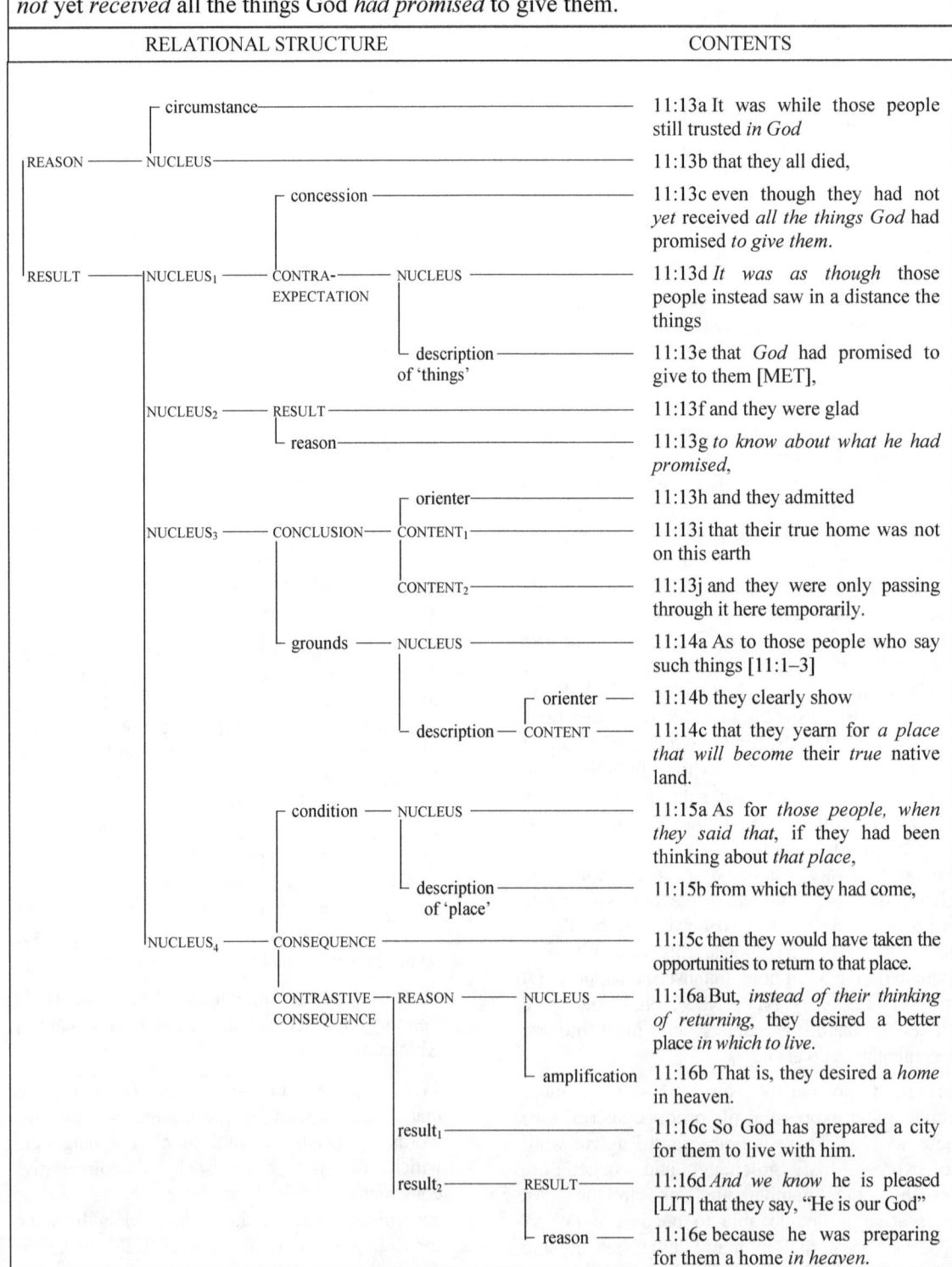

NOTES

11:13a those people Commentators agree that the referent of οὗτοι 'these' is Abraham and his family, not those mentioned before v. 8.

people still trusted *in God* This is an unskewed rendering of κατὰ πίστιν 'according to faith'. Although some commentators say this is simply a literary variation of πίστει 'by faith', the better interpretation is that the sense here is 'in a state of faith' (Ellingworth); CEV has "they still had faith" and Ellingworth and Nida (p. 263) suggest "trusted God until the time they died."

11:13c had not *yet* received *all* The problem here is that Abraham did live to see the fulfillment of one of the greatest of God's promises to him—the birth of his son Isaac. One solution is to supply 'not yet', as here; another one would be to follow LB, which has 'not all that God had promised him'.

***the things God* had promised** The phrase τὰς ἐπαγγελίας 'the promises' can be considered a sort of metonymy, the cause (promising) standing for the effect (what was promised); as Ellingworth says (p. 593), the phrase "must mean, here as in 4:1 (contrast 9:15), the content of the promises."

11:13d *It was as though* those people instead saw in a distance The words πόρρωθεν αὐτὰς ἰδόντες 'seeing them from afar' are not intended to be understood literally; hence 'it was as though'. As to 'them' (= the promises) meaning 'the things God promised', see the previous note.

11:13i that their true home was not on this earth There are two questions here. First, is the expression ξένοι καὶ παρεπίδημοι 'aliens and sojourners' to be considered a doublet? Moore (p. 39) considers them synonymous. Ellingworth says (p. 594) these two terms and πάροικος "are used interchangeably" (cf. Gen. 23:4; Ps. 39:12; Eph. 2:19; 1 Pet. 2:11, in all of which two of the three terms are used together). Although this is no doubt true, the display uses two expressions (the second being v. 13j) both because the writer seems to be making a clear reference to Gen. 23:4 and to make clear both the positive and negative connotations of the terms.

The second question is, does επὶ τῆς γῆς 'on the earth' refer to the earth as a whole or to Canaan? Most commentators ignore it, assuming the former, and nearly all versions render it 'on earth' or 'on this earth'. Miller tries to argue (p. 351) that the phrase ἐκείνης...ἐφ' ἧς 'that [land] from which' in v. 15 requires an antecedent 'land' different from the promised land, but the obvious referent there is their birthplaces, whether Canaan or not. The contrast in v. 13 is with ἐπουράνιος 'heavenly' in v. 16; furthermore, the use of ἐπί 'upon' would seem strange if the sense of the phrase were '*in* the land of Canaan'.

11:13i-j See previous discussion. LB's rendering of the two terms, "they agreed that this earth was not their real home but that they were just strangers visiting down here" is very similar to that given here.

11:14a those people who say such things The referent of 'those' is primarily Abraham and Jacob (so Ellingworth) and 'such things' refers to the comment about being aliens and sojourners.

11:14c *true* native land The word πατρίδα means 'homeland'; but since the sense here, which is made specific in v. 16, is heaven, and not their earthly land of origin, 'true native land' is implied. (cf. JB's 'real homeland').

11:15a if they had been thinking about *that place* The author used the expression εἰ μὲν ἐκείνης ἐμνημόνευον ἀφ' ἧς ἐξέβησαν 'if they were remembering that [country] from which they had come'. He indicated that they had an opportunity to turn away from their faith, but instead that they continued to trust God that they would enter heaven.

when they said that This is required by the context as an implicature of the argument. As Ellingworth notes, vv. 14–16 are a syllogism. Here is a modified, somewhat expanded version of what Ellingworth suggests:

They said they were seeking a true native land (v. 14b).

When they said that, they could not have meant any earthly native land (v. 15).

Therefore they must have meant a home in heaven (v. 16b).

11:15a-b *that place* from which they had come The text has no nominal referent, only ἀφ ἧς ἐξέβησαν 'from which they left'. Nearly all the versions supply 'country' or 'land' but since the reference is to Abraham and Jacob, it may be helpful, perhaps in a footnote, to list one of the names suggested by commentators: Ur (Ellingworth), Chaldea (Hughes, Louw and Nida, Brown), Mesopotamia (Kistemaker (p. 326), Bruce).

11:15c taken the opportunities The word καιρός in the clause εἶχον ἂν καιρόν 'they might have had time' means 'opportunity', but since the verb is in the imperfect, it signals 'over a period of time', hence 'opportunities'. For languages with no word for 'opportunity' the word could be omitted; CEV's 'they could have gone back at any time' captures the sense very well.

11:16a But, *instead* The author completed the contrast with νῦν δὲ κρείττονος ὀρέγονται 'but now a better (place) they stretch toward'. He indicated that those people had purposely chosen to continue faithfully.

they desired a better place The GNT has ὀρέγονται 'they stretch toward' to indicate that those people desired to arrive in heaven.

in which to live The words in italics make clear what is meant by 'they desired a better country'. For languages with no comparative degree, it may be necessary to say something like 'a very good country', or 'a country which surpassed the one they were born in'.

11:16d *we know* he is pleased The words 'we know' make this propositional relationship clearer. The phrase οὐκ ἐπαισχύνεται 'he is not ashamed' is a litotes, emphasizing the positive by denying the negative; (cf. Heb. 2:11; Rom. 1:16.)

that they say, "He is our God" Most commentators do not discuss the verb ἐπικαλεῖσθαι 'to be called'. Moffatt discusses it as though the sense were 'he called himself their God', but the passive must assume others are the agent, not God himself. The display recognizes and removes the passive and the secondary sense of 'call' and also changes what would be a resultant indirect quote, 'that he is their God', to a direct quote, 'he is our God'.

11:16e because he was preparing for them The γάρ in this verse introduces v. 16c as the evidential grounds of v. 16d, not the reason.

a home *in heaven* The Greek has only the words αὐτοῖς πόλις 'for them a city'. For 'to live in' see previous note. The words 'in heaven' are implied from the context (NLT has "heavenly").

(NUCLEUS₄: NUCLEUS₄ 11:17–19 of 11:8–19)

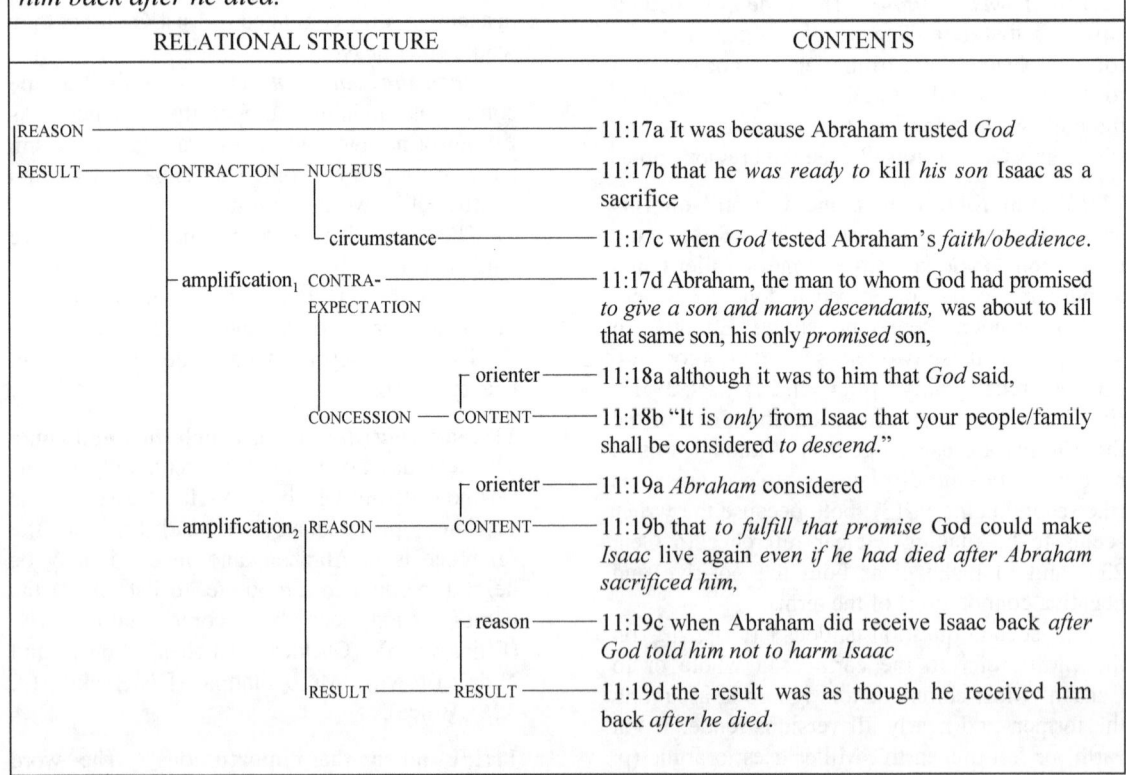

NOTES

11:17b *was ready to* **kill** *his son* **Isaac as a sacrifice** The text has προσενήνοχεν Ἀβραὰμ τὸν Ἰσαάκ 'Abraham offered up Isaac'. Lünemann says "The author could thus express himself, since the offering was really intended by Abraham," or as Montefiore says, "he was actually in the process of doing this when he was stopped," which is enough to explain why 'was ready to' is included. Of the versions only CEV deals with the problem by rendering 'was willing to'; 'prepared to' would be another good alternative. The words 'his son' again express the implied kinship relation that the author assumed his audience would know; TEV, CEV, and LB do likewise. The words 'as a sacrifice' are implied (see 5:1) and made explicit in NIV, TEV, JBP, and NCV.

11:17c *God* **tested Abraham's** *faith/obedience* The verb πειράζω here means "*try, make trial of, put to the test,* to discover what kind of a person someone is... b. in a good sense, of God or Christ, who put men to the test...so that they may prove themselves true" (BAGD p. 640.2b). The rendering in the display suggests that it may be necessary to spell out the meaning by something like 'allowed it to happen to him to see if he would continue to trust/obey God'. The verb form is 'a divine passive' (Hughes, p. 481) to avoid God's name.

There are a number of poorly attested textual variants here regarding the inclusion and position of the name 'Abraham', but almost none of them would affect the sense.

11:17d The καί here introduces this cluster as an amplification of 17b-c, but one which Miller calls 'ascensive'; the sense is almost 'and, incredibly,....'

God had promised *to give a son and many descendants* Abraham is described as ὁ τὰς ἐπαγγελίας ἀναδεξάμενος 'the one who had received the promises'. Unskewing the abstract noun 'promises' to make it a clause requires semantically not only supplying 'God' as the agent but a content: in this context both the giving of a son and the eventual giving of many descendants (Gen. 17:6, 18:10) are implied (so Ellingworth).

his only *promised* **son** The phrase τὸν μονογενῆ 'the only (one)' is forefronted giving it an emphasis conveyed in the display text by a similar forefronting. It is true as Ellingworth says (p. 601) that "Isaac was not in fact at this time Abraham's only son; but in Jewish tradition, Ishmael (Gen. 15:16) does not count as a 'child of promise'." In some languages it may be necessary to say 'who was considered his only son' or something comparable.

11:18a although It seems best to take the relative clause introducing this verse as expressing concession (as do Miller, Montefiore, Ellingworth and Nida).

11:18b It is *only* **from Isaac** The rest of the verse is cited from Gen. 21:12. The force of the forefronted phrase ἐν Ἰσαάκ 'in Isaac' is retained by a forefronted cleft construction here (and in TEV, JB; cf. NLT); and in the original OT passage (Gen. 21:12) the word 'only' is contextually implied (see also Miller, Ellingworth, and Alford).

considered *to descend* The verb κληθήσεται 'shall be called' is used here in a performative sense (so Ellingworth) so that "what is being named is what exists" (Miller, p. 353); one could shorten it to 'shall descend' except that in the original OT context this was God's reply to Abraham who was musing that 'Ishmael was also his son' (Gen. 21:13, CEV).

11:19a *Abraham* **considered** The present participle λογιζάμενος 'reckoning' is considered as introducing a second amplification of v. 17b (so Moffatt and Miller). All the modern versions start a new sentence here.

11:19b *to fulfill that promise* Although the great majority of older commentators say v. 19b is a general statement of what Abraham believed, the context demands more than that. The words in italics are a necessary implicature of the argument. Hughes restates this part of the verse as 'that is, that God was able to perform the greatest of all miracles if this was necessary for the preservation of his promise' (see also Montefiore, Bruce).

God could make *Isaac* **live again** Miller argues (p. 353) in support of the 'universal truth' notion that the present infinitive ἐγείρειν 'to rise' occurs, and if the reference were to raising Isaac only, the aorist infinitive with the pronoun 'him' would have occurred. There may be some truth to this, and one could well argue that the complete sense required from the context is 'since God can raise the dead, he could raise Isaac'. But since a conclusion is more naturally prominent than a grounds and since the context requires the conclusion mentioning Isaac to be understood more than the grounds here, that is what is stated in the display. This interpretation is supported by TEV, KJV, JBP, and LB, Hughes, Ellingworth, and Nida.

even if he had died As Kistemaker notes (p. 328), "Of course, Isaac did not die" and therefore this proposition is not only an implicature of the argument but OT knowledge the writer would assume his audience knew.

11:19c *after God told him not to harm Isaac* This is an implicature of OT knowledge which the author would count on his audience to know. It will probably be necessary to include it in some form for audiences totally unfamiliar with the account in Gen. 22:1–13.

11:19d the result was The conjunction ὅθεν usually has the locational sense 'from which' but is always used with a logical sense in its other five occurrences in Hebrews, and is assigned a logical sense here by BAGD (p. 555.2). In the argument v. 19c-d also fits much better as introducing the conclusion to be derived from v. 19a-b.

11:19d as though This renders the phrase ἐν παραβολῇ 'in a parable' which is somewhat of an idiom. Some versions use a quite idiomatic expression (e.g., "so to speak" in TEV, "in a manner of speaking" (JBP), the words "figuratively speaking" (NIV, JB, RSV) capture the sense but may be hard to translate. Some commentators (Moffatt, Bruce, Hughes) agree with Hewitt who says it means 'in a hidden sense,' because the sacrifice of Isaac was a type of our Lord's crucifixion. But Christ's death and resurrection is completely foreign to the context, and the notion of "the sacrifice and salvation of Isaac as a type of Christ's death and resurrection" is "nowhere found in the New Testament" (Montefiore).

back *after he died* The verb in the phrase αὐτὸν ἐκομίσατο 'he received him' means 'get back, recover' (BAGD p. 443.2b). Case requirements then demand an answer to the question, 'back from what'? Most of the versions supply 'from the dead' or its equivalent (e.g., NIV, NCV, TEV, CEV, JBP, JB).

(CLAIM₅: CONSTITUENT 11:20 of 11:4–31)

THEME: It was because Isaac trusted God that he prayed that God would bless his sons Jacob and Esau in the future.	
RELATIONAL STRUCTURE	CONTENTS
REASON	11:20a *Many years later*, it was because Isaac trusted God
RESULT	11:20b that he *prayed that God would* bless *his sons* Jacob and Esau in the future.

NOTES

11:20a *Many years later* This phrase is included to indicate the lapse of time between Abraham preparing to sacrifice Isaac and Isaac blessing his sons. Not in any versions consulted.

11:20b *prayed that God would* **bless** The word εὐλόγησεν 'blessed' may be translated literally 'in cultures in which blessings play an important part' (Louw and Nida) but semantically the sense is as in the display text. Where 'bless' is not a lexical item, one may have to translate 'ask that God would do good to.'

his sons **Jacob and Esau** The kinship relation which the writer would expect his readers to know is supplied.

in the future The phrase περὶ μελλόντων means 'about coming (things)' but it is difficult to know how to relate this to the word 'bless.' Another alternative would be the word 'later,' which appears to be almost redundant (cf. 'future blessings' in RSV, LB; CEV does not really express the phrase). An alternative involving a full clause would be 'as he spoke/by speaking about the things that would happen to them.'

(CLAIM₆: CONSTITUENT 11:21 of 11:4–31)

THEME: It was because Jacob trusted God that he blessed each of Joseph's sons, and he worshipped God as he leaned on his walking-stick *just before he died*.	
RELATIONAL STRUCTURE	CONTENTS
REASON	11:21a *Many years later* it was because Jacob trusted God
RESULT — NUCLEUS₁	11:21b that he *prayed that God would* bless each of Joseph's sons,
NUCLEUS₂	11:21c and he worshipped *God*
circumstance	11:21d as he leaned on his walking-stick *just before* he died.

NOTES

11:21a *Many years later* This phrase is included to indicate the lapse of time between Isaac blessing his sons and Jacob's death. Not in any versions consulted.

11:21b *prayed that God would* bless See note on v. 20b.

11:21c-d and he worshipped *God* as he leaned on his walking-stick *just before* he died The italicized words satisfy the case frame and supply an implicit event recalled from the OT narrative. One problem here is that the worshipping as he leaned on his staff (Gen. 47:31) took place some time before the blessing of Joseph's sons (Gen. 48:10–20). CEV places the events in correct chronological sequence, which is certainly better than NCV's rendering which presumes an incorrect order of events. Another problem is that the MT read the vowel pointing on the Hebrew word at Gen. 47:31 to be the word 'bed', whereas the compilers of the LXX read the pointing to be the word 'staff'. Translators are not at liberty to try to reconcile the two; the main thing to avoid is some wrong meaning being derived from the words προσεκύνησεν ἐπὶ τὸ ἄκρον τῆς ῥάβδου αὐτοῦ 'worshipped on the tip of his staff'. The display text supplies 'as he supported himself' as a good rendering of the implicit event (cf. Ellingworth and Nida p. 269); 'leaned on' (found in most versions) could be confusing.

(CLAIM₇: CONSTITUENT 11:22 of 11:4–31)

THEME: When Joseph was about to die, it was because he trusted in God that he told his fellow Israelis that their descendants would someday leave Egypt, and he commanded that those descendants must carry his bones with them when they left Egypt.	
RELATIONAL STRUCTURE	CONTENTS
circumstance	11:22a *Many years later,* when Joseph was about to die,
REASON — NUCLEUS	11:22b it was because he trusted in God
RESULT₁	11:22c that he told his fellow Israelis *that their descendants* would someday leave *Egypt,*
orienter	11:22d and he commanded
RESULT₂ — CONTENT	11:22e that *those descendants must carry* his bones *with them when they left Egypt.*

NOTES

11:22c that he told his fellow Israelis *that their descendants* would someday leave Egypt The verb μνημονεύω means 'remember, think about', but since the event being remembered 'in fact would not take place until another century and a half had passed' (Hughes), some other verb is needed. Many versions use 'spoke of'.

their descendants **would someday leave Egypt** The phrase υἱοί Ἰσραήλ 'sons of Israel' is rendered here as 'people of', but translators will have to follow the natural receptor language pattern for expressing the name of a people group (several versions use 'Israelis'). The noun ἔξοδος 'Exodus' is rendered by a verb since it expresses an event; the case frame of the motion verb is then satisfied by the word 'Egypt' (as in NIV, TEV, LB, NEB, CEV, and NCV).

11:22e that *those descendants must carry* **his bones** *with them when they left Egypt* The GNT has only περὶ τῶν ὀστέων αὐτοῦ 'concerning his bones', which is very elliptical. The writer assumed his readers would be able to supply the rest from their knowledge of Gen. 37:2ff. Of the versions, only CEV's "to take his bones with them" and LB and NLT's "to carry his bones with them when they left" are very clear.

(CLAIM$_8$: CONSTITUENT 11:23–30 of 11:3–31)

> THEME: *It was because Moses' parents trusted in God that they hid Moses for 3 months. It was because Moses trusted in God that he refused to accept the privileges of being the son of the king's daughter, he departed from Egypt not fearing the king, he instituted the feast called Passover, the people of Israel walked through the water called the Red Sea as though they walked over dry land, marched around the walls for seven days so that the walls around Jericho city collapsed.*

RELATIONAL STRUCTURE	CONTENTS
NUCLEUS$_1$	11:23 It was because *Moses' father and mother trusted in God* that they hid Moses (their son) for 3 months *shortly* after he was born. [See expanded display on page 193.]
NUCLEUS$_2$	11:24-26 It was because Moses trusted *God* that when he had grown up he refused to accept *the privileges he was entitled to if the king considered* that he was the son of his daughter. [See expanded display on page 193]
NUCLEUS$_3$	11:27 It was because Moses trusted *God* that he departed from Egypt, and he was not afraid that the king would be angry, but instead he did not turn back. [See expanded display on page 195]
NUCLEUS$_4$	11:28 It was because Moses believed that God would save his own people that he instituted the feast called Passover. [See expanded display on page 196.]
NUCLEUS$_5$	11:29-30a It was because the *people of Israel* trusted *in God* that they walked through *the water called* the Red Sea *as though they walked over* dry land. But when the Egyptian *army* also attempted to cross *this same water*, they drowned, *because the sea returned and covered them*. [See expanded display on page 197.]
NUCLEUS$_6$	11:30b-d It was because the Israeli people trusted God that the walls around Jericho city collapsed, after the Israelis marched around the walls for seven days. [See expanded display on page 197.]

(NUCLEUS₁: CONSTITUENT 11:23 of 11:23–30)

THEME: *It was because Moses' father and mother trusted in God that they hid Moses (their son) for 3 months shortly after he was born.*	
RELATIONAL STRUCTURE	CONTENTS

```
REASON──────────────────────────────  11:23a Many more years later, it was because Moses' father and
                                             mother trusted in God
RESULT ──── NUCLEUS₁ ──── NUCLEUS ──── 11:23b that they hid their son for 3 months
                        └─circumstance── 11:23c shortly after he was born,
                        ┌─orienter ────── 11:23d because they saw
            NUCLEUS₂ ───┴─CONTENT ─────── 11:23e that their child was beautiful,
                        ┌─orienter ────── 11:23f and they did not fear
            NUCLEUS₃ ───┤ CONTENT ─────── 11:23g what the king of Egypt had commanded,
                        └─specific ────── 11:23h namely that the Jewish male children must be killed.
```

NOTES

11:23a father and mother The display text uses this phrase because not all languages have an expression for πατέρες 'parents'.

11:23g king *of Egypt* The display specifies which king, information the writer would obviously expect his audience to know.

11:23h *namely that the Jewish male children must be killed* The text will not make much sense to anyone who does not know this implicit information from Ex. 1:16. LB conveys some of it by "the death the king commanded."

(NUCLEUS₂: CONSTITUENT 11:24–26 of 11:23–30)

THEME: *It was because Moses trusted God that when he had grown up he refused to accept the privileges he was entitled to if the king considered that he was the son of his daughter.*	
RELATIONAL STRUCTURE	CONTENTS

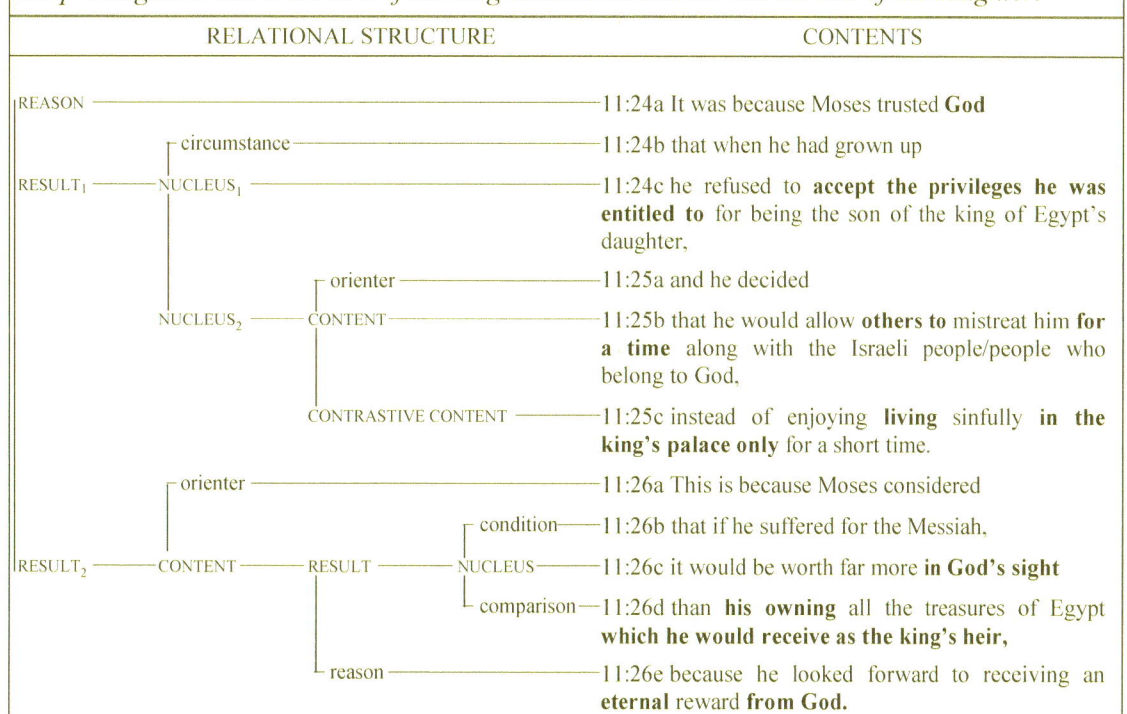

NOTES

11:24b grown up Stephen (Acts 7:23) says the event referred to took place when Moses was forty years old.

11:24c king of Egypt The clause ἠρνήσατο λέγεσθαι υἱός which is literally 'denied to be said the son' is not easy to render adequately. The verb, in its aorist tense, suggests a definite decision at a definite time, not a habitual action. Ellingworth suggests (p. 611) that in the light of Moses' actions reported in Exodus 2, the sense of the verb is more 'renounce' than 'deny', and this would fit the third sense of the verb given by BAGD (p. 107.3). But the main problem is that 'be called' is a metonymy, a literal translation of which is very likely to give wrong meaning. Peake suggests "The word implies deliberate rejection of a career which he was free to choose." Bruce says (p. 318) "Moses renounced the status which he enjoyed in Egypt as a member of the royal household." Hughes says (p. 494) "his calling was to relinquish his position of privilege." The display rendering is an attempt to express these notions.

king of Egypt The Greek has the word 'Pharaoh' but in many languages the word Pharaoh will be unknown and thus considered a personal name, which it was not. The display follows translations such as CEV ("The king's grandson") and NCV ("son of the king of Egypt's daughter"). In some translations it may be desired to include the word 'Pharaoh' and say 'the king who was called Pharaoh.'

11:25a-c he decided Israeli people...enjoying living sinfully *in the king's palace only* for a short time The grammatical comparative construction 'he chose X rather than Y' which can be represented easily in Greek and English is not possible in many languages; the display therefore expresses the sense of the two underlying semantic propositions differently, in the same way that NLT and CEV do.

11:25b Israeli people All the versions render the phrase λαός τοῦ θεοῦ 'people of God' literally, but this could be misunderstood. The sense is, as Kistemaker puts it, "the nation Israel."

11:25c enjoying *living* sinfully *in the king's palace only* for a short time The adjective in the phrase πρόσκαιρον ἔχειν ἁμαρτίας ἀπόλαυσιν 'to have the temporary enjoyment of sin' is forefronted. This emphasis is conveyed in the display by the word 'only' in the phrase 'only for a short time'. The display attempts to give an adequate rendering which removes the semantic mismatch in the abstract nouns 'enjoyment' and 'sin'. The words 'in the king's palace' seem to be implicit OT knowledge necessary to complete the contrast; Hughes says (p. 494) it refers to the "pleasures of the ease and affluence of the palace" and Lenski (p. 409) says it is "the earthly grandeur at Pharaoh's palace and court."

11:26a This is because None of the versions consulted have any logical connector introducing this verse, but the rendering here follows many commentators in considering that the aorist participle "gives the *reason* for the *result* expressed in the participle of the previous proposition" (Miller, p. 361).

11:26b if he suffered for the Messiah There are at least four interpretations of the genitive phrase τὸν ὀνειδισμὸν τοῦ Χριστοῦ 'the reproach of the Christ':

1. One is that it means Christ suffered when Moses suffered (Alford, Bruce); but the context is clearly focusing on what Moses endured, not what Christ endured.
2. The second, mostly based on the assumption that there is an allusion here to Psa. 89:50–51, is that 'the Christ' means the nation of Israel (cf. Montefiore, Brown, and Hughes); but nowhere else in the NT does ὁ Ξριστός have that meaning.
3. The third is that it means 'for the sake of' (Peake, Dods, Lenski (p. 409), Hewitt, Miller, Kistemaker (p. 337).
4. The fourth is that the sense is 'like Christ endured' (Davidson, Moffatt, Lünemann, Westcott).

Nearly all the versions choose the third interpretation. The problems with the fourth interpretation are that the reproaches Moses endured had little similarity with those Christ endured, and he could not have known about the insults hurled at Christ anyway. The third interpretation is not without difficulties, but it seems best to conclude that in the light of what God promised Moses in Deut. 18:15 and elsewhere, "even though Moses never used the name *Messiah*, he was fully aware of his presence and his coming" (Kistemaker (p. 337), and thus "Moses suffered the reproach, having the coming of Christ in view" (Hewitt). In any case, 'Christ' should not be transliterated but instead translators should use whatever expression they have decided on for Messiah, such as 'God's promised deliverer'.

11:26c worth far more *in God's sight* Since reproaches have no intrinsic worth, it is best to recognize with Kistemaker (p. 338) that "This is a comparison of spiritual riches and earthly treasures." Thus 'in God's sight' is implied.

11:26d than *his owning* all the treasures of Egypt *which he would receive as the king's heir* A verb such as 'owning' is an implicature of the argument (LB supplies "to own," NCV supplies "to have.") The final italicized part of the proposition is an implicature of OT knowledge; Barnes says "It is implied here that Moses had a prospect of inheriting large treasures in Egypt"; cf. also Kistemaker, (p. 338.)

11:26e he looked forward to receiving an *eternal* reward *from God* The verb ἀποβλέπω means "to fix one's attention on" (Louw and Nida, 30.31), which is somewhat figurative here; there is an "implicit future reference" (Ellingworth, p. 615) by which a future 'receiving' is implied. Several commentators (e.g., Peake, Barnes, Alford, and Nairne) suggest that 'eternal' or 'in heaven' is implied.

(NUCLEUS₃: CONSTITUENT 11:27 of 11:23–30)

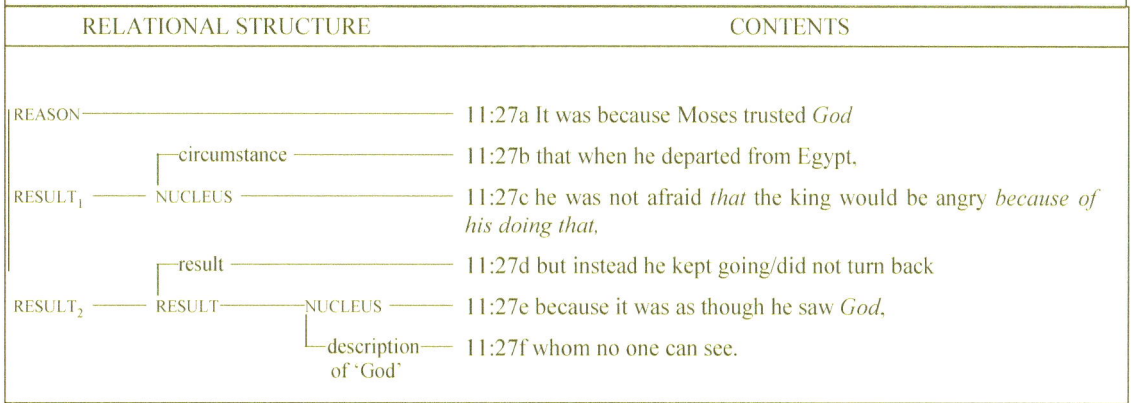

THEME: It was because Moses trusted God *that he departed from Egypt, and he was not afraid that the king would be angry, but instead he did not turn back.*

NOTES

11:27b departed from Egypt Commentators are divided as to whether this refers to his fleeing to Midian after he killed the Egyptian, or to the later Exodus. If the events listed in vv. 23–28 are in chronological order (and it seems clearly that they are), then this must refer to the former occasion. Furthermore, the statements in v. 27 all refer to Moses as an individual, with no reference to the rest of the Israelites. The great majority of commentators take this view. The only difficulty with it is that when Moses fled to Midian (Ex. 2:11–15) it says clearly that he *was* afraid, whereas here it says he was not. The solution seems to be as Hughes puts it, "that it was not personal fear of Pharaoh but the awareness of his destiny as the deliverer of the covenant people that caused him to take flight" (see also Peake, Ellingworth, Miller, Kistemaker, (p. 340).

11:27c he was not afraid The negated aorist participle μὴ φοβηθείς 'not having feared' is taken as expressing a negated or unfulfilled action. The rendering here follows that of NEB and the comments of Bruce, Hughes, and others.

***that* the king would be angry** Rendering the abstract noun θυμός 'anger' as a verb requires that some relationship with 'was not afraid' be expressed. Some have suggested a concession relationship ('even though the king was angry') but semantically this does not cohere as well as saying the anger was the cause for the fear.

because of his doing that These words are supplied to keep the reader from wondering why the king would be angry.

11:27d he kept going/did not turn back The γάρ here is taken as introducing an amplification of v. 27b because it does not relationally cohere as supplying either the reason for not being afraid (v. 27c) or the reason for departing (v. 27b). The verb here is ἐκαρτέρησεν for which BAGD (p. 405) and Louw and Nida (25.178) give the meaning 'he persevered'. As Ellingworth and Nida (p. 274) point out, there is some question as to exactly what it means here. Two alternatives are supplied: the first gives a more generic sense (as in JB's "he held to his purpose," Moffatt's "he never flinched," NCV's "continued strong;" and the second assumes a more specific reference to his journey (as in TEV's "would not turn back," LB's "kept right on going").

11:27e because it was as though he saw God The participle ὁρῶν 'seeing' is taken as expressing the reason. Ellingworth says (p. 617), "The question remains whether ὡς here means that Moses really did see the invisible God...or whether he persevered like...one who did see him." It seems far more natural to take the conjunction as expressing an irrealis comparison, 'as though'. That interpretation is followed by the vast majority of versions and commentators. The word 'God' is supplied as the referent of τὸν ἀόρατον 'the invisible' (v. 27g) as is done in NCV, TEV, CEV, LB, and NEB.

(NUCLEUS₄: CONSTITUENT 11:28 of 11:23–30)

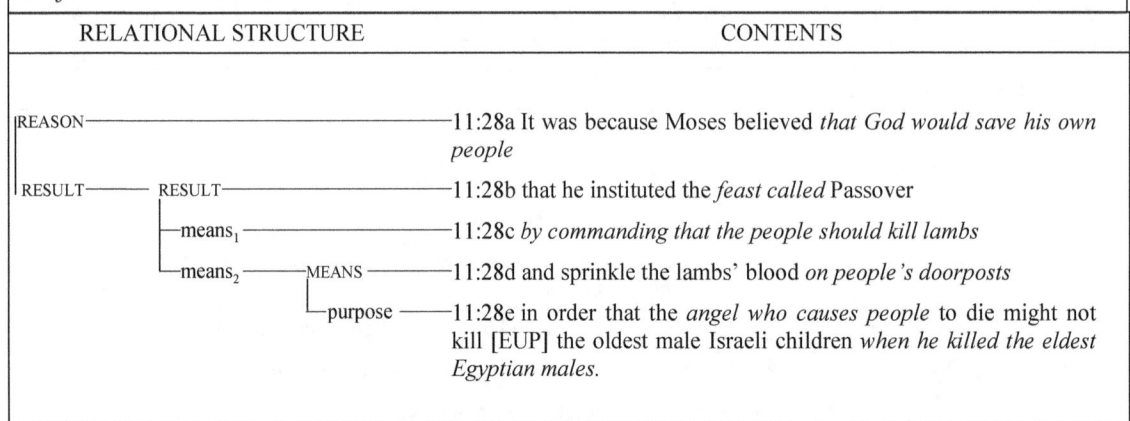

NOTES

11:28a believed *that God would save his own people* The display follows LB here in supplying a complete clause to satisfy the case frame of 'believe' as an implicature of OT information to fit the context of establishing the Passover.

11:28b instituted The verb here is πεποίηκεν 'he made'; several commentators (Louw and Nida, Miller, Ellingworth, Bruce, Kistemaker (p. 340–342), et al.) suggest the sense here is much more 'establish/institute' than 'kept/observed'. All the Israelis kept it, but because of his faith in what God had promised, Moses established it. As Miller observes (p. 365), "Moses was aware that the Passover was to be a permanent institution (Ex. 12:14–20)."

feast called **Passover** Since the immediately following context spells out exactly what was involved in the original incident, it is probably best here to transliterate the term or use an existing name such as Paska and indicate it was the name of a certain feast. The word 'Passover' did not occur in the LB but has been restored in the NLT.

11:28c *by commanding that the people should kill lambs* The display supplies further OT implicatures; if people do not know the story (Ex. 12:6-7) they would not know what blood was being referred to (LB supplied it, but unfortunately it is deleted in NLT).

11:28d sprinkle the lambs' *blood on people's doorposts* The GNT has only τὴν πρόσχυσιν τοῦ αἵματος 'the sprinkling of the blood.' Again, the writer assumes his readers will know where the blood was to be sprinkled. It is specified in TEV, LB, NLT, NCV, and CEV.

11:28e *angel who causes people* to die The phrase ὁ ὀλεθρεύων 'the one who destroys' is a literal rendering of the word in Ex. 12:23 which says "he (= the LORD) will not permit the destroyer to enter your houses and strike you down" (NIV). The word 'angel' is never mentioned as being the destroyer, but since some agent other than the Lord himself is being specified, it seems a reasonable assumption to identify him as an angel. The term here is translated as "Angel of Death" in TEV, LB, and JBP, as 'the one who brings death' in NCV, and as 'the destroying angel' in CEV. The verb phrase 'whom God sent' is supplied to clarify roles (cf. Louw and Nida, Miller).

oldest male Israeli children The phrase τὰ πρωτότοκα 'the firstborn' in the original account referred to the "firstborn farm animals" (Ex. 11:5, NCV) as well as the eldest sons of the Egyptians, but only the latter are really in focus. The GNT construction ἵνα μὴ ὁ ὀλεθρεύων τὰ πρωτότοκα θίγῃ αὐτῶν can be understood as 'lest the one destroying the firstborn touch them' '(as it is taken here since the verb separates 'firstborn' and 'their/them') or as 'lest the destroyer touch their firstborn,' but the question is moot: both must be understood from the OT passage to satisfy the case frames and supply the referent of 'their/them.'

not kill The phrase μὴ θίγῃ 'not touch' is considered a type of hyperbole in which there is an understatement. TEV, NCV, and CEV use 'kill.'

(NUCLEUS₅: CONSTITUENT 11:29–30a of 11:23–30)

THEME: It was because the people of Israel trusted in God that they walked through the water called the Red Sea as though they walked over dry land. But when the Egyptian army also attempted to cross this same water, they drowned, because the sea returned and covered them.

RELATIONAL STRUCTURE	CONTENTS
REASON	11:29a It was because *the people of Israel* trusted *in God*
RESULT₁ — NUCLEUS	11:29b that they walked through *the water called* the Red Sea
└comparison	11:29c *as though they walked over* dry land.
┌circumstance	11:29d But when the *army of the* Egyptians also attempted to cross *this same water*,
RESULT₂ — NUCLEUS	11:30a they drowned, *because the sea returned and covered them.*

NOTES

11:29a *the people of Israel* The display text specifies the subject of διέβησαν 'they went through'; cf. "people of Israel" (LB, NLT) and "Israelites" (TEV).

11:29ba *the water called* **the Red Sea** It is always called the Reed Sea in the Hebrew OT but the Red Sea in the LXX. The words 'water called' are supplied both to indicate this was how it came to be known and to help avoid the connotation that the water was actually red.

11:29c *as though they walked over* **dry land** Then display fills in the ellipsis; BAGD says (p. 897.I2a) "The Israelis went through the Red Sea as (one travels) over dry land."

11:29d the *army of the* **Egyptians** The word Αἰγύπτιοι 'Egyptians' is taken as a synecdoche (the whole standing for the part).

11:30a *because the sea returned and covered them* This supplies the implicature from Ex. 14:27–28.

(NUCLEUS₆: CONSTITUENT 11:30b–d of 11:23–30)

THEME: It was because the Israeli people trusted God that the walls around Jericho city collapsed, after the Israelis marched around the walls for seven days.

RELATIONAL STRUCTURE	CONTENTS
REASON	11:30b It was because the *Israeli* people trusted *God*
RESULT — NUCLEUS	11:30c that the walls around Jericho *city* collapsed,
└circumstance	11:30d after *the Israelis* marched around the walls *each day* for seven days.

NOTES

11:30d *the Israelis* **marched around the walls** *each day* **for seven days** The display supplies the agent of κυκλωθέντα 'having been encircled' (an alternative would be 'Joshua's army'). The phrase ἐπὶ ἑπτὰ ἡμέρας means 'during seven days,' but the translation 'for seven days' found in most versions would most naturally imply "the entire seven days were spent in marching round the walls" (Louw and Nida), which is untrue. They marched around once each day except the final day, when they marched around it seven times (Joshua 6:15).

(CLAIM₉: CONSTITUENT 11:31 of 11:4–31)

THEME: It was because Rahab, who had been a prostitute, trusted God that she did not perish with those within Jericho who disobeyed God.

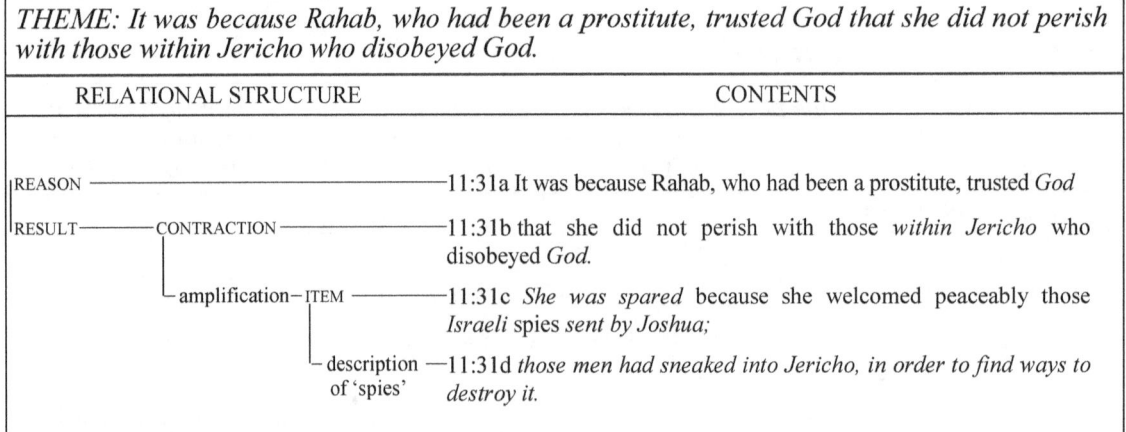

RELATIONAL STRUCTURE	CONTENTS
REASON	11:31a It was because Rahab, who had been a prostitute, trusted *God*
RESULT—CONTRACTION	11:31b that she did not perish with those *within Jericho* who disobeyed *God*.
└ amplification—ITEM	11:31c *She was spared* because she welcomed peaceably those *Israeli* spies *sent by Joshua*;
└ description of 'spies'	11:31d *those men had sneaked into Jericho, in order to find ways to destroy it.*

NOTES

11:31b those *within Jericho* **who disobeyed** *God* The word 'God' satisfies the case frame (cf. TEV, LB, NCV); an alternative is 'the unbelievers' (JB, NEB). The words 'within that city' make clear that the time and place are the same as in v. 30 (LB has 'all the others in her city').

11:31c those *Israeli* **spies** *sent by Joshua* Again the display text supplies crucial OT implicatures needed for identification and to avoid wrong meaning.

11:31d *those men had sneaked into Jericho, in order to find ways to destroy it* This proposition supplies more OT implicatures (Joshua 2:1-2). Louw and Nida suggest 'the Israelis who were spying out the land' or 'who had come to see what the land was like' but the reaction by the king of Jericho suggests the rendering in the display is closer to the truth.

(BASIS₂: CONSTITUENT 11:32–38 of 11:4–38)

THEME: Many more, including the judges and prophets lived trusting in God and doing great things for God, but others suffered for their faith.

MACROSTRUCTURE	CONTENTS
parenthesis	11:32 I cannot tell you about many others who trusted in God [RHQ] because it would take too much time to tell about several judges, David, Samuel, and the other prophets who trusted God.
CLAIM₁	11:33–35b It was because they trusted *in God* that some of them did valiant things for God.
CLAIM₂	11:35c–38 But other people who also trusted in God endured great hardships, much persecution and death.

INTENT AND RHETORICAL STRUCTURE

This is an expository paragraph in which the author continues his presentation of those who exhibited faith in God. His purpose is to remind his readers that under the old agreement, many exhibited faith and did great things for God, but others kept trusting God even while suffering for their faith – and God is calling his readers to do likewise.

BOUNDARIES AND COHERENCE

A new paragraph at v. 39 is indicated by the conjunction καί 'and' and a switch from discussing those who suffered for their faith to a discussion of those whom he has been discussing not receiving in their lifetime all that God had promised.

PROMINENCE AND THEME

The theme is a condensation of the two CLAIMS, which are more naturally prominent than the *parenthesis*.

(PARENTHESIS: CONSTITUENT 11:32: Paragraph₁ of 11:32–38)

THEME: *I cannot tell you about many others who trusted in God [RHQ] because it would take too much time to tell about several judges, David, Samuel, and the other prophets who trusted God.*

RELATIONAL STRUCTURE	CONTENTS
RESULT	11:32a I cannot tell you about many others who trusted *in God* [RHQ]
reason	11:32b because it would take too much time to tell about *the judges* Gideon, Barak, Samson, Jephthah, *king* David, *the prophet* Samuel, and the *other* prophets.

INTENT AND RHETORICAL STRUCTURE

This is a brief expository paragraph. The author's intent is to explain why he must cut short the descriptions of others who trusted in God. The paragraph consists of a RESULT and a r*eason*.

NOTES

11:32a I cannot tell you about many others who *trusted in* God The display spells out the force of the rhetorical question τί ἔτι λέγω 'what more shall I say?' and ties it to the context (NCV has "Do I need to give more examples?").

11:32b *the judges* Gideon... *king* David, *the prophet* Samuel, and the *other* prophets The GNT does not have any qualifiers with these various names, assuming his Jewish audience did not need any such, but for audiences with little or no knowledge of the OT, those supplied here may help (although a word like 'champion' is probably better than 'judge'). LB supplies "other prophets" to make clear that Samuel was also a prophet, but that information has been deleted in the NLT.

BOUNDARIES AND COHERENCE

A new paragraph in v. 33 is signaled by a new occurrence of the word πίστις 'faith' and a switch from a list of those who had faith to a list of positive exploits by those who had faith.

Coherence is provided by the list of other individuals who exhibited faith.

PROMINENCE AND THEME

The theme consists of a slightly abbreviated form of the RESULT and *reason* propositions.

(POSITIVE NUCLEUS: CONSTITUENT 11:33–35b: Paragraph₂ of 11:32–38)

THEME. It was because they trusted in God that some of them did valiant things for God.

¶ PTRN	RELATIONAL STRUCTURE	CONTENTS
justification	NUCLEUS	11:33a It was because they trusted *in God*
CLAIM₁	specific₁ — ITEM	11:33b that some of those people conquered lands
	└ identification of 'lands'	11:33c that other kings ruled.
	specific₂ — ITEM	11:33d Some ruled justly *over the areas*
	└ identification of 'areas'	11:33e *that they controlled.*
	specific₃ — ITEM	11:33f Some obtained *from God* the things
	└ identification of 'things'	11:33g which he promised to give to them.
	specific₄	11:33h Some kept lions from devouring them [MTY];
	specific₅	11:34a some kept a fierce fire from destroying them;
	specific₆	11:34b some of those people escaped from *men killing them* with a sword;
	specific₇ — NUCLEUS	11:34c some *of those people* became strong again
	└ circumstance	11:34d after they had once been weak;
	specific₈ — NUCLEUS	11:34e some became powerful
	└ circumstance	11:34f when *they fought* wars;
	specific₉	11:34g some caused armies which came from foreign *lands in order to kill them* to run away from them.
	specific₁₀ — NUCLEUS	11:35a Some women *who trusted in God* received their *relatives* again
	└ circumstance	11:35b when *God* enabled them to live *again after they had previously* died.
CLAIM₂ negative		11:35c–38 Other people endured hardships. [See expanded display on page 202.]

INTENT AND RHETORICAL STRUCTURE

This is an expository paragraph. The author's intent is to list a number of positive exploits of others who had faith in God.

NOTES

11:33b-c conquered lands that other kings ruled The display text is an attempt to soften the phrase 'conquered kingdoms', which seems to be somewhat of a collocational clash. TEV seems to recognize the problem, but its rendering "fought whole countries and won" is even more of a clash because of its metonymy.

11:33d-e ruled justly *over the areas that they controlled* There is a question as to what the phrase ἠργάσαντο δικαιοσύνην 'accomplished righteousness' means. The expression is at times used "of doing right with reference to personal integrity" (Hughes), but commentators agree that following the mention of subduing kingdoms it has a different sense here. It could refer to simply administration of justice within Israel itself, or to "public acts in behalf of Israel, the righteous nation, against the sinful, heathen world" (Davidson), or to both. The rendering here is an attempt to include both possibilities; Miller (p. 375) expresses well the sense taken here with "They established righteousness as the criterion of justice in the areas they gained control of."

11:33f-g obtained *from God* the things which he promised to give to them The phrase ἐπέτυχον ἐπαγγελιῶν 'obtained promises' is a metonymy, the cause standing for the effect. The rendering here is quite close to that of TEV and LB.

11:33h kept lions from devouring them The clause ἔφραξαν στόματα λεόντων 'stopped mouths of lions' is also considered a metonymy, the cause standing for the effect and mouths standing for the act associated with them. The obvious reference here is to Dan. 6:22, but could also refer to Judges 14:5ff. and 1 Sam. 17:34ff.

11:34a kept a fierce fire from destroying them The reference here is most likely to Dan. 3:23–28. Thus the clause ἔσβεσαν δύναμιν πυρός 'quenched the power of fire', like the previous one, refers not just to the act itself but the personal deliverance achieved thereby.

11:34b escaped from *men killing them* with a sword The clause ἔφυγον στόματα μαχαίρης 'escaped the mouths of a sword' is also a metonymy, the object standing for the action associated with it. Louw and Nida suggest a good alternative, 'escaped from people trying to kill them with swords', and also suggest that where swords are not known as weapons, 'escaped from those who were trying to kill them violently' may be better. JBP has "escaped death by the sword," CEV has "escaped from the swords of their enemies," and LB has "escaped death by the sword."

11:34c-d became strong again after they had once been weak This is a straightforward representation of ἐδυναμώθησαν ἀπὸ ἀσθενήθησαν 'were empowered from weakness'. It could refer to recovering from illness, (e.g., Isa. 38:16), but more probably from weakness in general, as in Judges 16:28. Some commentators suggest the reference here and those in the rest of the verse may well be to the Maccabean struggles.

11:34e-f became powerful when *they fought wars* The display supplies a verb for those situations in which the preposition in the clause ἐγενήθησαν ἰσχυροὶ ἐν πολέμῳ 'became strong in war' may not be translatable literally.

11:34g caused armies which came from foreign *lands in order to kill them* to run away This spells out in more detail the sense of παρεμβολὰς ἔκλιναν ἀλλοτρίων 'caused armies of foreigners to give way'. The word παρεμβολή usually means a fortified camp, but in some Biblical passages, as here, it means a battle line of soldiers. NIV's translation, "routed foreign armies," captures the sense well.

11:35a women *who trusted in God* received their *relatives* again The fact that these women trusted in God is implied by the context; TEV and LB also make it specific. (The same implicit information is supplied in vv. 35c, 36c, 37a, 37e, 38b, and 38d). As Louw and Nida note, 'relatives' is implied.

11:35b when *God* enabled them to live *again after they had previously* died The word 'God' satisfies the case frame, and the other parts in italics are an entailment of the argument. One could query also whether the 'receive' in v. 35a is really in focus or, as Louw and Nida suggest, it " 'is a grammatically active verb with a passive meaning,' or no real meaning at all; i.e., the sense is probably no more than 'God resurrected from the dead the relatives of some women who trusted God.' " The reference here is probably to 1 Kings 17:22–24 and 2 Kings 4:36.

BOUNDARIES AND COHERENCE

A new paragraph at v. 35c is signaled by the conjunction δέ 'but' and a switch from a list of positive exploits to a list of suffering experienced by others who had faith in God.

Coherence is achieved by there being a long series of exploits of those who had faith in God, without listing their names.

PROMINENCE AND THEME

The theme consists of an identification of the agent of the verb plus a clause summarizing what these people of faith did.

(NEGATIVE NUCLEUS: CONSTITUENT 11:35c–38: Paragraph₃ of 11:32–38)

THEME: *But other people who also trusted in God endured great hardships, much persecution and death.*

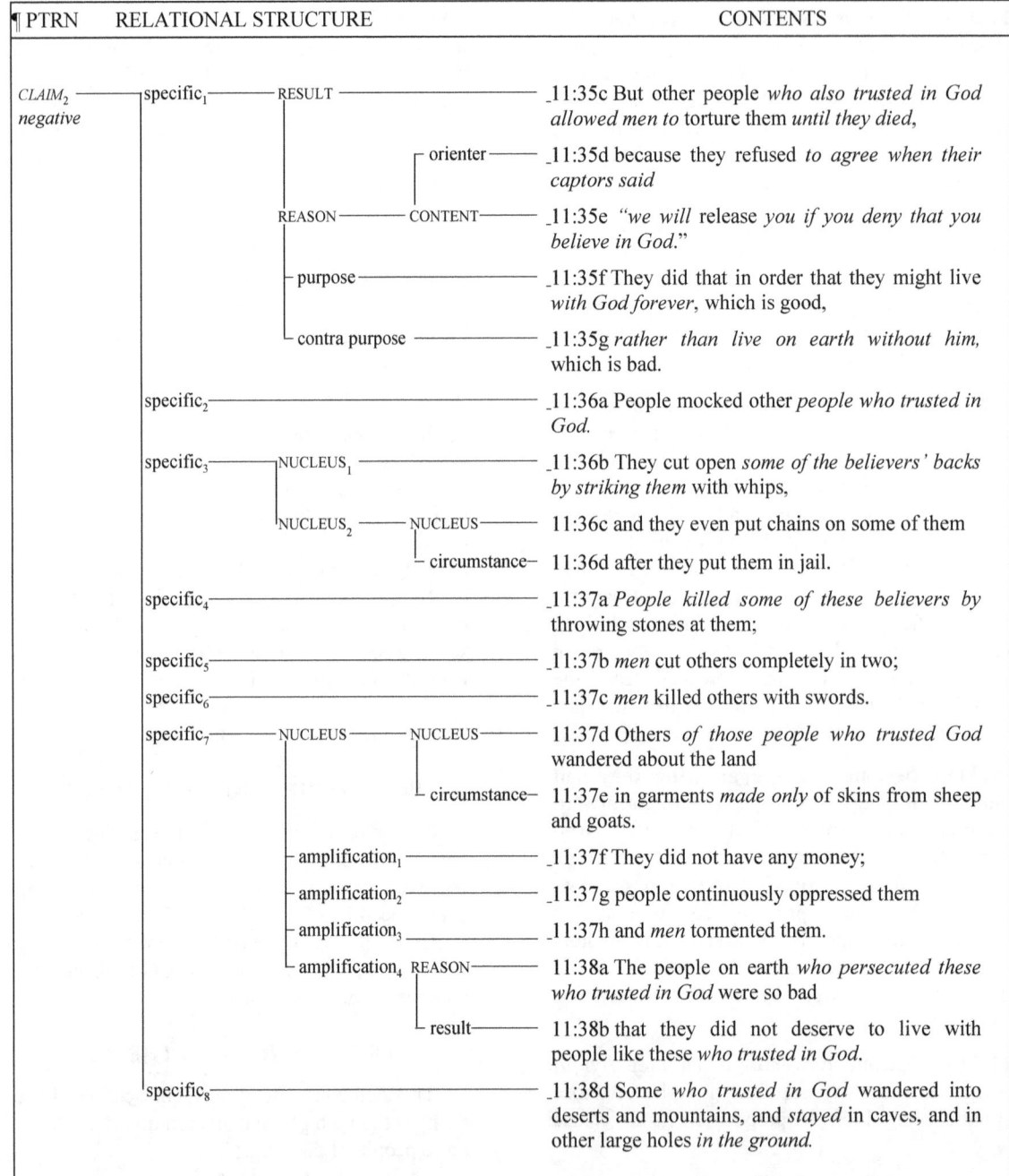

INTENT AND RHETORICAL STRUCTURE

This is an expository paragraph, with all main verbs being indicative in past tense. The author's purpose is to complete his listing of examples of those who exhibited faith in God by noting that there were many who suffered for their faith.

NOTES

11:35c *allowed men to* torture them *until they died* Though the verb τυμπανίζω means 'torture' in general, Bruce says (p. 337), "The particular form of torture indicated by the Greek verb is being stretched on the rack and beaten to death." Miller, Kistemaker (p. 354), Attridge and others concur. Commentators suggest that ill treatment suffered by the Maccabees is probably what is being referred to in vv. 35c–38.

11:35d-e because they refused *to agree when their captors said "we will* **release** *you if you deny that you believe in God."* The aorist participle expresses reason (so Miller, p. 377). The phrase οὐ προσδεξάμενοι τὴν ἀπολύτρωσιν 'not accepting deliverance' carries a good bit of implicit information which only LB/NLT do some justice to with 'preferring to die than turn from God and be free'. Hughes states it well as "restoration to life if they would deny their faith in God."

35f-g *live with God forever,* **which is good** *rather than live on earth without him,* **which is bad** The display attempts to be of help in languages where there is no comparative degree construction to render κρείττονος 'better'. The display unravels the GNT κρείττονος ἀναστάσεως τύχωσιν 'they might obtain a better resurrection', a literal translation of which could convey the idea that there were two resurrections. A rendering such as that given here removes the necessity of deciding whether 'better' refers to 'resurrection to a better life than this one' or "resurrection to a better state than their enemies" (Louw and Nida). They argue for the latter, assuming the reference is to 2 Macc. 7:14, but the immediately preceding context suggests the former and does not hint at all about the fate of their enemies. The rendering in the display could be taken either way.

11:36a People mocked other *people who trusted in God* The display removes the abstract noun and the awkward genitive construction of ἐμπαιγμῶν πεῖραν ἔλαβον 'they took trial of mockings'.

11:36b cut open *some of the believers' backs by striking them* **with whips** The display spells out the semantic components of μάστιγοι 'scourgings'.

11:36c-d put chains on some of them after they put them in jail Ellingworth suggests that δεσμῶν καὶ φυλακῆς 'of bonds and prison' could be a hendiadys. At any rate, as Louw and Nida note, it does not mean being chained only on the way to prison.

11:37a *killed some of these believers by* **throwing stones at them** The verb λιθάζω means "to kill or attempt to kill by means of hurling stones" (Louw and Nida 20.79); thus the words in italics are implied. JBP, NCV, and CEV make it clear. The reference is primarily to the stoning of the prophet Zechariah in 2 Chr. 24:20–21.

11:37b cut others completely in two This seems to refer to the tradition concerning the death of the prophet Isaiah.

There is a textual problem here. The word ἐπειράσθησαν 'were tempted/tested' is found in some manuscripts preceding ἐπρίσθησαν 'sawn asunder' and in other manuscripts following ἐπρίσθησαν. Most certainly ἐπειράσθησαν was added accidentally as a result of dittography. The fact that it occurs in two different positions and the fact that such a mild word as 'tempted' is very much out of place in a list of various kinds of violent death make the reading omitting ἐπειράσθησαν much more certain than the C 'difficulty in deciding' rating given it in the latest UBS text. It is included in KJV and evidently in LB but omitted in all other modern versions (including NLT).

11:37c killed others with swords The reference here may be to the murder of the prophets in the time of Ahab, recorded in 1 Kings 19:10. JB's rendering, "beheaded," is unwarranted.

11:37d wandered about the land The verb περιέρχομαι means 'to travel about, to wander about' (Louw and Nida 15:23). Some versions (NCV, JB, CEV) omit this verb altogether, but this seems unwarranted; the writer was probably recalling the flight of Elijah.

11:37e in garments *made only* **of skins** The phrase ἐν μηλωταῖς 'in sheepskins' implies 'wearing' and 'only' is an implicature of the argument: the sense is that they wore this because they could afford nothing better. JBP has "with nothing but...to cover them" and CEV has "had nothing but...to wear."

11:37f They did not have any money The verb ὑστερέω means "to be lacking in what is essential or needed" (Louw and Nida 57.37). NIV and RSV have "destitute" which is good; "poor" (TEV, CEV) is too mild.

11:37g-h oppressed...tormented There is probably little semantic difference between the verbs θλίβω 'afflict' and κακουχέω 'maltreat'.

11:38a-b The people on earth who persecuted *these who trusted in God* **were so bad that they did not deserve to live with people like these** *who trusted in God* Miller (p. 379) says the relative pronoun here "introduces a parenthetical proposition" (also Attridge); Louw and Nida call it "a quiet aside." The GNT has only ὧν οὐκ ἦν ἄξιος ὁ κόσμος 'of whom the world was not worthy', which is very elliptical, and commentaries and versions try to make sense of it in various ways. The question is, worthy of what? NCV and TV have "The world was not good enough for them" which is still unclear. Louw and Nida suggest as a possible translation "the world did not deserve to have such people" which is along the lines taken here, except that 'world' is both a metonymy standing for the people in the world but also a synecdoche, the whole standing for the part.

11:38c *stayed* in caves, and in other large holes in the ground The verb πλανάομαι 'wander about' which is applicable to deserts and mountains does not apply to caves; so 'stay' is supplied (TEV has "living in" but the caves would be more places of temporary refuge than permanent residences.)

BOUNDARIES AND COHERENCE

A new paragraph begins at v. 39 with the conjunction καί 'and', and a change of topic from those who suffered for their faith to a statement that God did not give these people during their lifetime all that he had promised.

PROMINENCE AND THEME

The theme for this paragraph is a very brief statement that summarizes what hardships and persecutions many others suffered.

SECTION CONSTITUENT 11:39–40 (SUMMARY of 11:1–40)

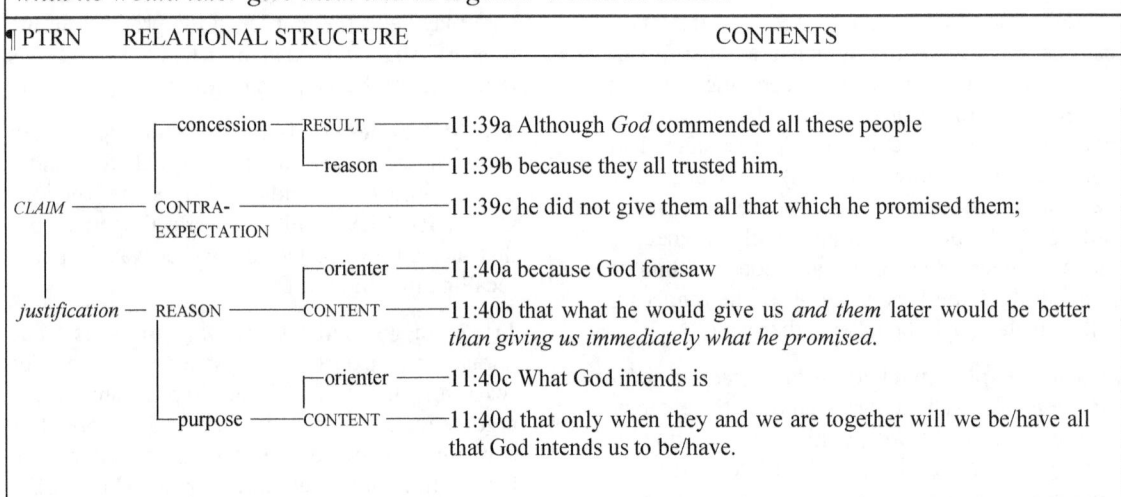

INTENT AND PARAGRAPH PATTERN

The verbs in this unit are all indicative; it is expository. It is a generic summary regarding faith, following the long list of examples of faith exhibited by the readers' ancestors.

NOTES

11:39a *God* commended The verb μαρτυέω has the same meaning, 'approve of', as it did in v. 2. "God" is supplied as the implied agent; only LB and NLT make this clear.

11:39c did not give them all that which he promised them The word ἐπαγγελία 'promise' is a metonymy, the cause standing for the effect, as all the modern versions make clear. God is the implied agent of the action cf. LB, TEV, and NCV. Commentators suggest that the singular 'promise' suggests the reference here is to the promise of a Messiah, and more specifically, salvation through him (so Kistemaker (p. 358).

11:40a because The display follows a number of commentators and versions in giving a causal sense to the genitive absolute construction τοῦ θεοῦ προβλεψαμένου 'God having foreseen' here.

11:40b give us *and them* The prepositional phrase περὶ ὑμῶν 'concerning us' leaves ambiguous in English whether the 'us' includes or excludes the people he has just been referring to. Most commentators do not mention the problem, but Kistemaker (p. 358) is surely correct: "He is saying that they (the heroes of the faith) and we (believers in Jesus Christ) are one." The display makes this clear with 'and them'. The alternate interpretation, that it refers to "the Writer and his readers" (Alford) does not give semantic coherence to the passage.

better *than giving us immediately what he promised* The questions here are, in the words of Ellingworth (p. 636), "(a) in what respect the situation of the present generation is better, and (b) in what the 'something better' consists." His comment here regarding (a) is as good as any, and better than most:

> "(a) In view of the positive tone of chap. 11 as a whole, the contrast must be between good and better, not, as in 6:9, between good and bad. The language of fulfillment in the present verse suggests a contrast with the OT as a period of non-fulfillment, of which the wandering of the patriarchs is a type (vv. 13–16), but which continues after the occupation of the promised land (v. 38). The present generation of believers, by contrast, is an age of fulfillment, at least by anticipation."

This is the interpretation of the great majority of commentators. Ellingworth suggests the author does not give an answer to (b), but Miller (p. 382) says that the writer has already in the epistle given a long list of things that are better under the New Agreement. That is the interpretation followed here, but the writer of Hebrews does not repeat them. The display attempts to be as general as possible.

11:40c-d What God intends is that This part of the verse is introduced by ἵνα which usually signals purpose. But a purpose relationship does not cohere relationally with 'God foresaw' in v. 40a. Louw and Nida suggest that "40b is logically related to verse 39b rather than to verse 40a," but a purpose relationship does not cohere with 'they did not receive what he promised' either; and furthermore, to do so would destroy the *CLAIM-justification* paragraph pattern. The solution taken here, which actually does follow Louw and Nida's interpretation ("This 'something better' is the fulfillment of God's promises by making them and us perfect together") by taking the ἵνα as explanatory, specifying what was 'better.' This is the interpretation followed in TEV, RSV, and NEB.

11:40d only when they and we are together The phrase μὴ χωρὶς ἡμῶν 'not without us' has two problems. First, it is a double negative 'essentially equal to a positive statement' (Kistemaker (p. 358–359) and is so translated here (also in NIV, NEB, NCV, and TEV). The next question is, what is meant by "only together with us" (NCV)? Peake seems to state it the most clearly: "What is meant is that all believers are to 'be made perfect' at the same time."

be/have all that God intends us to be/have For this rendering of the verb τελειόω see the note on 10:1e.

BOUNDARIES AND COHERENCE

The start of a new paragraph in 12:1 is indicated by a switch from indicative clauses to a hortatory clause introduced by a first person plural subjunctive. Cohesion in the 11:1–40 unit is provided by twenty-three occurrences of the noun πίστις 'faith' or its cognate verb.

PROMINENCE AND THEME

The theme consists of abbreviations of the two prominent propositions in the paragraph, the CONTRAEXPECTATION proposition of the *CLAIM*, plus the REASON proposition of the *justification*.

SUB-PART CONSTITUENT 12:1–6 (Paragraph: Appeal of 11:1—12:6)

THEME: Since we know so many people with faith like that, let us put aside anything, especially sin, which hinders us, and let us strive to achieve God's will and concentrate on Jesus.

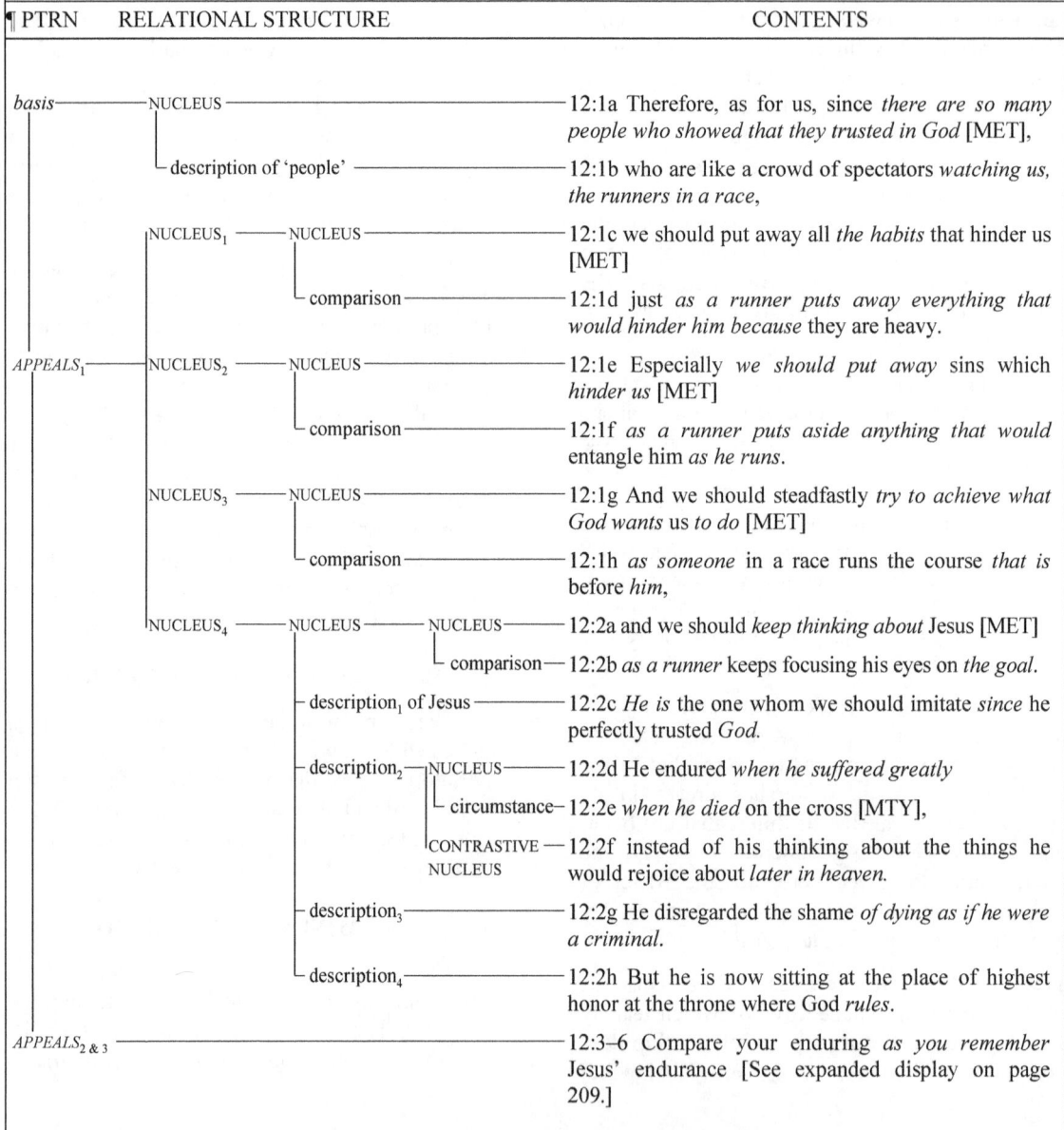

INTENT AND PARAGRAPH PATTERN

This paragraph consists of three *APPEALS* and an *introductory basis*. It is a hortatory paragraph, as signaled by the present subjunctive verb τρέχωμεν 'let us run' in v. 1 and a 2nd person plural imperative ἀναλογίσασθε 'consider' in v. 3. It is an exhortation to his readers on how they should conduct their lives in view of the list that he has just completed of those who trusted in God in ages past.

NOTES

12:1a Therefore The conjunction pair Τοιγαροῦν καὶ is very rare, so it seems to point to what the author is about to say being extremely important.

as for us The pronoun 'we' is emphatic, with additional emphasis from being forefronted. The wording which conveys this emphasis follows TEV cf. NEB's "And what of ourselves?". The word highlights a comparison between the Old Testament believers and those living in New Testament times (so Miller, Ellingworth).

there are *so many people who showed that they trusted in God* The words τοσοῦντον ἔχοντες περικείμενον ἡμῖν μαρτύρων 'having such a cloud of witnesses surrounding us' are taken as a metaphor (see v. 1b). In the context the witnesses are those listed in chapter 11. The point is that we know about them from the Scriptural record. As many commentators note, 'witnesses' here means specifically people who were "examples of much-enduring but triumphant faith" (Dods); NEB has "witnesses to faith," LB has "men of faith," NCV has "people whose lives tell us what faith means."

12:1b who are like a crowd The word νέφος means literally 'cloud', but here it has a figurative sense of "a compact, numberless throng" (BAGD p. 537); Louw and Nida (11.3) give only the sense of "large crowd" since the sense of 'cloud' does not occur in the NT.

of spectators who are watching the runners in a race. The sense of 'crowd' plus 'surround' plus the plural of the word μάρτυς 'witness' plus the following context about running a race require that the metaphor be understood as denoting a crowd witnessing a sporting event; (so Hughes, Ellingworth, Guthrie, Brown, Kistemaker, and several others.) The use of 'spectators', 'runners', and 'race' then requires some verb to express what the spectators are doing; the display supplies two alternatives. LB makes the metaphor clear with "watching us from the grandstands" cf. also Barclay, Knox. It may be appropriate to use some expression such as 'cheering for' instead of just 'watching'; the spectators in this case are not neutral in their attitude towards the runners.

12:1c-d we should put away all *the habits* that hinder us just *as a runner puts away everything that would hinder him because* they are heavy The words ὄγκον ἀποθέμενοι πάντα 'laying aside every impediment' continue the metaphor of running a race. As Miller notes, the participle here has "the same mood semantically as the leading verb," here τρέχωμεν 'let us run'. Most versions maintain the metaphor, but CEV states very nicely the topic of the metaphor, "We should remove from our lives anything that would get in the way."

12:1e Especially Most versions render the καί here simply as 'and'. The problem with this is that it would signal connecting two things that are very different; there are many hindrances that are not sins. The καί must then be taken as explicative, indicating either 'namely' or 'especially'. The discussion by Kistemaker which supports the sense of 'especially' is good here: "there are things which hinder us spiritually which are not necessarily sinful in and of themselves."

The word ἁμαρτία 'sin' is personified. In languages where one cannot do this, it may be necessary to say something like 'let us stop doing sinful things'.

12:1f *as a runner puts aside anything that would entangle him as he runs* There are a very few manuscripts which read the participle εὐπερίσπαστος 'easily distracting' instead of εὐπερίστατος 'easily surrounding', but the latter verb is chosen by the GNT with an A 'certain' rating. Since this participle occurs nowhere else (and was probably coined by the writer), it is difficult to assign a meaning to it. BAGD (p. 324) assigns the senses "constricting, obstructing" and Louw and Nida (37.6) give a similar sense, "controlling tightly." Nearly all commentators choose something similar giving the sense of 'encumbering/ entangling'.

12:1g we should steadfastly *try to achieve what God wants* us *to do* This proposition spells out what the writer intends to convey by dia hupomene 'through endurance'.

12:1f *as a runner puts aside anything that would* entangle him *as he runs* This material spells out the figurative part of the metaphor on 'running a race'.

12:2c *He is* the one whom we should imitate *since* he perfectly trusted *God* There are two interpretations of the words τὸν τῆς πίστεως ἀρχηγὸν καὶ τελειωτὴν 'the author and finisher of faith'. Some (including most versions) take it quite literally to mean that Jesus is the originator and completer of what we believe. The problems with that interpretation are first of all that the word 'our' is not in the text. Secondly, Christ is, in other passages in the New Testament, the goal of our faith. No apostle referred to him as the originator. Furthermore, following the previous chapter in which many examples of faith of individuals are cited, it would seem that the author was urging the believers to imitate them, and especially Jesus, whose trust in God was perfect. The phrase is thus seen as a an idiom meaning that Jesus was the perfect example of faith; hence 'perfectly trusted'. The sense of ἀρχηγός as 'role model' is suggested by the verb ἀφοράω, 'to fix one's eyes on', and the following context regarding Christ's sufferings, which the writer calls on his readers to imitate. Hughes states well the sense of the phrase taken by most commentators: "...who is the supreme exponent of faith, the one who, beyond all others, not only set out on the course of faith but also pursued it without wavering to the end." A somewhat idiomatic way of expressing the sense would be 'our best example of faith, from beginning to end'.

12:2d-e He endured *when he suffered greatly when he died* on the cross The clause ὑπέμεινεν σταυρόν 'he endured a cross' is taken as a metonymy, the object or instrument standing for the event of death which was associated with it cf. NCV's "He suffered death on the cross," CEV's "he endured the shame of being nailed to a cross".

12:2f instead of his thinking about the things he would rejoice about *later* The interpretation of this verse hangs very much on the meaning of the preposition ἀντί. Its usual sense is to indicate substitution, 'instead of'. Commentators and lexicons that support this interpretation include BAGD, Louw and Nida, Montefiore, and Lane. Some suggest that sense does not fit here and prefer a causal sense, 'for/because of'. All versions examined except the Twentieth Century New Testament and TT translate it using a causal sense here. But to accept a causal sense, one has to show if it can have that sense in the NT, and why the normal sense is not to be chosen. It does have a causal sense in many Greek documents besides those of the Bible, and supposedly ἀντί has a causal sense in Eph. 5:31, but that passage is a quotation from Gen. 2:24 and probably cited from the LXX and is not very good support. The other passage usually cited supporting a causal sense for ἀντί is Matt. 17:27, where Jesus tells Peter to take the coin he will find in a fish's mouth and offer it ἀντὶ ἐμοῦ καὶ σοῦ 'for me and you;' but the sense of 'for' could also be 'as a substitute for coins we would both have to give otherwise.' Some even suggest that ἀντί has a causal sense in v. 16 of this chapter where it says that Esau sold his birthright ἀντί one meal, but clearly the one was exchanged for the other; he did not sell a birthright *on behalf of* a meal. So a causal sense is extremely suspect. The next question is then, why do people interpret that the author did not mean 'instead' (the substitutionary sense)? If one takes the sense to be 'instead of the joy that was set before him', then we must ask, "What joy?" Two answers have been suggested: "either the joy of his heavenly status or the joy that he might have had on earth" (Attridge). The latter would not seem to have any Biblical support, but the former might be supported by Phil. 2:6–8; indeed, the two passages then seem to be stating something similar. The display therefore takes the substitutionary interpretation, and supplies 'in heaven' to make the time and location explicit. If one prefers the other sense, the proposition would read 'because of the joyful things God placed before him'. The question then again arises, "What joys?" Miller suggests it was "His exaltation to the right hand of God." Others suggest the joy was the reward he would receive after enduring all the sufferings of death. This is possible, but to suggest that Jesus' motivation for enduring the cross was to receive a reward seems unacceptable.

With either interpretation, 'God' is to be taken as the implied agent of πρόκειμαι 'set before' if the word is given a transitive sense. But if it is given an intransitive sense, as seems preferable from the lexicons (e.g., Louw and Nida, 13.76, "to lie before (someone), to lie ahead,") it should be translated as 'lay ahead of, awaited, potentially available'.

12:2g He disregarded the shame *of dying as if he were a criminal* The participial phrase αἰσχύνης καταφρονήσας is taken as expressing a "coordinating circumstance" with ὑπέμεινεν σταυρόν 'he endured a cross' (Miller). The words 'as if he were a criminal' are included as culturally implicit information; Barnes says "it was regarded as the appropriate punishment of [only] the most infamous of mankind."

12:2h at the place of highest honor For this rendering of ἐν δεξιᾷ see the note on 1:3.

at the throne where God *rules* The verb 'rules' is supplied to spell out the implicit event in the genitive phrase τοῦ θρόνου τοῦ θεοῦ 'the throne of God': the throne is not just something God possesses.

EXPANSION OF *APPEALS*₂₋₃ IN THE 12:1–6 DISPLAY

¶ PTRN	RELATIONAL STRUCTURE	CONTENTS
APPEAL₂ — MEANS — NUCLEUS		12:3a You should keep thinking about Jesus because **you should** compare your **enduring to his enduring.**
└ description of 'Jesus' — NUCLEUS		12:3b He **patiently** endured
└ circumstance		12:3c when sinful **people** acted/spoke so hostilely against him.
└ purpose		12:3d Do that [3a] in order that you do not give up **trusting God** or become discouraged.
┌ circumstance		12:4a While you have struggled to resist **being influenced by** sinful **people,**
basis — NUCLEUS — RESULT		12:4b you have not yet bled **and died as Jesus did**
└ reason		12:4c because of your resisting **evil.**
┌ orienter		12:5a And **I don't want** you to forget [RHQ] these words that **King Solomon spoke to his own** son
├ description of 'words'		12:5b **which are the same as** God would exhort you **because you are his children**:
APPEAL₃ — CONTENT — NUCLEUS₁		12:5c "My son, do not disregard/despise the Lord **God** disciplining **you,**
NUCLEUS₂ — NUCLEUS		12:5d and do not be discouraged
└ circumstance		12:5e when **the Lord God** corrects [DOU] you(pl) **for your wrong actions,**
├ REASON₁		12:6a because it is everyone whom he loves whom the Lord disciplines
└ REASON₂ — NUCLEUS		12:6b and he punishes everyone whom he accepts as his child
└ circumstance		12:6c **when they do wrong.**"

NOTES

12:3a You should keep thinking about Jesus because Since this is an exhortation, the γάρ here can not signal reason. It simply introduces another *APPEAL*. The other words in the propositionalization are just a repetition of what was given in v. 2a.

you should* compare your *enduring to his enduring The great majority of commentators suggest the imperative verb ἀναλογίσασθε 'consider' involves making a comparison; Kistemaker says, "He literally tells them to compare their lives with that of Jesus."

12:3b He *patiently* endured The verb ὑπομένω carries the sense both of submitting to trials and remaining steadfast in the midst of them.

12:3c when sinful *people* acted/spoke so hostilely against him There is a serious textual problem here. All the versions follow the GNT reading, εἰς ἑαυτόν 'against himself', which is given a C "difficulty in deciding" rating. Even here, Wikgren disagrees with the majority in Metzger's *A Textual Commentary on the Greek New Testament*. Since either of the plural forms, εἰς ἑαυτούς 'against themselves' or εἰς αὐτούς 'against them' has better manuscript support than the singular variants (either that followed by GNT or εἰς αὐτόν 'against him'), he says "The plural is the qualitatively best supported and the more difficult (though meaningful) reading, and the one more likely to be altered." The problem with the plural is, as Ellingworth so succinctly states it, "it is difficult to see what that might mean." Some have taken the plural to mean that in opposing God, sinners only harm themselves; but as Attridge notes, such an idea is completely foreign to the context. Since 'against himself' obviously fits the context so well, the display follows the GNT and assumes there was an early scribal change, perhaps on the assumption of an allusion to Num. 16:36 where it states that Korah, Dathan, and Abiram were "sinners at the cost of their lives."

The other problem here is whether ἀντιλογία 'hostility' refers to an action involving words only or actions only or both words and actions. Considering the various kinds of things Christ endured at his trial and crucifixion, and the context here, there is no reason to limit the term. Etymologically the word refers to speech, but as Hughes says, "What Christ endured was far more than words." LB's rendering, "as sinful men did such terrible things to him," is excellent.

12:3d in order that you do not give up *trusting God* **or become discouraged** The main problems with the Greek text, ἵνα μὴ κάμητε ταῖς ψυχαῖς ὑμῶν ἐκλυόμενοι 'lest you grow weary in your souls fainting' are whether 'fainting' explains 'grow weary' or is coordinate with it, and whether 'in your souls' is to be connected only with 'fainting' or with both 'grow weary' and 'fainting'. The sense is not affected much in any case, but semantically 'in your souls' would seem to better collocate with and be explained by κάμνω 'grow weary' than with 'give up'. By rendering the verb and participle non-figuratively the 'in your souls' becomes a redundant figure anyway (the words "in your souls" are not rendered in any version examined except KJV).

Grammatically it is probably true that the participle following the aorist subjunctive verb expresses attendant action, and nearly all English translations render the whole expression by two verbs joined by 'and'. But since κάμνω τῇ ψυχῇ means 'become discouraged' (Louw and Nida, 25.291) and ἐκλύομαι also means 'become discouraged' (Louw and Nida, 25.288), a good case may be made for considering the expression a doublet. The rendering here follows BAGD (p. 243) in assigning the meaning 'give out' (i.e., 'give up') to ἐκλύομαι and thus, since 'be discouraged' and 'give up' are two different actions, they are both given in the display and connected with 'or' (as in JBP). The words 'trusting God' specify the sphere of 'giving up'.

12:4a While you have struggled to resist *being influenced by* **sinful** *people* Commentators note that the writer's figurative language shifts from the foot races to boxing matches. The word ἁμαρτία 'sin' is a personification. Commentators are divided as to whether the phrase πρὸς τὴν ἁμαρτίαν ἀνταγωνιζόμενοι 'struggling against sin' refers to an inner struggle to commit sin, here probably unbelief or apostasy, or a struggle against the opponents of their faith, or even both. In the light of what the author has said in 10:32–33 about their sufferings at the hands of those opposed to the Christian message, it seems best to go with Bruce who says, "This does not exclude the constant inner conflicts, but the emphasis is clearly on those antagonistic to the Christian faith." Ellingworth and Nida suggest it could be translated as "in defending yourself against sinners," but this sounds too much like the attacks were purely physical, whereas the immediate context of not being discouraged and giving up the faith suggests that whatever the nature of the attacks, the danger was that the believers might give up their faith as a result. The words 'be influenced by' seem the best to capture this sense. If one prefers the other interpretation, he could put 'While you have struggled against *being tempted to* sin…'.

12:4b you have not yet bled *and died as Jesus did* The phrase μέχρις αἵματος 'unto blood' is elliptical, the verb 'shedding' being supplied here as in most versions. There are two questions here: first, is 'blood' a metonymy standing for 'being killed'? It is so taken by TEV and JB, and BAGD (p. 22.2a) takes the whole clause to mean "resist unto death." Several commentators suggest that death by martyrdom is meant, and thus 'and died' is supplied here. The next question is: Is a reference to Christ's death intended? The context of 'looking to Jesus who endured the cross' (v. 2) and 'compare yourselves with Jesus' (v. 3) leave little doubt that this is so. LB makes the reference overly clear in rendering "until you sweat great drops of blood," a reference to the events in Gethsemane (Luke 22:44), but the writer is probably not meaning to be that specific. Some have suggested the writer is referring to other early martyrs in the church or to those mentioned in chapter 11 who had died for their faith, but in the immediate context the reference is much more clearly to Christ.

12:5a *I don't want* **you to forget** Commentators are almost equally divided as to whether this verse is a statement or a rhetorical question. However it cannot be a statement, because if it were a statement it would be an accusation, which it is not. The author used a rhetorical question to emphasize this specific way in which he wanted the audience to hold a proper attitude like the attitudes of Jesus. The clause ἐκλέλησθε τῆς παρακλήσεως 'Have you/You have forgotten the exhortation' must not be translated as an accusation, but positively as an encouragement.

Commentators and versions are fairly evenly divided as to whether to read a question here or a statement. Following the asyndeton introducing v. 4, the καί 'and' here fits very well as an *orienter* for the APPEAL to follow in vv. 5c–6. Even if it were taken as a question, the semantic force would still be a statement like 'it seems that you have forgotten'. The wording in the display, "I don't want you to forget" is trying to convey the same sense in a somewhat different way.

these words *that King Solomon spoke to his own son* The display identifies the author and recipient of the quotation and thus avoids a personification involved in the words παρακλήσεως διαλέγεται 'exhortation speaks'. Most versions signal that the quotation comes from Scripture by orthographic devices; CEV has "the Scriptures say," and some translators might want to use this shortened wording.

which are the same as **God would exhort you** *because you are his children* The GNT has ὡς υἱοῖς διαλέγεται 'as he speaks with sons'. The ὡς is taken as introducing a comparison, which is here made a full clause expressing a simile (so Miller, Barnes). The word 'sons' is rendered more generically to refer to both males and females.

12:5c My son The GNT has υἱέ μου 'my son'. Solomon was advising his own son, but the author of Hebrews wants Solomon's admonition to apply to all of his readers. The author cited Proverbs 3:11–12 from the Septuagint.

do not disregard/despise the Lord *God* **disciplining** *you* The Greek μὴ ὀλιγώρει παιδείας 'do not despise discipline' is taken as a negative prohibition. The present imperative "demands that action in progress be stopped" (Miller). But it could be taken as a litotes, in which case it would be translated as a positive command; (e.g., 'you(pl) should continue to accept gladly') (cf. the TEV, "Pay attention when the Lord corrects you").

Lord *God* The display indicates that Solomon was referring to Yahweh, the Father.

disciplining *you* The participial phrase ὑπ' αὐτοῦ ἐλεγχόμενος 'being reproved by him' is taken as expressing circumstance (so Miller). There is very little semantic difference between the event being expressed by παιδεία 'discipline" in v. 5c and the verb here; see note on v. 6b. The phrase 'disciplining you' means "punishes you in order to make you realize that you have done wrong" (Ellingworth and Nida).

12:6a it is everyone whom he loves The words ὃν ἀγαπᾷ 'whom he loves' are forefronted. The emphasis thus conveyed is represented in the display by a cleft construction. The relative pronoun is singular, but with a generic sense, and is thus rendered as 'everyone'.

12:6b punishes The verb here, μαστιγόω, in its primary sense means to whip and thus here, in an extended sense, "to punish severely" (Louw and Nida, 38:11). The two clauses of v. 6 are considered a doublet (Moore, p. 59) but both are kept in the display because the passage cited is a poetic one.

12:6c *when they do wrong* This matches the verb 'punishes', so that the display does not imply that God beats his children routinely, as many versions imply.

BOUNDARIES AND COHERENCE

It is not easy to decide where to end the first paragraph in this chapter. TEV, NEB, and RSV start a new paragraph at v. 3, while NIV, JBP, NCV, and CEV start one at v. 4. JB and LB begin the second paragraph at v. 5. There are several bits of evidence pointing to the break being before v. 3. The ἀναλογίζασθε 'compare yourselves with' in v. 3 seems clearly to refer to a specific comparison between ourselves and Jesus in v.4. The material in vv. 3–6 is 'the discipline of suffering'. Furthermore, metaphorical references to racing (the crowd in the stadium and 'run the race' in v. 1, 'keeping our eyes on the goal' in v. 2,) are not continued in v. 3.

But, because of the indecision of various versions, and because vv. 1–6 all center around 'enduring suffering', starting a new paragraph in the middle of this unit, does not seem justified.

PROMINENCE AND THEME

The main feature of prominence in this unit (vv. 1–6) is the emphatic free pronoun 'we' at the beginning, preceded only by two conjunctions. The theme is drawn from the NUCLEUS of the *basis* and the most naturally prominent propositions in each of the APPEALS.

PART CONSTITUENT 12:7–11 (Paragraph: Appeal₆ of 1:4—12:29)

THEME: Endure what you suffer, because our sufferings are to discipline us, and if we haven't experienced God's discipline we are not his true children. We should accept God's discipline since it is always to help us.

¶ PTRN	RELATIONAL STRUCTURE	CONTENTS

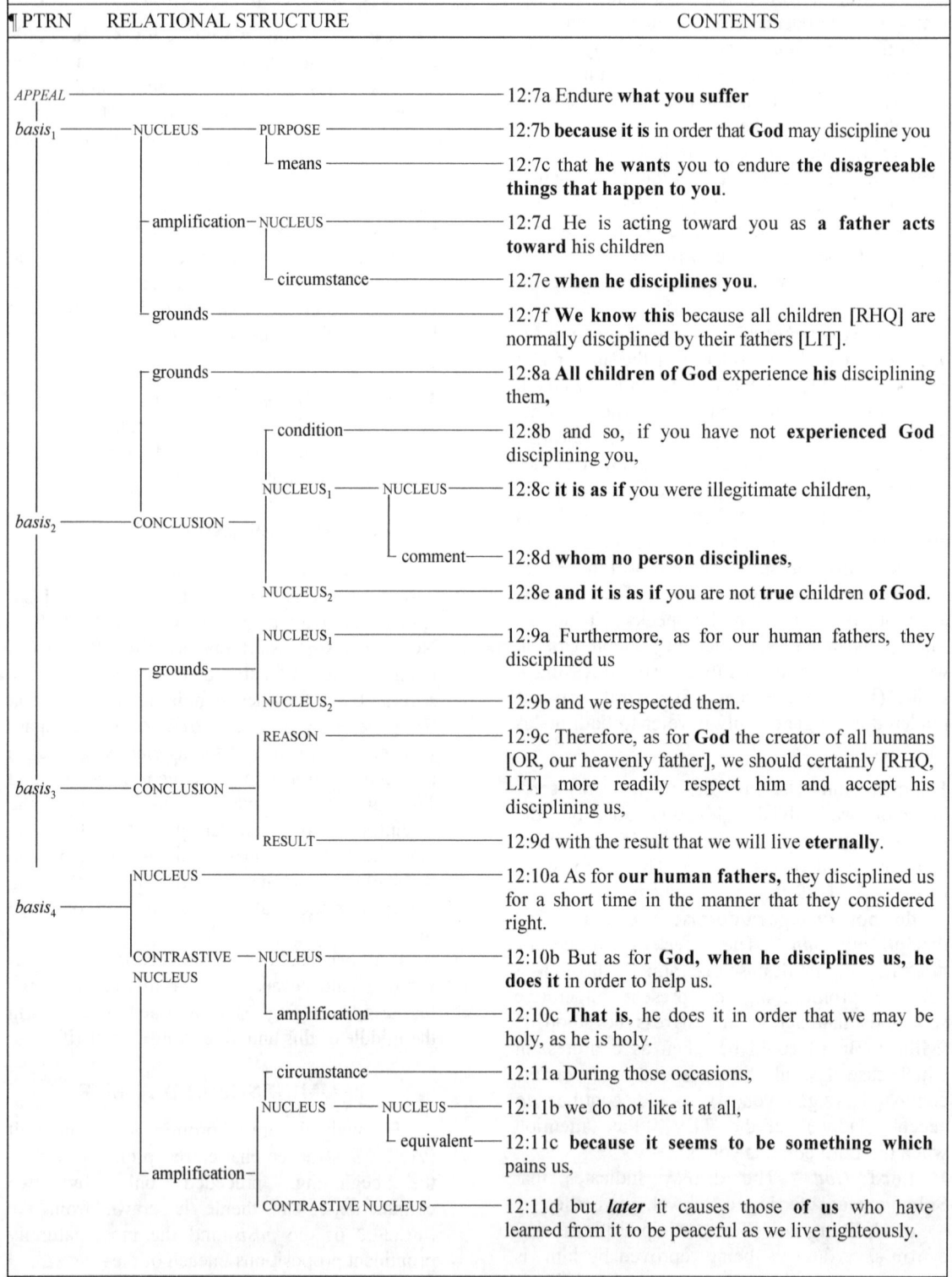

INTENT AND PARAGRAPH PATTERN

This paragraph consists of one *APPEAL* and four subsequent *bases*. The *APPEAL* is signaled by the 2nd person plural imperative ὑπομένετε 'endure'. It is thus a hortatory paragraph.

NOTES

12:7b it is in order that *God* may discipline There are a few Greek manuscripts that begin the verse with εἰ 'if' and this is reflected in the KJV. Most manuscripts have εἰς 'toward, in the direction of'. The evidence for εἰς is so strong that the variant is not even mentioned in the GNT.

12:7c *he wants* you to endure There is a question of whether ὑπομένετε is to be taken as indicative, 'you are enduring', or as an imperative, 'endur'. It can be taken in an imperative sense here, functioning as a somewhat mitigated *APPEAL*; the whole chapter is basically hortatory in nature. Many versions express a somewhat mitigated exhortation here: e.g., "you have to" (RSV), "you must" (NEB), and many others have a straight imperative. Perhaps the main reason it is taken here as a statement is that v. 12 starts with διό 'therefore' and an imperative, suggesting that vv. 4–11 form the basis for the list of *APPEALS* which follow. A bit of the mitigated *APPEAL* force is retained by rendering the verb as 'God wants you to endure'.

the disagreeable things that happen to you These words are supplied to satisfy the case frame; NIV supplies "hardship," JBP supplies "what you have to bear," and TEV "what you suffer."

12:7c Though there is no conjunction here, communication relations in Greek are not always signaled by conjunctions.

12:7f *We know this* because The γάρ here introduces the grounds for the statement in 7b-c; the words 'we know this because' make the relationship clear.

all children [RHQ] are normally disciplined by their fathers The rhetorical question τίς γὰρ υἱὸς ὃν οὐ παιδεύει 'what son is not disciplined?' is rendered as a positive statement cf. also NCV and JBP. The implied double negative (a litotes) is also removed in the display and the sense conveyed by 'normally'. NCV and CEV represent this with "all children." In some cases it may be better to translate πατήρ 'father' as 'parents' (as in CEV and The Message) instead of 'fathers'.

12:8a All *children of God* experience *his* disciplining This states the semantic content of ἧς μέτοχοι/μέτεχοι γεγόνασιν πάντες 'of which all have become sharers' in an unskewed manner. There is a question as to whom the 'all' refers. It cannot refer to 'all people in general' (as NCV and LB imply) because the writer has just said this in v. 7. It is clear, in Ellingworth's words (p. 651), that "The immediate context requires πάντες to mean 'all legitimate sons', " As Miller notes, the grammatical construction here is a somewhat skewed way of presenting a logical syllogism:

All God's true children experience being disciplined.

Therefore you are not a true child of God if you are not experiencing his discipline.

12:8b if you have not *experienced God disciplining* you The display expresses by a verb and supplies a subject for the abstract noun in the phrase χωρὶς παιδείας 'without discipline'.

12:8c *it is as if* you were illegitimate children The word νόθοι 'child conceived out of wedlock' is expressing a metaphor (cf. Louw and Nida, 10:39), and thus the implied point of comparison is supplied as a cultural implicature. As Guthrie notes (p. 253), "The father does not give the illegitimate son the same rights and privileges, neither does he bother to discipline him" cf. also Kistemaker (p. 376), Moffatt.

12:8d *whom no person disciplines* This phrase expresses a crucial cultural implicature cf. Ellingworth, Bruce, Kistemaker (p. 376).

12:8e *it is as if* you are not *true* children of God The word 'true' is supplied as an implicature of the argument; either 'true' or 'real' is supplied in NIV, TEV, NEB, and NCV. 'Accepted as children of God' would be a good alternative. It is possible that in some places the metaphorical sense of 'children' (υἱοί 'sons' in the Greek) may not be acceptable or understood, in which case it may be necessary to translate something like CEV's "you don't really belong to him."

12:9a-b as for our human fathers The author uses again the μέν construction to indicate that we should respect God even more than we respect our biological fathers. He writes τοὺς μὲν τῆς σαρκὸς ἡμῶν πατέρας εἴχομεν παιδευτὰς καὶ ἐνετρεπόμεθα οὐ πολὺ [δὲ] μᾶλλον ὑποταγησόμεθα τῷ πατρὶ τῶν πνευμάτων 'as for our flesh fathers, we have had fathers who disciplined us and we respected them. Even much more as for the Father of spirits we should respect.'

12:9a our human fathers This is the sense of the expression τῆς σαρκὸς ἡμῶν πατέρας 'our fathers of the flesh'. Several of the versions have either 'human fathers' or 'earthly fathers'.

12:9c Therefore The second half of the verse supplies the CONCLUSION for which 9a-b supply the grounds.

as for God The author completes the μὲν...δέ construction.

the creator of all humans [OR, our heavenly father] It is very difficult to decide which sense the writer intends by τῷ πατρὶ τῶν πνευμάτων 'to the father of spirits'.

Commentators suggest 1) the creator of our human spirits, 2) the creator of all spirits, whether human or non-human; or 3) our spiritual father (= creator of spiritual life). The expression occurs nowhere else in the NT. As to interpretation 2), it has been suggested that the absence of ἡμῶν 'our' points to a reference to supernatural spirits, but the ἡμῶν does occur in the previous clause with the phrase 'our fathers of the flesh'; and since there is clearly a contrast being stated between human fathers and God, the pronoun would not need repeating. And that contrast must determine the sense of 'father of spirits'. Therefore interpretation 2) is not included here. Interpretation 1) is much more likely, but even then, in this context it would have to mean 'creator of our spirits which have the potential of experiencing eternal life'. This would give a sense very close to interpretation 3). The display gives two alternatives. Several versions (e.g., CEV, TEV, JB, and NEB) have "spiritual Father" but as Ellingworth and Nida point out, translators may have difficulty in translating such a phrase meaningfully.

we should certainly [RHQ, LIT] more readily The writer uses a rhetorical question here "to emphasize the writer's evaluation of the heavenly Father's superior discipline" (Miller). The wording 'not much more' is also a litotes. The display reflects both of these devices by an emphatic positive statement.

respect him and accept his disciplining us The GNT has ὑποταγησόμεθα 'shall we be subject', but in the context the writer is not talking about submission in general but about the need to "accept discipline from" (NCV); cf. also JBP, CEV.

12:9d with the result that we will live *eternally* The καί 'and' here is semantically expressing result cf. NEB's "and so attain life". The contrast between physical and spiritual life being expressed in the verse requires that 'eternally' or something equivalent be understood as modifying the verb ζήσομεν 'we shall live': BAGD give the sense here as "*live*, of the sanctified life of the child of God... in the glory of the life to come" (p. 336.2bα).

12:10a As for *our human fathers* The author uses the same μέν construction to indicate another reason why the believers should accept discipline from God. He wrote οἱ μὲν...πρὸς ὀλίγας ἡμέρας κατὰ τὸ δοκοῦν αὐτοῖς ἐπαίδευον, ὁ δὲ ἐπὶ τὸ συμφέρον 'as for them, for a few days, according to the manners they supposed good, they disciplined us. And as for him, (he disciplines us) to help us'. The author indicated that God trains us for our benefit, certainly more beneficially than our human fathers disciplined us.

our human fathers The relative pronoun οἱ 'they' refers to 'natural fathers' in v. 10a, its full antecedent being in v. 9a.

for a short time The phrase πρὸς ὀλίγας ἡμέρας is an understatement meaning 'for a brief period'. Commentators are mostly agreed that the phrase means, in Dods' words, "during the brief period of youth."

12:10b But as for *God* The author completes his comparison of the benefits that our fathers caused us through their disciplining us and the benefits that God gives.

to help us The phrase ἐπὶ τὸ συμφέρον 'for the profit' means 'for our (own) good', as it is rendered in most versions; but since that expression is also somewhat idiomatic, it is rendered here in a non-idiomatic way.

12:10c in order that we may be holy, as he is holy Most commentators agree that the purpose phrase εἰς τὸ μεταλαβεῖν τῆς ἁγιότητος αὐτοῦ 'for the sharing of his holiness' is explanatory of 'for our profit'. The phrase does not mean that God will apportion out bits of his holiness, but, as Alford says, our "becoming holy like him."

12:11a During those occasions This verse, introduced by the conjunction δέ, is an amplification of the preceding verse. The author indicates that 12:11a is in contrast with 12:11d, using the construction μὲν...δέ. Here the meaning of the construction seems to be 'During the occasions/events when...but later...'

The phrase πρὸς τὸ παρόν 'for the present' can be considered a type of metonymy, a generic expression standing for "when we are punished" (TEV).

12:11b we do not like it at all The GNT has πᾶσα δὲ παιδεία...οὐ δοκεῖ χαρᾶς εἶναι ἀλλὰ λύπης 'but any discipline...seems not to be a matter of joy'. This is a Hebrew negative understatement that emphasizes the natural response from children when their parents correct them.

12:11d but <u>later</u> The μέν...δέ construction which relates v. 11a and v. 11d is usually considered one indicating contrast, but here the contrast is between the previous situations and the later results.

it causes...to be peaceful as we live righteously The clause καρπὸν εἰρηνικὸν ἀποδίδωσιν δικαιοσύνης 'gives back the peaceful fruit of righteousness' presents several problems. 'Yield fruit' is a dead metaphor meaning 'to produce', or as here, to cause something. The adjective 'peaceful' is semantically conveying a state, thus 'be peaceful'. The word 'righteousness' here means "a righteous life" (TEV), "the practical righteousness which springs from faith, not the forensic righteousness which comes by faith" (Alford). The main problem is the relationship between peace and righteousness. The genitive could be one of apposition, 'the fruit (i.e., peace), which is righteous living', or a genitive of cause, "a righteous life that brings peace" (TCNT). The latter is supported by the context and directly reflects Isa. 32:17, "the fruit of righteousness will be peace" (NIV).

causes those *of us* who have learned from it The phrase τοῖς δι' αὐτῆς γεγυμνασμένοις 'to those who have been trained by it' not only involves an athletic metaphor but a personification. The former is removed by considering training as a means of teaching someone to do something; and then using 'learn' as the reciprocal of 'teach'. Louw and Nida (36.11) concur, stating that here "it may be important in some languages to translate 'those who have learned by such punishment'."

BOUNDARIES AND COHERENCE

A new paragraph is indicated at v. 12 by a new imperative and a new set of metaphors referring to body parts. The next paragraph begins at v. 14 with a new set of imperatives and a new topic. Coherence in the 12:7–11 paragraph is seen in six occurrences of the noun παιδεία 'discipline' and its cognate verb, and three occurrences of the kinship terms for 'father' and 'son'.

PROMINENCE AND THEME

Prominence is given to the phrase εἰς παιδείαν 'unto discipline' being forefronted, and that prominence is indicated in the display by a cleft construction. The rhetorical question in v. 7 also probably indicates prominence, and use of the word 'all' in the display is an attempt to convey that prominence. The theme is drawn from the APPEAL and a very abbreviated form of the most prominent propositions in the *bases*.

PART CONSTITUENT 12:12–29 (Paragraph: Summary Appeals of 1:4—12:29)

THEME: Renew yourselves spiritually; go forward in your Christian life; endeavor to live peacefully with everyone; seek to be holy; guard against bitterness; do not be immoral; and do not refuse to listen to God.

¶ PTRN	RELATIONAL STRUCTURE	CONTENTS
APPEAL₁ — MEANS ┬ NUCLEUS₁		12:12 Therefore, even when you feel spiritually exhausted, renew yourselves [MET] **in your trust in Jesus**,
└ NUCLEUS₂		12:13a and continue to believe **the truth you have been taught** [MET],
├ purpose (negative)		12:13b in order that none **of you** who is uncertain **about continuing to trust in Christ** will leave **God's** way (OR, become eternally lost) [MET],
└ purpose (positive) ┬ NUCLEUS		12:13c but instead allow God to restore *your faith in Christ* [MET]
└ comparison		12:13d as an injured limb is restored.
APPEAL₂ ┬ NUCLEUS₁		12:14a Endeavor to live peacefully with all people,
└ NUCLEUS₂ ┬ EXHORTATION		12:14b and endeavor to be holy
└ grounds		12:14c since no one will ever see the Lord **Jesus/God** if he is not holy.
APPEAL₃		12:15a Make sure that none of you stops believing, **with the result that** you reject **God's** gracious **offer to save you.**
APPEAL₄ ┬ EXHORTATION		12:15b Beware of allowing anyone to teach you what is evil/false doctrine [MET],
├ grounds₁		12:15c **since anyone who does that** will cause many others to believe his wrong teaching, **like** a root **of a weed spreads and produces plants which choke the good plants around it,**
└ grounds₂		12:15d **and since there is danger that such a person** will cause trouble **among you** and as a result cause many **believers to sin and become** unacceptable to God.
APPEAL₅ ┬ NUCLEUS		12:16a Make sure that none of you is immoral, or is irreligious/godless as Esau was,
└ description of 'Esau' ┬ NUCLEUS		12:16b who considered that the rights he had **as a firstborn son to be so small in value** that he gave them away in exchange for **only** one meal.
├ amplification₁ ┬ circumstance		12:17a You know that afterwards, when he wished **his father to** bless him,
│ └ NUCLEUS		12:17b **his father** rejected **his request.**
└ amplification₂ ┬ CONTRAEXPECTATION		12:17c Esau found no way to change **his having given away his birthright,**
└ concession		12:17d even though he tried tearfully **to convince his father to change what he had done.**

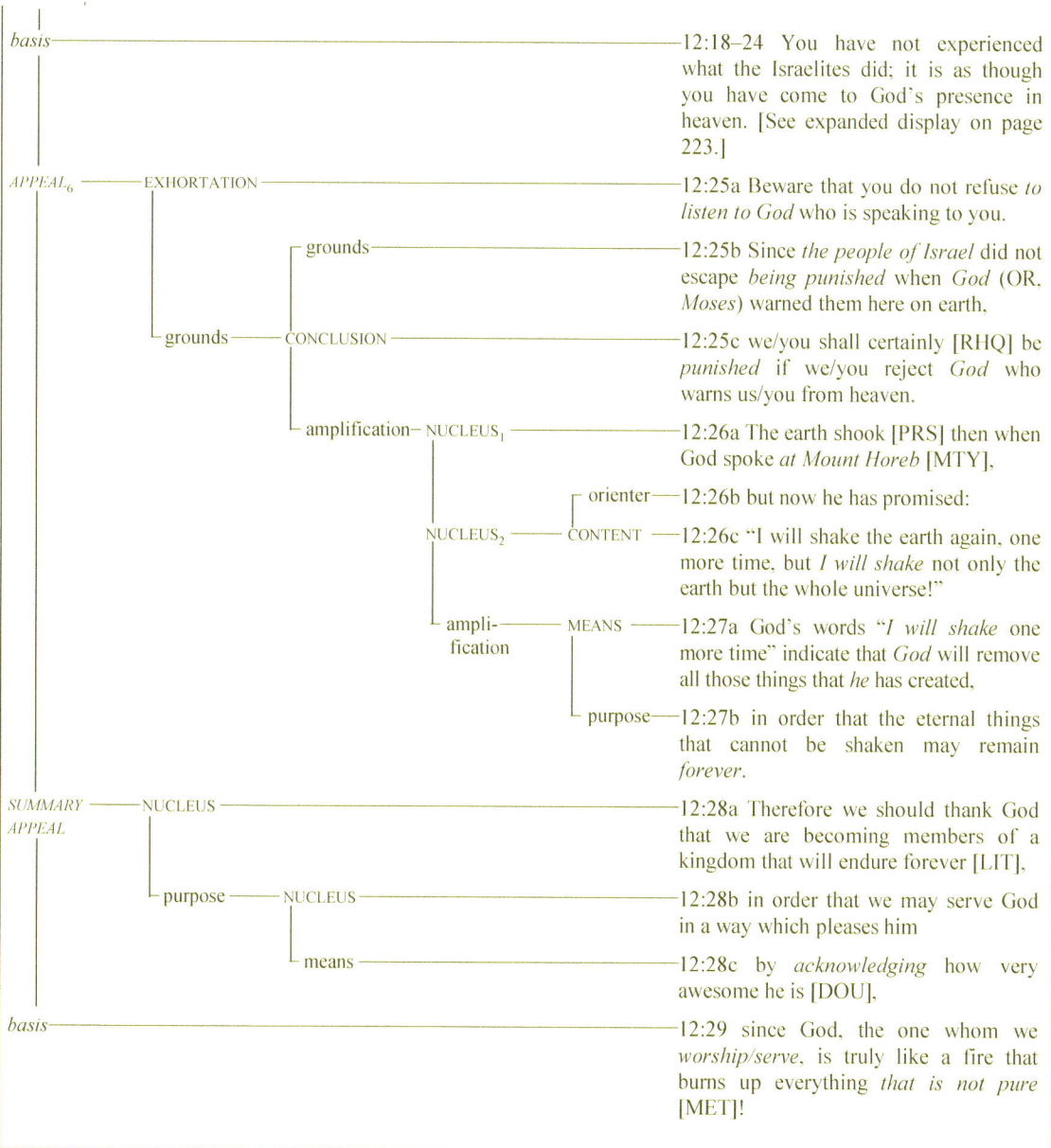

INTENT AND PARAGRAPH PATTERN

This unit is a hortatory paragraph; it consists of six specific APPEALS and a final SUMMARY APPEAL followed by one *basis* for that SUMMARY APPEAL. There are four 2nd person plural imperatives, one 1st person plural subjunctive, and one implied imperative. They constitute the first set of general exhortations with which the writer concludes his epistle.

NOTES

12:12 Therefore, even when you feel spiritually exhausted, renew yourselves [MET] *in your trust in Jesus* The GNT wording παρειμένας χεῖρας καὶ τὰ παραλελυμένα γόνατα ἀνορθώσατε 'straighten the drooping hands and the paralyzed knees' is very metaphorical, probably continuing the figure of runners who are nearly totally exhausted. As Ellingworth and Nida (p. 301) suggest, "It is in fact rare that one can reproduce the metaphors in v. 12" and still communicate. The display has shown the meaning in a non-metaphorical fashion. If one wishes to retain something of the images of the metaphors, one could say 'strengthen yourselves, even when you feel exhausted like those runners whose arms are drooping and their knees collapsing'.

It could be noted as Ellingworth and Nida point out that much of verse v. 12 echoes words from Isaiah 35:3. JB puts this material in italics; none of the other versions examined use any such device.

12:13a continue to believe *the truth you have been taught* The author's words are based on Prov. 4:26. The GNT wording here, τροχιὰς ὀρθὰς ποιεῖτε τοῖς ποσὶν ὑμῶν 'make straight tracks for your feet', continues the metaphor involving a runner. The interpretation is very difficult to determine, and depends a good bit on how the verb ἐκτραπῇ in the next clause is rendered. The basic sense of ἐκτρέπω is 'turn away', which does not seem to collocate in any meaningful way with the phrase τὸ χωλόν 'that which is lame' which is its subject. BAGD (p. 246) suggests that in the context it might be best understood as 'be dislocated', which is the way it is taken in most modern versions which retain the figure. But the commentators are about equally divided between that extended meaning and a literal meaning of 'deviating from the way'. If the meaning 'be dislocated' is chosen, then 'make straight tracks' in the previous clause can be taken as an exhortation that the believers were to maintain a consistent Christian life and avoid "hesitations and vacillations between Christian faith and Judaism" (Davidson), otherwise their spiritual 'lameness' would result in permanent 'dislocation' from the faith. If the meaning 'deviate from the way' is chosen in the second clause, the sense of the first clause would be that "everything should be removed [from a person's own life] which would hinder ... [that person] from walking in the path to life" (Barnes).

Louw and Nida (23.178) accept the medical sense of ἐκτρέπω here as "to wrench or sprain the ligaments of a joint." In view of so many references to bodily ailments in the context, the decision here has been to go with the majority of more recent commentators and follow Ellingworth, who says (p. 659–660) that here ἐκτρέπω "is almost certainly used in a technical medical sense, of a foot turning so as to become dislocated... This meaning also suits the general purpose of the epistle, which presupposes that ailing members of the community must either progress to maturity, or fall back to a state worse than that in which they began their Christian life." The display attempts to express the meaning in a non-figurative way with 'continue to believe the truth you have been taught'.

12:13b in order that none *of you* who is uncertain *about continuing to trust in Christ* will leave *God's* way (OR, become eternally lost) Much of this wording has been covered in the previous note. The GNT wording ἵνα μὴ τὸ χωλὸν ἐκτραπῇ 'in order that the lame may not be dislocated' obviously continues the metaphor about the runner's exhausted body. Miller states that 'the lame' refers to those who "were limping back and forth between two opinions" (i.e., between Christianity and Judaism;) cf. also Hughes, Montefiore. The display makes clear the topic of the metaphor, giving two alternatives. The first of these, 'may leave God's way', is somewhat metaphorical, while the second 'become spiritually lost' is less so. NCV takes the latter approach, rendering "will not cause you to be lost," which is a rather strong rendering of 'become disabled' but probably carries the sense well.

12:13c but instead The author recommended a positive action, one which is somewhat a restatement of the first APPEAL.

allow God to restore *your faith in Christ* The Greek continues the metaphor about a runner, and the display makes the topic specific. NCV's rendering, "so that you will be saved" is non-metaphorical but rather biased theologically. It seems that the author wanted to imply that the doubting person should actively do whatever was needful in order to continue believing, imitating whatever a long distance runner does in order to finish the race.

12:13d as an injured limb is restored This continues the metaphor referring to physical health, but expresses the topic of the metaphor as ἰαθῇ 'be healed'. JB has "grow strong again."

In some languages it may be necessary to complete the athletic metaphor by including '*in order that the runner can continue running*'.

12:14a-b Endeavor to live peacefully with all people and...to be holy The display uses verb phrases to avoid the abstract nouns εἰρήνη 'peace' and ἁγιασμός 'holiness'. The word 'people', following JB and NCV, is used to be more generic than 'men' which is used in most translations to render the Greek adjective πάντων 'all'. NLT has 'everyone'.

12:14c since The causal relation here expresses in a straightforward manner the Greek οὗ χωρὶς 'without which'; versions that render similarly include TEV, NEB, LB.

no one will ever see the Lord *Jesus/God* if he is not holy A literal translation of this seemingly simple clause has two translation problems. One is that it could imply seeing the Lord in this life; the display supplies 'ever'.

Actually the sense could probably be as well expressed by something like 'go to heaven'. The other difficulty is the double negative; if that causes problems, one could render it positively as 'only if people are holy will they eventually see the Lord'. A final query here is, does 'Lord' refer to Christ or to God? It is hard to know which the writer had in mind. Both options are given in the display; Ellingworth and Nida (p. 303) say "a reference to God is slightly more probable."

12:15a Make sure that The Greek participle ἐπισκοποῦντες 'taking care' is taken to have imperatival force following the imperative verb διώκετε 'seek' at the beginning of the sentence. All English versions examined except KJV start a new imperative sentence here.

One question which many commentators do not address well is whether the warning in this verse is addressed to individual believers who might be in this spiritual peril or to the spiritual companions of such an individual who should be actively counseling such an individual. Miller (p. 403) strongly suggests the latter: "Community responsibility and mutual influence is exactly what the author is seeking to promote in this exhortation as so often elsewhere in the epistle. He is seeking a united forward thrust of the *whole* community…as the only effective antidote for apostasy by a return to Judaism…on the part of some." See also Kistemaker (p. 385). The display has tried to capture this sense of the verb by rendering it 'make sure that' (as in CEV) and the pronoun τὶς 'anyone' is rendered 'none from among you'.12:15a. NLT makes the sense extremely clear with 'Look after each other so that'.

none of you stops believing, *with the result that* **you reject** *God's* **gracious** *offer to save you* The Greek word ὑστερέω means 'fail to reach, be excluded from' (BAGD p. 849.1a). One of the main difficulties in translating the passage is how to avoid using some abstract noun by which to render χάρις 'grace' as the object of the verb. Another problem is whether the Greek verb should sort of be considered a euphemistic cause-effect metonymy: that is, does the writer not really mean "forfeit" (NEB) or "turns back from" (TEV) by rejecting God's way of salvation through faith in Christ? The display attempts to handle both of these problems, supplying 'God's gracious offer' and 'stop believing' (OR, 'reject') as the implied cause part of the metonymy. A shorter version might be 'stop trusting in Christ to graciously redeem him'.

Ellingworth and Nida (p. 304) state that "the wider context (including 6.4, 10.39, 12.25) supports the idea of receiving God's grace and then letting it go rather than that of missing it altogether ."

12:15b Beware of The GNT has no conjunction here, simply a repetition of μή τις 'lest' which introduced the content of the previous warning. It is thus considered a parallel APPEAL to the one in v. 14.

allowing anyone to teach you what is evil/false doctrine The expression ῥίζα πικρίας ἄνω φύουσα 'a root of bitterness growing' is a reference to Deut. 29:18 in which there is warning against idolatry, saying that those who worship idols are like a plant that grows bitter fruit. But it is not a direct quotation, and thus there is no need to indicate in the text as RSV does that this is a Scripture citation. There are several interpretations of this metaphor:

1. Some have proposed that the writer is talking about bitter feelings or attitudes. But most commentators do not support that the writer is talking about believers having bitter feelings toward other believers.
2. Lenski (p. 445) says "Himself bitter against Christ, he embitters others against Christ." However, it would seem strange that the author would imply a reference to Christ in this context.
3. Attridge says (p. 368) "Such bitterness may have arisen from the persecution that they had experienced, or perhaps from the disappointment of their eschatological hopes." This seems strange also that the author would imply a person's anger arising out of disappointment.

All these interpretations suffer from attempting to separate the meaning of 'bitter' from the meaning of 'root' instead of trying to determine the meaning of the whole phrase. The vast majority of commentaries say that the metaphor is referring to an individual who might introduce evil behavior or false doctrine to the group.

The text has 'root of bitterness' as though it were referring to an inanimate thing, but the author was warning about individuals, and thus the display has 'any person'.

12:15c *since anyone who does that* **will cause many others to believe his wrong teaching,** *like* **a** root *of a weed spreads and produces plants which choke the good plants around it*

The display states the topic and point of comparison of the metaphor involving 'root'. Kistemaker states (p. 385), "The roots of many weed plants spread rapidly and produce plants in all the places where the roots grow."

12:15d cause trouble *among you* The verb ἐνοχλέω, 'trouble, annoy' is found nowhere else in the N.T. The trouble is, says Kistemaker (p. 386), that he ends up "disturbing the peace" among the believers.

cause many *believers to sin and become unacceptable to God* The fact that (οἱ) πολλοί 'the many' refers to believers is made specific. The expression could be taken literally or as an understatement meaning "the entire congregation" (Alford, Dods). CEV renders it as "the rest of you." The verb μιαίνω means 'stain, defile' and the passive here has a figurative sense: what is defiled becomes unacceptable to God. The display attempts to make the meaning quite clear; Dods suggests it means to become unfit for fellowship with God.

12:16a Make sure that none of you is immoral The GNT has no verb here; it is governed by the participle in v. 15a which was also rendered 'make sure that'. Commentators agree that the word πόρνος means one who practices sexual immorality.

irreligious The word βέβηλος means "caring for nothing that is sacred or holy, treating it as secular or common" (Lenski, p. 447).

12:16b rights he had *as a firstborn son* The meaning of πρωτοτόκια 'birthright' could be described as 'things a man was obliged to give to his oldest son' for cultures where the concept is unfamiliar.

***only* one meal** The word βρῶσις means food, but here means a meal, "helping of food" (Bruce). The word 'only' is implied from the context cf. CEV "for only one meal;" Ellingworth and Nida quoting RSV has (p. 305) "a single meal".

12:17a when he wished *his father to* bless him This represents the phrase κληρονομῆσαι τὴν εὐλογίαν 'to inherit the blessing'. As several commentators point out, the word 'blessing' refers to the specific blessing that the first-born son was entitled to. It might be necessary in some cases to say 'the things his father would promise to give him if he blessed him'. Ellingworth and Nida (p. 306) also suggest this could be rendered simply as "wanted his father to bless him" which recognizes that the verb 'inherit' is used somewhat metaphorically.

12:17b his father rejected *his request* The GNT has only ἀπεδοκιμάσθη 'he was rejected', but as Bloomfield noted, it was the request that was rejected, not Esau. Commentators are divided as to whether the implied agent of the passive verb is 'God' or 'his father'; but when 'his request' is recognized as the implied goal of the event, there is no need from the context of the account in Gen. 27:33-37 to make God the agent.

12:17c Esau found no way to change *his having given away his birthright* The Greek is μετανοίας τόπον οὐχ εὗρεν, literally 'he did not find a place of repentance' but the great majority of commentators render it as in the display, or alternatively 'to get his decision changed' (cf. also NCV, TEV).

This clause can be taken as expressing a metonymy; that is, the cause (not getting the decision changed) standing for the effect of Esau not realizing the long lasting consequences of his giving away his birthright.

12:17d tried tearfully *to convince his father to change what he had done* It is uncertain what the pronoun in ἐκζητήσας αὐτήν 'seeking it' refers to. Some suggest repentance = 'change his mind'; some suggest the blessing, some suggest both. The display follows the former. Ellingworth and Nida's arguments (p. 306) seem conclusive:

> "In favor of this interpretation is the fact that the writer is accustomed to drawing from the Old Testament stories a moral different from the main message or intention of the original story. Also, in Greek 'repentance' is closer than **blessing** to the phrase **looked for it with tears**. Note also that the writer is concerned in other places with the impossibility of repentance after certain particularly serious sins (note 6.4 and 'repentance' in 6.6). Finally, if it is the **blessing** he sought, the clause 'he found no chance to repent' would be an awkward parenthetical expression, spoiling the contrast between 'found' and 'sought.' "

12:18-24 See note at 12:18.

12:25a refuse *to listen* The GNT has only παραιτήσησθε 'refuse', but many modern English versions supply some verb; e.g., "to listen" (NCV, JB), "to hear" (TEV, JBP, NEB). Another approach is to consider the expression a litotes and translate it positively; e.g., "make sure that you obey" (CEV).

***to God* who is speaking to you** The GNT has only τὸν λαλοῦντα 'the one who is speaking'. Nearly all the commentators say the reference is to God, though GNT suggests that the speaker here could be God or Christ (only NCV of versions examined states a referent and gives it as God). In some cases it may be confusing to say 'who is speaking' as though God is currently continuously speaking to people. CEV takes note of this and renders it as "when God speaks" (cf. also JB).

12:25b *the people of Israel* The subject of the verb is not specified in the GNT; LB also makes "people of Israel" specific.

escape *being punished* The words in italics complete the case frame; JB supplies "escape their punishment."

when *God* (OR, *Moses*) warned them Commentators are divided as to who the agent of τὸν χρηματίζοντα 'the one warning' is. The majority say it is God. In favor of that interpretation is the fact, as Westcott (p. 419) notes, that "the contrast is not between the two mediators Moses and Christ, but between the character of these two revelations which God made." Furthermore it is stated in v. 26 that when the first warning was given it shook the earth, which was obviously God's voice, not that of Moses.

12:25c we/you shall certainly [RHQ] be *punished* The GNT wording πολὺ μᾶλλον 'much more', with no verb, is very elliptical. Even KJV supplies "shall not escape" in parentheses. The expression is taken as a litotes, with 'shall not escape punishment' being rendered as an emphatic positive statement, 'shall certainly be punished'; (cf. NCV.)

The author makes a shift from 2nd person plural at the beginning of this verse to 1st person plural in the latter part of the verse. The display gives both options; a literal translation might make the readers think the writer was including himself among those who needed this warning.

if we/you reject *God* The great majority of commentators suggest the agent of the unexpressed verb 'warns' is God, though a few say it refers to "God speaking in Christ" (so Miller, p. 418). The fact that none of the pronominal referents are specified in the verse seems to indicate that the same one is intended for all; and 'from heaven' seems a clear reference to God.

12:26a when God spoke *at Mount Horeb* The words οὗ ἡ φωνὴ τὴν γῆν ἐσάλευσεν 'whose voice shook the earth' are considered a metonymy meaning that the earth shook when God spoke. The words 'at Mt. Horeb' are included to supply reference to the occasion being referred to (Exodus 19:18); LB has "from Mount Sinai." But the Greek does not specify the location, and all the O.T. references to this Mount are to Mt. Horeb in Arabia.

12:26c the whole universe The Greek word here is οὐρανός 'sky, heaven', but it means the whole universe, not heaven. See Lünemann, Alford.

12:27a God's words "*I will shake* one more time" indicate that *God* will remove all those things that *he* has created The display supplies words necessary to complete the case frames.

12:27b in order that The commentators consulted do not discuss the ἵνα 'in order that', but there seems no good reason to consider it as indicating result, instead of its usual meaning, of purpose.

eternal things that cannot be shaken Commentators do not for the most part specify what the 'unshakable things' are. Montefiore says a new heaven and new earth (also Lenski, p. 465, Kistemaker p. 399, Hughes); Hewitt suggests "God's heavenly kingdom" (also Lane, cf. v. 28); Attridge (p. 381) suggests "Christ's priesthood and the eschatological inheritance of his followers." It would be best not to specify the things being referred to unless one is forced to.

may remain *forever* The word 'forever' is an implicature of the argument. Guthrie says "Clearly what is unshakable must be eternal;" also Wilson, Brown.

12:28a we should thank God The noun in the clause ἔχωμεν χάριν 'let us have grace' here means "thanks, gratitude" (BAGD p. 878.5). Many versions avoid stating a referent and simply translate as 'let us be thankful'.

we are becoming members of a kingdom The participle in the phrase βασιλείαν... παραλαμβάνοντες 'receiving a kingdom' is present tense, indicating a presently continuing process. But since 'receiving a kingdom' is a fairly severe collocational clash, it is rendered here as 'becoming members of'.

that will endure forever The Greek word ἀσάλευτον means 'unshakable' but it is taken as a litotes (cf. Louw and Nida, 13.31 "enduring").

12:28b we may serve God The words δι' ἧς 'through which' signal the preceding clause as indicating the *means* of the following PURPOSE clause (see Miller, p. 422).

12:28c by Most commentators who discuss what μετά 'with' is signaling suggest it is indicating means.

***acknowledging* how very awesome he is** The phrase εὐλαβείας... καὶ δέους 'reverence and reverence' is considered a doublet by Moore (p. 59). Since both words mean 'awe'; the force of the doublet is indicated by 'very awesome.'. Ellingworth, suggesting it is a hendiadys, renders it as "with reverent fear."

12:29 God, the one whom we *worship* The rendering in the display is to explicate the genitive ὁ θεὸς ἡμῶν 'our God' which does not indicate possession.

is truly Several commentators note that the expression καὶ γάρ puts emphasis on the basis clause. TEV indicates this with "is indeed" and JBP by "it is perfectly true that."

like a fire that burns up everything *that is not pure* The participle in the phrase πῦρ καταναλίσκον 'a consuming fire' is here spelled out using a verb, with 'that is not pure' supplying the implied identification of 'everything'. Bruce (p. 384) suggests "everything that is unworthy of Himself" and Westcott (p. 423) as "all that is unfit to abide in His Presence."

EXPANSION OF BASIS OF *APPEAL*₅ IN THE 12:12–29 DISPLAY

¶ PTRN	RELATIONAL STRUCTURE	CONTENTS
NEGATIVE CLAIM — NUCLEUS		12:18a *After you trusted in Jesus*, you did not experience *terrifying events like our ancestors experienced at Mount Horeb*.
├ specific₁		12:18b Specifically, they approached an actual blazing mountain;
├ specific₂		12:18c it was very dark [DOU];
├ specific₃		12:18d there was a fierce wind;
├ specific₄		12:19a they heard a trumpet blast
├ specific₅ — REASON		12:19b and they heard *God* speak,
└ result		12:19c with the result that those who heard it pleaded that he not speak *directly* to them again.
├ amplification ─ orienter		12:20a God commanded them,
circumstance — content — NUCLEUS₁		12:20b "*Do not climb up* this mountain!
NUCLEUS₂		12:20c If *a person or* an animal touches *even the edge of it* [HYP], you must *kill that person or animal by* throwing stones *at them*."
NUCLEUS₁		12:20d Those people could not endure [HYP] *their terror*.
├ reason		12:21a Moses *himself also* was very afraid when he saw those terrifying events *happen*.
NUCLEUS₂ — RESULT		12:21b He said, "I am so afraid that I am trembling!"
POSITIVE CLAIM — NUCLEUS₁		12:22a Instead, *when you trusted in Christ, it is as though* you came [MET] to the Jerusalem in heaven, the City where God who is all-powerful *lives, which is like* Mount Zion *on earth*.
NUCLEUS₂		12:22b *It is as though you have come to where there are* countless angels, who have gathered and are rejoicing.
NUCLEUS₃		12:23a *It is as though you have joined* a group of believers who *have privileges like* first-born sons, whose names are written down in heaven.
NUCLEUS₄		12:23b *It is as though you have come* to God who will judge all people.
NUCLEUS₅		12:23c *It is as though you have come to where* the spirits *of God's people are*, people who lived righteously *who have died and* who are now made perfect *by God in heaven*.

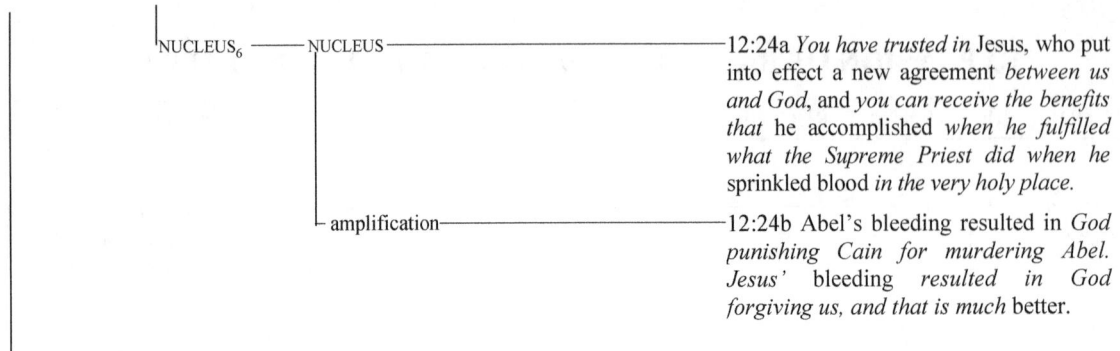

NOTES

12:18–24 This is separated from the 12–24 unit only because the number of levels of indentation in the relational structure require it. This is a very long negative-positive summary statement. There is an emphasis on the positive affirmation. The negative part (12:18–21) negates the validity of the old Israelite system, which the author has already affirmed that God has abandoned (OR declared it to be ineffective). The positive part (12:22–24) focuses on the many benefits that we may have if we follow Jesus.

In some languages, the people prefer to know the positive idea before the negative idea. Even if your language is like that, it is recommended that you do not put the positive first in order. It is important that the strong warning that the author wrote in 12:25–27 should follow closely the message of 12:22–24.

12:18a After *you trusted in Jesus,* you did not experience *terrifying* events like our ancestors experienced The GNT has οὐ προσεληλύθατε 'you have not come near', and the verb is repeated in v. 22. But though the ancient Israelites 'came near' the mountain, one can hardly say they 'came near' many of the other things mentioned in vv. 18–19 (darkness, gloom, sound of a trumpet, a voice). These were events the Israelites experienced

at Mount Horeb This phrase is supplied to make explicit the Old Testament knowledge the author assumed his readers would know (Exodus 19). CEV has "a place like Mount Sinai" cf. also TEV; LB's "as the Israelites did at Mount Sinai" is very close to what the display has. But the Greek does not specify the location, and all the OT references to this Mount are to Mt. Horeb in Arabia.

12:18b an actual blazing mountain There is somewhat of a textual problem here, though its solution is irrelevant. Many manuscripts add the word ὄρει 'mountain', (its omission is now given a B 'almost certain' rating in the 4th edition GNT), but the fact that they do not agree on its placement is proof that it was added later to make clear the implied object of ψηλαφωμένῳ 'what is being touched'. Although many commentators say that the verb refers only in a general way to something which was tangible, even the majority of these admit the indirect reference is to Mount Sinai. ψηλαφάω 'to be touched' BAGD (892) says, "even if the ὄρει...is dropped, the reference is to Mt. Sinai, where God revealed himself in the OT with manifestations that *could be felt* or *touched, were tangible*." Among the versions which state 'mountain' or Mount Sinai are CEV, TEV, and NLT.

actual The GNT has ψηλαφωμένῳ 'which could be touched', but commentaries agree that what is meant is 'available to the senses'. The word 'actual' attempts to convey that connotation. It seems that the author was contrasting events that were physically experienced with the events that are only spiritually experienced (verses 22–25).

12:18c it was very dark Regarding the expression γνόφῳ καὶ ζόφῳ 'blackness and darkness', Moore (p. 59) calls them a near-synonymous doublet. Several commentators suggest the doubling of terms is for emphasis, and Ellingworth and Nida suggest (p. 308) rendering the one set by "the intense darkness."

12:18d fierce wind The word θύελλα means "storm, whirlwind" (BAGD p. 365), "windstorm, whirlwind, squall" (Louw and Nida 14.6). The term does not seem to imply that rain accompanied the wind.

12:19a heard a trumpet blast The phrase σάλπιγγος ἤχῳ 'to the sound of a trumpet' is governed by the verb προσεληλύθατε 'come near' in v. 18, but again, the trumpet is something the Israelites experienced, or specifically that they heard. NLT's rendering, "they heard an awesome trumpet blast," is excellent cf. NIV, JBP, NEB.

12:19b heard *God* speak The expression φωνῇ ῥημάτων 'voice of words' is quite tautological. It is taken as a metonymy, 'voice' standing for the person who spoke: the voice was God's. Ellingworth and Nida (p. 309) suggest it could be rendered as "heard God speaking" or "heard God's voice."

12:19c not speak *directly* to them again The GNT has μὴ προστεθῆναι αὐτοῖς λόγον 'not to be added a word to them' is very idiomatic; NLT has "begged God to stop speaking." But the point of the Ex. 20:19 passage was not that they did not want God to ever speak to them again, but that the experience of hearing God speak through the thunder was so awesome that they did not want God to speak to them directly.

12:20a God commanded The display renders the abstract phrase τὸ διαστελλόμενον 'that which was commanded' as a clause in which God is supplied as the agent. NLT has "God's command."

12:20b *Do not climb up* this mountain The words 'do not climb up' are an implicature of the hyperbole 'Do not touch' given in Exodus 19.

12:20c If *a person or* an animal touches *even the edge of it* The phrase κἂν θηρίον 'if even an animal' implies something more expected than an animal, namely, a person. This is explicitly stated in Ex. 19:13. In some languages it might be necessary to say 'if people touch the mountain they must be killed by stoning them; if animals touch it, you must do the same to them'.

12:20c you must *kill that person or animal by* throwing stones *at them* This spells out what is meant by λιθοβοληθήσεται 'shall be stoned' and removes the passive form.

12:20d Those people could not endure This conveys the sense of the Greek verb φέρω given in the lexicons, but Ellingworth and Nida (p. 309) suggest the sense could be expressed by "they refused to accept."

12:21a Moses *himself* The καί 'and' is five words removed from 'Moses', but the force of καί here seems to be 'even,', though it is not so rendered in the versions. Guthrie (p. 260) says, "It was not only the people, but Moses himself who was terrified." See also Kistemaker and Bruce for similar comments. Miller's note (p. 411) has "even Moses said." It might be necessary to make this explicit in some translations.

when he saw those terrifying events happen This wording clarifies what the writer meant by the expression τὸ φανταζόμενον 'that which became visible'. Most English translations render the phrase as 'the sight'.

12:22–24 An accurate translation should not imply that the author supposed that his people had already arrived in heaven, or that they have seen thousands of angels or they have met the many Christians who have died. A literal version with 'but you have come to…' is likely to be understood as implying arrival in heaven.

12:22a *when you trusted in Christ* This proposition simply repeats what was stated in 12:18a.

***it is as though* you came** It is difficult to know how to do justice to the perfect tense of the verb προσεληλύθατε 'you approached'. Hagner (p. 210) says "it indicates arrival some time in the past with continued enjoyment of the results of that arrival in the present." The difficulty is that nearly all the things they have 'come to' in the list that follows are what believers will experience in heaven. Montefiore says "his readers have not actually arrived at Mount Zion; they have drawn close." Hagner (p. 212) has similar comments. The author seems to be saying that since their conversion they have in some sense begun to experience these things spiritually. The rendering in the display seems the best solution to the problem. The same rendering is used in v. 22c and v. 23b and c. Hewitt says, "the verb προσεληλύθατε 'you are come' or 'you have come', being in the perfect, does not refer to some communion into which believers enter after death but to a communion into which they enter when Christianity is embraced. Those who have this experience have already come to the celestial order…"

the Jerusalem in heaven, the City where God who is all-powerful *lives, which is like* Mount Zion *on earth* The GNT has Σιὼν ὄρει…Ἰερουσαλὴμ ἐπουρανίῳ 'to Mount Zion…, to heavenly Jerusalem'. This is taken as a metaphor since the believers had not literally come to these places. The ancestors of his audience had come to the earthly Jerusalem, but not the heavenly one.

Most of the phenomena listed in the rest of vv. 22–23 are events that believers will experience in heaven. Rev. 21:2 describes "the new Jerusalem, coming down out of heaven from God" (NCV). Several commentators say the reference to Mount Zion here is because it was known as the place of God's presence.

For a discussion of the rendering of 'God who is all-powerful' for θεοῦ ζῶντος 'of the living God', see the notes on 10:31. The verb 'lives' is supplied to make explicit the relationship implied by the genitive (so Kistemaker (p. 392–396); see also the comment on the same phrase at 10:31.

12:22b *where there are* **countless angels** Following the rendering in v. 22a, μυριάσιν ἀγγέλων 'to myriads of angels' is taken to refer to the place where these angels are located, viz. heaven. The same rendering is made in v. 23c.

who have gathered and are rejoicing There is a question of whether the πανηγύρει 'festal gathering' is to be taken with 'angels' which precedes it or with 'assembly of the firstborn' which follows it. The GNT suggests the latter in its punctuation. The problem is that καί 'and' is used consistently in this passage to introduce new items in the list, but there is no καί preceding 'festal gathering' as there is preceding 'assembly of the firstborn'. Therefore following the vast majority of commentators, 'festal gathering' is taken as a further description of the angels.

12:23a a group of believers who *have privileges like* **first-born sons** Nearly all commentators agree that the phrase ἐκκλησία πρωτοτόκων 'to a gathering of first-born ones' refers to believers. It would scarcely be appropriate to say it refers to angels, for it is believers, not angels, whose names are written in heaven. But the first question is, whether it refers to fellow believers among the author's audience cf. Miller, p. 416, "it is the present living church on earth that is meant", or whether it is looking forward to the completed company of believers in heaven (so Lane). All the others in this list are ones who will be in heaven, but since those to whom he is writing **have** joined other believers, the latter is preferred, though it would include the former too. Therefore 'it is as though you have joined' is repeated to start this proposition.

The second question is, why are they referred to as 'first-born'? Several commentators (e.g., Lenski (p. 457), and especially Kistemaker (p. 394) say it refers to the privileges and inheritance that first-born sons received. This is the interpretation followed here; the display spells out the metaphor.

whose names are written down in heaven The phrase ἀπογεγραμμένων ἐν οὐρανοῖς 'having been enrolled in heaven' means their names were recorded; if necessary, 'God' could be supplied as the agent to avoid the euphemistic passive.

12:23b God who will judge all people All versions except RSV ("a judge who is God of all") ignore the fact that the wording of the Greek, κριτῇ θεῷ πάντων 'to a judge, God of all' seems to require a translation other than 'to God, the judge of all people'. Nearly all commentators recognize the wording, but fail to give a corresponding wording. They do suggest that in this context the writer is not talking about condemnation so much as giving fair judgment to all believers. The wording in the display follows this idea in spelling out the relationship intended by the genitive construction.

12:23c the spirits *of God's people are, people ...who have died* The wording in the display makes specific whose spirits the writer is referring to. Alternatives to 'God's people' would be 'believers' or "the redeemed" (LB). Since they will be in heaven, it is implied that they have previously died. Some commentators debate whether it refers to Old Testament saints or those of the New Agreement, but the question is irrelevant; most commentators say it refers to both.

Most commentators assume that 'spirits' is to be taken literally; that is, they are believers who are still awaiting their resurrection bodies. Ellingworth and Nida (p. 312) strongly object and say that rather than referring to disembodied spirits, it is an expression which would be better rendered "those good people who died." It is hard to decide which is the better interpretation.

who lived righteously The word δίκαιος here means upright, righteous in one's character; thus the sense is 'lived righteously' and not 'who were declared righteous'.

made perfect *by God* The display supplies the implied agent.

12:24a who put into effect The word μεσίτης 'mediator' means "one who mediates between two parties to remove a disagreement or reach a common goal" (BAGD, p. 506). The display specifies the two parties involved.

when he fulfilled what the Supreme Priest did when he sprinkled blood in the very holy place It may be a collocational clash to say 'we have come to the blood'. Although the Greek begins this phrase with καί 'and', 'coming to' the blood of Christ is not different from coming to Christ as mediator. It is by his blood that he establishes the new agreement.

The expression 'the sprinkled blood' is a reference to what the Supreme Priest did in the Most Holy Place to prove that the required offering had been made. The information in italics would have been clear to the author's Jewish readers.

12:24b Abel's bleeding resulted in *God punishing Cain for murdering Abel. Jesus'* **bleeding** *resulted in God forgiving us, and that is much* **better** There are two translation problems arising from the words κρεῖττον λαλοῦντι παρὰ τὸν Ἄβελ 'better things speaking than (the blood of) Abel'. One is the personification of blood speaking; this is handled by the words 'The result of Abel's bleeding was....' The other problem is, in what way is the blood of Christ better? Various commentators use various words to express it: "peace and salvation" (Brown, p. 656), "mercy and forgiveness" (Miller, p. 415), "cleansing, forgiveness and peace with God" (Bruce, p. 379), "reconciliation and peace between God and man" (Kistemaker, p. 395), "eternal redemption" (Hughes), "expiation, reconciliation, pardon" (Lenski, p. 459), "most conspicuously of the forgiveness of sins" (Hagner). The display supplies 'forgives' (cf. LB's "which graciously forgives.") Much of the implicit material supplied here is from knowledge of the Old Testament, as found in Gen. 4:10–11.

for murdering Abel This is also implicit knowledge of the Old Testament, and supplied in footnotes in CEV and NCV.

BOUNDARIES AND COHERENCE

Chapter 13 starts with another set of imperatives, but a new unit is signaled by the fact that these injunctions refer to how to act toward fellow believers, not to general moral conduct. Coherence is signaled by references to several individuals and places mentioned in the Old Testament (Esau, Moses (twice), Horeb, Zion Hill, and Jerusalem).

PROMINENCE AND THEME

The theme statement is comprised of slightly abbreviated forms of all the most naturally prominent propositions of all seven of the APPEALS in the paragraph.

EPISTLE CONSTITUENT 13:1–19 (Part: Final Appeals of 1:1—13:25)

THEME: I appeal to you that you love and help one another, respect your marriages, and be content. Imitate your former leaders and obey well their teachings about Christ. Also I want you to praise God. I want you to do good to others, and share with others. Submit to your spiritual leaders, and pray for me.

MACROSTRUCTURE	CONTENTS
APPEAL₁	13:1–14 I appeal to you to love one another, be hospitable, help imprisoned and other mistreated believers, respect the marriage relationship; avoid covetousness; remember the manner of life of your former spiritual leaders and imitate their faith. Since Christ never changes, don't be diverted to believe strange teachings.
APPEAL₂	13:15 We should continually praise God. Specifically, we should say openly that we belong to Jesus.
APPEAL₃	13:16 Be continually doing good for others and be continually sharing your things with people who lack.
APPEAL₄	13:17–19 Submit to your spiritual leaders, and pray for me.

INTENT AND MACROSTRUCTURE

The 13:1–19 unit is a hortatory one which consists of a series of *APPEALS*, in the form of 2nd person plural imperatives or 1st or 3rd person subjunctives, or else implied by ellipsis.

BOUNDARIES AND COHERENCE

The next paragraph at 13:20 is a prayer for God to bless his readers. Coherence is shown by the long list of brief exhortations, not by lexical content.

PROMINENCE AND THEME

The theme is drawn from each of the *APPEALS*, by taking what is the most naturally prominent part of each, and by abbreviating all of them.

PART CONSTITUENT 13:1–14 (Hortatory Paragraph: Appeal₁ of 13:1–19)

THEME: I appeal to you to love one another, be hospitable, help imprisoned and other mistreated believers, respect the marriage relationship; avoid covetousness; remember the manner of life of your former spiritual leaders and imitate their faith. Since Christ never changes, don't be diverted to believe strange teachings.

¶ PTRN	RELATIONAL STRUCTURE	CONTENTS
EXHORTATION₁		13:1 You should continue to love your fellow believers.
EXHORTATION₂ — EXHORTATION		13:2a You should continue to be hospitable [LIT] **to people, even** people whom you do not know,
┕ grounds		13:2b since by **being hospitable,** some people have provided food and shelter for people without knowing **that they were really** angels.
EXHORTATION₃ ┌ NUCLEUS₁ ─ NUCLEUS		13:3a You should be concerned about **and give help to** those who have been put in prison **because they are Christians,**
┕ MANNER		13:3b thinking about **what it would be like for you** if you were in prison with them.
┕ NUCLEUS₂ ─ NUCLEUS		13:3c You should help those who are being mistreated **for believing in Christ**
┕ manner		13:3d as you consider that you are still alive **and others might cause you to suffer as the mistreated ones are suffering**.
EXHORTATION₄ ┌ NUCLEUS₁		13:4a Each of you **must** respect the marriage relationship [EUP]. (OR, You **must** respect the marriage relationship in every way,)
┕ NUCLEUS₂ ─ EXHORTATION		13:4b and you must keep your sexual relations pure [EUP],
┕ grounds		13:4c since God will surely punish people who are sexually immoral and those who commit adultery.
EXHORTATION₅ ┌ EXHORTATION₁		13:5a Live without coveting money
┕ EXHORTATION₂		13:5b and be content with the things you possess.
	┌ orienter	13:5c You should do this because God said **in the Scriptures**:
	┌ grounds ── CONTENT	13:5d "I certainly will never leave you; I will never stop *taking care of* you" [DOU].
	┌ orienter	13:6a Therefore, **knowing that God will certainly supply whatever we need,** we can say **to ourselves** confidently **the same words that the Psalmist wrote,**
	┌ reason₁	13:6b "The Lord **God** is the one who helps me.
	┕ reason₂	13:6c Nothing [RHQ] can be taken from me by humans.
┕ evidential grounds ── CONCLUSION ── CONTENT ── RESULT		13:6d **So I am not afraid."**

```
| EXHORTATION₆ ──────────────────────── | 13:7–9 Remember how your spiritual leaders lived and imitate their faith. [See expansion on page 232] |
| EXHORTATION₇ ──────────────────────── | 13:10–14 We must stop **supposing that we will be saved by** practicing Jewish sacrifices and rituals, and we must keep trusting only in **Jesus**. [See expansion on page 234] |
```

INTENT AND PARAGRAPH PATTERN

The 13:1–14 unit consists of a set of seven *EXHORTATIONS*, all basically unrelated to each other; and all but the final exhortation are not related to the central theme of the book. Most of the exhortations are expressed by 3rd person plural imperatives; one is by a 1st person plural subjunctive and one by a 3rd person singular imperative. Several are clauses that have no expressed verb.

NOTES

13:1 continue to love your fellow believers The wording here replaces the imperative μενέτω 'let continue' and the abstract noun φιλαδελφία 'brotherly love' with a clause, as is done in most modern English versions. NEB has "Never cease to love your fellow-Christians."

13:2a You should continue to be hospitable [LIT] *to people, even* **people whom you do not know** The display replaces the litotes expressed in μὴ ἐπιλανθάνεσθε 'do not be forgetful' by a positive one, as is done by GNB, JB, NEB, NCV, and CEV. The word φιλοξενία 'hospitality' has the notion 'to strangers' involved and is so rendered by CEV, NIV, JB, RSV, LB, et al. In some languages it may be necessary to spell out 'be hospitable' by something like 'provide meals and a place to sleep'.

13:3a You should be concerned about *and give help to* A number of commentators suggest that μιμνῄσκεσθε 'be mindful' means not just "don't forget" (NLT,) but "by praying for them and by ministering as far as possible to them in their need" (Hughes, p. 564). Hence 'and give help to' is included in the display.

because they are Christians The reference is not to those who had been imprisoned because of committing some crime, but presumably "Christians who are suffering for their faith" (Guthrie; see also Lenski, p. 470).

13:3b thinking about *what it would be like for you* **if you were in prison with them** This tries to make more sense out of a literal rendering, 'as though you were…' It might also mean 'as you would like others to do for you if you were also in prison'.

13:3c mistreated *for believing in Christ* See previous note. Lane (p. 515) says the reference is "to that larger company of men and women who experienced abuse in any form because of their Christian faith."

13:3d as you consider that you are still alive and others might cause you to suffer as the mistreated ones are suffering A great many commentators suggest that the clause ὡς καὶ αὐτοὶ ὄντες ἐν σώματι 'as also yourselves being in body' refers not just to being in a physical body but as a result "the same fate can happen to you" (Hagner, p. 220).

13:4a Each of you Commentators are about equally divided as to whether the phrase ἐν πᾶσιν 'in all' means 'by all persons' or 'in all aspects'. There seems no good way of deciding which was meant. The display gives both alternatives.

***must* respect the marriage relationship** It does not seem possible to avoid an abstract noun in rendering the noun γάμος 'marriage'. But the adjective τίμιος "held in honor, respected" (BAGD, p. 818.1c) can be rendered as a verb. The subject 'each of you' refers to believers. Commentators are agreed that the implied verb is to be considered a command, rendered here as 'must'.

13:4b and you must keep your sexual relations pure The verbless clause καὶ ἡ κοίτη ἀμίαντος 'and the marriage-bed undefiled' is either a euphemism or a metonymy (the place standing for the event which occurs there) or both. Greenlee (p. 576) summarizes what the commentators say "It means that the marriage relationship must not be defiled by adultery or any other illicit sexual acts."

13:4c God will surely punish Several commentators note that the subject, 'God', is emphatic by virtue of being placed last in the clause, which is an aberration of the normal VSO order. This emphasis is indicated by 'surely' in the display (cf. LB).

13:5a Live without coveting money This is an unskewed way of expressing the verbless clause Ἀφιλάργυρος ὁ τρόπος 'without-love-silver the way-of-life'. Most English versions have something similar to NCV's "Keep your lives free from the love of money."

13:5b be content with the things you possess The participle ἀρκούμενοι 'being satisfied with' has the function of an imperative; see Miller, Bruce, Lane, and Ellingworth.

13:5c You should do this because The γάρ 'for' here introduces the grounds for 3:5a-b.

God said *in the Scriptures* The display includes a lot of information that the writer expected his audience to know: that what follows was an OT quote of which God was the speaker. Most modern English versions state God as the speaker and use orthographic devices to indicate it is an OT quote.

13:5d I certainly will never leave you; I will never stop *taking care of you* The word 'providing' is again supplied to make it more relevant to the context. Quite a few modern versions similarly translate v. 5e as 'I will never fail you', although the word ἀνίημι means "abandon, desert" (BAGD p. 69.2), not 'fail'. Since the meaning of the two statements in v. 13d-e is identical (they have the same entry in Louw and Nida 35:54), they should be considered a semantic doublet (although it is not mentioned by Moore). The words seem to be taken in a modified form from Deut. 31:6, 8.

I will never stop *taking care of* you These words are supplied as a contextual implicature to indicate how what follows relates to the subject of not coveting money.

13:6a *knowing that God will certainly supply whatever we need* These words supply the implied conclusion that the author expects his readers to draw from the Scripture he has just quoted.

the same words that the Psalmist wrote The words in italics are to signify the application of the referent 'me' in the quote to the author's audience. It also indicates that the author is citing another OT reference (here cited exactly from Psalm 118:6).

13:6b-c The Lord God is the one who... humans The order of elements in the two clauses of the Greek text here, with 'Lord' coming first and 'man' coming last, puts an emphatic contrast between these two elements. The cleft structure using 'is the one who' and putting 'humans' at the end of v.6c to preserve the Greek order as closely as possible attempts to bring out this contrast. NLT captures the contrast nicely by rendering the last word as "mere mortals."

13:6c Nothing [RHQ] can be taken from me by humans The display transforms the rhetorical question into a negative statement, as is done by LB and NCV. But the bare negative statement, such as is done in those two versions, is patently false, because persecution of believers is a constant reality. The SSA of Romans 8:1 expresses a similar thought by "since God is acting on our behalf, no one can prevail against us." An alternative is to combine v. 6c-d as is done by LB: "I am not afraid of anything that mere man can do to me." Hagner and Hughes suggest that the thought is more "people can do nothing to deprive me of my eternal spiritual riches," but in this context 'take nothing from me' is more in focus.

13:6d *So* I am not afraid There is asyndeton between the two clauses in the Greek text, but there is clearly a reason-result relationship between them. NCV reverses the order and implies a causal connection.

EXPANSION OF EXHORTATION₆ IN THE 13:1–14 DISPLAY

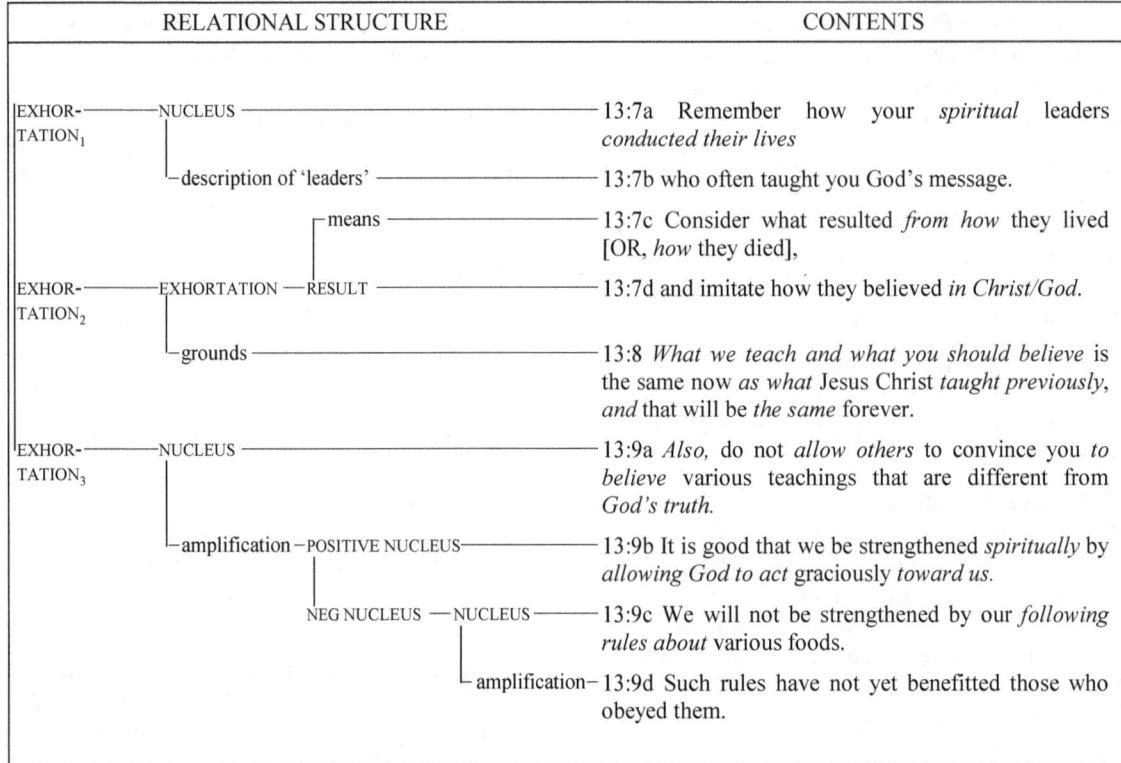

NOTES

13:7a Remember how your *spiritual* leaders *conducted their lives* The literal translation of the Greek is simply 'remember your leaders'. The word 'spiritual' makes clear, as Miller (p. 431) points out, that although the word ἡγούμενοι can be used for political and military leaders, it "is used three times in Hebrews 13 (7, 17, 24) for past and present church leaders." NLT also has "spiritual leaders;" The Message has "pastoral leaders." The phrase 'conducted their lives' is included to specify what they were to remember; Barnes says it was "their counsel; their instructions; their example."

13:7b who often taught you God's message The reference could include present spiritual leaders, (so Miller and Wilson), but the reference is almost certainly mainly confined to "those leaders whom death has taken away" (Kistemaker p. 414); all the other commentators consulted agree. If translators wish to make that specific, they could add the words 'before they died' at the end.

13:7c Consider Though Miller suggests the present participle indicates the grounds for the exhortation which follows, several commentators consider it an exhortation parallel with the one which follows, and the analysis here does likewise. Ellingworth says (p. 703), "Ἀναθεωροῦντες... μιμεῖσθε may be a stylistically more attractive equivalent for ἀναθεωρεῖτε... μιμεῖσθε compare the imperative participle ἀρκούμενοι in v. 5."

what resulted *from how they lived* [OR, *how* they died] Commentators are pretty well divided on the meaning of the words τὴν ἔκβασιν τῆς ἀναστροφῆς 'the outcome of (their) way of life'. Some suggest that 'outcome' refers to "how their lives ended" (NEB); for example, Westcott (p. 434) says "The reference here seems to be to some scene of martyrdom." But there is much stronger support for "what kind of lives they lived" (CEV). Perhaps it means both (e.g., "how they lived and died" TEV); cf. also TFT. The display gives two alternatives, but the first one, which follows an interpretation which is more literal and which seems more likely, is preferred.

13:7d imitate how they believed *in Christ/God* The display renders the abstract noun 'faith' as a clause and supplies two alternatives for the goal of the action for languages which require it.

13:8 *What we teach and what you should believe* A major question here is, to what does this verse relate? Some commentators suggest it is independent, not related to v. 7a or v. 7d. This is most unlikely. The wording of this sentence is much like a liturgical expression, but that does not help in deciding relationships. Some say it is related to both the preceding reference to the faith of their former leaders and then to the following exhortation, as its grounds. Such an interpretation is semantically also very unlikely. Some suggest that it relates to the preceding verse alone, giving either the grounds for imitating the faith of their former leaders or the content of their faith. This is possible, but there are no lexemes in v. 8 which point to this. But there is one phrase in v. 8, ὁ αὐτός 'the same', which is in a clear contrast with the words 'various and strange' in v. 9. For this reason the display includes the words 'what we teach'. Hewitt says that the connection with v. 7 is that the audience must not "allow any doctrines opposed to the doctrines which have been taught them to find a place in their thoughts." Hence the display includes the implied words 'and what you should believe'.

is the same now *as what* **Jesus Christ** *taught previously, and* **that will be** *the same* **forever** A literal translation of the GNT with the familiar words 'the same yesterday, today, and forever' has several problems. First, there is no verb; the verb 'to be' is supplied, and as suggested by most versions and commentators, inserted between 'Christ' and 'yesterday' The words 'yesterday' and 'today' are figurative; the former refers to "the past in general" and 'today' refers to "the present in general" (Greenlee, p. 584).

13:9a do not *allow others* **to convince you** *to believe* The passive of the verb παραφέρω means 'to be carried away' but it has a figurative sense here (BAGD p. 623.2b). NCV states the meaning of the verb nicely with "lead you into the wrong way." The wording in the display also removes the personification found in the Greek by making 'others' the agent of the 'carrying away' instead of 'strange teachings'.

various teachings that are different from God's truth The words ποικίλαις and ξέναις are quite different in meaning: the former means 'of various kinds' and the latter 'strange.' Specifically the latter implies "alien to and incompatible with the truth" (Hughes). The word does not mean 'peculiar' (JBP) but it does mean "previously unheard of" (Louw and Nida 28.34).

13:9b It is good It is difficult to determine whether the γάρ here is introducing an amplification of what precedes it or a grounds for the preceding exhortation. This analysis has chosen amplification because semantically it does not cohere if taken as grounds.

we be strengthened *spiritually* The phrase τὴν καρδίαν 'the heart' is a common NT term standing for the whole person; hence 'we'. The verb βεβαιόω 'strengthen' as is usual in the NT has a secondary sense here.

by *allowing God to act* **graciously** *toward us* The display avoids translating the noun χάρις literally by the word 'grace' as most English translations do. CEV has "from God's undeserved kindness." Since a MEANS proposition introduced with 'by' requires that the agent of the event to follow be the same as the subject of the RESULT clause to which it relates, the words 'by our allowing' are supplied. This makes good sense: our spiritual strengthening entails our doing something to achieve it.

13:9c by our *following rules about* **various foods** The italicized words are implied cf. "by obeying rules about foods" TEV, NCV. The writer in this paragraph continues his main theme about not going back to the former Jewish rules and regulations. Some writers say the reference here is to various sacrificial meals, and some say it is to rules about which foods were permissible to eat and which were not.

EXPANSION OF EXHORTATION₇ IN THE 13:1-14 DISPLAY

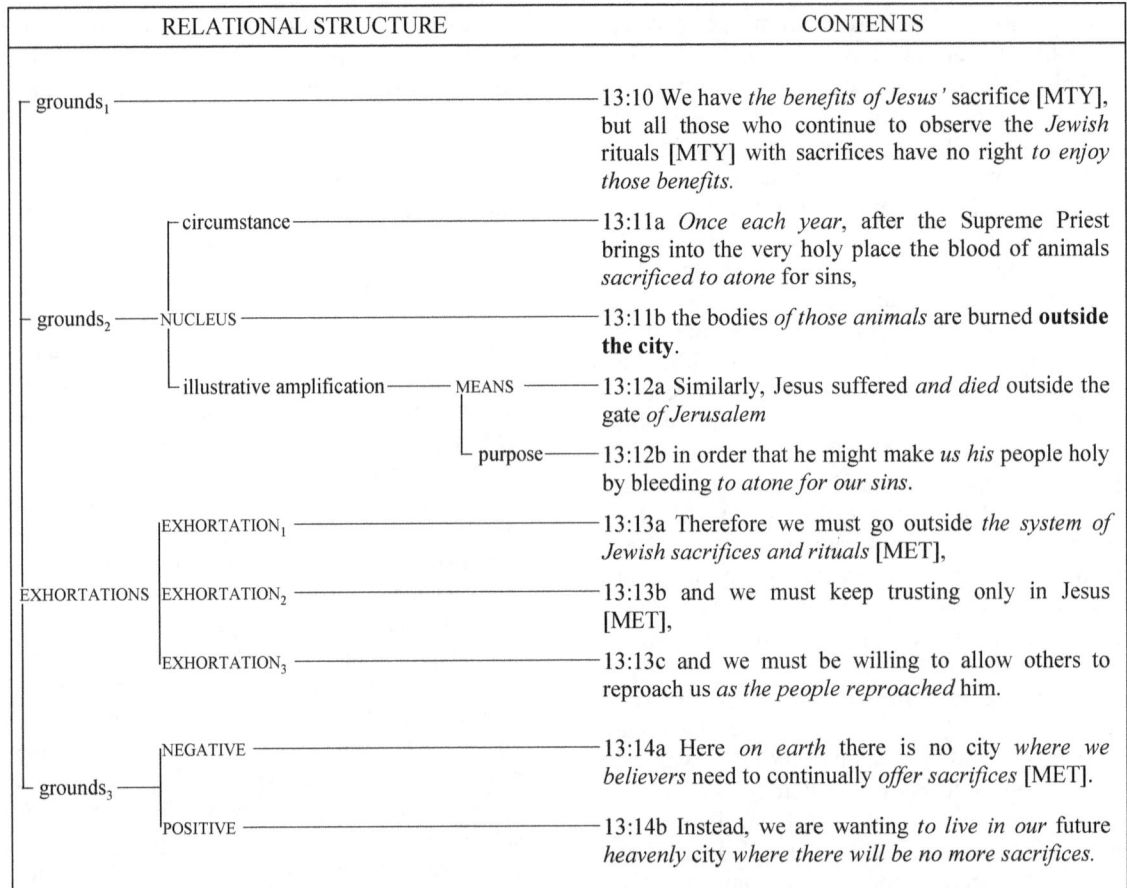

NOTES

13:10 We have *the benefits of Jesus' sacrifice* The GNT has ἔχομεν θυσιαστήριον ἐξ οὗ φαγεῖν οὐκ ἔχουσιν ἐξουσίαν 'we have an altar from which they have no authority to eat'. This is very figurative. Several commentators suggest 'altar' means the cross on which Christ died, but this would still be figurative. The word 'altar' is a metonymy, the place standing for the event, Christ's sacrifice, which took place there. What we have, then, is Christ, who was sacrificed for us. Then 'eating from the altar' is figurative, its non-figurative meaning being "to partake of the benefits of the sacrifice of Christ" (Hagner, p. 228). Eating is metaphorical for 'taking and enjoying something as one enjoys eating food'.

all those who continue to observe the Jewish rituals [MTY] with sacrifices have no right *to enjoy those benefits* The GNT has οἱ τῇ σκηνῇ λατρεύοντες 'the ones serving in the tabernacle'. The word σκηνή is a somewhat anachronistic metonymy, referring to the tent of worship set up by Moses in the wilderness but which was replaced by the temple under Solomon's rule. This reference of 'Jewish rituals', harks back to v. 9 where these rituals are declared to be non-beneficial. Almost all commentators agree the phrase refers to the Jewish priests and/or Jewish worshipers. The display makes no attempt to specify which.

13:11a It is very difficult to see how vv. 11–12 relate to what precedes or follows. Commentators are very divided. But these two verses do not seem to relate to v. 10 at all. The best solution seems to take the γάρ here as introducing an additional grounds for what follows in v. 13.

animals *sacrificed* The word in italics is implied from the culture; LB has "slain animals."

***to atone* for sins** The GNT has only περὶ ἁμαρτίας; the words 'to atone' provide the event implied by the preposition. BAGD (p. 644.1g) suggests this is the meaning of περί here. TEV, RSV, and NLT have "as a sacrifice for," JB has "for the atonement of."

the very holy place The display follows the wording of NIV and TEV; it refers to the inner room or 'Holy of Holies' in the tent.

13:11b are burned <u>outside the city</u> (Leviticus 16:27) The Greek word παρεμβολῆς 'camp' "refers to the time when Israel was encamped in the wilderness: the enclosure of the camp was afterwards replaced by the walls of Jerusalem" (Alford). The verb κατακαίεται 'burned' is in the present tense, though the tent and the camp had long ceased to operate. That is why the present tense is used in the display (as in NLT). The writer uses the present tense probably because the whole sacrificial system was still in operation at the time he wrote, but he wanted to use the word παρεμβολή 'camp' because he wants to make a play on the word in v. 13. The word 'camp' "represents the Jewish community/Judaism, which surrounded the tabernacle in Israel's encampments and centered around the temple in Jerusalem in Israel's later national and religious life" (Miller, p. 437). The words ἔξω τῆς παρεμβολῆς 'outside the camp' (repeated in v. 13) are emphatic by their final position in their clauses. The author introduces a new topic 'outside' which he develops in the next two verses. This emphasis is indicated by bold type in the display.

13:12a suffered *and died* The word ἔπαθεν 'suffered' is probably a form of metonymy, the one action standing for the other which was associated with it. TEV simply has "died;" NLT and JBP have "suffered and died."

outside the gate *of Jerusalem* The display makes specific what gate was being referred to by the word πύλη: TEV and CEV have "city gate" and NLT and JBP "city gates," while NCV and LB simply have "city." Lane (p. 542) is probably correct in suggesting that the phrase connotes the shame of crucifixion (criminals had to be executed 'outside the camp', Num. 15:35) and that "Jesus died as one rejected by his people."

13:12b make *us his* people holy The GNT has ἁγιάσῃ...τὸν λαόν 'sanctify the people'. But what people is this referring to? Surely it is believers, of whom the writer was one, and therefore the display has 'us, his people'.

by bleeding *to atone for our sins* The display conveys the implied event signaled by the preposition διά. JBP also has "by the shedding of his own blood." The final purpose clause (see the third note under v. 11a) will probably not be needed in most translations; an alternative would be 'as a sacrifice'.

13:13a The Greek has the text for v. 13b preceding that for v. 13a, but the order is reversed here because v. 13b-c both refer to Jesus.

we must go outside the system of Jewish sacrifices and rituals The text does not have these words, but the word ἔξω 'outside' implies leaving something, and the whole context implies it, too. Ellingworth, Guthrie (p. 274–275), Montefiore and Lane all support this view. The phrase is thus considered a metaphor; but since the literal meaning of the same phrase is in v. 11, it is not repeated here. Attridge says (p. 399) the word 'camp' "is frequently seen to be Judaism and the summons to go out must be understood as a call to leave behind the tempting security of the ancestral religion."

13:13b we must keep trusting only in Jesus The pronominal referent of πρὸς αὐτόν 'to him' is specified as in NCV and CEV. The word 'trusting' expresses the implied purpose of 'going to Jesus'; an even more general statement of purpose, if one were needed, would be 'to have all our spiritual needs met'.

13:13c we must be willing to allow others to reproach us The present participle φέροντες 'bearing' is considered to signal attendant circumstance (so Miller, p. 438). The alternative is to consider it as expressing condition, in which case the translation would be 'even if'. The words 'willing to' are an implicature of the argument; Guthrie (p. 274) says it means we "must be prepared to" and Lane (p. 544) suggests "Readiness to bear Jesus' shame."

***as the people reproached* him** Greenlee (p. 594) summarizes the views of several commentators on the genitive phrase τὸν ὀνειδισμὸν αὐτοῦ 'his reproach' by saying it means "to suffer the same kind of abuse that Christ suffered," or as Greenlee (summarizing Ellingworth) puts it, "to bear humiliation in the way that Jesus bore it."

13:14a Here *on earth* The words 'on earth' make clear what the author means by ὧδε 'here'. TEV, NCV and JBP do likewise.

no city *where we believers* need to continually *offer sacrifices* Although commentators are agreed that the author is not referring to the destruction of Jerusalem, it is clear that he is referring to Jerusalem. Some translators may feel that 'such as Jerusalem' ought to be supplied. Hagner (p. 230) says the implication here is that "the importance of the literal Jerusalem, symbolic of the temple and the levitical sacrifices, must give way to that of the heavenly Jerusalem."

The word 'city' is taken in a sense as a metonymy, the place standing for the events associated with it, namely the whole Judaic sacrificial system. Wilson says (p. 194) the force of the appeal is, "They must abandon the rites and ceremonies of Judaism." The writer is not referring in this context to the question of a lasting city but the lasting set of sacrifices to earn God's favor that was located there.

we believers The display specifies who 'we' refers to cf. Ellingworth, Lünemann.

13:14b *our* **future** *heavenly* **city** As commentators all suggest, the reference is to the heavenly city, the new Jerusalem (Rev. 21:3). NLT has "our city in heaven, which is yet to come."

where there will be no more sacrifices The commentators all suggest the writer here is simply talking about our future heavenly home. But the whole context is talking about the Jewish sacrificial system, not about looking forward to heaven. The writer is saying that the need for all the Jewish rituals and sacrifices ended with Jesus' sacrifice, and it will remain that way in heaven. The following verse continues the topic of sacrifices.

BOUNDARIES AND COHERENCE

The introductory conjunction οὖν at v. 15 is given only a C 'considerable doubt' notation in the GNT, but semantically it is implied; this verse begins a conclusion to what precedes it. Coherence within this paragraph is provided by two occurrences of the phrase ἔξω τῆς παρεμβολῆς 'outside the camp' and one additional occurrence of the same preposition ἔξω 'outside'.

PROMINENCE AND THEME

The theme is drawn from all four of the APPEALS, but each is somewhat abbreviated. 'Help one another' summarizes the two individual exhortations that follow. From v. 15 only the more prominent generic proposition is included.

PART CONSTITUENT 13:15 (Hortatory Paragraph: Appeal₂ of 13:1–19)

THEME: We should continually praise God. Specifically, we should say openly that we belong to Jesus.

¶PTRN	RELATIONAL STRUCTURE	CONTENTS
APPEAL	┌ circumstance ───────	13:15a As we ask Jesus *to help us,*
	├ NUCLEUS ───────────	13:15b we should continually praise God,
	├ description of 'praise' ───	13:15c which will be something we can sacrifice to him [MET] *instead of our sacrificing animals only at specific times.*
	└ specific ───────────	13:15d *Specifically,* we should say openly *that we belong to* Jesus [MTY].

INTENT AND PARAGRAPH PATTERN

This brief paragraph consists of one APPEAL, expressed as a 1st person plural subjunctive, urging his readers to continually praise God.

NOTES

13:15a As we ask Jesus *to help us* Commentators are little help in explaining the phrase δι' αὐτοῦ 'through him', but NLT has "with Jesus' help." Miller (p. 441) says it expresses means, and this is fine, except that a means requires a whole proposition with the agent the same as the main clause to follow. The display attempts to do this as generically as possible. Other possibilities might be 'by calling on Jesus' or even "because of what Jesus did" (Ellingworth and Nida, p. 331). By forefronting this phrase, the author places emphasis on it. As many commentators suggest, the writer is saying that Christ's sacrifice alone is sufficient to enable us to enter God's presence; efforts of other Jewish priests are of no avail now.

13:15c which will be something we can sacrifice to him [MET] *instead of our sacrificing animals only at specific times* The author continues the theme of sacrifice. He states that, under the new agreement, we do not make thank offerings (Lev. 7:12–18) of animals and bread from time to time, but we can offer something to God, and we can do it continually. A few commentators suggest the implied contrast here is between what we can do continually and the sacrifice of Christ, which was made only once. But in this context the writer is contrasting the new order with the old sacrificial system. Ellingworth and Nida (p. 331) say the phrase διὰ παντός 'always' "may suggest some contrast with the Old Testament sacrifices which were offered at set times;" see also Hughes, Brown, Alford, Moffatt.

13:15d we should say openly The GNT phrase καρπὸν χειλέων 'fruit of lips' is a Hebraistic metonymy, the body part standing for what it produces, speech. The verb ὁμολογέω carries the sense of making a public declaration.

that we belong to **Jesus** The word 'name' is a metonymy, standing for a person's nature or for the person himself. To confess the name of Christ thus means to "confess him as our Lord" (Ellingworth and Nida, p. 331); (also TEV, 1976 edition). An alternative would be 'that we have trusted in Christ'.

BOUNDARIES AND COHERENCE

A new brief paragraph at v. 16 is signaled by an imperative which is presenting a new topic. Prominence in this proposition is indicated by it being a litotes 'do not be forgetful'.

PROMINENCE AND THEME

The theme statement is taken from the prominent nucleus of the APPEAL.

PART CONSTITUENT 13:16 (Hortatory Paragraph: Appeal₃ of 13:1–19)

THEME: *Be continually doing good for others and be continually sharing your things with people who lack.*		
¶ PTRN	RELATIONAL STRUCTURE	CONTENTS
APPEAL	NUCLEUS₁	13:16a You should be continually [LIT] doing good *for others*
	NUCLEUS₂	13:16b and be continually sharing *your things with people who lack them,*
basis		13:16c since your doing actions like that will please God very much, *as though you were offering* sacrifices.

INTENT AND PARAGRAPH PATTERN

This paragraph also consists of one APPEAL, expressed by a 1st person plural subjunctive, and the *basis* for the APPEAL.

NOTES

13:16a You should be continually [LIT] doing good *for others* The phrase μὴ ἐπιλανθάνεσθε 'do not let it escape your notice' is a litotes, a forceful way of stating the positive. It is rendered by a positive statement in TEV, NCV, and JB.

13:16b sharing *your things with people who lack* The word κοινωνία here is very complex semantically and hard to translate in many languages. BAGD (p. 439.2) gives the meaning here as 'generosity' which would mean 'share generously'; but Louw and Nida's definition (57.98, though not listing this passage as a reference) is much better: "to share one's possessions." But the added implied case role components, "with those in need" (Wilson, p. 196), are what make it difficult to translate. The display suggests 'people who lack them' but it also implies 'and who cannot get along without them' or 'who will not survive if they don't have them'.

13:16c your doing actions like that...*offering* sacrifices The GNT has τοιαύταις θυσίαις 'with such sacrifices'. Since the author has mentioned praise as a sacrifice in the previous verse, 'also' is implied; CEV has "too." But since such good works are not literally sacrifices; the term is considered a metaphor and it is made a simile in the display.

BOUNDARIES AND COHERENCE

A new paragraph at v. 17 is signaled by another imperative verb expressing a new topic.

PROMINENCE AND THEME

The theme of this paragraph is drawn from the two nuclei of the APPEAL; the *basis* of the APPEAL is less thematic.

PART CONSTITUENT 13:17–19 (Hortatory Paragraph: Appeal₄ of 13:1–19)

THEME: *Submit to your spiritual leaders, and pray for me.*

¶ PTRN RELATIONAL STRUCTURE CONTENTS

- GENERAL APPEAL
  - EXHORTATION — 13:17a Obey your *spiritual* leaders and be submissive to them,
  - grounds
    - NUCLEUS — 13:17b since they are the ones who are guarding your spiritual life/welfare.
    - amplification — 13:17c *They know that God* will decide whether their actions were good or not [IDI].
  - purpose
    - RESULT
      - POSITIVE — 13:17d *You should obey them well* in order that they may do their work *of guarding you* joyfully
      - negative — 13:17e instead *of their doing it* sadly *because you are not obeying them,*
    - reason — 13:17f because *if you cause them to do it* sadly, *God will punish you.*

- PERSONAL APPEAL
  - APPEAL
    - EXHORTATION — 13:18a Pray *to God* concerning me
    - grounds
      - GENERIC — 13:18b since I am certain that I have not done anything *toward you* that displeases God.
      - specific — 13:18c I have desired to act honorably *toward you* in all ways.
  - AMPLIFIED APPEAL
    - orienter — 13:19a I implore you earnestly
    - MEANS — 13:19b that you do that [18a]
    - purpose — 13:19c in order that God will quickly remove the things that hinder my coming to you.

INTENT AND PARAGRAPH PATTERN

The 13:17–19 unit consists of two APPEALS each expressed by a second person plural imperative. The first one is a general appeal to his readers; the second is a personal appeal for prayer for himself.

NOTES

13:17a *spiritual* leaders See the note on v. 7a cf. NLT.

13:17b spiritual life The problem with the clause ἀγρυπνοῦσιν ὑπὲρ τῶν ψυχῶν ὑμῶν 'they keep watch over your souls' is how to translate 'souls'. Some versions simply say "you" (CEV, NCV, NIV, and NEB) but this does not make clear the nature of the guarding. Bruce (p. 407) suggests "spiritual well-being," Kistemaker (p. 426) says "spiritual welfare."

13:17c *God* will decide whether their actions were good or not The words λόγον ἀποδώσοντες mean 'giving an account' but this is an idiom. It has been expressed as "they must answer to God" (CEV), "they are accountable to God" (NLT), but these are also somewhat idiomatic. It might be expressed more fully as 'explain to God why they have done what they have done'. The implied time is at the return of Christ or the Judgment Day.

13:17d their work *of guarding you* joyfully The word τοῦτο 'this' refers to the work of spiritual oversight.

13:17e *because you are not obeying them* These words supply the contextual reason for the 'sadly'.

13:17f *if you cause them to do it* sadly The τοῦτο here refers to the preceding word στενάζοντες 'groaning'; Hughes says it refers to a "sad report of disharmony and spiritual decline;" NCV has "to make their work hard."

***God* will punish you** The word ἀλυσιτελές 'profitless' is a negative understatement that means "you will suffer for it" (LB); Lünemann says very clearly it means "causing punishment from God."

13:18a Pray *to God* concerning me The ἡμῶν 'us' is taken as an epistolary or editorial 'we' by the majority of commentators. As noted by Ellingworth and Nida (p. 333), the best evidence for this is probably the mention of 'conscience' later in the verse, "which almost by definition is something inward and therefore individual." Among versions examined, only Williams has 'me', which is not surprising, because versions almost never adjust the 'editorial we'.

13:18b I am certain that I have not done anything *toward you* that displeases God The words καλὴν συνείδησιν 'good conscience' sound simple enough, but what do they mean semantically? Ellingworth and Nida (p. 333) suggest "our heart has no guilt," but this is very figurative. However, to feel guilt is to be aware of doing wrong. In the light of the author's prayer request in v. 19 about visiting them, the words 'to you' seem implied. Lane says (p. 557) the words 'we have a clear conscience' signify "in the specific matter of our conduct toward you."

13:19c in order that *God* will quickly remove the things that hinder my coming to you The verb in the clause ἵνα τάχιον ἀποκατασταθῶ ὑμῖν 'that I may be restored to you quickly' is passive and somewhat figurative; NCV has God "will send me back to you soon." But the verb implies some sort of hindrance that the author is asking God to remove; Hewitt says, "there appears to have been some obstacle in the way."

BOUNDARIES AND COHERENCE

The new paragraph in v. 20 is indicated by a switch from a 2nd person plural imperative to a 3rd person singular optative, and a change from a prayer request to a benediction. Coherence consists of a reference to 'those leading them' and several subsequent pronominal references to the same group, and several pronominal references to the writer.

PROMINENCE AND THEME

The theme is taken from the two most naturally prominent exhortation propositions of the two *APPEALS*.

EPISTLE CONSTITUENT 13:20–25 (Paragraph: Conclusion of the Epistle)

THEME: *May God equip you with everything good you need. Timothy will be able to come with me to see you. Greet the believers; those from Italy send their greetings. May God act graciously to you all.*

MACROSTRUCTURE	CONTENTS
generic prayer	13:20–21 I desire that God will equip you with everything good you need to do what he desires, and that you will exalt him/Christ forever. [See expansion on page 240]
APPEAL	13:22 I appeal to you that you pay careful attention to this teaching that I have written. [See expansion on page 242]
personal plans	13:23 Timothy has been released from prison, so he will come with me to see you. [See expansion on page 243]
GREETINGS	13:24 Greet your spiritual leaders and other fellow-believers for me. Those here from Italy send their greetings to you. [See expansion on page 243]
BENEDICTION	13:25 May *God* continually act kindly toward you all.

INTENT AND MACROSTRUCTURE

The conclusion of this epistle has five distinct parts: a *generic prayer* that God will bless the readers, a SUMMARY APPEAL, a *personal word* about his helper Timothy, a set of GREETINGS from the writer and those who are with him, and a final brief BENEDICTION.

NOTES

13:25 May *God* continually act kindly toward you all See notes on 13:20 and 4:16c-d. CEV has "I pray that God will be kind…."

EXPANSION OF GENERIC PRAYER 13:20–21 IN THE 13:20–25 DISPLAY

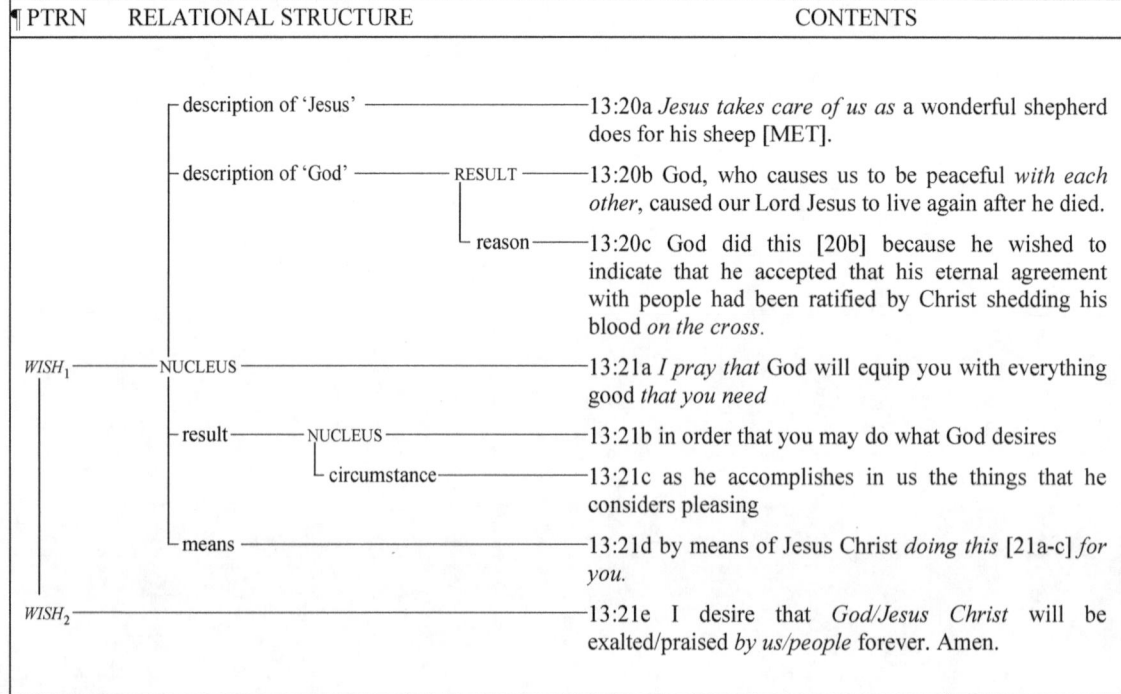

NOTES

13:20–21 The one independent verb καταρτίσαι 'equip' in these two verses occurs at the start of v. 21; v. 20 consists basically of descriptions of God and of Jesus using a chiastic structure. In many languages it is very difficult and confusing to translate such a passage of descriptive clauses before the main verb occurs. For this reason, the rendering of 'equip' is left until v. 21. CEV does the same thing; NCV does a fair amount of reordering and combines the two verse numbers.

13:20a *takes care of us as* **a wonderful shepherd does for his sheep** The phrase τὸν ποιμένα τῶν προβάτων τὸν μέγαν 'the great shepherd of the sheep' (Ezekiel 34:23) is clearly metaphorical. The question is, what are the points of similarity in the figure? The display suggests a generic one; more specifically one could say, '*provides for us, protects us, and guides us*'.

13:20b causes us to be peaceful *with each other* The display spells out the meaning of the genitive phrase Ὁ Θεὸς τῆς εἰρήνης 'the God of peace'. There is no doubt that the phrase "encodes an implicit event with God as the agent in the sense: 'God who causes you to be peaceful' " (Miller, p. 448), but does it refer to an inward peace, an external peace with respect to relations with God and others, or both inward and external peace? Commentators are divided all three ways. But in view of the fact that throughout the epistle there are references to the "dissentions and dangers of apostasy among the readers of the Epistle" (Montefiore; see also Hughes, Guthrie (p. 278) it seems best to take it as referring to harmony between believers. One could translate as 'act peacefully toward each other'. If translators prefer to retain the ambiguity, they would not translate 'with each other'.

13:20c God did this [20b] because he wished to indicate that he accepted that his eternal agreement with people had been ratified by Christ shedding his blood *on the cross* There are a number of problems with the phrase ἐν αἵματι διαθήκης αἰωνίου 'by the blood of an eternal agreement'. First of all, 'blood' stands for the blood shed by Christ in his sacrificial death on the cross; NCV has "blood of his death." Then there is an implied event in the genitive phrase 'blood of an agreement': the blood seals or ratifies the agreement cf. NJB "the blood that seals an eternal covenant". Then there is the question of whether the phrase; 'by the blood of the eternal agreement' relates to 'the great shepherd of the sheep' or to 'raised from the dead'. The latter is much more likely because of collocational improbability: one does not become a shepherd by dying for his sheep. On the other hand, the death and resurrection of Christ are constantly linked in the New Testament.

Finally, what is the meaning of the preposition ἐν? "It is generally agreed that the ἐν is used in a *causal* sense here" (Miller, p. 449). Miller quotes Dods who says "This covenant was sealed when 'our Lord Jesus'...was brought up again from the dead 'in virtue of the perfect and accepted sacrifice'." Miller adds on her own, "When God raised Jesus from the dead, He was signifying the acceptance of the Covenant blood." Note also Deibler's rendering of Romans 4:25: "...was raised up from being dead because God wanted to show he had accepted the death of Jesus as the grounds by which he would declare us righteous."

13:21a *I pray that* The aorist optative of καταρτίζω is usually translated in English by a verb phrase beginning with 'May...' but many languages do not have a third person optative or imperative. Since it is expressing a prayer, the rendering here does likewise (as is done in CEV, NCV, and JB).

everything good *that you need* The Majority Text has ἐν παντὶ ἔργῳ ἀγαθῷ 'in every good work' but the textual support for the inclusion of 'work' is so poor that the reading without it is given an A 'certain' rating in the Fourth Edition GNT. The text then reads 'with everything good' but something like 'that is necessary' or 'that you need' (as in TEV, NCV, and NLT) is clearly implied as an implicature of the argument.

13:21c as he accomplishes in us The present participle ποιῶν 'doing' has been interpreted as conveying various relationships. Miller suggests result, but since the 'result' is an anticipated or hoped-for one, she means purpose. This fits the context well but it is very doubtful this is a function of a present participle. Most suggest it conveys an additional wish, and this is how it is rendered in most English translations. This is a legitimate function of a present participle, and fits the context well, but the clauses are so closely related semantically that a closer relationship seems more likely. Bruce suggests a temporal relationship, and that is how it is rendered here. The writer wants God to work through us, and at the same time he wants God to accomplish things in us.

Some manuscripts read 'in you' instead of 'in us', but the evidence for 'us' is so strong that it is given an A 'certain' rating in the fourth edition of the GNT. In view of the 'you' in the first part of the verse it is easy to see how scribes would have changed it.

13:21d by means of Jesus Christ *doing this* [21a-c] *for you* The preposition in the phrase διὰ Ἰησοῦ Ξριστοῦ 'through Jesus Christ' is expressing means (which is related to the result in v. 21b; so Miller) which then requires a full proposition. Ellingworth and Nida (p. 337) suggest as a translation "he will do this by causing Jesus Christ to accomplish it."

13:21e I desire that *God/Jesus Christ* will be exalted/praised *by us/people* There is no overt verb in the phrase ᾧ ἡ δόξα 'to whom the glory'. It is easy enough to suggest, as commentators do, that an imperative or optative form of the verb 'be' needs to be supplied, but who is the implied agent of giving the praise? The display suggests a couple options. Then there is the question, who is the implied object of the praise? Many commentaries suggest Christ on the basis that Jesus Christ is the nearest referent. A larger number suggest God on the grounds that God is the main subject of the sentence. Other reasons supporting each can be listed (see Miller) but with the immediately preceding referent being Jesus Christ, one would think that if the author meant the referent to be God, he would have made that specific. The punctuation of the GNT also supports Christ as the referent.

forever There is a difficult textual problem of whether the reading should be εἰς τοὺς αἰῶμας 'unto the ages' or whether the added words τῶν αἰώνων 'of the ages' should follow. The fourth edition of the GNT prefers the longer reading with a C "difficult to decide" rating; but there is very little difference in meaning between 'forever' and 'forever and ever'.

EXPANSION OF *APPEAL* 3:22 IN THE 13:20–25 DISPLAY

RELATIONAL STRUCTURE	CONTENTS
orienter	13:22a My fellow believers, I appeal to you
CONTENT — RESULT	13:22b that you patiently consider *what* I have just written to you in order to exhort/encourage you
reason	13:22c since this is a short letter that I have written to you.

NOTES

13:22a My fellow believers See the note on 3:1a.

13:22b patiently consider The verb ἀνέχομαι usually means 'to endure, bear with'. Here it can be taken to mean to "listen to willingly" (BAGD p. 66.2); but since it is being put in written form, 'listen' is appropriate to express the meaning only if one assumes the letter will be read to the recipients. CEV has "pay close attention to," but the words seem to imply either that the writer feared that the recipients might not welcome its contents (so Wilson) or that they might object to its length (Moffatt, Bruce).

what I have just written to you Commentators agree that the words τοῦ λόγου 'the word' mean 'this letter I have just written you'. NCV has "this message;" LB has "in this letter."

in order to exhort/encourage you The noun παράκλησις can mean either 'exhortation or encouragement', but since the whole book is a hortatory work, the former is much more likely the intended meaning here.

13:22c a short letter This represents the phrase διὰ βραχέων 'through a few', meaning 'through a few words' but the sense is "only a short letter" (CEV).

EXPANSION OF *PERSONAL PLANS* 13:23 IN THE 13:20–25 DISPLAY

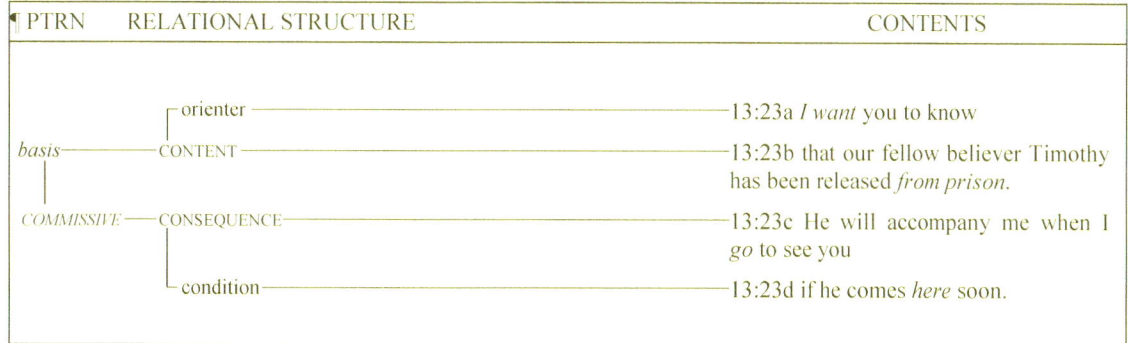

NOTES

13:23a *I want* you to know The GNT has an imperative Γινώσκετε 'know' but this cannot be an imperative in English (OR probably in many other languages); most English versions render it as is done here.

13:23b released *from prison* The display completes the case frame and supplies 'from prison' which nearly all commentators agree is a situational implicature cf. "let out of prison" NCV, TEV; "out of jail" NLT, CEV.

13:23c He will accompany me when I *go* to see you This is a clearer way of stating μεθ᾽ οὗ...ὄψομαι ὑμᾶς 'with whom I shall see you' cf. "he will be with me" (REB, JB).

EXPANSION OF *GREETINGS* 13:24–25 IN THE 13:20–25 DISPLAY

RELATIONAL STRUCTURE	CONTENTS
WISH₁	13:24a Tell all your *spiritual* leaders and all the *other* fellow-believers *in your various cities* that I hope things will go well for them.
WISH₂	13:24b Those *believers in this area* who have come from Italy want you to know they hope things will go well for you.
WISH₃	13:25 May *God* continually act kindly toward you all [WISH].

NOTES

13:24a Tell...that I hope things will go well for them The verb ἀσπάζομαι 'greet' is often very difficult to translate. In the first place, in many languages greeting people is an action which is performed but there is no lexeme for it. Here there is no action, only words. It is complicated here by the fact that The writer is 'sending' his greetings cf. CEV "Give my greetings to", whereas 'greet' usually means to perform a certain action when you see people you know but have not seen for some time. Ellingworth and Nida (p. 333) suggest that in some cases it could be rendered "greet all your leaders as though we were greeting them," but this does not solve the problem of how to render 'greet'. This epistle was written to Jews. When Jews greeted one another, they used the word 'shalom', which is usually translated 'peace' but really means 'may things go well for you'. The display tries to convey this meaning.

all your *spiritual* leaders and all the *other* fellow-believers For 'leaders' see note on 13:7a. The word 'other' is implied; the leaders were believers too. NLT has "other," CEV has "the rest of."

13:24b Those *believers in this area* who have come from Italy The phrase οἱ ἀπὸ τῆς Ἰταλίας 'those from Italy' refers to believers cf. "the Christians" NLT, JBP; "God's people" (NEB). The phrase "can mean either 'residents in Italy', in which case the author is also in Italy and is writing to a Church outside Italy; or it can mean 'those who belong to Italy but who are for the time being resident outside Italy'. If this latter interpretation is correct then the author is outside Italy and writing to Christians in Italy" (Hewitt). The great majority of commentators favor this latter interpretation, which is the most natural way to understand the preposition.

BOUNDARIES AND COHERENCE

The beginning of this unit is signaled by a switch from a personal request concerning himself to a generic prayer. The end of the unit is the end of the letter. Because of the wider range of topics in this unit, there is very little in the way of features of coherence, other than closing remarks appropriate to a letter.

PROMINENCE AND THEME

The theme for this unit is drawn from the most naturally prominent propositions in each of the subdivisions of the unit.

APPENDIX

The following material suggesting involvement by Luke in the Epistle to the Hebrews was written by Tom Henstock. Tom has an MBA from Northeastern University in Boston and an Ed. D. from SUNY in Buffalo. He has been teaching in Sunday Schools for fifty years. He wrote two teachers' guides for the Assemblies of God quarterlies, and has been preparing his own teaching materials since 1970. Although not a Bible translator, he is competent in Greek and has made other contributions to this SSA. Tom Henstock presents here a view of Hebrews different from that presented in this SSA. This has been included to allow you the reader to see a point of view that results from researching the Biblical literature.

Overview

Contemporary commentaries on the "Epistle to the Hebrews" offer thorough analyses of probable identification and location of respondents, author, and date and place of writing. Internal evidence points to Hebrew Christians as the recipients. Where they lived ranges from Rome to Jerusalem. The place of writing is unknown. The date of writing ranges from 48 A.D. to 96 A.D.

Most effort is given to identifying the author. Sources include Origen and the views of the Eastern and Western churches. Calvin and Luther suggest someone other than Paul, differing from Origen and the Church. Current commentators seem certain that "Paul did not write Hebrews." Into this vacuum of a hung jury over a dozen author nominees emerge.

Textual analysis and form criticism point away from Paul. Otherwise, the anonymous author, date of writing, the recipients, and place of its writing suggest that this introduction should abbreviate the commentaries' analyses. A review of their circumstantial evidence and speculation in support of the author do not require a level of thoroughness herein for it will leave the reader wondering.

Outline of the Epistle's Content

Hebrews' commentaries all give an overview of content. All compare and contrast Christ with things Hebrew. The following outline notes warnings, then encouragement. Warnings address loss of faith, failing to meet, pray, work, endure and listen to God. Others stress neglecting salvation and rejecting the gospel. Encouragement is to endure and trust Christ. The tendency to "go back" to Judaism is strongly checked in Hebrews: remain in Christ and the new covenant. The Hebrews content brings to completion the words of the risen Christ to two disciples.

> NAU **Luke 24:25–27** And He said to them, "O foolish men and slow of heart to believe in all that the prophets have spoken! [26] "Was it not necessary for the Christ to suffer these things and to enter into His glory?" [27] Then beginning with Moses and with all the prophets, He explained to them the things concerning Himself in all the Scriptures.

THE UNMATCHED EXCELLENCE OF CHRIST

Christ excels the prophets: (1:1–3).
Christ the man is superior to the angels: (1:4—2:18)
    Warning: the danger of neglecting the great salvation: 2:1–4.
    Encouragement: receive aid from Christ when tempted: 2:18.
Christ excels Moses: (3:1—4:13).
    Warning: the danger of following the Hebrews example in the wilderness: 3:6—4:2.
    Encouragement: keep confidence secure and do not harden your hearts: 3:6—4:8.
Christ the heavenly high priest excels the Aaronic priesthood: (4:14—10:18).
    Warning: the dangers of remaining immature and committing apostasy: 5:11—6:8.
    Encouragement: continue to diligently minister: 6:9–20.
    Contrast: The priesthood of Melchizedek excels the imperfect Levitical priesthood: 7:1–28.
    Warning: The old covenant is superseded by the realities of the new covenant: 8:1—9:10.
    Encouragement: Redemption through Christ's sacrifice is complete and eternal: 9:11—10:18.
Christ excels as the new and living way to God in heaven: (10:19—12:29).
    Encouragement: enter boldly to the throne of grace for help: 10:19–25.
    Warning: the terror of rejecting the once-received gospel: 10:26–31.

Encouragement: endure and triumph through faith: 10:32—11:39.
Encouragement: consider the supreme endurance of Christ: 12:1–4.
Encouragement: work hard, pray much, walk upright, and be holy: 12:12–14.
Warning: the danger of imitating the disregard of Esau: 12:15–17.
Encouragement: we will receive the kingdom—show gratitude to God: 12:28.
Warning: the danger of not listening to God: 12:25–29.
Final encouragement, requests, and greetings: (13:1–25).

Hebrew Christian Recipients and Their Location

The environment of the New Testament gospels is Jewish with roots in the Hebrew Scriptures. Jesus was a Jew—of the tribe of Judah. He proclaimed, "Salvation is from the Jews." (John 4:22) The magi sought the "king of the Jews." Pilate wrote, "Jesus of Nazareth, the king of the Jews."

Pentecost revealed the wide geographical range of the nations (Acts 2:7–11) in which Jews lived. They came from all around the Great Sea to Jerusalem for Shauvot (Feast of Weeks). At these feasts, news spread out to the whole Hebrew world, including Jewish Christians. Shortly after, *scattered Christian Jews* settled in Judea, Samaria, Phoenicia, Cyprus, Antioch, and Cyrene (Acts 8:1; 11:19f).

Those *diaspora* Jews knew Jesus' prophecy that the temple would be utterly demolished and that Rome would surround and besiege Jerusalem. They knew to flee, and did so. These Jews learned of the soon and awful fulfillment of these prophecies. They could not return, for nothing would remain of their former faith. The Hebrews' writer sees this disaster making the Levitical sacrifices obsolete. He feels the anxiety, terror and confusion filling their daily lives—threatening the salvation put there by Christ. He explains the relation between the old and new covenants—the two great epochs of God dealing directly with His human creation. Jeremiah foretold the new covenant. Now, the new covenant superseded the old leaving no access. The author explains this singular access to God for everyone through Jesus the Christ—the new and living way. To explain this new covenant, the author leads the recipients through the Torah, into Kings and Chronicles, into the Psalms and introduces several prophets—all of the foregoing pointing to Jesus fulfilling every Hebrew messianic prophecy and the new covenant to the fullest extent in Christ.

Hebrews does not offer again the gospel or *didachē* to the *diaspora*. Instead it refers to the old and new covenants fifteen times. Only Paul (3) and Luke-Acts (3) mention "covenant." Diaspora Jews understand "covenant" and "unshakable kingdom" far better than gospel or *didachē*.

In sum, the recipients are Jewish Christians who represent the *diaspora*. Their spiritual situation changed from instability to impossible with the soon destruction of Jerusalem. It did not matter where they lived because their culture never depended on location, but on their faith. Bruce replaces the mass of unverifiable opinion with: "Where did they live? We do not know."

Place and Date of Writing

Internal evidence is clouded by the words "they of Italy" (13:24). Is it Rome? Lenski thinks so. Does this mean "they of Italy here with me" or "they with me here in Italy?" Perhaps it refers to Italians elsewhere. Does it mean Priscilla and Aquila, Italians who were with the author and send greetings? The "Timothy" reference suggests Ephesus, but not as the place of writing. Negating Ephesus yields nothing new. Rather than list places of writing and scenarios supporting each, it will shorten this section to leave this question unanswered—to avoid a guessing game. Scenarios may identify a place, but none finds evidence of the sole place of writing. The least important and most unlikely to advance our knowledge of "The Epistle to the Hebrews" is the place of its writing.

The writing of Hebrews is within the first century (Bruce, et al.) since Clement of Rome quoted it in A.D. 96. Kistemaker puts the date range at A.D. 80–85. Attridge chooses A.D. 60-100. This is the *terminus ad quem* (the final time limit). Timothy is still alive. The recipients of the letter endured a persecution (10:32–36). Three Roman "persecutions" took place in the first century: Claudius (A.D. 49–54), Nero (A.D. 58–64) and Domitian (A.D. 81–96). The destruction of Jerusalem (A.D. 66–70) exceeds all persecution definitions. Most commentators look to Claudius for the *terminus a quo* (the earliest date). The persecutions of Nero and Domitian were murderous and not distant. The Claudian was recent. The Sanhedrin persecution in A.D. 33 began the *diaspora*. The Jewish Christians are told to "Remember those earlier days..." This is a distant past persecution—removed from the writing of Hebrews. Persecution cannot date the composition. The text in Hebrews 10:32–34 uses (*athlēsis* - contest, struggle or fight) denoting resistance, but not bloodshed.

> SEV-32 Remember those earlier days after you had received the light, when *you stood your ground in a great contest in the face of suffering. 33 Sometimes you were publicly exposed to insult and persecution; at other times you stood side by side with those who were so treated. 34 You sympathized with those in prison and joyfully accepted the confiscation of your property, because you knew that you yourselves had better and lasting possessions.* [Italics added]

Hughes (1977) lists eighteen Hebrews' passages that pertain to the "still operative" Levitical priesthood services, such as: "...what is obsolete and aging will soon disappear;" (8:13) "... the high priest enters the Most Holy Place every year with blood..." (8:25) and, "...every priest stands and performs his religious duties..." (10:11). The siege and destruction horror described by Josephus provides the fulfillment of the sentence of Christ "on this generation." (Luke 11 :29–32, 50, 51) The destruction of Jerusalem and the temple in A.D. 70 casts doubt on later dates.

To sum up: to date the Hebrews writing beyond A.D. 66 is inconceivable for any first century Jewish Christian of the *diaspora*. They knew Jesus' prophecy concerning Jerusalem, and now it was imminent. This puts Hebrews within the apostles' lifetimes. The Roman siege sets the date of Hebrews well after the Acts persecution and within sight of the destruction of Jerusalem.

The Author of the Epistle to the Hebrews

Contention governs the identity of the author of Hebrews, with many current scholars removing Paul as a possibility. Hence, nominations abound. In sum, nearly every candidate nominated as author lacks convincing evidence to be "elected." Early church leaders held to Paul, Apollos and Barnabas. Origen named Luke and Clement of Rome as possible writers. The Eastern Church stuck with Paul; the Western Church followed three centuries later. Luther picked Apollos; so did Lo Bue, and Montfiore—and with impressive, but inconclusive documentation. Spicq gave ten reasons for Barnabas. Guthrie agreed, and lists Apollos, Priscilla, Philip, Peter, Silvanus, Ariston and Jude as modern guesses. Bruce quotes Manson: "...attempts to discover the writer's identity have no greater interest than a parlour-game." *(Epistle to the Hebrews,* p. 171f.)

Paul is disqualified in the minds of scholars because: 1) of a missing Pauline salutation; 2) Hebrews 2:3 makes the author a "second-generation" Christian; 3) textual criticism points elsewhere; 4) Origen said, "...*who wrote the epistle, in truth, God knows.*" and 5) of Origen's damaging word, "... *the style and composition belonged to one who called to mind the apostle's teachings...*"

Defenders of Paul suggest that identifying him as author would offend the Jews who knew him as "the apostle to the Gentiles." They also note Paul's ubiquitous form of greeting at the end of every epistle and found in Hebrews: "The grace of our Lord Jesus Christ be with you."

Origen is lightly regarded today. He identified three factors to consider later in this introduction. 1) the author (known by the *apostle's thoughts*), 2) the *writer* of Hebrews. His truncated quote often found is "...*who wrote the epistle, in truth, God knows...*" and 3) the style and diction of the Greek text of the Epistle to the Hebrews.

One by one each nominee drops out as the evidence or argument fails to convince. A question germane to identifying the author or writer is, "What prior writing do we have of this person?" A few apostles, Mark and Luke wrote treatises that became part of the canon and are considered to be inspired by God. An argument that an excellent speaker (Apollos) could have written Hebrews begs the question of whether speaking and writing are identical twin gifts.

Further discussion results in checkmating every author candidate. An alternate approach follows.

Asking a Different Research Question

All commentary introductions ask pointed questions: Who is the author? When and from where was it written? And so forth. These questions form a deductive analysis with blinders looking for the *one* answer. The unstated question behind the open one is, "Who authored the Hebrews monograph?" If this limitation were removed, the restated question begins an inductive analysis, "How did Hebrews come about?" Or, "In what context was Hebrews written?" Either of these questions casts the net broadly by looking into the context out of which Hebrews came. This reasonable approach governs much literature: sound non-fiction writing takes place in time and in a cultural context. Writing with a paucity of facts may produce at best only interesting reading.

The Culture That Jesus Created

People who follow a set of common values, ideas and practices partially define a culture. The first place to seek facts on the Hebrews' questions starts with Jesus' followers. He began the new culture with, "Follow me." The followers left all to become learners. He taught them a curriculum never before heard on earth (John 7:16–17 —*tē didachē tou Christou*). Healings and miraculous signs confirmed his teaching. He avoided claiming to be the Christ, but acknowledged those who so identified him.

Great crowds followed Jesus everywhere. His teaching amazed them; his mighty works astonished all. Division arose on who Jesus was. The crowds and his teaching alarmed the religious leaders. They contested his teaching and tried to discredit it. They lost face and became discredited. One sign of an emerging culture is overreaction by a threatened host culture fearing what it hears and sees. The large numbers of followers caused alarm and demanded swift action. The night before the leaders took violent action, Jesus initiated the "new covenant in his blood." Moses' covenant created the Jewish culture after deliverance from Egypt. The new covenant opened the way for anyone to become "His people" and He "their God." The common teaching and experience caused the new culture to expand. The death of Jesus dispersed the crowds and scattered his disciples.

The resurrection of Jesus drew the disciples back. The crowds remained aloof. Pentecost changed everything. Perplexity marked the leadership of the traditional culture. The twelve apostles spoke boldly that "Jesus is the Christ" proclaiming forgiveness in his name. Many new disciples followed the apostles' teaching. Peter and the other apostles withstood the hierarchy. Panic gripped the leaders who could not silence the apostles, nor stop the growth of the new culture. After stoning the deacon, Stephen, they persecuted the disciples causing a *diaspora* from Jerusalem. The apostles remained in Jerusalem, but carried the teaching of Christ beyond the city.

Luke records three main parts of the new culture in the New Testament: local groups, evangelism and apostolic missionary teams. Local churches sprang from apostolic teaching. Luke records the evangelistic work of Philip and Stephen, but cuts short that history. Apostolic missionary teams spread the teaching of Christ broadly founding new local churches. One team, led by Peter and John took the gospel to the Jews. Another, led by Paul and Barnabas took the gospel to Jews first, then to Gentiles. The context or culture of the apostles offers the best prospects for identifying the author or writer of Hebrews, since almost every present-day nominee is either an apostle, or one with close connections to the apostles. The place to ask the question, "In what context was Hebrews written?" is within the first century apostolic missionary culture. This culture is described below largely from the Acts of the Apostles and the epistles.

The Apostolic Missionary Culture

Luke offers the most complete account of the travel and ministries of the apostolic missionary culture (AMC). He wrote what he received from "eyewitnesses and ministers of the word." (Luke 1:2) He was not present for everything in his gospel. He was present for a large part of the ministry of the AMC that he recorded in Acts. Witnesses, predominantly Paul, filled in the rest.

The Common Culture

Many factors created the AMC. The apostles and those with them had these things in common: revelation, faith, unity, theme, teaching, and suffering.

The Common Revelation

When the Holy Spirit communicates what only God knows; it is *revelation*. Scripture did not originate in the minds of those who wrote it (2 Peter 1:19–2:1). The Spirit of God moved the prophet to speak or write. Revelation presupposes activity of the Holy Spirit in the life of the writer, making the unknowable open and now known. Paul defends the gospel as revelation:

> ESV **Galatians 1:11, 12** For I would have you know, brothers, that the gospel that was preached by me is not man's gospel. [12] For I did not receive it from any man, nor was I taught it, but I received it through a *revelation* of Jesus Christ.

Peter, James and John confirmed the gospel Paul preached to Gentiles to be the same as they preached to the Jews (Gal. 2:1–9). Paul went up to Jerusalem by revelation. Barnabas and Titus accompanied him. The revelation of the gospel did not begin and end with Paul. He notes the common revelation to the apostles and prophets—not just Peter, James and John.

> ESV **Ephesians 3:3–6** how the mystery was made known to me by revelation, as I have written briefly. ⁴ When you read this, you can perceive my insight into the mystery of Christ, ⁵ which was not made known to the sons of men in other generations as it has now been revealed to his holy apostles and prophets by the Spirit. ⁶ This mystery is that the Gentiles are fellow heirs, members of the same body, and partakers of the promise in Christ Jesus through the gospel.

The gospel preached by the apostles and prophets in the first century exceeded the death, burial and resurrection of Jesus Christ. This is its core, but the foundational history (Scripture), present followers' life and walk, and eschatology contained teaching about the messiah, new covenant, the kingdom of God, the coming of Christ, salvation and shaking this present world. These are integrated in the Hebrews' revelation.

The Common Faith

Jesus spoke to his disciples about faith and believing in him—especially who he was. Paul wrote: "To Titus, my true child in a common faith: Grace and peace from God the Father and Christ Jesus our Savior." (Titus 1:4) See also: John 11:27; 20:31; Romans 3:22 and Ephesians 4:4–6. In the broadest terms, the common faith held Jesus to be the prophesied Christ, the Son of God—and no alternate Christ's were considered, preached or taught—under penalty of a curse (Galatians 1:8, 9).

The Common Unity

Jesus prayed for unity for his followers (John 17:11, 21, 22). Paul and Peter emphasized this unity to the churches in different exhortations: in Rome: "Live in harmony with one another–one heart and mouth. (Romans 12:16, 15:6 and 1 Peter 3:8); in Corinth: "Agree with one another ... no divisions among you ...." (1 Corinthians 1:10); in Philippi: "perfectly united in mind and thought...." (Philippians 4:2); and in Ephesus: "keep the unity of the Spirit through the bond of peace ...." (Ephesians 4:3)

The degree of common unity for the churches did not exempt the AMC. Paul exhorted the churches to imitate him and those with him. There is no hint of "do as I say..." In his epistles, Paul identifies people traveling and ministering with him as *sunergos*, "fellow-workers." They are Priscilla, Aquila, Urbanus, Timothy, Titus, Epaphroditus, Clement, Jesus (Justus), Philemon, Mark, Aristarchus, Demas and Luke. Others worked with the apostles Paul, Apollos, Barnabas and Silas. Many women, the "rest of my fellow workers," and those who gave generously are anonymous.

The Common Theme and Teaching

Luke notes that Paul and Apollos defended the common theme, "Jesus is the Christ." The messiah prophesied early in Genesis and throughout the OT culminated in the life, death, resurrection and ascension of Jesus of Nazareth. This is the core and common theme (1 Corinthians 15:1–11).

Teaching bound together all elements of the AMC. Indeed, the teaching of Christ (John 7:16, 17) was unknown on earth before Jesus taught it. Jesus said that God, the one who sent him, was the source of his teaching, not himself. The primary word used to designate Jesus' teaching is *didachē*. Jesus' *didachē* astonished the crowds (Mark 1:22, 11:18; and Luke 4:32). The high priest asked Jesus (John 18:19) of his *didachē*, showing his own failure to hear Jesus' public teaching. After Jesus ascended, 3,000 new believers assembled to obey the apostles' *didachē* (Acts 2:42). Believers multiplied so rapidly that the high priest (correctly) accused the apostles of filling Jerusalem with their *didachē* (Acts 5:28). This *didachē* shifted the demographics. In response the rulers persecuted the Hebrew Christians beginning the *diaspora* from Jerusalem.

Paul praised the Christians at Rome because they obeyed the *didachē* from their hearts (Romans 6:17). Years later, John wrote defending the *didachē* with these severe words:

> ESV **2 John 1:9, 10** Everyone who goes on ahead and does not abide in the teaching of Christ (*tē didachē tou Xristou*), does not have God. Whoever abides in the teaching (*en tē didachē*) has both the Father and the Son.

¹⁰ If anyone comes to you and does not bring this teaching (*tēn didachēn*), do not receive him into your house or give him any greeting,

The struggle to maintain the purity of the gospel and the teaching of Christ remains to this day, but the Epistle to the Hebrews serves as a strong bulwark against the many hetero-gospels and other false teachings. The purity of this teaching held the apostles together and resulted in the Lord adding to their number. John gave the best test for discerning who has and does not have God.

The Common Suffering

Jesus predicted that his followers would be hated—certifying the approval of God. All who live godly lives will be persecuted. The obverse of suffering, especially suffering together is the lasting friendship that can be won in no other way. Suffering, struggling and serving together enabled Paul and Silas to sing. The preferred response is to rejoice in the face of suffering for Christ.

The *diaspora* Jewish Christians were of the apostles' generation. Although widely scattered they foresaw Jerusalem's destruction. The familial tone of Hebrews shows the author(s) identifying with the recipients. Well over 70 times the pronouns "we," "us," and "our" connect them. They hear of "our Lord" and "our Lord Jesus." The recipients read of those who drifted from the faith by the use of the pronouns "they" or "them." Thus, the epistle shows family warmth and warnings to their wavering brothers. Those who lost earthly things gained eternal riches in Christ.

Summary on the Common Culture of the Apostolic Mission

These factors describe the AMC and the manner in which it spread the gospel. Everyone possessed access to the same revelation, teaching and suffering for Christ. This formed the context out of which the Epistle to the Hebrews most likely came.

Jesus sent out his disciples two by two. The apostles followed this pattern. The Holy Spirit chose Paul and Barnabas as the first pair. Barnabas qualifies as a prophet as he fulfills the 1 Cor. 14:3 descriptors. Barnabas stood up for Saul, rescuing him. Later he rescued his nephew, Mark. Paul and Silas traveled together. Paul traveled with Timothy for 15 years. Priscilla and her husband Aquila ministered together, instructing Apollos and making tents with Paul. Paul and Luke speak well of Apollos. Luke enters the AMC in Acts 16:10 using "we" instead of "they." Luke remains with Paul from Acts 20:5 to Rome. It is hard to deny that Luke heard everyone who ministered the gospel, the *didachē* as he traveled with the AMC. The *didachē* "strengthened the disciples." Their common message gave Luke time to make "short notes" of all that was said and taught. The "we" verses (2:3, 5, 4:2, 5:11, 6:9(2), 11, 8:1, 9:5, 13:8) reveal "insiders relating to insiders," that is the author(s) of Hebrews were known to the recipients by their common message, faith and love.

Issues Raised For and Against Paul as Author

Hebrews 2:3

Three responses pertain to the exegesis of Hebrews 2:3. First, verse 4 continues the thought began in verse 3. Second, the meaning of "confirm" (*bebaioō*) must be made clear. Third, the impact of revelation on the apostles and prophets negates a "second-hand" gospel.

The source of revelation is not open to research or study; the content of revelation may be studied and taught. The first century apostles (before A.D. 66) had the revelation of the gospel: they spoke it in one accord because they were "taught of God" (John 6:45). Apollos seems to be an exception. Perhaps he followed John until Jesus appeared. He may not have known all the Scriptures that Jesus fulfilled until Priscilla and Aquila taught him. His scriptural deficit is only partially known, but as an apostle he received the same revelation of the gospel as the apostles.

To confirm in Scripture means to prove that two independent entities are the same. Peter testified that the Holy Spirit fell on the Gentiles, "...so if God gave them the *same* gift..." (Acts 11:1–17). Words spoken may be false, but God "confirmed the word with the signs that followed" (Mark 16:20). The Acts 15 apostolic meeting sent a message to Antioch but Judas and Silas spoke words confirming it. A better exegesis of Hebrews 2:3 is that the meeting of the apostles with the "us" of the Hebrews demonstrated that they both had the same salvation gospel. No knowledge transfer took place at this meeting. The meeting of

Paul, Barnabas and Titus with the Jerusalem apostles confirms that the gospel to both Jews and Gentiles is the same (Gal 2:1–9).

Finally, verse four continues the confirmation process with God also "testifying with them, both by signs and wonders and . . . miracles and by gifts of the Holy Spirit according to his own will."

The light exegesis of Hebrews 2:3 cannot fit either the verbal meaning or the contextual meaning of *bebaioō* in the two verses. Perhaps the "us" included Luke, but this is not known.

Absent Salutation – Present Greeting

In all of Paul's Epistles, he begins with this salutation: Paul. Why is this absent in the Epistle to the Hebrews? This argument against Paul is based on logic and silence. Since Paul is methodical, then why did he break here? The answers are many and weak—all based on supposition. Would the apostle to the Gentiles write to Hebrews? Arguments for Paul are weak since silence governs as well. Supposition posits that the Jews would never accept Paul authoring Hebrews, as he was now their arch enemy having become a turncoat after being their key defender. Indeed, Paul was a poisoned well, and nothing good could come from him to Jews—so goes the argument. To Paul, the gospel was to the Jews first. But without a word from Paul, his motives are unknown.

Paul includes a greeting at the end of every epistle—and in Hebrews 13:25 Paul's ubiquitous trademark appears. In 2 Thessalonians 3:17, 18, he states: "*I, Paul, write this greeting in my own hand, which is the distinguishing mark in all my letters. This is how I write.* [18] *The grace of our Lord Jesus Christ be with you all.*" The wording differs somewhat, but essentially is: "Grace be with you." Paul's writing (rarely found) makes his mark certain and proves the source. This is evidence for Paul.

Grace distinguished the work of God in the eyes of the apostles. To them it meant more than unmerited favor. Grace was God changing lives by pouring out the Holy Spirit and doing things thought impossible: miracles, healings and signs. Paul and Barnabas told Peter, James and John how the Holy Spirit fell on the Gentiles, and how miracles occurred. The original apostles noted that grace was evident in the ministry of Paul and Barnabas. Grace was the power of God that brought full new covenant change to the one who believed. (Ephesians 2:8–10). The Word of God, the gospel of Jesus Christ, the *didachē tou Xristou* brought forth the power of God.

Three Words from Origen

Of note is the often truncated quote of Origen: "*who wrote the epistle, In truth, God knows.*" We begin with Origen. Since the testimony of Origen is used both against and for Paul, it is best to provide more depth to his statement on the source of the epistle to the Hebrews. He considers the contents of Hebrews in accord with the *thoughts* of the apostle Paul. He evaluates the writing of Hebrews to be of *better Greek* than that of Paul and that the *diction, differences of style* and *composition* belong to someone other than Paul. Calvin and Spicq noticed differences between composition of Hebrews and other writings of Paul. Calvin chose Apollos as author. The misquote of Origen obscures what he wrote. Origen links author and writer: "*... the style and composition belonged to one who called to mind the apostle's teachings and ... made short notes of what his master said.*" [Italics added.] To Origen, the writer was either Luke or Clement. [Eusebius, Church History 6.25.11–14]

The three words are thoughts, writer and style of composition. To Origen, Paul provided the thoughts, but did not write Hebrews. He names either Luke or Clement as writer. His qualifications of style and composition were someone who "…called to mind the apostle's teaching…and made short notes…" This elevates Luke and virtually eliminates Clement.

He forthrightly chooses Paul as the Hebrews source author. In his theology, *First Principles*, he attributes the Hebrews quotes to Paul. Does this prove Paul to be the author of Hebrews? No, not unless the attributions are unique to Paul. Attributions may equal nominations. Direct evidence with supporting arguments comes closer to proof. Mounds of circumstantial evidence pointing in one direction may convince an unbiased jurist to decide whether Paul or someone else is author.

The short version is simply, anyone naming Paul as the author of Hebrews does not make him so. This holds even if the naming person is the smartest in the world. The reverse holds: denying that Paul is the author of Hebrews does not exclude him. Nominations guarantee nothing to find the unknown identity. They do set the person forward in the eyes of others—then count noses. If majority vote cannot establish truth, neither can minority opinion.

By identifying the source author as Paul, he supported the apostolic authority of the letter as well as its place in the canon. These two conclusive decisions far outweighed the perplexing and supposed anonymity of the epistle. However others of the apostles may serve as sources.

Summary of Arguments and Evidence For and Against Paul as Author

Origen's word about the style and diction of Hebrews is strong argument and evidence excluding Paul as its writer. Commentators cite the variance between the better Greek of the epistle and Paul's more direct (*idiōtēs*) *speaking* style. Paul admits his rudeness of speech, but the Corinthians said his letters terrify and are weighty and powerful. They deemed his speech contemptible, but this was intentional. Paul saw the Lord confirm the direct message of the cross with signs and wonders. He wanted their faith to be in the power of God and not in human wisdom. Greeks seek wisdom and Jews a sign, but the power of God shown in the gospel of Jesus Christ trumps both. Paul uses the Hebrew text, but Hebrews uses the LXX in all but two of thirty references. Gamaliel trained the Pharisee, Paul in Tarsus. He was not an Alexandrian, nor a Hellenist.

Chapter thirteen suggests Paul through linkage with "they of Italy," and years of traveling with Timothy, his protégé. Prisoners are chained but no one frequented them more than Paul.

Paul's greeting at the end of the epistle to the Hebrews consistently appears as his trademark in all of his other epistles, essentially: "Grace be with you." Paul's own writing (rarely found in his letters) makes his mark certain and its presence in all his epistles proves this point. This self-evident greeting needs no argument. Only Paul, as expected, but also Peter and John use similar words. Peter's formula is "Grace and peace…be". Paul never adds in *peace*.

It is not doublespeak or equivocation to conclude that the above arguments and evidence 1) do not rule Paul out, but, 2) they do not rule Paul in as the author of Hebrews. What they strongly suggest is that Paul had input into the ideas of the epistle to the Hebrews. But what part?

Earlier in this introduction, nominations and counting of votes for or against this or that candidate were categorically excluded as having no place in identifying the author. This still stands. Ruling out or ruling in are valuable pieces of any research. Medical research keeps records of all the substances that fail to affect the malicious condition. This prevents going back over the same ground countless times in further research.

Evidence and Arguments Supporting Both Writer and Authors of Hebrews

This summation discards nominations for their numerical value: voting cannot establish truth; and rarely selects the best candidate. Relying on arguments with scant evidence puts the research in a precarious position. Some of the evidence is circumstantial. Some points in different directions. The best arguments flow from the evidence. Some of the evidence is explicit; some implicit; but they yielded the summary that follows. An inductive method seeks the simplest answer that takes in all the facts. The facts and evidence from the foregoing are many:

- that the author and writer of Hebrews most assuredly must be different persons.
- that Origen cannot lightly be dismissed, as he spoke, read, wrote and understood the Koinē when it was a living language, and in it he wrote a number of OT and NT works.
- that Origen's choice of Luke as writer of Hebrews stands, while that of Clement does not.
- that the recipients of Hebrews were the Jewish Christians of the Acts 8 persecution and subsequent *diaspora*.
- that Peter and James wrote to the *diaspora*. Peter references Paul writing to those he did in Cappadocia, Bithynia, Asia and Galatia. Paul compares the two covenants in Galatians.
- that the date of writing cannot be later than the siege of Jerusalem, but must be close to it.
- that any of the Roman persecutions cannot date the composition of Hebrews.
- that Paul, exclusively, identifies Christ as both mediator and high priest in his other works.
- that chapter 13 of Hebrews hints that Paul may be speaking of Timothy and the Italians.
- that chapter 13 bears Paul's ubiquitous trademark: *The grace of our Lord Jesus be with you.*
- that the confirmation in 2:3 is not a transfer, but a confirmation that the salvation heard by the apostles and that of the "us" of Hebrews were equal. Galatians 2 may record this event.

- that the AMC provided the environment for the writer to collect information necessary to write Hebrews. It was cohesive and cooperative (*sunergos*), and fellow sufferers were with him. It was united with one heart and mind—not having many and varying opinions regarding Christ. And it built its presentation of "Jesus is the Christ" from the revelation of the risen Christ (Luke 24:46) and further revelations by the Holy Spirit to all apostles and prophets.

- that imprisoned Roman citizens receive privileges: visits from friends, including physicians.

- that Luke's method of collecting information for his gospel fits well with the AMC context.

- that Luke heard the encouragement of Barnabas, the teaching of Priscilla and Aquila and the preaching of Apollos.

- that the new covenant replaced a passing old covenant with a heavenly high priest, temple, and the high priest's blood taken into the most holy place was one sacrifice for sins forever.

- that Luke recorded speeches throughout the gospel and Acts and that both preaching and teaching were the primary methods used to convey the gospel at that time.

- that the *didachē* is equivalent to the gospel, the truth that Jesus Christ is come in the flesh.

- that the main message of the epistle to the Hebrews is equivalent to the *didache* of Christ

- that Luke blends the various speakers' messages into a single smoothly written document thus hiding personal idiosyncrasies—except for the unknown source of the better Greek.

- that Luke reported Hebrews in Greek with an Alexandrian and Septuagint coloring.

- that the message of scripture always towers above its messenger: "He must increase; I must decrease." Therefore, Christ stands above everything Jewish, including its Jewish-Christian apostles and his disciples, and, indeed, all present and past scholars and their works.

This constitutes most of the evidence and argument. The inductive process led the summation. Other evidence may have escaped notice. It is possible that errors are in the summation. All of these belong with me and are attributable to no one else.

- Paul was the apostle to the Gentiles. How did the AMC take the gospel to Gentiles and also produce the epistle to the Hebrews?

- The AMC may be inaccurate in describing the behavior and missionary work of the apostles.

- The source of revelation and the power of God are causes beyond research. Causes remain hidden. Their effects are open to research. These limits mask the dynamics of the AMC.

- Rigorous testing with hypotheses in this type of research will always prove difficult.

- Luke may not have been able to adjust the quality of his Greek. This is unknowable.

- Some evidence may be opinion or speculation.

Conclusion on the Author of Hebrews

Common factors detailed above bound the apostolic missionary culture (AMC) together. The resulting AMC is rare if not unique in all of Scripture. Most others were single men or women of faith (Hebrews 11). Their singular theme, "Jesus is the Christ" and the revelation of the gospel and *didachē* made possible a range of contributors in the development of Hebrews. Within this environment lived the authors of Hebrews. Their singleness of mind and heart resulted from their risen Lord and the gospel linking him with all the prophets foretold of the coming Christ. In short, they had one subject that captivated their thinking and speaking, one purpose of heart and mind.

The evidence and argument for Paul do not exclude him as a source author; they exclude him as the sole source author. The same is true of Apollos and Barnabas, Priscilla and Aquila, and other members of the AMC. Looking for one stand-alone author produces hypotheses and speculation which must follow from a faulted research question: "Who authored Hebrews?" This question begs the process of finding the sole author. By asking, "How did Hebrews come about?" we look for a cultural context and a most likely process of writing Hebrews.

The writing style of Hebrews suggests one person who imperfectly fits none of the members of the AMC, except one—Luke. This writer of the gospel and Acts joined the AMC at Troas. His powers of observation and recording are without peer. In his gospel, he sought eyewitnesses (*autoptai*) who were also "servants of the word." (Luke 1:2) In this culture, Luke needed no eyewitnesses—he saw and heard for himself. Every day and in every place, he heard witnesses, and all were "servants of the word." We know Luke evaluated Apollos' preaching as superior in eloquence and presentation. Luke heard the exhortations and encouragement of Barnabas—the rescuer of failed lives. Luke never missed hearing Paul. Paul and Luke were very close for years. Luke the *iatros* continued his practice while with Paul.

Origen nominated only two writers: Clement must be dismissed. The process Luke employed in writing both Luke and Acts required interviewing individuals and serving as a reporter and recorder who witnessed the events, signs and especially the teaching and preaching. The missionary journeys placed him directly in the face of many people who spoke the same message, but with different styles, levels of skill, and degrees of delivery. The quality of the Greek, Alexandrian and Septuagint, suggests that Luke adopted the Greek of Apollos. The exhortations and encouragement of Barnabas are strategic in the Hebrews text. The exegesis of OT prophecies preached by both Apollos and Paul provided Luke with ample ways of expressing their relationship with their fulfillment in Christ. Perhaps nuances provided by other fellow workers such as the didactics of Priscilla and Aquila entered Hebrews, but only Luke knows where they may be.

In sum, the apostolic missionary culture provided the environment and context in which the Holy Spirit by widespread revelation of the mystery of Christ differentially qualified a number of its fellow workers to "author" the epistle to the Hebrews. Luke served as the reporter who collected the data; the transcriber who faithfully put on parchment the content and style of the preaching and teaching he heard; and the editor who gave a smooth standard text that provides the appearance of a single polished, highly educated and well-researched author. The fact of revelation points always to the single author of all scripture: the Holy Spirit.

BIBLIOGRAPHY

Commentaries, Lexicons, and Other General References

Alford, Henry. *The Epistle to the Hebrews, and the Catholic Epistles of St. James and St. Peter.* The Greek Testament, Vol. 4. London: Rivingtons, 1859.

Attridge, Harold W. *Hebrews: A Commentary on the Epistle to the Hebrews* (Hermeneia: A Critical and Historical Commentary on the Bible, ed. Helmut Koester). Philadelphia: Fortress, 1989.

Barnes, Albert. *Notes on the New Testament; Explanatory and practical.* Grand Rapids: Baker Book House, 1949. [vol. 9 is Hebrews]

Bauer, Walter. *A Greek-English Lexicon of the New Testament and Other Early Christian Literature.* Second ed. Revised and edited by Fredrick William Danker based on Walter Bauer's 5th ed. Chicago and London: University of Chicago Press, 1979.

Beekman, John, John C. Callow and Michael F. Kopesec, *The Semantic Structure of Written Communication*, 5th rev.; Dallas, Summer Institute of Linguistics; 1981

Brown, John. *Hebrews.* Edinburgh: The Banner of Truth Trust, 1862.

Bruce, F. F. *The Epistle to the Hebrews: The English Text with Introduction, Exposition, and Notes.* Grand Rapids: Wm. B. Eerdmans, 1964.

Büchsel, Friedrich. *Die Christologie des Hebräerbriefs.* BiblioBazaar, [2009]. [the original edition was published in 1922 by Gutersloh; C. Bertelsmann]

Callow, Kathleen, *Man and Message: A Guide to Meaning-Based Text Analysis*; Lanham, MD/Dallas, University Press of America and Summer Institute of Linguistics; 1998

Davidson, A.B. [1831-1902]. *The Epistle to the Hebrews with Introduction and Notes.* Edinburgh: T. & T. Clark, 1900.

Davies, J. H. *A Letter to Hebrews.* Cambridge Bible Commentary. Cambridge: Cambridge University Press, 1967.

Dods, Marcus. "The Epistle to the Hebrews." In vol. 4 of *The Expositor's Greek Testament*, edited by W. Robertson Nicoll, n.d. Reprint. Grand Rapids: Eerdmans, 1980.

Ellingworth, Paul. *The Epistle to the Hebrews: A Commentary on the Greek Text.* Grand Rapids: Wm. B. Eerdmans Publishing Co., 1993.

Ellingworth, Paul, and Eugene A. Nida. *A Translator's Handbook on the Letter to the Hebrews.* New York: United Bible Societies, 1983.

Geytenbeek, Brian and Helen Geytenbeek, Larry Clark, Ron Olson; Richard Blight, ed. *Exegetical Helps on the Epistle to the Hebrews.* Unpublished.

Greenlee, J. Harold. *An Exegetical Summary of Hebrews.* Dallas: SIL, 1998.

Guthrie, Donald. *The Letter to the Hebrews.* Tyndale New Testament Commentaries, edited by Leon Morris. Grand Rapids: Eerdmans, 1983.

Hagner, Donald A. *Hebrews.* New International Biblical Commentary. Peabody, Mass.: Hendrickson Publishers, 1983.

Hewitt, Thomas. *The Epistle to the Hebrews.* Grand Rapids: Eerdmans, 1970.

Hughes, Philip Edgecumbe. *A Commentary on the Epistle to the Hebrews.* Grand Rapids: Wm. B. Eerdmans, 1977.

Kistemaker, Simon J. *Exposition of the Epistle to the Hebrews.* New Testament Commentary. Grand Rapids: Baker, 1984.

Lane, William. *Hebrews 1-8.* Word Biblical Commentary, vol. 47a. Dallas: Word, 1981.

Lane, William. *Hebrews 9-13.* Word Biblical Commentary, vol. 4b. Dallas: Word, 1991.

Lenski, R. C. H. *The Interpretation of the Epistle to the Hebrews and The Epistle of James.* Minneapolis: Augsburg Publishing House, 1986.

Louw, Johannes, and Eugene Nida, *Greek-English Lexicon of the New Testament Based on Semantic Domains,* United Bible Societies: New York, 1988

Lünemann, Göttlieb. *Critical and Exegetical Hand-book to the Epistle to the Hebrews.* Meyer's Commentary on the New Testament, edited by Heinrich August Wilhelm Meyer. Translated by Maurice J. Evans, with supplementary notes by Timothy Dwight indicated by My(D). New York and London: Funk and Wagnalls, 1890.

Metzger, Bruce M. *A Textual Commentary on the Greek New Testament.* 2d ed. Stuttgart: German Bible Society, 1994.

Miller, Neva F. *The Epistle to the Hebrews; An Analytical and Exegetical Handbook*. Dallas: Summer Institute of Linguistics, 1988.

Moffatt, James. *A Critical and Exegetical Commentary on the Epistle to the Hebrews*. The International Critical Commentary. Edinburgh: T. & T. Clark, 1924.

Montefiore, Hugh. *A Commentary on the Epistle to the Hebrews*. Black's New Testament Commentaries (Harper's New Testament Commentary in USA), Henry Chadwick, general editor. London: Adam and Charles Black, 1964.

Moore, Bruce, *Doublets in the New Testament,* Summer Institute of Linguistics: Dallas, 1993

Morris, Leon. "Hebrews." In vol. 12 of *The Expositor's Bible Commentary*, edited by Frank E. Gaebelein. Grand Rapids: Zondervan, 1981.

Murray, Andrew. *The Holiest of All: An Exposition of the Epistle to the Hebrews*. Old Tappan, New Jersey: Fleming H. Revell, n.d.

Peake, Arthur S. *Hebrews: Introduction, Authorized Version, Revised Version with notes, Illustrations*. London: Blackwood Le Bas & Co., 1901.

Trail, Ronald. *An Exegetical Summary of 1 Corinthians 1–9*. Dallas: SIL, 1995.

Trail, Ronald. *An Exegetical Summary of 1 Corinthians 10–16*. Dallas: SIL, 2001.

Tuggy, John C, "Semantic paragraph patterns: a fundamental communication concept and interpretation tool"; in David A. Black (ed.), *Linguistics and New Testament interpretation*, pp. 45–67; Nashville, Broadman; 1992

Westcott, Brooke Foss. *The Epistle to the Hebrews: The Greek Text with Notes and Essays*. 3rd edition. London: Macmillan and Co., 1903.

Wilson, Geoffrey B. *Hebrews: A Digest of Reformed Comment*. Edinburgh: The Banner of Truth Trust, 1979.

Wilson, Robert McLelland. *Hebrews*. New Century Bible Commentary, edited by Matthew Black. Grand Rapids: Eerdmans, 1987.

Wiley, H. Orton. *The epistle to the Hebrews*. Kansas City, MO: Beacon Hill Press, 1984.

Greek Texts and Translations

Aland, Barbara, Kurt Aland, Johannes Karavidopoulos, Carlo M. Martini, and Bruce M. Metzger, eds. *The Greek New Testament*. 4th rev. ed. Stuttgart: United Bible Societies, Stuttgart, 1993.

Barclay, William. *The New Testament. Volume Two, The Letters and the Revelation*. London-New York: Collins, 1969.

Contemporary English Version, New York: American Bible Society, 1995.

Deibler, Ellis W. Jr. *A Translation for Translators of the New Testament: A Source Text for Translators*. Ann Arbor: Cummins Works, 2008.

Eight Translation New Testament: King James Version, The Living Bible, Phillips Modern English, Revised Standard Version, Today's English Version, New International Version, Jerusalem Bible, New English Bible. Wheaton: Tyndale House Publishers, 1974.

Holy Bible: New International Version, Colorado Springs: Biblica, Inc., 1973, 1978, 1984.

Holy Bible: New Living Translation, Second Edition, Wheaton: Tyndale House Publishers, 1996, 2004.

Knox, Ronald. *The Holy Bible: A Translation from the Latin Vulgate in the light of the Hebrew and Greek originals*. New York: Sheed and Ward, 1950.

Norlie, Olaf M. *Simplified New Testament*. Grand Rapids: Zondervan, 1961.

New Century Version, Dallas: Word Publishing Company, 1991, 1993.

Peterson, Eugene. *The Message: The Bible in Contemporary Language*. Colorado Springs: NavPress, 2002.

J. B. Phillips, *The New Testament in Modern English*. New York: Macmillan, 1958.

Revised English Bible, Oxford University Press & Cambridge University Press, 1989.

Revised Standard Version. New York: Thomas Nelson, 1952.

The Jerusalem Bible, Garden City, N. Y.: Doubleday, 1966.

The Living Bible, Paraphrased. Wheaton: Tyndale House, 1971.

New English Bible, New York: Oxford University Press, 1972.

The NIV Study Bible, Grand Rapids: Zondervan, 1985.

Twentieth Century New Testament, New York: Revell, 1902.

Today's English Version, New York: American Bible Society, 1976

Today's New International Version, Colorado Springs: Biblica, 2005.

Weymouth, Richard Francis. *The New Testament in Modern Speech*. New York: Baker and Taylor Co, 1903.

www.ingramcontent.com/pod-product-compliance
Lightning Source LLC
Chambersburg PA
CBHW080537300426
44111CB00017B/2763